Dr. Salomon Fritz Forkel
ד״ר שלמה פריץ פורקל

Biblical Hebrew for Students of Modern Israeli Hebrew

MARC ZVI BRETTLER

YALE UNIVERSITY PRESS   NEW HAVEN & LONDON

To
NAHUM M. SARNA,
*who taught me to appreciate the beauty of
biblical Hebrew and the importance of a
precise understanding of the
Bible's grammar*

Copyright © 2002 by Yale University.
All rights reserved.
This book may not be reproduced, in whole or in part, including illustrations, in any form (beyond that copying permitted by Sections 107 and 108 of the U.S. Copyright Law and except by reviewers for the public press), without written permission from the publishers.

Publisher: Mary Jane Peluso
Production Controller: Joyce Ippolito
Editorial Assistant: Emily Saglimbeni
Designer: James J. Johnson
Set in Minion, Hebraica, and TranslitLS types by Integrated Publishing Solutions, Grand Rapids, Michigan.
Printed in the United States of America by Sheridan Books, Ann Arbor, Michigan.

Library of Congress Cataloging-in-Publication Data

Brettler, Marc Zvi.
    Biblical Hebrew for students of modern Israeli Hebrew / Marc Zvi Brettler.
       p.   cm. — (Yale language series)
    Includes bibliographical references and index.
    ISBN 0-300-08440-4 (cloth: alk. paper)

    1. Hebrew language—Grammar. 2. Bible. O.T.—Language, style.   I. Title.   II. Series.
PJ4567.3 .B74   2002
492.4'82421—dc21   00-050323

A catalogue record for this book is available from the British Library.

The paper in this book meets the guidelines for permanence and durability of the Committee on Production Guidelines for Book Longevity of the Council on Library Resources.

10 9 8 7 6 5 4 3 2 1

Contents

List of Charts	vii
Preface	ix
Introduction: Biblical Hebrew as a Language	1
1. The Consonants of Biblical Hebrew	5
2. The Vowels	11
3. The Cantillation Marks	19
4. Other Written Symbols	26
5. Syllabification	30
6. Some Principles of Hebrew Phonology (Part One)	40
7. Some Principles of Hebrew Phonology (Part Two)	44
8. The Definite Article, the Interrogative הֲ, and Other Interrogative Pronouns	54
9. The Vocalization of the Prepositions בְּ, כְּ, לְ, and מִן; the Conjunction וְ	61
10. The Morphology of the Noun and the Adjective	70
11. The Syntax of the Noun and the Adjective	80
12. The Bound Form (Construct): Morphology and Syntax	92
13. The Participle	105

14. The Independent, Demonstrative, and Relative Pronouns	120
15. The Possessive Pronominal Suffixes: The Singular	129
16. The Possessive Pronominal Suffixes: The Plural	143
17. The Numerals	159
18. Introduction to the Verb	169
19. The קַל of Healthy Verbs	178
20. The קַל of Verbs with Gutturals	194
21. The קַל of פֿנ, פֿי, and פֿא Verbs	209
22. The קַל of Hollow Verbs, לא and לי Verbs, and Geminates	225
23. Combined Deficiencies and the קַל with Verbal Suffixes	243
24. The Derived Conjugations (בִּנְיָנִים): Healthy Verbs	260
25. The Derived Conjugations (בִּנְיָנִים): Other Verbs	280
Cumulative Exercises	297
Glossary of Grammatical Terms and Abbreviations	305
Hebrew Grammatical Terms and Their English Equivalents	315
Hebrew-English Glossary	317
English-Hebrew Glossary	334
Index	353

Charts

The Consonants, Their Names, and Their Transliteration	6
The Classes of Hebrew Consonants	8
The Hebrew Vowels	12
Vowel Class and Quantity	13
The Transliteration of Hebrew Vowels	14
Disjunctive Cantillation Marks	21
Conjunctive Cantillation Marks	22
Distinguishing Between the שְׁוָא נָח and the שְׁוָא נָע	32
The Insertion of a דָּגֵשׁ קַל in the Letters ב, ג, ד, כ, פ, and ת	33
Some Basic Phonological Principles of Biblical Hebrew	48
Vocalization of the Definite Article	56
Vocalization of the Interrogative הֲא	57
Vocalization of the Bound Prepositions ב, כ, and ל	63
Vocalization of the Conjunctive וְ	64
Vocalization of the Preposition מִן	65
Forms of Nouns and Adjectives	76
Distinguishing Between Attributive and Predicative Adjectives	82
Changes in Form of the Noun in the Construct	95
The קַל Active Participle	109
The Independent Subjective Personal Pronoun	120
Pronominal Suffixes Added to the Singular	130
Pronominal Suffixes Added to the Plural	144
Comparison of Pronominal Suffixes Added to Singular and Plural	145
The Numerals 1–10	160

The Numerals 11–19	161
The Numerals 100, 1,000, and 10,000	161
The Ordinal Numbers 1–10	163
Translation of the Perfect and the Converted Imperfect	173
Translation of the Imperfect and the Converted Perfect	173
Healthy Verbs in the Perfect	179
Healthy Verbs in the Imperfect	181
Imperatives of Healthy Verbs as Derived from Imperfects	182
The Active Participle of Healthy Verbs	183
The Passive Participle of Healthy Verbs	184
The Infinitive Construct of Healthy Verbs with Suffixes	185
Gutturals in the Perfect	195
Gutturals in the Imperfect	196
Gutturals in the Imperative	197
Active Participles of Gutturals	198
Passive Participles of Gutturals	198
The Imperfect and Converted Perfect of פנ, פי, and פא Verbs	210
The Imperative of פנ, פי, and פא Verbs	212
The Infinitive Construct of פנ, פי, and פא Verbs	213
The Verb נתן	214
The Perfect of Hollow Verbs, לא and לי Verbs, and Geminates	226
The Imperfect of Hollow Verbs, לא and לי Verbs, and Geminates	228
The Imperative of Hollow Verbs, לא and לי Verbs, and Geminates	231
Active Participles of Hollow Verbs, לא and לי Verbs, and Geminates	231
Pronominal Suffixes	246
The Strong Verb with Suffixes	248
לי Verbs with Suffixes	250
The Perfect in the Various בִּנְיָנִים	263
The Imperfect in the Various בִּנְיָנִים	265
Identifying the בִּנְיָן of Perfect and Imperfect Verbs	266
The Jussive in the Various בִּנְיָנִים	267
The Imperative in the Various בִּנְיָנִים	267
The Cohortative in the Various בִּנְיָנִים	268
The Participle in the Various בִּנְיָנִים	269
The Infinitives in the Various בִּנְיָנִים	269

Preface

עֲשׂוֹת סְפָרִים הַרְבֵּה אֵין קֵץ, "The making of many books is without limit." It is to this thought in Ecclesiastes that I have returned so many times in the midst of this project, as piles of previous grammars began to obscure my computer screen. Yet I persevered, not because I believe that this grammar is better than others, but because it fills a significant void.

At some college campuses, and at most seminaries, biblical Hebrew (BH) is the only kind of Hebrew taught. Many textbooks have been written to teach BH as a dead language to beginning students; this is not my aim. Instead, my book is addressed to two types of students: those who have read or studied some of the Bible in Hebrew but have not studied formal biblical grammar, and those who have learned at least one year of modern Israeli Hebrew (MIH) and are now interested in studying the Bible in its original Hebrew. These students do not need an introduction to the alphabet, extensively transliterated texts, or an introduction to the basic syntactic rules that distinguish all dialects of Hebrew from English. Because modern Hebrew and the biblical lexicon overlap significantly, such students know much of the basic vocabulary of the Bible. Yet BH and MIH are two different languages—or at the very least, two substantially different dialects of the same language. MIH is certainly useful for reading the Bible, but no one can understand the Hebrew Bible knowing only MIH. There are significant differences in vocabulary, spelling, verb formation, use of verbal suffixes, and word order. The goal of this book is to offer the supplement to a foundation of MIH or casual knowledge of BH that is necessary for reading the Hebrew Bible.

This textbook is unique not only in terms of audience but in terms of structure. An overview of biblical phonology serves as the backdrop for the rest of the text, which emphasizes the application of these phonological principles, and thus the logic of biblical Hebrew.

The underlying principle is that biblical Hebrew is a real language that follows real linguistic rules and makes much more sense than is usually presumed. For this reason, the section on the derived conjugations (the בִּנְיָנִים other than קַל) is shorter than in other texts; these may be derived using phonological principles from the קַל. This innovative structure also makes the textbook suitable for use as a review text for students who have studied the language using a different method or book.

The book is divided into two main sections: chapters 1–7 outline BH phonology (the study of sound patterns), and chapters 8–25 deal with morphology (the study of linguistic forms) and syntax (the study of relations between words). Reference grammars traditionally separate morphology and syntax; I have kept them together because I feel it is best to describe the forms of words and the use of these forms at the same time. Each chapter is followed by a vocabulary list. Many of these words will already be known to most students of MIH, though I have noted some cases in which the use of a word differs in the two languages. Exceptional plurals and the forms that verbs typically take are also noted in these lists. The vocabulary is followed by exercises. These are both Hebrew-English and English-Hebrew; my teaching experience has convinced me that a passive knowledge of a language, even of a literary or "dead" language, is not sufficient.

Although this textbook is not typically inductive in its method, I have included examples from biblical texts throughout, and beginning with chapter 11, I have included many glossed biblical passages in the exercises. These exercises are of fundamental importance; they reinforce and sometimes introduce many crucial points, especially with regard to syntax. Some of the later chapters also use paradigms from two of the standard reference grammars, in order to encourage students to become more comfortable with the basic tools of serious biblical scholarship and to use these fundamental works at an early stage.

Readings in Biblical Hebrew: An Intermediate Textbook, by Ehud Ben Zvi, Maxine Hancock, and Richard Beinert (Yale University Press, 1993), which offers a well-chosen selection of carefully glossed texts, could easily be used as a continuation of this textbook for those interested in reading more texts and acquiring greater facility in BH. Ideally, the two could be used together in a single year.

Although this book is the first grammar of its type, it has obviously been influenced by other grammars. Most prominent among them is Thomas O. Lambdin, *Introduction to Biblical Hebrew* (Scribner's, 1971), the textbook that I previously used when I taught biblical Hebrew. I have also found the second, amended edition of Joshua Blau, *A Grammar of Biblical Hebrew,* Porta Linguarum Orientalium, n.s. 12 (Harrasowitz, 1993), most useful. In writing this textbook, I have constantly referred to these grammars, along with many more specialized works. Much of my terminology and many of my examples are taken from various student and reference grammars; in an introductory text of this sort, it is not possible to acknowledge these borrowings individually. I would like to thank Oxford University Press for permission to reproduce several paradigms from *Gesenius' Hebrew Grammar,* and the Pontifical Biblical Institute for permission to reproduce paradigms from Paul Joüon and T. Muraoka, *A Grammar of Biblical Hebrew.*

In my teaching experience, I have found that the exercises that accompany many biblical Hebrew textbooks are inadequate. I recognize that I have, in some cases, included an excessive number of exercises. Students and teachers should use their discretion about which exercises must be completed and which should be seen as optional.

Although this text is in many ways modeled after *Readings in Biblical Hebrew,* the formats of these two books are different. One of the most significant features of Ben Zvi's book is its suggestions for further reading. These allow the intermediate student to be introduced to the world of serious biblical scholarship. Although I was sorely tempted to include such sections after each chapter, I concluded that bibliographical lists would not be appropriate for the beginning student. I have made an exception only in some of the early chapters, where I have cited a small number of general works published in English concerning biblical Hebrew.

Mary Jane Peluso, publisher at Yale University Press, shepherded this book through all stages of the publishing process. I am very thankful for the support that she gave me at all times, and for her ability to understand the big picture while making sure it is realized through countless details. As a result of the careful work of Dan Heaton, senior manuscript editor at the Press, this is a much more clear manuscript. Tak Toyoshima drew the illustrations of translation tips that decorate this book. It was a pleasure to work with him, as his whimsical drawings captured perfectly various types of errors that I hope future students will avoid.

I would like to acknowledge the work of the many reviewers who have provided encouragement as well as insightful comments and constructive criticism for improving this text, including Ehud Ben Zvi, University of Alberta, Edmonton; Carl Ehrlich, York University, Toronto; Christine Hayes, Yale University; Victoria Hoffer, Yale University; and William Schniedewind, UCLA. The extensive comments of Adele Berlin, University of Maryland, were particularly helpful. W. Randall Garr of the University of California at Santa Barbara offered detailed comments on the manuscript, saved me from many errors, and taught me much. I am very happy that such a knowledgeable and careful reader of texts participated in this project.

Several graduate students have proofread the entirety of the manuscript in one version or another and have saved me from many factual mistakes and stylistic infelicities. I would like to thank Benjamin Studevent-Hickman and Chris Wyckoff, and especially Alan Lenzi, who commented on several drafts of this book, assisted with the proofreading, and compiled the Hebrew-English and English-Hebrew glossaries, as well as the index. Harvey N. Bock, a Hebraist, offered valuable comments and proofreading assistance. My brother Eli and my niece Avital Ordan helped me read second proofs. Many students who used the typescript version of this textbook at Brandeis and other institutions offered useful suggestions and corrections, which I have tried to incorporate. I cannot thank them all by name, but I am deeply appreciative of their contributions. Pamela Barmash of Washington University, a friend and a former student, read an early draft of this textbook and offered useful advice. John Huehnergard of Harvard University offered an important model for this book in his Akkadian grammar and was gracious enough to discuss with me many of the issues concerning writing a language textbook. My wife, Monica, helped smooth my writing style; along with our children, Talya and Ezra, she heard much too much about different types of דְּגֵשִׁים over the past few years. I am deeply appreciative of my family's support and patience. In spite of my best efforts, errors are present in this book; I encourage all readers to contact me with further suggestions or corrections for future editions.

Writing a beginning language textbook is not an easy task. I had to consider many issues—whether I should be linguistically precise or retain the standard older terminology, whether I wanted to present detailed historical reconstructions or synchronic explanations. This book does not offer a uniform stance on such questions; in each case, I did what I felt would best facilitate the students' acquisition of BH and would offer a useful foundation for further study. Others, I am sure, would make different judgments at various points; I look forward to their comments, and the discussion that this textbook might generate about methods of teaching BH.

Introduction
Biblical Hebrew as a Language

Biblical Hebrew (BH) is a scholarly construct, based on the collection of books now found in the Hebrew Bible. (The small portion of the Bible written in Aramaic will not concern us here.) These books constitute a rather incomplete representation of the range of languages spoken in ancient Israel. Nor do they truly represent a single language or dialect, for they reflect the diversity of time periods, places, and genres that are exhibited in the Hebrew Bible.

The Bible, by its nature, is a largely theological book; in the everyday lives of ancient Israelites, religion played an important but not an exclusive role. Thus it is not surprising that all sorts of words reflecting basic nontheological realia are missing from the Hebrew Bible. These include words for household items that we know existed in ancient Israel, such as *spoon* (rabbinic כַּף; biblical כַּף is used only in the sense of "palm of the hand") or *comb* (מַשְׂרֵק; the biblical feminine plural adjective שְׂרִיקוֹת, *combed* [flax], is found once, but the noun מַשְׂרֵק is lacking). Because locust plagues are an important tool of divine punishment in the Bible, we have four names for types of locusts in a single biblical verse (Joel 1:4). In contrast, we only have the general word דָּג for fish, because fish are not typical tools for God's anger, nor do they require detailed listings in the catalogues of permitted and prohibited foods (for example, the lists of birds in Leviticus 11 and Deuteronomy 14). This does not mean necessarily that ancient Israel had no vocabulary to distinguish among different kinds of fish; words for specific kinds of fish simply have not been preserved. In sum, we must always remember that BH is a "linguistic fragment"; we can supplement this fragment with caution given what we know from the small number of extrabiblical inscriptions, from later Hebrew, and from other Semitic languages, which are closely related to Hebrew. Still, even with these resources, we have an incomplete picture of ancient Israelite Hebrew.

What the previous examples illustrate in terms of vocabulary, or lexicon, is true for grammar as well. Biblical texts are predominantly concerned with males, either singly or in groups; furthermore, a mixed group of men and women (for example, "[the nation of] Israel") is treated as masculine in BH, as in MIH. (Masculine, in other words, is the "default" or "prior" gender in BH.) Thus, statistically, we have a huge number of masculine singular and plural forms, a small number of feminine singular forms, and a still smaller number of feminine plural forms. The form known from postbiblical, including modern, Hebrew of לָכֶן (*to you* [feminine plural]), for example, never appears in the Hebrew Bible; we may surmise that it existed in ancient Israel, and we may reconstruct it by analogy to forms like לָכֶם (*to you* [masculine plural]) and לָהֶן (*to them* [feminine plural]). Similarly, we can only guess that if an ancient Israelite wanted to tell a group of women to eat, he or she would have said אֱכֹלְנָה (the sign ˋ indicates that the stress is on the next to last syllable; see p. 20), because such forms (קֹל, imperative, feminine plural of פ״א verbs) never appear. Unlike lexical items, these grammatical forms may be reconstructed with some certainty, but we must remember that languages are not fully predictable.

The second problem alluded to in the term *biblical Hebrew* was that it implies that we have a single, unified language. On the contrary, we actually have several dialects that are merged in the Hebrew Bible. These dialects may be distinguished mainly in terms of chronology, geography, and genre.

All languages change over time; at certain points, these changes are rapid, especially if exacerbated by various historical events; at other times, languages can remain *relatively* stable over a long period of time. The scholarly consensus is that the Hebrew Bible incorporates works composed in approximately a thousand-year time period from the twelfth to the second pre-Christian centuries. That time period includes the years 586–538 BCE, during which a significant segment of the Judean population was exiled to Babylonia, and was influenced by Aramaic, the *lingua franca* of the ancient Near East at that time. It is thus customary to distinguish between pre-exilic Hebrew, which precedes the exile of 586, and postexilic Hebrew, which follows the return to Zion in 538. The middle period is represented by exilic Hebrew, which is a transition between these two dialects. The influence of Aramaic was far-reaching, sparking changes in the vocabulary and many elements of grammar. Under the influence of Aramaic, for example, words like זְמָן (*time*) entered BH by the post-exilic period. Many other changes may be seen on the syntactic level; in fact, in some significant ways, the syntax of postexilic Hebrew is closer to MIH than to earlier BH. Even the script used by the population changed; the so-called paleo-Hebrew script was replaced by its cousin, the Aramaic script, a descendent of which is now used to write Hebrew.

There are also substantial differences between the very earliest layers of BH and the typical dialect, which scholars call Standard Biblical Hebrew. The earliest levels are likely attested in several poems, such as the Song of Deborah in Judges 5. Because these poems were probably recited in antiquity, they retained certain archaic features; in contrast, old prose material was likely updated in its transmission. In terms of grammar, for example, the word שַׁקַּמְתִּי, with the suffix תִּי, is found in the Song of Deborah in Judges 5:7; this is not, as in modern and typical biblical Hebrew, a first-person suffix ("I arose") but an archaic second-person feminine suffix ("you arose"). There is some specialized vocabulary in this corpus as well. Because the corpus of archaic biblical poetry (ABP) is limited, and some of these texts may have been corrupted over time and are extremely difficult to understand, they will not be studied in this textbook.

According to the biblical tradition, a civil war ensued after the kingship of Solomon ended (ca. 920), and his former kingdom was ruled by two kings. The southern area was called Judea (יְהוּדָה) and the northern area Israel (יִשְׂרָאֵל). For two centuries, until the exile of the northern kingdom by the Assyrians, these areas existed as separate, typically antagonistic, political bodies. There is some evidence within the Bible, as well as from ancient inscriptions excavated in Israel, to indicate that a different dialect of Hebrew was spoken in each kingdom. So in the stories about the northern prophet Elisha in 2 Kings 4:2, for example, we find the expression מַה־יֶּשׁ־לָכִי instead of the expected מַה־יֶּשׁ־לָךְ ("what do you [feminine singular] have?"). The feminine singular suffix ־כִי is known in Aramaic, the language of ancient Syria that was adjacent to the northern kingdom. It is likely that the Bible has preserved a dialectical feature of northern Hebrew. Most texts that deal with the northern kingdom are not preserved in this dialect, however, because northern texts were ultimately passed down through Judah after the destruction of the northern kingdom in the late eighth century and have thus been adjusted to a large extent to Judean Hebrew. For this reason, there is no biblical text that accurately represents the northern dialect.

Although most of the Bible is prose, a substantial portion is in poetry. These poetic texts are quite distinct from a linguistic point of view from their prose counterparts. For example, in the first section of Isaiah chapter 5, called by modern scholars "The Song of the Vineyard," Israel is threatened with severe punishment. The first verse of that poem declares, "my beloved had a vineyard." Biblical prose would usually express this as וַיְהִי לִידִידִי כֶּרֶם, but in fact the poem begins כֶּרֶם הָיָה לִידִידִי. Many other syntactic differences exist; much as in English-language poetry, biblical poetry is not constrained by the "rules" of "standard" prose. In addition, a substantial vocabulary of biblical Hebrew is found only in poetry. There are two words for gold in biblical Hebrew—זָהָב and חָרוּץ. זָהָב may be used in any context, but חָרוּץ is confined to poetry. Words found only in poetic contexts will not be emphasized in this grammar.

Other distinctions can be made—between spoken and written ancient Hebrew, for example. Most of the Hebrew prose in the Bible is quite formal, and, especially in its use of the verb, it is unlikely to have been used when ancient Israelites spoke. Indeed, some scholars have suggested that a careful look at quoted narration preserved in the Bible, in contrast to other biblical prose, indicates that quoted speech follows slightly different rules. The case here is reminiscent of what was noted above concerning northern vs. southern Hebrew: it is likely that different dialects—spoken as opposed to formal or written—did exist, but the history and nature of the Bible's composition and transmission render these differences nearly invisible.

Indeed, it must be emphasized that although the Bible contains works from a thousand-year period and from several geographical locales (Judea, northern Israel, Babylonia, Egypt), and although some differences may be perceived through careful study, the language of the Hebrew Bible is much more uniform than expected. Because the text remained flexible to some extent as it was transmitted, certain archaic or unusual forms were normalized. Additionally, the vowel points were inserted into the biblical text only toward the end of the first millennium CE, further leveling dialectical differences.

A complete grammar of the Hebrew Bible should distinguish to the extent now possible among these dialects, just as an English grammar should distinguish among the languages of Chaucer, Shakespeare, and contemporary English, among written English, spoken formal English, and slang, among British and northern and southern American English, and between poetry and prose. The typical biblical reference grammars have, in fact, not done so, and this is one of the features that makes them so difficult to use—one is never quite sure whether the rules adduced are relevant to the corpus one is studying. The grammatical section in this book emphasizes (Judean) Standard Biblical Hebrew (SBH) prose–the language of the largest block of material in the Hebrew Bible. The foundation offered in this textbook should allow the interested student to use the standard grammars and other tools in order to study texts composed in dialects not represented here.

For Further Reading

Kutscher, E. Y. *A History of the Hebrew Language.* Jerusalem: Magnes, 1982.
Naveh, Joseph. *Early History of the Alphabet: An Introduction to West Semitic Epigraphy and Paleography.* Jerusalem: Magnes, 1982.
Sáenz-Badillos, Angel. *A History of the Hebrew Language.* Cambridge: Cambridge University Press, 1993.
Ullendorff, Eduard. *Is Biblical Hebrew a Language? Studies in Semitic Languages.* Wiesbaden: Harrassowitz, 1977.
Young, Ian. *Diversity in Pre-Exilic Hebrew.* Tübingen: J. C. B. Mohr, 1993.

1 The Consonants of Biblical Hebrew

Counting only written signs, the biblical alphabet has twenty-two letters. Linguists, however, distinguish between letters and phonemes; a letter is a type of written sign, whereas a phoneme is a sound that is significant in terms of distinguishing the meaning of one word from another. We know that ק and ד are distinct phonemes in biblical Hebrew, for example, because the word קָם, "he[1] arose" (with a ק), is distinct in meaning from דָּם, "blood" (with a ד). If we take a closer look at the idea of phonemes in relation to biblical Hebrew, we see that the distinction the Bible makes between שׁ and שׂ is significant—take for example שָׁם, "there," versus שָׂם, "he placed." Thus, שׁ and שׂ represent two different phonemes in biblical Hebrew—or, to put it differently, the contrast between שׁ and שׂ is phonemic. (It is only in the late first millennium CE, however, that the dot was used to distinguished between these two letters; earlier, they were both written simply ש.) This stands in contrast to the letters כ and ⟨ב-variant⟩, for example; this difference never determines a difference in meaning. Instead, various speech or sound (phonological) rules determine whether in any particular situation we find כ or ⟨ב-variant⟩. (The technical term for such a pair is *allophone*: they represent the same phoneme, but articulated differently depending on their phonological environment—that is, their placement within the word.) Once we understand phonemes as meaningful sounds, we realize that there are twenty-three consonantal phonemes in biblical Hebrew, for both שׁ and שׂ must be counted.

The twenty-three consonantal phonemes are listed below, along with their corresponding written sign or representation in standard Hebrew transliteration. Transliteration is often used in the scholarly world because it allows Hebrew to be expressed without the expense of typesetting in a separate font. In addition, transliteration demonstrates certain aspects of Hebrew words (especially syllable structure) more clearly than script; this textbook will use transliteration occasionally for that reason.

---

1. Or *it*. Throughout this textbook, *he* and *she* will typically be used instead of *it* for inanimate subjects, depending on that subject's grammatical gender.

The Consonants, Their Names, and Their Transliteration

Letter	Transliterated value	(postbiblical) Name
א	ʾ	אָלֶף
בּ (and its allophone ב)	b (and b̠)	בֵּית (and בֵית)
גּ (and its allophone ג)	g (and g̠)	גִּימֶל (and גִימֶל)
דּ (and its allophone ד)	d (and d̠)	דָּלֶת (and דָלֶת)
ה	h	הֵא
ו	w	וָו
ז	z	זַיִן
ח	ḥ	חֵית
ט	ṭ	טֵית
י	y	יוֹד
כּ (and its allophone כ)	k (and k̠)	כָּף (and כָף)
ל	l	לָמֶד
מ	m	מֵם
נ	n	נוּן
ס	s	סָמֶךְ
ע	ʿ	עַיִן
פּ (and its allophone פ)	p (and p̠)	פֵּא (and פֵא)
צ	ṣ	צָדִי
ק	q	קוֹף
ר	r	רֵישׁ
שׂ	ś	שִׂין
שׁ	š	שִׁין
תּ (and its allophone ת)	t (and t̠)	תָּו (and תָו)

The six letters ב, ג, ד, כ, פ, and ת come in pairs (בּ, גּ, דּ, כּ, פּ, and תּ, as well as ב, ג, ד, כ, פ, and ת), as is discussed in chapter 4. MIH distinguishes only between the pronunciations of בּ, כּ, and פּ, on the one hand, and ב, כ, and פ on the other. Ashkenazic (East European) pronunciation distinguishes ת from ת. Yemenite Jews, when chanting liturgically from the Torah, distinguish each of the letters in the six pairs. Without question, the fact that these six pairs are marked shows that there once was a distinction made between them, but the distinction at this point is largely of historical interest.

There are five Hebrew letters that have different final forms: ך, ם, ן, ף, and ץ. They are typically cited in the order מנצפך because of the rabbinic understanding of their origin as deriving "from (מִן) your prophets" (צֹפֶךָ; צוֹפִים are those who gaze into the future). Each of these forms is called a סוֹפִית in modern Hebrew (ך, for example, is a כַּף סוֹפִית). In Arabic, another language in the Semitic language family to which Hebrew belongs, most letters have three forms: initial, medial (in the middle of the word), and final. From a historical perspective, we know that the forms of the letters דוץף are earlier than the corresponding כבנ, and that the latter arose at the beginning and the middle of words for simple graphic reasons—when writing a ד followed with another letter, it is natural to pull the tail to the left toward the next letter, resulting in a horizontal stroke instead of a tail below the line. For this reason, in all but the final forms, the tails of the letters דוץף became horizontal strokes. (The history of מ and ם is somewhat different; both forms existed in antiquity, and, by analogy to כבנ and דוץף, one form was assigned to the final position, while the other became the initial-medial form.) In sum, the variant forms of such letters as כ and ב, צ and ץ do not affect the tally of twenty-three consonantal phonemes in biblical Hebrew.

In all languages, we may divide the consonantal inventory into classes on the basis of how particular clusters of consonants are pronounced, in order to help explain certain phonetic patterns. In English, for example, we might want to explain why the plural suffix is sometimes written *s* but on other occasions *es*. It would then be helpful to note that the *es* form of the plural follows *s, x, z, ch,* and *sh,* and to realize that the corresponding sounds, called sibilants, are all pronounced from a similar point in the mouth. We might then expect these letters to share other characteristics or to cause other phonetic or spelling changes as well.

Hebrew consonants, too, may be divided into classes, based on the way they are articulated using the mouth, tongue, and throat. All Hebrew sounds can be categorized along several axes; I note the following groups which are especially important.

> ### The Classes of Hebrew Consonants
>
> - Labials (pronounced using the lips): ב, ו, מ, and פ.
> - Gutturals (a sound originating in the throat): א, ה, ח, and ע. (The letter ר is not formally a guttural but shares several phonetic features with the gutturals. We therefore sometimes speak of "the gutturals plus ר." The mnemonic הָאָח רַע—"the brother is bad"—may help in remembering this important class.) These letters are sometimes (imprecisely) called laryngeals.
> - Dentals (pronounced with the tongue touching the tips of the upper teeth): ד, ט, and ת.
> - Sibilants (pronounced by narrowing the air passages and produced on the hard palate): ז, ס, צ, שׁ, and שׂ.
> - Emphatics or velars (pronounced in the soft palate, in a region farther back than the corresponding letters כ, ס, and ת): ט, צ, and ק.
> - Sonants (voiced consonants—that is, pronounced with a vibration of the vocal cords): ל, מ, נ, and ר.

For now, a single example will illustrate the importance of putting the consonants into such categories. The typical form of the conjunction *and* in biblical Hebrew, as in modern Hebrew, is וְ; so, for example, "and a book" is וְסֵפֶר. Yet it may be difficult to pronounce two labials in a row, so before labials, the conjunction takes the form וּ—for example, וּמַיִם, "and water." The same principle applies to all labials, thus וּבַיִת, "and a house," and וּפֹה, "and here."

Vocabulary Lists

The vocabulary lists in this book review the common words used in the Bible; the most frequently used words are found in the earliest chapters. These words, however, are used extensively in the chapter exercises only following chapter 8, after issues of morphology and syntax are introduced. Verbs are introduced into the vocabulary beginning with chapter 13, which treats the participle. The vocabulary lists illustrate certain features that are discussed in detail only in later chapters (for example, irregular gender, irregular plural forms, verb conjugation forms), but these issues should be familiar from MIH. It is important to learn the vocabulary words (and the irregular plurals) from these early chapters gradually, along with the grammatical material in them, rather than waiting until chapter 8.

Vocabulary for chapter 1

אָדָם	person, humanity (a collective—no plural)
אִישׁ	man, person (irregular plural אֲנָשִׁים)[2]
אֵל	god, God
אֱלֹהִים	god, gods, God
אֱנוֹשׁ	humanity (a collective, mostly poetic)
אִשָּׁה	woman (irregular plural נָשִׁים)
גָּדוֹל	big, great
דָּבָר	word, matter, thing
הַר	mountain (plural הָרִים)
טוֹב	good
לַיְלָה	night (irregular plural לֵילוֹת)
מַלְאָךְ	messenger, angel (= divine messenger)
מֶלֶךְ	king
מָקוֹם	place (masculine; irregular plural מְקוֹמוֹת)
עַיִן	eye
עִיר	city (feminine; irregular plural עָרִים)
עַם	nation (plural עַמִּים)
צַדִּיק	righteous
קָטֹן (less often קָטָן)	small (feminine קְטַנָּה; plurals קְטַנִּים and קְטַנּוֹת)
רַע	evil, bad (plural רָעִים)
שָׁלוֹם	peace, well-being
שֵׁם	name (masculine; irregular plural שֵׁמוֹת)
שָׁנָה	year (feminine; irregular plural שָׁנִים)
תּוֹרָה	instruction, law, teaching, Torah (in this sense, rare and LBH [Late Biblical Hebrew])

---

2. Irregular plural is used to indicate either that the word changes in form in some unexpected way, as in this case, or that a masculine noun takes the typically feminine ending (as in שֵׁם שֵׁמוֹת), or vice versa (as in שָׁנָה שָׁנִים).

Exercises for chapter 1

1. Using the chart on p. 6, offer a consonantal transliteration of the prophetic verse Zephaniah 3:8, which contains all the consonants of the Hebrew alphabet:

   לָכֵן חַכּוּ־לִי֙ נְאֻם־יְהוָ֔ה לְי֖וֹם קוּמִ֣י לְעַ֑ד כִּ֣י מִשְׁפָּטִי֩ לֶאֱסֹ֨ף גּוֹיִ֜ם לְקָבְצִ֣י מַמְלָכ֗וֹת לִשְׁפֹּ֨ךְ עֲלֵיהֶ֤ם זַעְמִי֙ כֹּ֚ל חֲר֣וֹן אַפִּ֔י כִּ֚י בְּאֵ֣שׁ קִנְאָתִ֔י תֵּאָכֵ֖ל כָּל־הָאָֽרֶץ׃

2. Transcribe the following transliterated words into (consonantal) Hebrew:

šmʿ	qdwš
yld	śr
ʾbqš	sr
ʾḥwt	ṣr
gdwl	šr
ṭwb	hmzbḥ
tʿmdy	kḥ
npš	ḥk

3. Identify the category (or categories) to which each of these letters belongs:

נ	א
ע	ב
פ	ד
צ	ה
ק	ז
ר	ח
שׂ	ט
שׁ	ל
ת	מ

2   The Vowels

The picture of Hebrew vowels is much more complex and uncertain than that of the consonants. Although both consonantal and vocalic sounds have always been a part of spoken BH, written Hebrew for centuries included consonants only. The meager corpus of pre-exilic letters on ostraca (broken pieces of pottery), for example, contains only consonants. Similarly, none of the Dead Sea scrolls, which date from the third century BCE to the first century CE, contain vowel signs above or below the consonants. Vowel signs began to appear in the second half of the first millennium CE, most likely by the seventh century. They were developed as groups of Jews became concerned that the correct tradition of liturgical readings for the Hebrew Bible would be lost: the consonantal text presents but a shell, and in BH, as in MIH, a group of consonants is open to several readings with different meanings (דבר, for example, may reflect דָּבָר, *thing;* דְּבַר, *thing of;* דֶּבֶר, *pestilence;* דֹּבֶר, *speaking;* דִּבֶּר, *he spoke,* and so on). The scholars who developed these systems of vocalization are called Masoretes, from the Hebrew בַּעֲלֵי הַמָּסוֹרָה, "masters of the tradition." The term Masorete is often used in a broad sense, comprising the individuals who were concerned with all aspects of the precise reading and writing of the biblical text; some prefer to use the term נַקְדָנִים, *pointers,* for those concerned specifically with the vocalization of the Hebrew Bible.

This concern for precisely preserving the tradition of reading by a more complete marking of the sounds of the word originated in two main geographical centers of Jewry: Babylonia and Israel. Within Israel, in fact, it was realized in different ways in various centers of learning. The system that we now use for vowels is the winner, so to speak, of several competing systems. These systems differ mainly in the number of signs marking vowels, in the shape of the vowel signs, and in the positioning of the signs in relation to the consonants. The system we use was developed in Tiberias, in the Galilee region of (northern) Israel, and is called the Tiberian system. Other systems developed in other areas of Israel (the Palestinian system[s]) and in Babylonia (the Babylonian system[s]).

The Tiberian system is largely infralinear—that is, most of the vowels are below the line. The names given to these vowel names vary significantly; only the most frequent variants are noted below. The consonant בֵּית is used below to illustrate the position of the vowels.

The Hebrew Vowels

בָּ	קָמֶץ (frequently called קָמָץ)
בַּ	פַּתַח (frequently called פֶּתַח)
בֶּ	סֶגוֹל
בֵּ	צֵרִי
בִּ	חִירִק (frequently called חִירֶק)
בֹּ	חֹלֶם (frequently called חוֹלָם); when written וֹ called חוֹלָם מָלֵא
בּוּ	שׁוּרֶק (frequently called שׁוּרוּק)
בֻּ	קִבּוּץ (frequently called קָבּוּץ)
בְּ	שְׁוָא
בֲּ	חֲטַף פַּתַח
בֱּ	חֱטַף סֶגוֹל
בֳּ	חֳטַף קָמֶץ

The vowels are pronounced after the consonant they are written with. There are two exceptions to this rule. A final פַּתַח under the letters החע is called a furtive *pátaḥ*—in Hebrew פַּתַח גְּנוּבָה—and is pronounced *before* the final consonant of the word. For example, שָׂמֵחַ is pronounced as if it were written שָׂמַאח. (Thus the word אֱלוֹהַּ should be pronounced אֱלוֹאַהּ, not, as commonly heard, אֱלוֹהָה.) In good biblical manuscripts and in several printed editions, the furtive *pataḥ*, or פַּתַח גְּנוּבָה, is written to the right of the center of the consonant that it is under (for example, שָׂמֵֽחַ), reflecting the fact that it is pronounced before rather than after the consonant. The second exception is the conjunctive וַ which in certain cases is written as וּ, but is pronounced אוּ.

The number of phonemes that these twelve signs represent continues to be the focus of scholarly debate. In addition, the Tiberian system is confusing in that at least two of its signs are ambiguous to us in terms of their pronunciation: the שְׁוָא may be pronounced either as an ultrashort vowel (as in דְּבָרִים) or may have no pronunciation at all (as in הִשְׁמִיד), and the קָמֵץ may be pronounced as a short *a*, identical to the פַּתַח (as in כָּתַב) or may be pronounced as a long *o*, as in the first קָמֵץ in the word חָכְמָה, *wisdom*. The first type of קָמֵץ, which is much more common than the second, is sometimes called a קָמֵץ גָּדוֹל, while the second is called a קָמֵץ קָטָן. (A קָמֵץ is pronounced as a קָמֵץ קָטָן when it is found in a closed, unaccented syllable; syllable structure is explained in the following chapters.) The type of שְׁוָא that is pronounced is called a שְׁוָא נָע, or a mobile *sheva*, while the type that is silent is called a שְׁוָא נָח, or a quiescent *sheva*. (Distinguishing between these pairs is summarized on p. 32.) It is likely that the שְׁוָא and the קָמֵץ originally did not have these double pronunciations, and that this doubling emerged as the written Tiberian system came into contact with non-Tiberian systems of Hebrew pronunciation.

Although there is no consensus concerning the exact number of vocalic phonemes, scholars generally agree that Hebrew vowels may be distinguished along two axes: quality and quantity. Quality refers to the fact that within Semitic languages there are three basic categories of vocalic sounds: *a* sounds, *i* sounds, and *u* sounds; indeed, in Arabic (except for a sign marking the equivalent of a שְׁוָא נָח), only these three vowel sounds may be found. In addition, it is customary to categorize Semitic vowels in terms of quantity as "long" or "short"; thus, in Arabic, there are a total of six vowels, short and long *a*, short and long *i*, and short and long *u*. With Arabic, "short" and "long" actually refer to the duration for which the vowel sound is held. In the case of Hebrew, the terms do not refer to actual vowel length; nevertheless, the *concept* of vowel length is useful. The following chart uses the letters ח and ט with various vowels to illustrate the quality and quantity of the Hebrew vowels.

Vowel Class and Quantity

	a-class	*i-class*	*u-class*	other
Long	חָ (קָמֵץ גָּדוֹל)	חֵ חֵי חִי חוֹ חוּ		
Short	חַ	חֶ	חָ חֻ (קָמֵץ קָטָן)	
Ultrashort	חֲ	חֱ	חֳ	טְ (שְׁוָא נָע)

(Note: Some scholars have suggested that in certain cases the vowels צֵרִי [חֵ] and חֹלֶם [חֹ] may be classified as short.)

There are many different systems of transliterating Hebrew vowels. The system adopted here is the one used in the *Journal of Biblical Literature*.

The Transliteration of Hebrew Vowels

A-class vowels

קָמֵץ גָּדוֹל *ā* (final הָ, *â*); פַּתַח *a*; חֲטַף פַּתַח *ă*.

The furtive *paṭaḥ* or פַּתַח גְּנוּבָה is written as an *a* before the consonant that it is associated with (for example, שָׂמֵחַ *śāmēaḥ*).

I-class vowels

סֶגוֹל *e*; צֵרִי *ē* (final and medial יִ and medial יֶ, are *ê*); חִירֶק חָסֵר *i* (medial or final יִ is *î*); חֲטַף סֶגוֹל *ĕ*.

U-class vowels

חֲטַף קָמֵץ *ŏ*; חוֹלֶם חָסֵר *ō*; חוֹלֶם מָלֵא *ô*; קָמֵץ קָטָן *o*; שׁוּרֶק *û*; קִבּוּץ *u* or *ū*; חֲטַף קָמֵץ *ŏ*.

In addition, שְׁוָא, when pronounced, is written *ĕ*. (In other systems, it is written ə). Words with penultimate stress, namely, stress on the next to last syllable (Hebrew מִלְעֵיל), are marked with the sign ´ on the stressed syllable.

The problem of helping the reader decide the proper pronunciation of ambiguous words existed long before the development of the various written vowel systems in the second half of the first millennium CE. Already in the biblical period, the four consonants א, ה, ו, and י began to be used to mark particular vowel sounds connected to the previous consonant. This may be seen in various Hebrew inscriptions. In one pre-exilic inscription, for example, the word *cursed* is written ארור, with the ו indicating that the previous ר is followed by a u-class vowel (we would vocalize it אָרוּר); in another, "the man" is written האיש (later הָאִישׁ); in another, the numeral 6 is written ששה (later שִׁשָּׁה), indicating that there is an *ā* after the second ש; in yet another the negative *not* is written לא (later לֹא). These consonants, which help the reader determine which vowel sounds should be read, are called vowel letters in English and are frequently called by the Latin name *matres lectionis* or the Hebrew אִמּוֹת הַקְּרִיאָה (singular: *mater lectionis*, אֵם קְרִיאָה). Usually, ו represents a u-class vowel, while י represents the i-class vowels, and ה typically represents final $\bar{a}$, $\bar{e}$ or e (as in the words שָׂדֶה, בָּנָה, or יִבְנֶה). א most often represents o, as in רֹאשׁ. The *matres lectionis* developed over a long period of time and are not employed consistently in the Hebrew Bible. There is tremendous variation in their use between books and even within the same book. This is seen, for example, in the second half of Genesis 26:18, where the word שמות is spelled two ways: וַיִּקְרָא לָהֶן שֵׁמוֹת כַּשֵּׁמֹת אֲשֶׁר־קָרָא לָהֶן אָבִיו׃.

The English *full*, the Latin *plene*, and the Hebrew מָלֵא describe words in which a *mater lectionis* is used, while words that lack a *mater* are called defective (in the sense of short, not marred) or חָסֵר. Sometimes individual vowels are also characterized as מָלֵא (or less frequently חָסֵר); in the verse cited above, for example, we may say that the word שֵׁמוֹת has a חוֹלֶם מָלֵא, while כַּשֵּׁמֹת appears with a חֹלֶם חָסֵר.

For Further Reading

Barr, James. *The Variable Spellings of the Hebrew Bible*. Oxford: Oxford University Press, 1989.

Gibson, John C. L. *Textbook of Syrian Semitic Inscriptions*. Vol. 1, *Hebrew and Moabite Inscriptions*. Oxford: Oxford University Press, 1973.

Zevit, Ziony. *Matres Lectionis in Ancient Hebrew Epigraphs*. Cambridge, Mass.: American Schools for Oriental Research, 1980.

Vocabulary for chapter 2

אָדוֹן	master, lord
אֲדֹנָי	God (literally "my masters")
אָז	then
אֶרֶץ	land, the Earth (feminine, with expected plural אֲרָצוֹת)
בַּיִת	house (masculine; irregular plural בָּתִּים)
גּוֹי	nation
חַי	alive, living
חַיִּים	life (plural only)
יָד	hand (in dual, יָדַיִם, "hands," and in plural יָדוֹת, "times")
יהוה	Yahweh, a name of God in the Hebrew Bible, often translated (the) LORD. It is not known how this name was originally pronounced. At a certain point, it became taboo to pronounce this name, and it was vocalized with the vowels of אֲדֹנָי (as יְהֹוָה), and pronounced אֲדֹנָי. Less frequently, it is written with the vowels of אֱלֹהִים (as יֱהֹוִה), in which case it is pronounced אֱלֹהִים.
יוֹם	day (irregular plural יָמִים)
כֹּהֵן	priest
לֵב (also לְבָב)	heart (plurals לְבָבוֹת and לִבּוֹת).
מַיִם	water
עֶבֶד	servant, slave
פָּנִים	face (plural only)
קוֹל	voice (masculine; irregular plural קֹלֹת)
קָדוֹשׁ	holy
קֹדֶשׁ	holy thing
רֹאשׁ	head (irregular plural רָאשִׁים)

THE VOWELS

Exercises for chapter 2:

1. Read the following words (from Genesis 22), identify the names of all of the vowels they contain, and note whether each vowel is long, short or ultrashort:

לָכֶם פֹּה עִם־הַחֲמוֹר

אַיִל אַחַר נֶאֱחַז

אֶל־בְּאֵר שָׁבַע

2. Transliterate the following words into Hebrew:

ʾaḇrāhām	yaʿăqōḏ
ʾeṯ	ḥāśaḵtā
ḥămōrô	ṭĕmēʾîm
qaḥ	ʾayil
yiṣḥaq	sôrēr
hāʾēš	

3. Transliterate the following Hebrew words:

שְׁנֵיהֶם	סָבַךְ
מֵרָחֹק	שֹׁמֵעַ
יַחֲבֹשׁ	שֶׂה
הֶהָרִים	שֵׁנִית
אַחַר	יֵאָמֵר
	לְעֵצִים

4. Note where the letters אהוי are consonantal, and when they function as vowel letters:

	וְיָקוּם
	מִי
	רֵאשִׁית
	חַיִל
	דּוֹד
	דָּוִד
	יֵצֵא
	בֵּין
	בָּנָה
	וְיֹשִׁיב
	הַפֶּה
	רוּחַ
	בְּיַד
	בִּידֵי
	עָוֹן
	וַיִּמְצָא
	יְהִי
	הֵנָּה

5. Circle the vowel letters in the first two verses of the Bible:

בְּרֵאשִׁית בָּרָא אֱלֹהִים אֵת הַשָּׁמַיִם וְאֵת הָאָרֶץ: וְהָאָרֶץ הָיְתָה תֹהוּ וָבֹהוּ וְחֹשֶׁךְ עַל־פְּנֵי תְהוֹם וְרוּחַ אֱלֹהִים מְרַחֶפֶת עַל־פְּנֵי הַמָּיִם:

3 The Cantillation Marks

Several additional signs beyond the consonants and the vowels were developed by the Masoretes and are used in biblical manuscripts and printed Bibles. The most noteworthy among these are the cantillation marks. To better prepare students for encountering regular biblical texts, these signs are included in all quotations of biblical passages in this book. Like the vocalization marks, these signs developed in different ways in various centers of world Jewry in the second half of the first millennium CE. Ultimately the Tiberian cantillation signs were adopted, along with that system of vocalization. Even the Tiberian system includes two fundamentally different subsystems: one that is used for Psalms, Proverbs, and most of Job, and another that is found in all other biblical books. This chapter will survey only the more typical system, sometimes called the cantillation or accents of the twenty-one books.[1]

The opening of the Hebrew Bible follows, with the consonantal text, vowels, and cantillation marks:

1:1 בְּרֵאשִׁ֖ית בָּרָ֣א אֱלֹהִ֑ים אֵ֥ת הַשָּׁמַ֖יִם וְאֵ֥ת הָאָֽרֶץ׃ 2 וְהָאָ֗רֶץ הָיְתָ֥ה תֹ֙הוּ֙ וָבֹ֔הוּ וְחֹ֖שֶׁךְ עַל־פְּנֵ֣י תְה֑וֹם וְר֣וּחַ אֱלֹהִ֔ים מְרַחֶ֖פֶת עַל־פְּנֵ֥י הַמָּֽיִם׃ 3 וַיֹּ֥אמֶר אֱלֹהִ֖ים יְהִ֣י א֑וֹר וַֽיְהִי־אֽוֹר׃ 4 וַיַּ֧רְא אֱלֹהִ֛ים אֶת־הָא֖וֹר כִּי־ט֑וֹב וַיַּבְדֵּ֣ל אֱלֹהִ֔ים בֵּ֥ין הָא֖וֹר וּבֵ֥ין הַחֹֽשֶׁךְ׃ 5 וַיִּקְרָ֨א אֱלֹהִ֤ים ׀ לָאוֹר֙ י֔וֹם וְלַחֹ֖שֶׁךְ קָ֣רָא לָ֑יְלָה וַֽיְהִי־עֶ֥רֶב וַֽיְהִי־בֹ֖קֶר י֥וֹם אֶחָֽד׃

These signs have three significant functions: they describe how the text should be cantillated or chanted, they specify where words should be accented or stressed, and they divide the biblical verse into sections, functioning like punctuation.

1. According to traditional Jewish enumeration, the biblical canon contains twenty-four books; subtracting Psalms, Proverbs, and Job leaves twenty-one.

Various geographical groupings of Jews have different traditions for the musical value of particular Tiberian cantillation marks, and most traditions interpret the same cantillation marks in five ways, depending on what corpus is being read: one interpretation is used when chanting the Torah, another for Esther, a third for Lamentations (אֵיכָה), a fourth for Ruth, Song of Songs (שִׁיר הַשִּׁירִים), and Ecclesiastes (קֹהֶלֶת), and a fifth for all other books. In addition, there are special forms of cantillation for the High Holidays—Rosh Hashanah (the New Year) and Yom Kippur (the Day of Atonement)—and for special sections of the Bible (for example, the Song of the Sea in Exodus 15). The musical transcriptions of the cantillation marks will not be explored here.

A key function of the cantillation marks is to show where words are accented. For this purpose it is important to remember that Hebrew words, in contrast to English words, may be accented only on their last or next-to-last syllables. (On syllabification, see pp. 30–34.) Because the last syllable is called the ultima, accent on the last syllable is called ultimate stress. In Hebrew the term מִלְּרַע (borrowed from Aramaic) is used. Accent on the next-to-last syllable is called penultimate stress, in Hebrew מִלְּעֵל. Most Tiberian cantillation marks appear on the accented or "tonic" syllable. (Biblical Hebrew textbooks and grammars conventionally mark penultimately stressed words with the sign ˋ ; for example, בַּ֫עַל, "husband, owner," is accented on the penultima—in this case, the first—syllable. When words are cited without cantillation marks, this convention for marking penultimate stress will be followed here.)

Cantillation marks can be divided into two categories: conjunctive and disjunctive. Conjunctive accents tell the reader to keep going, while disjunctive accents suggest that the reader must pause or stop. The disjunctives are arranged according to a hierarchy that may be viewed as a gradient from full stop to slow down or yield. The conjunctives have no such arrangement; instead, particular conjunctives tend to appear with specific disjunctives.

Below is a list of the names of most of the Tiberian cantillation marks. I have listed the disjunctive and conjunctive signs separately, and for the sake of convenience, I have put all of the signs over or under the letter ק. There is some variation between biblical manuscripts and some printed editions in the shapes of some of the signs; the illustrations used here are those found in the standard scholarly reference Bible, *Biblia Hebraica Stuttgartensia*.

Disjunctive Cantillation Marks

סִלּוּק ק֑ This ends every biblical verse and is the most powerful disjunctive accent. Each biblical verse is also followed by what looks like a colon (:). This is called a סוֹף פָּסוּק.

אַתְנַחְתָּא ק֑ or אַתְנַח This is the second most powerful disjunctive and divides almost all biblical verses in two sections.

זָקֵף קָטֹן ק֔ A common major disjunctive, which typically divides each "half" of the verse into two sections.

זָקֵף גָּדוֹל ק֕

רְבִיעַ ק֗

טִפְחָא ק֖

תְּבִיר ק֛

גֶּרֶשׁ ק֜

גֵּרְשַׁיִם ק֞

שַׁלְשֶׁלֶת ק֓

פָּזֵר ק֡

All of the disjunctive accents listed above appear on (above or below) the tonic syllable. In addition, there are several cantillation marks that do not mark the word's tone. These are of two types: postpositive signs, which appear on the last syllable of the word, and prepositive signs, which appear on the first syllable. It is crucial to remember which signs are prepositive and postpositive, because in these cases you must determine where the stress falls by some means other than the placement of the cantillation mark.

The prepositive and postpositive marks are listed below:

סֶגּוֹלְתָּא ק֒ or סֶגּוֹל postpositive (see Genesis 1:7 הָרָקִיעַ)

זַרְקָא ק֮ postpositive

פַּשְׁטָא ק֙ postpositive

יְתִיב ק֚ prepositive

תְּלִישָׁא גְדוֹלָה ק֠ prepositive

Sometimes these cantillation marks are written twice, once at the beginning or the end of the word, and again on the tonic syllable, as in Genesis 1:2 תֹ֙הוּ֙. The פַּשְׁטָא is postpositive, so it *must* appear on the final syllable, but it is repeated over the first syllable as well to indicate that this syllable is tonic.

Conjunctive Cantillation Marks

מוּנַח ק֣

מְהֻפָּךְ ק֤ This is identical in form with the prepositive יְתִיב. In Genesis 1:5, the cantillation mark on אֱלֹהִים is a מְהֻפָּךְ, because it is written on the tonic syllable rather than at the beginning of the word.

מֵירְכָא ק֥

דַּרְגָּא ק֧

קַדְמָא or אַזְלָא ק֨ This is identical in form with the postpositive פַּשְׁטָא.

תְּלִישָׁא קְטַנָּה ק֩ postpositive

Before moving on to other Tiberian signs, it must be noted that these cantillation marks are of substantial importance, even outside of liturgical occasions. They help guide the punctuation of the verse, and to the extent that punctuation is key to interpreting many verses, they represent an early interpretive tradition. (For example, the Masoretic tradition suggests that the famous words of Isaiah in 40:3, קוֹל קוֹרֵא בַּמִּדְבָּר, should be understood as "A voice calls out, 'In the wilderness . . .'" rather than the early Christian understanding as a reference to John the Baptist: "A voice calls out in the wilderness.") Additionally, accent in biblical Hebrew is sometimes phonemic—that is, the same word may have a different meaning depending on whether its stress is ultimate or penultimate. This may be seen, for example, in the contrast between שָׂמָה, "she places," with ultimate stress and שָׂמָה, "she placed," with penultimate stress. The pair קוּמִי, "arise" and קוּמִי, "my arising," is similar. Given that the cantillation marks may determine the meaning of a word or how a sentence should be punctuated, it is important to learn the names of the more common accents, whether they are tonic, pre- or postpositive, and conjunctive or disjunctive.

For Further Reading

Kelley, Page H., Daniel S. Mynatt, and Timothy G. Crawford. *The Masorah of Biblia Hebraica Stuttgartensia: Introduction and Annotated Glossary*. Grand Rapids, Mich.: Eerdmans, 1998.

Yeivin, Israel. *Introduction to the Tiberian Masorah*. Masoretic Studies 5. Trans. and ed. E. J. Revell. Chico, Calif.: Scholars Press, 1980.

Vocabulary for chapter 3

אֹהֶל	tent
דָּם	blood
זָהָב	gold
חָדָשׁ	new
חֹדֶשׁ	month, new moon
יָם	sea
כֹּל, כָּל־	all, every, everything, any
כְּלִי	vessel (plural כֵּלִים)
כֶּסֶף	silver (contrast MIH, "money")
מִזְבֵּחַ	altar (masculine, but plural is מִזְבְּחוֹת)
מִלְחָמָה	war
מִשְׁפָּט	justice
נְאֻם	utterance (often in prophetic books in the idiom נְאֻם יהוה), the declaration of YHWH (contrast MIH, "speech")
נָבִיא	prophet
סָבִיב	around
עֵץ	tree, wood
פֶּה	mouth (irregular plurals פִּיפִיּוֹת פֵּיוֹת פִּיּוֹת)
צָבָא	army (masculine, but plural is צְבָאוֹת)
צְדָקָה, צֶדֶק	righteousness
רוּחַ	wind, spirit (mostly feminine, though sometimes masculine; plural is רוּחוֹת)
שַׂר	officer (plural שָׂרִים)
שָׁמַיִם	heavens, sky

Exercise for chapter 3

1. Identify the cantillation marks in the following verses (Genesis 22:1–6); note whether each word has ultimate or penultimate stress, and divide the verses into their major sections based on the placement of their major disjunctive accents:

22:1 וַיְהִ֗י אַחַר֙ הַדְּבָרִ֣ים הָאֵ֔לֶּה וְהָ֣אֱלֹהִ֔ים נִסָּ֖ה אֶת־אַבְרָהָ֑ם וַיֹּ֣אמֶר אֵלָ֔יו אַבְרָהָ֖ם וַיֹּ֥אמֶר הִנֵּֽנִי׃ 2 וַיֹּ֡אמֶר קַח־נָ֠א אֶת־בִּנְךָ֨ אֶת־יְחִֽידְךָ֤ אֲשֶׁר־אָהַ֙בְתָּ֙ אֶת־יִצְחָ֔ק וְלֶ֨ךְ־לְךָ֔ אֶל־אֶ֖רֶץ הַמֹּרִיָּ֑ה וְהַעֲלֵ֤הוּ שָׁם֙ לְעֹלָ֔ה עַ֚ל אַחַ֣ד הֶֽהָרִ֔ים אֲשֶׁ֖ר אֹמַ֥ר אֵלֶֽיךָ׃ 3 וַיַּשְׁכֵּ֨ם אַבְרָהָ֜ם בַּבֹּ֗קֶר וַֽיַּחֲבֹשׁ֙ אֶת־חֲמֹר֔וֹ וַיִּקַּ֞ח אֶת־שְׁנֵ֤י נְעָרָיו֙ אִתּ֔וֹ וְאֵ֖ת יִצְחָ֣ק בְּנ֑וֹ וַיְבַקַּע֙ עֲצֵ֣י עֹלָ֔ה וַיָּ֣קָם וַיֵּ֔לֶךְ אֶל־הַמָּק֖וֹם אֲשֶׁר־אָֽמַר־ל֥וֹ הָאֱלֹהִֽים׃ 4 בַּיּ֣וֹם הַשְּׁלִישִׁ֗י וַיִּשָּׂ֨א אַבְרָהָ֧ם אֶת־עֵינָ֛יו וַיַּ֥רְא אֶת־הַמָּק֖וֹם מֵרָחֹֽק׃ 5 וַיֹּ֨אמֶר אַבְרָהָ֜ם אֶל־נְעָרָ֗יו שְׁבוּ־לָכֶ֥ם פֹּה֙ עִֽם־הַחֲמ֔וֹר וַאֲנִ֣י וְהַנַּ֔עַר נֵלְכָ֖ה עַד־כֹּ֑ה וְנִֽשְׁתַּחֲוֶ֖ה וְנָשׁ֥וּבָה אֲלֵיכֶֽם׃ 6 וַיִּקַּ֨ח אַבְרָהָ֜ם אֶת־עֲצֵ֣י הָעֹלָ֗ה וַיָּ֙שֶׂם֙ עַל־יִצְחָ֣ק בְּנ֔וֹ וַיִּקַּ֣ח בְּיָד֔וֹ אֶת־הָאֵ֖שׁ וְאֶת־הַֽמַּאֲכֶ֑לֶת וַיֵּלְכ֥וּ שְׁנֵיהֶ֖ם יַחְדָּֽו׃

Note: In v. 1 and elsewhere where the same disjunctive accent repeats in adjacent words (הָאֵ֔לֶּה וְהָ֣אֱלֹהִ֔ים) or in the same half-verse, the first occurrence is more disjunctive than the second.

4 Other Written Symbols

The Masoretes devised several other symbols in addition to the consonants, vowels, and cantillation marks. Of these, the most common is the דָּגֵשׁ (*dagesh*), which comes in two main varieties: the strong *dagesh* (also called *dagesh forte*, or in Hebrew דָּגֵשׁ חָזָק) and the weak *dagesh* (also called the *dagesh lene*, or in Hebrew דָּגֵשׁ קַל).

The דָּגֵשׁ קַל appears only in the letters ב, ג, ד, כ, פ, and ת (ב, ג, ד, כ, פ, and ת). It was used by the Masoretes to distinguish between the two ways these letters were pronounced. (In linguistic terms, the paired forms of each letter are allophones, not separate phonemes; see p. 5.) In transliteration, the forms without a *dagesh* are indicated with underlining (that is, as *b̲*, *g̲*, *d̲*, *k̲*, *p̲*, and *t̲*), while those with a *dagesh* are written without the line. In contrast, the דָּגֵשׁ חָזָק may appear in any letter except the gutturals א, ה, ח, ע, and ר (and even in these, in several rare exceptions). Its function is to indicate that the letters should be pronounced as doubled, as in the letter *n* in the English word *unnecessary*; the doubled letter both closes the first syllable and opens the second, but is not truly "doubled" in the sense of being pronounced distinctly twice. So, for example, the Hebrew word הַמָּקוֹם, "the place," would be transliterated as *hammāqôm*, and וַיִּשָּׂא, "he lifted," as *wayyiśśā'*.

In some circumstances, biblical manuscripts mark the absence of a *dagesh* on a particular letter with a רָפֶה, a horizontal stroke over that letter. The רָפֶה is mostly found to mark the absence of a דָּגֵשׁ קַל, but it is found in other contexts as well. Different biblical manuscripts show wide variation in the marking of the רָפֶה. *Biblia Hebraica Stuttgartensia*, the standard scholarly Bible edition, does not typically use the רָפֶה.

The letter ה at the end of a word is typically a vowel letter and is silent. When it is pronounced (aspirated), it is written הּ, as in בְּנָהּ, "her son," or גָּבַהּ, "he was high or lofty."[1]

---

1. This form גָּבַהּ (with a final פַּתַח) contrasts with forms such as בָּנָה (with a final קָמֵץ), where the final ה is a vowel letter only, and the root is really בני. In contrast, the root of גָּבַהּ is גבה. (See chapter 22.)

Although the same dot is used as with the שׁ֫גֵ, this particular type of dot in a ה at the end of a word is called a מַפִּיק.

Several words may be joined together into a single accent unit by a hyphen that is called a מַקֵּף or מַקָּף. Up to four words may be joined together in this way; those words have a single accent—that is, they are marked by a single cantillation mark. So, for example, in Genesis 22:2, we have אֶת־אַבְרָהָם. The מַקֵּף generally is used with monosyllabic words, such as אַל־, אִם־, אֶת־, בֶּן־, מִן־, פֶּן־, עַד־, עַל־, עִם־, and נָא־. It is important to pay attention to the מַקֵּף, because when two words are joined together, the first word loses its accent, and the vocalization of a biblical word may change as a result. For example, the marker of the definite direct object when it is not bound to the following word is אֵת, whereas in the example cited above, אֶת־אַבְרָהָם, it appears as אֶת־. The loss of accent is responsible for the change from צֵרִי to סֶגוֹל. In transliteration, the מַקֵּף is marked by a hyphen; thus אֶת־אַבְרָהָם would be ʾet-ʾaḇrāhām.

An additional sign that appears in biblical manuscripts is a short vertical line, typically to the left of a vowel. This was first called a גַּעְיָה but is typically known by its later name, מֶ֫תֶג. The rules concerning the application of this sign are quite complex and differ widely between manuscripts. The sign is often a warning to be careful concerning the pronunciation of a particular vowel. It is used in some modern grammars and biblical text editions after a קָמֵץ to indicate that the קָמֵץ in an ambiguous situation is a קָמֵץ גָּדוֹל rather than a קָמֵץ קָטָן (for example, חָכְמָה, hā ḵĕmâ, "she was wise," rather than חָכְמָה, ḥoḵ mâ, "wisdom"). I have not followed this modern convention, which is apt to confuse anyone reading actual biblical texts.[2]

A larger vertical line separating two biblical words is called a פָּסֵק, and it tells the reader to pause slightly. It is found in various contexts, including between two words, the second of which begins with the same letter or a letter similar to the end of the previous word. In Song of Songs 4:12, גַּן ׀ נָעוּל, "a locked garden," for example, the פָּסֵק warns the reader not to slur the words together. The line is also found when a word is repeated, to ensure that the reader pays attention and does not skip over the second occurrence, as in Genesis 22:11, where the messenger of YHWH calls Abraham's name twice: אַבְרָהָם ׀ אַבְרָהָם.

Finally, there are many cases where a marginal reading corrects the main reading of the text. This phenomenon is called קְרִי־כְּתִיב (in English, Qere-Kethib): קְרִי, the Aramaic passive participle for "it is read" refers to the marginal reading that is substituted for the כְּתִיב (the Aramaic passive participle for "what is written"). The historical origin of this phenome-

---

2. The description of the use of the גַּעְיָה or מֶ֫תֶג in most of the standard grammars is incorrect; for a reliable description, see Israel Yeivin, *Introduction to the Tiberian Masorah*, Masoretic Studies 5, trans. and ed. E. J. Revell (Chico, Calif.: Scholars Press, 1980), 240–64 (§§311–57).

non is complex and unclear; in some cases the two readings likely represent the collation of alternative ancient readings (the collation theory), while in other cases the קְרִי seems to be a correction of the כְּתִיב (the correction theory). The differences in sound between the כְּתִיב and קְרִי are usually minimal, though the differences in meaning may be great, as when we have variation between לֹא ("not") and לוֹ ("to him"), as in Job 13:15. This ambiguity yields two possible translations: "Though he may slay me I have no hope" and "Though he may slay me, I will trust in him." Additionally, there are several words that are always read differently than they are written (perpetual *Qere*); these include the Tetragrammaton, the four letter name of God, יהוה, which is read as either אֲדֹנָי or אֱלֹהִים, and Jerusalem, which is almost always written יְרוּשָׁלַם, though it is read יְרוּשָׁלַיִם. There are several perpetual *Qere*s that are unique to the Torah; the most frequent of these is the third-person singular feminine pronoun that is written הוא, though it is read הִיא.

Vocabulary for chapter 4

אֶבֶן	rock (feminine, but plural is אֲבָנִים)
אֲדָמָה	cultivable land
אַף	nose (also used in idioms concerning anger)
בְּרִית	treaty, covenant
בָּשָׂר	meat, flesh
חַג	pilgrimage festival (with a suffix, for example, חַגִּי)
חַטָּאת	purification offering (traditionally translated as "sin offering"; plural חַטָּאוֹת)
חֶרֶב	sword (feminine)
לֶחֶם	bread, food (no plural; may be a collective)
מִדְבָּר	wilderness (typically not "desert" in the sense of totally dry)
מוֹעֵד	appointed place, feast time
מִנְחָה	gift, offering, cereal offering
מַעֲשֶׂה	deed, work
נַחֲלָה	inheritance
נַעַר	young man
נַעֲרָה	young girl
עוֹלָם	eternity (not "world," as in MIH)
עֹלָה	burnt offering
צֹאן	small cattle (typically goats, sheep; frequently collective)
רֶגֶל	foot, leg
רָשָׁע	wicked
שָׂדֶה	field
שַׁעַר	gate

There are no exercises for this chapter. Be sure that you know the names of all of the symbols introduced in the chapter. The exercises in the next chapter are cumulative, covering the points introduced in chapters 4 and 5.

5 Syllabification

All Hebrew words consist of one or more syllables. Syllables start with a consonant and are of two main types: consonant plus vowel (CV), called open syllables, and consonant plus vowel plus consonant (CVC), called closed syllables.[1] The word הָאִישׁ (hā'îš), "the person (or man)," for example, is composed of two syllables; the first, הָ (hā), is open, because it ends with a vowel (ā), while the second, אִישׁ ('îš), is closed, because it ends with a consonant (š). (It is often easier to understand rules of syllabification in transliteration, so in this chapter I make extensive use of transliteration.) For the sake of syllabification, the ultrashort vowels בְ, בֱ, בֲ, and בֳ do not count as full vowels, and the consonant containing them is attached to the following syllable.[2] Thus, וְכַחוֹל (wĕkaḥôl), "like the sand," has two syllables: וְכַ (wĕka), which is open, and חוֹל (ḥôl), which is closed. (Others consider these syllables with a compound שְׁוָא to be half-syllables; this is also a reasonable analysis. The distinction between these two possibilities is not important for our purposes.) Most closed, unaccented syllables contain short vowels, while most open, unaccented syllables contain long vowels. (See the division into long and short vowels, p. 13.) The words דָּבָר and קָמְתֶּם, for example, are both accented on the last syllable. In the first case, דָּבָר, we have a long vowel in an open, unaccented syllable (דָּ), while in קָמְתֶּם, we have a short vowel in a closed, unaccented syllable (קָמְ).

Intimately connected to the issue of syllabification is the nature of the ambiguous sign שְׁוָא. The שְׁוָא is a syllable divider. It may be pronounced in two ways: at the beginning of a syllable, it is an ultrashort vowel that is called a שְׁוָא נָע, a mobile שְׁוָא, while at the end of a syllable it is silent (a zero, ∅), in which case it is called a שְׁוָא נָח, or a quiescent (silent) שְׁוָא. It is important to differentiate between the two types of שְׁוָאִים when pronouncing biblical

---

1. The only exception to this is the conjunction "and" when it is vocalized וּ.
2. Here and elsewhere, for typographical reasons I have used a consonant along with the vowel. The principle is true for any consonant, not just בֵּית.

Hebrew. If the שְׁוָא is at the beginning of a syllable, it is a שְׁוָא נָע (mobile שְׁוָא), while if it ends a syllable, it is a שְׁוָא נָח (quiescent [silent] שְׁוָא). For example, if we take the words לְךָ־לֵךְ (note how these two words share a single accent, and are joined with a מַקֵּף), the first word, לֵךְ, contains a שְׁוָא נָח, and would be transliterated as lek̲, while the second word, לְךָ, contains a שְׁוָא נָע, and would be transliterated as lĕk̲ā.

Thus when a שְׁוָא either begins or ends a word, it is easy to tell whether it is quiescent or mobile. Determining the nature of the שְׁוָא in other cases is more difficult. Yet it is important to determine the quality of the שְׁוָא because in some instances the contrast between a שְׁוָא נָע and a שְׁוָא נָח can be phonemic—that is, it may make a difference in meaning. This may be seen, for example, in the pair יִירְאוּ (yî rĕʾû), "they will fear" (from the root ירא), and יִרְאוּ (yir ʾû), "they will see" (from the root ראי).[3] In the middle of a word, it is not unusual to find two שְׁוָאִים in a row; in this case, the first is a שְׁוָא נָח, and the second is a שְׁוָא נָע. יִשְׁמְרוּ, "they will guard," for example, would be syllabified as יִשׁ מְרוּ (yiš mĕrû), with the first שְׁוָא a שְׁוָא נָח and the second a שְׁוָא נָע. A word can end in consecutive שְׁוָאִים, as in וַיֵּשְׁתְּ, "he drank"; in such a case, both are a שְׁוָא נָח, and we may say that the final syllable (or the entire word) is doubly closed. The principle that unaccented, open syllables usually have long vowels, whereas unaccented, closed syllables usually have short vowels is helpful in determining the quality of the שְׁוָא. For example, the word יִשְׁמֹר, which has ultimate stress, contains a שְׁוָא under the שׁ. In theory it could be analyzed as either יִשׁ מֹר or יִ שְׁמֹר. However, the second option, יִ שְׁמֹר, would leave a short vowel in an open, unaccented syllable (יִ yi), and thus should be discarded in favor of יִשׁ מֹר, that has a more typical closed, unaccented syllable with a short vowel (יִשׁ yiš). Finally, if the first of two identical consecutive consonants is vocalized with a שְׁוָא, that שְׁוָא must be a שְׁוָא נָע, as in הִנְנִי, which should be syllabified הִ נְנִי (hi nĕnî); if it were a שְׁוָא נָח, the two consonants would have coalesced in the writing system into a single consonant with a דָּגֵשׁ חָזָק (הִנִּי hin nî).

A special case of the שְׁוָא נָע is the חֲטָף vowel, which is typically found under a guttural consonant. (In some cases, the חֲטָף replaces a guttural that would have been vocalized with a שְׁוָא נָח; a שְׁוָא נָח under a guttural is permissible but is in many cases avoided.) The חֲטָף vowel thus *always* opens a syllable.

As noted earlier, the main function of a דָּגֵשׁ חָזָק is to double a consonant. This can be better understood now that the two different types of שְׁוָא have been introduced. The word יִקָּרֵא, "he will be called," a נִפְעַל from the root קרא, has a דָּגֵשׁ חָזָק in the ק, which doubles it. It would thus be transliterated as yiqqārēʾ, which would be syllabified as yiq qā rēʾ (יִק קָ רֵא). The דָּגֵשׁ חָזָק masks the (silent) שְׁוָא נָח in the first syllable, yiq. The word יְבַקֵּשׁ,

---

3. Many lexica would consider the root of this to be ראה, though this is not accurate. See the discussion on p. 225.

"he will seek," a פָּעַל from בקש, has a דָּגֵשׁ חָזָק in the ק that effectively doubles it. It would thus be transliterated as yĕbaqqēš, which would be syllabified as yĕbaq qēš. The דָּגֵשׁ חָזָק masks the (silent) שְׁוָא נָח in the second syllable, baq.

The following chart summarizes the rules for distinguishing the two types of שְׁוָא.

Distinguishing Between the שְׁוָא נָח and the שְׁוָא נָע

A שְׁוָא is a שְׁוָא נָע when:

1. It opens a word.
2. It is the second of two consecutive שְׁוָאִים in the middle of the word.
3. It is under the first of two identical consonants (e.g. הִנְנִי).

A שְׁוָא is a שְׁוָא נָח when:

1. It closes a word.
2. It is the first of two consecutive שְׁוָאִים in the middle of the word.
3. It is the next-to-last vowel in a word, immediately preceding a final שְׁוָא (for example, נֵרְדְּ).
4. It follows a short vowel, thereby closing the unaccented syllable (for example, יִשְׁמֹר).
5. A word has a דָּגֵשׁ חָזָק, which serves to double a consonant, thereby both closing one syllable and opening another.

Understanding the types of Hebrew syllables and the nature of the שְׁוָא also allows us to understand the rules concerning the insertion of a דָּגֵשׁ קַל in the letters ב, ג, ד, כ, פ, and ת. These letters will take the דָּגֵשׁ קַל (1) at the beginning of the word or (2) after a closed syllable. Thus we have דָּגֵשׁ קַל opening the word כָּתַב, "he wrote," because the letter כ/ך begins the word. In contrast, the ת that opens the second syllable follows an open syllable, so it does not take a דָּגֵשׁ. The final ב ends the syllable, so it too does not take the דָּגֵשׁ קַל. In the word תִּכְתֹּב, "you (masculine singular) or she will write," each letter could in theory take a דָּגֵשׁ קַל. The initial ת takes a דָּגֵשׁ קַל because it opens the word. The following כ does not, because it ends the syllable, following the short vowel. The next ת does because it follows a closed syllable, while the final ב does not because it closes the syllable.

The rule that בּ, גּ, דּ, כּ, פּ, and תּ take the דָּגֵשׁ קַל at the beginning of the word has one important exception: when a word beginning with בּ, גּ, דּ, כּ, פּ, or תּ (1) follows a word that ends with a vowel *and* (2) the preceding word has a conjunctive accent. In such a case, it is *as if* the word beginning with בּ, גּ, דּ, כּ, פּ, or תּ follows an open syllable within a word, so the דָּגֵשׁ קַל is not inserted. This explains why there is no *dagesh* in the ב of בְזַרְעֲךָ in Genesis 22:18, וְהִתְבָּרֲכוּ בְזַרְעֲךָ, "they will bless themselves through your children."

The pronunciation of בּ, גּ, דּ, כּ, פּ, and תּ with a דָּגֵשׁ is called a stop, while without the דָּגֵשׁ, these letters are called spirants. The process of "dropping" the דָּגֵשׁ is called spirantization. It is important to remember that we are dealing with a phonological process that is visible in terms of its graphic representation; in other words, the writing system reflects the way in which syllable structure influenced the pronunciation of בּ, גּ, דּ, כּ, פּ, and תּ at some point in the history of biblical Hebrew. Thus, when we speak of dropping a דָּגֵשׁ, this is a type of shorthand for the phonological process involved.

The principles that determine whether the letters בּ, גּ, דּ, כּ, פּ, and תּ are vocalized as spirants or as stops—that is, with or without a דָּגֵשׁ קַל—are summarized below.

The Insertion of a דָּגֵשׁ קַל in the Letters בּ, גּ, דּ, כּ, פּ, and תּ

Any of the letters בּ, גּ, דּ, כּ, פּ, and תּ will take a דָּגֵשׁ קַל when it:

1. Begins a word (unless it is closely connected to the previous word, which ends in an open syllable).
2. Immediately follows a closed syllable.

Seeing a דָּגֵשׁ קַל in the middle of the word can also help establish syllabification by determining the nature of a שְׁוָא that precedes the דָּגֵשׁ. For example, one might wonder about the nature of the שְׁוָא under the ב of יִבְכֶּה, "he will cry," until noticing that the כ takes a דָּגֵשׁ, so the previous syllable must be closed. This immediately suggests the syllabification of יִב כֶּה (*yib keh*), with a שְׁוָא נָח. Phrased differently, if the שְׁוָא were a שְׁוָא נָע, suggesting the (incorrect) syllabification of יְ בְכֶה (*yi bĕkeh*), why would there be a דָּגֵשׁ in the כ? Thus, the שְׁוָא must be closing the syllable, in which case it is a שְׁוָא נָח. There are, however, some exceptions to this rule. (Some grammars will use the term *medial shewa* or שְׁוָא מְרַחֵף to describe these exceptions.; see p. 94 n.2.)

A variant of the שְׁוָא נָע is the set of three ultrashort חֲטָף vowels, בֱ, בֲ, and בֳ. The gutturals א, ה, ח, and ע cannot be vocalized with a שְׁוָא נָע; in cases where this would be expected, a חֲטָף is substituted. (Note that ר is excluded here, and that we are only speaking of the שְׁוָא נָע, not the שְׁוָא נָח.) In most such cases, the חֲטָף פַּתַח (e.g., חֲ) is substituted for the שְׁוָא נָע, as may be seen from the following pairs: כְּתַבְתֶּם (kĕtab̲ tem, "you wrote") but עֲמַדְתֶּם (ʿămad̲ tem, "you stood"); כֹּתְבִים (kō t̲ĕb̲îm, "writing") but אֹהֲבִים (ʾō hăb̲îm, "liking/loving").

Vocabulary for chapter 5

אַיִל	ram (plural אֵילִים)
אֵם	mother
אַמָּה	cubit
בֶּגֶד	garment
בָּקָר	large cattle (collective)
בֹּקֶר	morning, daybreak
גְּבוּל	border
זֶרַע	seed, descendants
חַיִל	strength, power
חֶסֶד	loyalty, kindness (usually from the stronger party to the weaker party)
מַחֲנֶה	camp
מַטֶּה	staff, tribe
מִשְׁכָּן	dwelling, Tabernacle
מִשְׁפָּחָה	family, extended family (clan)
עָוֹן	sin (plural עֲוֹנֹת)
עֶרֶב	evening, dusk
עֵת	time
עַתָּה	now
פֹּה	here
קֶרֶב	midst
רֵעַ	friend, neighbor
שַׁבָּת	Sabbath
שָׁם	there

TRANSLATION TIP #1

Do not assume that a word has the same meaning in biblical Hebrew as in modern Hebrew.

Song of Songs 4:1: שַׂעְרֵךְ כְּעֵדֶר הָעִזִּים שֶׁגָּלְשׁוּ מֵהַר גִּלְעָד

In biblical Hebrew, the root גלשׁ means "to descend," not "to ski" as in modern Hebrew. Thus the proper translation is: "Your hair is like a flock of goats descending from Mount Gilead," not "Your hair is like a flock of goats skiing down Mount Gilead."

Exercises for chapter 5

1. Transliterate and syllabify the following words. Then distinguish between a דָּגֵשׁ קַל, דָּגֵשׁ חָזָק, and מַפִּיק in them:

	מִדְבַּר
	שִׁשָּׁה
	בָּנָהּ
	שִׁבֵּר
	גֻּבַהּ
	בָּנְתָה
	הִכְתִּיב
	וַיֵּשְׁתְּ
	יִכְתֹּב
	בֶּגֶד
	יִבְגְּדוּ
	נְתַתֶּם
	עָבַרְתָּ
	מַלְכִּי
	סַבּוֹתָ
	גַּנִּים
	דִּבַּרְתִּי
	כִּי־כָבֵד־פֶּה

2. Explain why there is or is not a דָּגֵשׁ קַל in the letters בגדכפת of the following words:

	בֹּגֶדֶת
	תִּבְגְּדוּ
	בְּגַדְתֶּם
	יִכְתְּבוּ־בוֹ
	תִּכְתֹּבְנָה

3. Distinguish between שְׁוָא נָח and שְׁוָא נָע in the following words:

תִּשְׁכַּ֫חְנָה
תִּשְׁכְּבוּ
נֵרְדְּ
אֱנוֹשׁ
מַלְאָךְ
יִרְאוּ
יִירְאוּ
לִבְנָה
לְבֵנָה
יִשְׁלְחוּ

4. Insert a דָּגֵשׁ קַל as required in these words:

כְּתַבְתֶּם	כָּתַב
תּוֹרָתִי	כָּתְבָ֫נָה
עַבְדִּי	יִכְתִּיב
לֹא־תֹאכַל	תִּכְתְּבִי

5. Write in Hebrew:

saddîq	ʾŏhālîm
gāḏôl	wayyā́qom
ʿăḇāḏîm	ʾiššâ
pĕnê	malʾāḵ
nĕʾum	ʿēṣ
šĕmî	yaʿăśû
śām	pāṯûaḥ
ʾĕnôš	ṭāman

6. Transliterate:

מֶ֫לֶךְ	נְאֻם
כְּלִי	מִשְׁפָּט
נַעֲרָה	מַעֲשֶׂה
עַמִּים	בְּרִית
פָּתוּחַ	מִשְׁפָּחָה
	חַטָּאת

6 Some Principles of Hebrew Phonology (Part One)

The phonological system of Hebrew is quite complex, and substantial knowledge of historical linguistics and Semitic languages is needed to understand it. Yet several fundamental principles are important for the beginning student and can be explained without recourse to comparative linguistics. These are typically ignored in the teaching of modern Hebrew but are worth conveying because they decrease the number of exceptions that need to be memorized: such exceptions are then seen within the structure of the language as cases in which particular phonological rules apply. For this reason I offer a selection of these rules in my final chapters on phonology, immediately before I introduce the section on morphology, where these rules will be seen operating.

Phonology, like many aspects of linguistics, may be explained historically, by observing how and when particular principles evolved, or synchronically, by describing the rules that seem to apply within a single stratum of the language. The first type of study is called diachronic, while the second is synchronic. Most of the explanations in this section are synchronic, and thus are imprecise from a historical perspective; a diachronic presentation would require knowledge of other ancient Semitic languages that may not be assumed here.

To facilitate this description, it is useful to introduce two symbols that are used in linguistic study: * and >. The * is used in front of a reconstructed or hypothetical form; it means that the particular form is not attested, or, in some cases, never existed but is useful to posit for theoretical or pedagogical reasons. The > sign indicates that the form at the left of the sign has changed to the form at the right of the sign. (The < sign indicates that the form at the right of the sign has changed to the form at the left of the sign.) To put these two signs together: the statement "דְּבָרִים* > דְּבָרִים" means that the hypothetical form דָּבָרִים, with an initial קָמֵץ, has changed to the current form, דְּבָרִים, with an initial שְׁוָא.

Several principles of phonology have already been noted in passing; we have seen, for example, that Hebrew stress may only occur in the final syllable (ultima) or in the next-to-last syllable (penultima). We have also seen that the typical structure of atonic syllables is consonant plus short vowel plus consonant (a closed syllable with a short vowel) or consonant plus long vowel (an open syllable with a long vowel). Using the symbols C for a consonant and V for a vowel, the two typical syllable structures are CV(short)C and CV(long). Below, I adduce several other rules, and bring examples shared by modern and biblical Hebrew that illustrate them. Although these rules refer to the language in its written form, it is important to remember that they reflect issues connected to the speaking of the language.

Vowel Reduction

Several vowels appear only toward the end of Hebrew words. This is particularly true of the $\bar{a}$ (קָמֵץ), which typically needs to be close to the accent in order to exist. More specifically, the $\bar{a}$ (קָמֵץ) is typically found in the tonic or the pretonic syllable (the stressed syllable or the syllable before the stressed syllable, respectively). If, as a result of changes to a word, the $\bar{a}$ (קָמֵץ) becomes more distant from the stress, it changes to a שְׁוָא נָע (mobile שְׁוָא). We call such changes reduction because the vowel quantity has changed from an $\bar{a}$ (קָמֵץ), a long vowel, to the שְׁוָא נָע, an ultrashort vowel. Because such reduction typically transpires when the קָמֵץ finds itself two syllables (or more) before the tone, we call this phenomenon propretonic reduction—that is reduction taking place two syllables before the tone.

An example of propretonic reduction was noted above: the plural for *thing*, דָּבָר, is דְּבָרִים. The stress on דָּבָר is ultimate; thus one קָמֵץ is in the ultimate syllable (בָר), while the other (דָ) is in the penultima. This is perfectly acceptable. If we add the plural suffix, (accented) ־ִים, however, the relation between the קְמָצִים and the tone changes. One would have expected the plural to be דָּבָרִים*, but that would have three syllables (דָ בָ רִים), with stress on the final syllable (רִים). The קָמֵץ under the ב is fine because it is pretonic (one syllable before the tone); the קָמֵץ that stood under the initial ד, however, is difficult to pronounce and shortened because it is now propretonic (two syllables before the tone). For this reason, it is reduced to a שְׁוָא; phrased differently, דָּבָרִים* > דְּבָרִים because of propretonic reduction.

The plural is not the only context in which this happens. Biblical words may be joined with the following word to express "of" and similar ideas. This form is called the construct form, or in Hebrew סְמִיכוּת. (See pp. 92–97.) In such a case, the first word of the pair is often connected to the following word with a מַקֵּף (the hyphen sign—see p. 27), indicating that it has lost its accent. Even in cases where there is no מַקֵּף, the first word in the construct chain *acts as if* it has lost its accent; it is proclitic—that is, closely dependent on the following word. This explains the form of the first word in the phrase נְבִיא הָעִיר, "the prophet of the city." *Prophet* is typically written as נָבִיא, with a קָמֶץ in its first syllable; this קָמֶץ is pretonic. When it is in construct with הָעִיר, however, the whole word נָבִיא acts as if it were part of a single word ending with הָעִיר and, therefore, loses its accent; thus through propretonic reduction it becomes נְבִיא. Propretonic reduction will be especially frequent when words are in construct.

Propretonic reduction may also be seen in verbs. It explains, for example, why in biblical Hebrew the third-person masculine singular form is כָּתַב, "he wrote," while the second-person plural form is כְּתַבְתֶּם, rather than כָּתַבְתֶּם*—as a result of the addition of the accented (or "heavy") suffix תֶּם־, the initial כָּ syllable, which in כָּתַב was pretonic, is now propretonic (tonic תֶּם; pretonic תַב; propretonic כָּ*), so the קָמֶץ is reduced to a שְׁוָא.

Propretonic reduction happens with the צֵרִי as well as with the קָמֶץ. Note, for example, the singular for *name*, שֵׁם (with a tonic צֵרִי), and the plural שֵׁמוֹת (with a pretonic צֵרִי), in contrast to the form with a suffix ("their names") שְׁמוֹתָם or the phrase "the name of the people," שְׁמוֹת־הָאֲנָשִׁים. As a result of the addition of the accented suffix תָם or of the word הָאֲנָשִׁים, the initial שֵׁ is in a propretonic position and is reduced to a שְׁוָא.

Propretonic reduction is especially common in nouns. Pretonic reduction is found more often in verbs and is not as predictable as propretonic reduction. It may be seen, for example, in the change from יִשְׁמֹר to יִשְׁמְרוּ (< יִשְׁמֹרוּ*). This type of reduction will be highlighted later in the review of the verb paradigms.

The Law of the שְׁוָא

No biblical Hebrew word may begin with two שְׁוָאִים. If, for example, a preposition vocalized with a שְׁוָא is added before a word that begins with a שְׁוָא, as in "to" (לְ) "Solomon" (שְׁלֹמֹה), the form would be לְשְׁלֹמֹה*, but instead we get לִשְׁלֹמֹה. In other words, initial Cĕ +Cĕ > CiC; in this case, לְשְׁ* > לִשְׁ. Similarly, for "in" (בְּ) "the things" (דְּבָרִים), we have בַּדְּבָרִים instead of בְּדְבָרִים*. (Note that the ד has no דָּגֵשׁ because it is no longer word initial; furthermore, the application of the law of the שְׁוָא has created an irregular initial syllable that has a short vowel in an open syllable.)

Vocabulary for chapter 6

אוֹר	light
בְּהֵמָה	(domesticated) animal
בְּכוֹר	firstborn
הַרְבֵּה	much
זֶבַח	sacrifice
חָכָם	wise, skillful
חָכְמָה	wisdom (note: the first vowel is a קָמֶץ קָטָן)
כָּבוֹד	glory, honor
כֶּבֶשׂ	lamb (feminine כַּבְשָׂה or כִּבְשָׂה)
לָשׁוֹן	tongue (rarely, language; masculine but plural is לְשֹׁנוֹת)
מְלָאכָה	work
מַמְלָכָה	kingdom
מִצְוָה	commandment
סוּס	horse
עֲבוֹדָה	service, work, labor
פַּעַם	time (rarely, footstep)
פַּר	bull (feminine פָּרָה)
רֶכֶב	chariots, charioteer (collective)
שָׂפָה	lip, speech, shore
שֶׁמֶשׁ	sun (mostly feminine; rarely masculine)
תּוֹעֵבָה	abomination

There are no exercises for this chapter. The exercises after chapter 7 are cumulative for both chapters 6 and 7.

7 Some Principles of Hebrew Phonology (Part Two)

Behavior of the Gutturals

As we have seen (p. 26), the gutturals א, ה, ח, ע, and ר cannot usually be doubled. In addition, the gutturals א, ה, ח, and ע cannot take a שְׁוָא נָע, though ר can. The expected שְׁוָא נָע is typically replaced by a חֲטַף פַּתַח (אֲ). For example, a frequent nominal pattern—that is, a pattern for nouns—in Hebrew is $C\bar{a}C\bar{a}C$, as in דָּבָר, "thing," "matter," or "word" or חָכָם, "wise person." We saw earlier that as a result of propretonic reduction, the plural is $C\check{e}C\bar{a}C\hat{i}m$. Thus the plural of דָּבָר is דְּבָרִים; we should then expect the plural of חָכָם to be חְכָמִים*, but this is impossible, for the initial guttural cannot be vocalized with a שְׁוָא. (Reminder: an initial שְׁוָא is by definition a שְׁוָא נָע because it must start a syllable.) Instead, the plural is חֲכָמִים, because, following the principle we just adduced, the initial הְ is changed to a הֲ under a guttural. In effect, two phonological principles are at work: חְכָמִים* > חָכָמִים* (propretonic reduction) > חֲכָמִים (הֲ > הְ under a guttural). This same rule may also be seen in the formation of nouns in the singular. Nouns fall into patterns of consonants with particular vowels. One such pattern—seen, for example, in the word בְּכוֹר, "firstborn"—is $C\check{e}C\hat{o}C$. The Hebrew word for dream falls into the same pattern, but because it opens with a guttural, it is vocalized as חֲלוֹם. (חְלוֹם* > חֲלוֹם.)

The fact that gutturals cannot be doubled conflicts with certain cases where doubling (gemination) would be expected, as in the formation of the פִּעֵל conjugation that is marked by the doubling of the middle root letter, indicated by a דָּגֵשׁ חָזָק (for example, the דָּגֵשׁ in the מ of טִמֵּא, "he made ritually impure"). In addition, when the preposition מִן, "from," is added to a word, the נוּן typically assimilates (see p. 65) and is replaced by a דָּגֵשׁ חָזָק (for example, מִמֶּלֶךְ* > מִן־מֶלֶךְ, "from a king"). In such cases, one of two things can happen:

either the vowel that precedes the consonant that should have been doubled is lengthened (for example, from a חִירֶק to a צֵרִי), or there is no change. The first circumstance is called compensatory lengthening, because the vowel is lengthened to compensate for the lack of doubling (consonant plus short vowel plus consonant > consonant plus long vowel). The second is called virtual doubling—we must *imagine* that the guttural is doubled, for it cannot actually be doubled, and there is no compensation for the lack of doubling. Some examples will make these two concepts of compensatory lengthening and virtual doubling clearer.

The word "you spoke," from the root דבר in the פִּעֵל, would be expressed as דִּבַּרְתָּ (*dibbartā*). (Note the דָּגֵשׁ חָזָק in the בּ.) By analogy to that, "you blessed," from the root ברך, also in the פִּעֵל, should be בִּרַּכְתָּ* (*birraktā*). That form, however, is not found (thus the *) because the ר is not typically doubled. Instead, we find בֵּרַכְתָּ—the initial short-i vowel (חִירֶק) of the closed syllable has been lengthened to a long "i-class" vowel (צֵרִי) of the open syllable to compensate for the fact that the ר could not be doubled. This explains why we have דִּ, with a short vowel, in the first (closed) syllable of דִּבַּרְתָּ, but בֵּ, with a long vowel, in the first (open) syllable of בֵּרַכְתָּ. Through compensatory lengthening, the short חִירֶק has been lengthened to a צֵרִי. An example using the definite article (הֵא הַיְדִיעָה) best illustrates virtual doubling. The typical manifestation of the definite article is an initial ה vocalized with a פַּתַח and followed by a דָּגֵשׁ חָזָק, as in "the king," הַמֶּלֶךְ. Thus we would expect "the temple/palace" (from הֵיכָל) to be vocalized as הַהֵּיכָל*; this is not the case, because ה cannot be doubled (that is, cannot take a דָּגֵשׁ חָזָק). In this case, no compensatory lengthening is found, and the definite form is הַהֵיכָל; we explain the lack of compensatory lengthening by saying that the ה is virtually doubled. Unlike compensatory lengthening, virtual doubling is invisible. In general, compensatory lengthening is applied before the letters א, ר, and ע, while virtual doubling is seen before ה and ח.

Assimilation and Elision

Assimilation occurs when one sound or letter changes into a different sound or letter under the influence of another—usually adjacent—sound or letter. This may be seen in English, for example, in the negative prefix in- (as in *indecent*), which becomes ir- before an *r* (as in *irresponsible*), il- before an *l* (*illegitimate*) and im- before labials (*imbalance, immature*). In Hebrew the letter נוּן is prone to assimilation; in fact, in a situation in which נוּן would have ended a closed syllable in the middle of a word, it almost always assimilates into the following letter. This may be expressed in terms of $C_1Vn+C_2V(C_3) > C_1VC_2+C_2V(C_3)$; in other words, the נוּן assimilates into the following consonant. (In the notation of the previous sentence, recall that V = vowel and C = consonant; C_1 indicates the first consonant, C_2 the second, and so on.) We have seen that מִן־מֶלֶךְ* (*min-mélek*) is expressed as מִמֶּלֶךְ (*mim-mélek*); that is, the נ assimilates into the following מ, and the assimilated נ is expressed through the מ by דָּגֵשׁ חָזָק. Another type of example may be seen using a verb that has a נוּן as its first radical (root letter), such as נגשׁ, "to draw near." We would expect "he will draw near" to be expressed as יְנַגֵּשׁ* by analogy, for example, to יִכְבַּד, "he will grow heavy." יִנְגַּשׁ* is of the form $C_1Vn+C_2VC_3$, (*yin+gaš*), however, and according to the rule adduced above, the נוּן that closes the syllable is typically assimilated into the following consonant, resulting in יִגַּשׁ (*yig+gaš*). (Note: the דָּגֵשׁ in the ג of the theoretical form יִנְגַּשׁ* is a דָּגֵשׁ קַל—it appears in the letters ב, ג, ד, כ, פ, and ת after a closed syllable—while the דָּגֵשׁ of יִגַּשׁ is a דָּגֵשׁ חָזָק— it serves to double the letter.) The principle of the assimilation of the נוּן is frequently seen in verbs derived from roots with נוּן as their first root letter (radical) and in the נִפְעַל conjugation. For example, the נִפְעַל imperfect (future) from the root לחם is יִלָּחֵם instead of יִנְלָחֵם*.

Assimilation can also occur with vowels. For example, the guttural consonants are pronounced in an area of the mouth that is close to that needed for the pronunciation of the פַּתַח. For this reason, certain words with the gutturals א, ה, ח, and ע have a פַּתַח instead of the vowel found in the nonguttural parallel. This explains, for example, why we have יִכְתֹּב, "he will write," with a final *ō* vowel (the חוֹלָם), but have יִשְׁמַע, with a final *a* vowel (the פַּתַח). We may say that the *ō* has partially assimilated into the following guttural, resulting in a change to the פַּתַח. This is also why we specifically have a (furtive) פַּתַח inserted as a helping vowel or glide in certain cases before a final ה, ח, or ע (as in שָׁבוּעַ, week, לוּחַ, tablet, or גָּבוֹהַּ, high; see p. 12).

Another type of vocalic assimilation may be seen when a prefix that usually takes a שְׁוָא נָע is added to a guttural with a חֲטָף. The preposition could not be vocalized with a שְׁוָא, because we would then have two שְׁוָאִים at the beginning of a word; this is never permitted in biblical Hebrew. (The חֲטָף as a compound שְׁוָא is considered to be a שְׁוָא.) For example, the form לְחֲמִשָּׁה* ("to five") is inadmissible. In such cases, the שְׁוָא assimilates into the full vowel of the compound שְׁוָא that follows it; in other words, if the preposition is followed by a guttural with a חֲטָף פַּתַח the preposition is vocalized with a פַּתַח. Similarly, a guttural with a חֲטָף סֶגוֹל is preceded by a preposition vocalized with a סֶגוֹל, and a guttural with a חֲטָף קָמֵץ is preceded by a preposition vocalized with a קָמֵץ. Thus the form לְחֲמִשָּׁה* is resolved to לַחֲמִשָּׁה, while instead of בְּאֱמֶת*, we find בֶּאֱמֶת, "in truth." This also explains why the plural "in tents" is expressed as בָּאֳהָלִים, with the preposition בּ vocalized with a קָמֵץ (קָמָץ קָטָן) to match the following full vowel. (On the קָמֵץ קָטָן, see p. 13). All these examples illustrate (partial) vocalic assimilation, where the expected שְׁוָא under the preposition is assimilated to the same quality of the following vowel. This is called the law of the שְׁוָא with gutturals.

Related to assimilation, but not identical to it, is a phenomenon called elision, also called syncope, in which a consonant is lost. In contrast to assimilation, elided letters do not leave behind a דָּגֵשׁ חָזָק. Elision is frequently seen with the letter הַ, especially in CĕhV(C), which is resolved as CV (the middle *ĕh* is lost, and the word is shortened). So, for example, "in the place" should include the preposition "in" (בְּ), followed by the definite article (הַ plus דָּגֵשׁ חָזָק), followed by "place" (מָקוֹם), thus בְּהַמָּקוֹם* (*bĕhammāqôm). In fact, the הַ is lost or elided, and the vowel under it is thrown backward, replacing the שְׁוָא, resulting in בַּמָּקוֹם. This process of elision is important not only in considering the common definite article, but also in understanding the הִפְעִיל conjugation.

Pause

As we have seen, cantillation marks also function as punctuation, dividing the verse into several sections. The marks סִלּוּק (ק,) and אַתְנַחְתָּא (ק,), and often זָקֵף קָטֹן (ק׳) and סֶגוֹל (ק֒) are considered to be major disjunctive accents, and they may influence the form of certain Hebrew words. (Other cantillation marks exert this influence in a less consistent fashion.) In conjunction with these signs, words often retain more conservative or historically ancient forms, in terms both of the place of the accent and of vocalization. These are called pausal forms. For example, instead of כֶּסֶף, we may find כָּסֶף, as in Genesis 37:28, when Joseph is sold for twenty pieces of silver, בְּעֶשְׂרִים כָּסֶף. In the case of the pronoun אַתָּה, *you*, the form changes to אָתָּה—we have both a change of vowel from פַּתָּח to קָמֵץ and a change from ultimate to penultimate stress. In Jeremiah 16:11, we have: וְאֹתִי עָזָבוּ וְאֶת־תּוֹרָתִי לֹא שָׁמָרוּ, "they have abandoned me and not observed my teaching"; note עָזָבוּ instead of the expected עָזְבוּ and שָׁמָרוּ instead of the expected שָׁמְרוּ. This is an example of the pausal form retaining a more ancient form due to the (older) penultimate, rather than ultimate, stress. (Note that because of the different stress, there was no pretonic reduction of קָמֵץ to שְׁוָא in עָזָבוּ and שָׁמָרוּ.) For the person reading biblical texts, it is sufficient to know of the existence of pausal forms, and to expect slightly different vocalization and stress patterns in conjunction with the major disjunctive accents. The pausal form that a word might take is listed in lexica of BH.

The following chart summarizes the phonological principles developed in chapters 6 and 7.

Some Basic Phonological Principles of Biblical Hebrew

- The קָמֵץ and צֵרִי are typically reduced to a שְׁוָא in a propretonic syllable (propretonic reduction).
- If a word would otherwise begin with consecutive שְׁוָאִים, the law of the שְׁוָא is applied, changing the initial שְׁוָא to a חִירֶק. In other words, initial Cĕ +Cĕ > CiC.
- Before a חֲטָף vowel, the expected initial שְׁוָא is written as the whole vowel of the same quality of the following חֲטָף (for example, בֶּאֱמֶת); this is caused by assimilation.
- The gutturals א, ה, ח, ע, and ר may not be doubled (that is, take a דָּגֵשׁ חָזָק).
- The gutturals א, ה, ח, and ע may never be vocalized with שְׁוָא נָע. The expected שְׁוָא נָע is replaced with a חֲטָף.
- The gutturals א, ה, ח, and ע *may* be vocalized with שְׁוָא נָח, though this too is *sometimes* replaced with a חֲטָף.
- Gutturals prefer the vowel פַּתַח.
- A נוּן that would have ended a syllable typically assimilates to the following consonant ($C_1Vn+C_2V[C_3] > C_1VC_2+CV[C_3]$).
- The letter הֵא is prone to elision when it is immediately preceded by a שְׁוָא נָע. (CĕhV[C]>CV[C].)
- The pauses in the verse at major disjunctive accents cause many words to change forms slightly in terms of accent and vocalization, often reverting to older forms.

Vocabulary for chapter 7

אָחוֹת	sister
אָרוֹן	chest, Ark
אֹרֶךְ	length
גִּבּוֹר	warrior
דּוֹר	generation (plural דּוֹרִים and דּוֹרוֹת)
הוֹי	woe
זָקֵן	old, elder
חֹק	ordinance (plural חֻקִּים)
יַיִן	wine
יָשָׁר	straight, upright
כֹּה	thus
כִּסֵּא	seat, throne (masculine, but plural is כִּסְאוֹת)
מָוֶת	death
מִסְפָּר	number
נָהָר	river, stream (masculine, but plural is usually נְהָרוֹת)
נְחֹשֶׁת	copper, bronze
סֵפֶר	document, scroll (in contrast to MIH, not "book" in the modern sense of the word)
עָפָר	dust, soil
פֶּתַח	opening, entrance
רֹחַב	breadth
שֵׁבֶט	staff, tribe
שֶׁמֶן	oil

Exercises for chapter 7

1. Following the example below, write the resultant form in Hebrew, and explain the phonetic principles involved:

   Example: בְּרִית + בְּ = בִּבְרִית.

   The law of the שְׁוָא is applied, so the initial שְׁוָא becomes a חִירֶק. In addition, the דָּגֵשׁ קַל of the בֵּית of בְּרִית is dropped, because the בֵּית no longer opens the word or follows a closed syllable.

נָהָר + וֹת (plural suffix) =
מִן + קוֹל =
בְּ + נְחֹשֶׁת =
בְּ + כֶּסֶף =
כְּ + הָאִישׁ =
יָשָׁר + ִים (plural suffix) =
לְ + אֲנָשִׁים =
לְ + עֲבוֹדָה =

לְ + הָעֲבוֹדָה =
לְ + מְלָכִים =
כְּ + אֱנוֹשׁ =
כְּ + נְאֻם =

2. Explain why these parallel forms are not identical:

Example: אֲדָמָה ‖ בְּרָכָה. The initial אָלֶף of אֲדָמָה is vocalized with a חֲטַף פַּתַח because אָלֶף, as a guttural, may not be vocalized with a שְׁוָא נָע.

הַחַיִּים ‖ הָעִיר ‖ הַשֶּׁמֶשׁ
חָכְמוֹת ‖ חָכָם
כְּבוֹד־יהוה ‖ כָּבוֹד
לִגְבוּל ‖ לְשֹׁר
מִיַּחֵל ‖ מְבָרֵךְ ‖ מְדַבֵּר
פָּתוּחַ ‖ כָּתוּב
יִגֹּף ‖ יִשְׁמֹר (from נגף)
מְלָכִים ‖ חֲסָדִים
תִּכְתְּבִי ‖ תִּכְתֹּב

תִּשְׁלַח ‖ תִּכְתֹּב
תּוֹעֲבַת־יהוה ‖ תּוֹעֵבָה
צְדָקָה ‖ אֲדָמָה
כָּתְבוּ ‖ כָּתְבוּ
כָּסֶף ‖ כֶּסֶף
שְׁמַרְתֶּן ‖ שָׁמַר

8 The Definite Article, the Interrogative הַא, and Other Interrogative Pronouns

The Definite Article

In BH, as in MIH, there is no separate word for "the" and its function of establishing that a particular, definite object is in the mind of the speaker or narrator is expressed most often by prefixing a הַא to the word in mind. This usage of the הַא is called the definite article, or in Hebrew, הַא הַיְדִיעָה.

This הַא may not usually be prefixed to a personal name or place name, because these are already definite, nor may it appear before the first element of a construct chain. Thus the following are inadmissible in Hebrew: הַדָּוִד*, "the David," or הַדְּבַר־הַסֵּפֶר*, which would have to be translated "the the word of the scroll." Stated differently, personal names, geographical names, construct chains that contain a definite article (for example, דְּבַר הַסֵּפֶר, "the word of the scroll"), and nouns with pronominal suffixes (for example, צֹאנוֹ, "his small cattle") are already considered definite, so they may not appear with (a redundant) הַא הַיְדִיעָה.

The definite article is typically marked by a הַא vocalized with a פַּתַח, and a דָּגֵשׁ חָזָק in the following letter. This addition creates an extra syllable in the word of the type CV[short]C, which, as we have seen, is one of the typical types of syllables in an unaccented position. Thus the דָּגֵשׁ חָזָק, or the doubling of the letter following the definite article, is an integral part of the structure of the word with the definite article. This doubling may be seen, for example, in הַקּוֹל, "the voice," or הַמֶּלֶךְ, "the king." Words that begin with a דָּגֵשׁ קַל will keep their *dagesh*, but it will now become a דָּגֵשׁ חָזָק. For example, from "house," בַּיִת, with a (word-initial) דָּגֵשׁ קַל in the ב, we find הַבַּיִת, with a דָּגֵשׁ חָזָק in the ב, or from "nation," גּוֹי, with a דָּגֵשׁ קַל in the ג, we get הַגּוֹי, with a דָּגֵשׁ חָזָק in the ג.

Because the gutturals and ר cannot be doubled, the definite article needs to be expressed in a different fashion before them. As expected, we find either compensatory lengthening or virtual doubling in these circumstances. Before the letters א, ע, and ר, we find compensatory lengthening; that is, instead of הַ plus פַּתָח plus doubling (a CV[short]C syllable), we have הָ plus קָמֵץ (a CV[long] syllable). Instead of the "expected" הַרֹאשׁ*, for example, we have הָרֹאשׁ, "the head." Similarly, "the person/man" is הָאִישׁ and "the city" is הָעִיר. Before ה and ח, however, we have virtual doubling, thus הַהֵיכָל, "the palace/temple," or הַחֹדֶשׁ, "the new moon/month."

There are several exceptions to the general principles concerning the definite article with the gutturals. If the article precedes an unaccented עָ, an unaccented הָ, or an accented or unaccented הָ or חָ, it is vocalized הֶ. (This may be a case of dissimilation, in which the vowel of the definite article changes from an a-quality vowel to an e-quality vowel to distinguish itself from the guttural with the following a-quality vowel.) This may be seen in the following examples: "the cities," הֶעָרִים; "the mountains," הֶהָרִים; "the wise man," הֶחָכָם; "the wisdom," הֶחָכְמָה; and "the months," הֶחֳדָשִׁים.

In certain cases, the doubling that follows the definite article is also missing in the letters י and מ. "The children," for example, is הַיְלָדִים (instead of the expected הַיְּלָדִים*), and similarly, we find הַמְרַגְּלִים ("the spies"). In general, the syllable and a half *hay yĕ* (הַיְ) is reduced to the single syllable *hay* (הַי). (If the י or מ is followed by a הָ or עָ, however, the doubling is preserved, as in "the Judeans," הַיְּהוּדִים, "the tired," הַיְּעֵפִים, and "the cave," הַמְּעָרָה.)

Finally, there are certain relatively common nouns in which the vocalization of the noun itself changes as a result of the addition of the definite article. These include:

אֶרֶץ	(land, country)	הָאָרֶץ
הַר	(hill, mountain)	הָהָר
עַם	(nation)	הָעָם
חַג	(festival)	הֶחָג
אָרוֹן	(ark, box)	הָאָרוֹן

The following chart summarizes the vocalization of the definite article.

> ### Vocalization of the Definite Article
>
> - Typically: הָא with a פַּתַח, and a דָּגֵשׁ חָזָק in the following letter (for example, הַקּוֹל).
> - Before the letters א, ע, and ר: Usually הָא with a קָמֵץ (compensatory lengthening, for example, הָרֹאשׁ).
> - Before the letters ה and ח: Usually הָא with a פַּתַח (virtual doubling, for example, הַחֹדֶשׁ).
> - Before unaccented עָ, unaccented הָ, הֳ, or חָ: הָא with a סֶגּוֹל (for example, הֶחָכָם).
> - Before the letters י and מ (not followed by הָא or עַיִן): הָא with a פַּתַח and no דָּגֵשׁ חָזָק (for example, הַיְלָדִים).
> - Words that change when the article is added: אֶרֶץ, but הָאָרֶץ; הַר, but הָהָר; עַם, but הָעָם; חַג, but הֶחָג; אָרוֹן, but הָאָרוֹן.

The Interrogative הֲא

As in English, there are several different ways to ask questions. Several special particles may introduce questions; these include לָמָּה, why?, and מִי, "who[m]?" Alternatively, the question might lack a formal marker, and spoken intonation might indicate that it was a question (in 1 Samuel 11:12, for example: שָׁאוּל יִמְלֹךְ עָלֵינוּ, "Will Saul reign over us?"). Finally, questions may be introduced by the interrogative הֲא (Hebrew הֵא הַשְּׁאֵלָה). The vocalization of the הֲא is typically הֲ, as in הֲתִתְּנֵם בְּיָדִי, "Will you give them into my hand?" (2 Samuel 5:19). There are two main changes in this vocalization. The first is expected—because a word may not open with two שְׁוָאִים, the interrogative הֲא before a word opening with a שְׁוָא (or a compound שְׁוָא) is vocalized הַ, as in Genesis 18:17, הַמְכַסֶּה אֲנִי מֵאַבְרָהָם אֲשֶׁר אֲנִי עֹשֶׂה, "Should I hide from Abraham what I am about to do?" Infrequently, the following consonant may be doubled. (This doubling cannot be predicted.) This could lead to some confusion between the definite article and the interrogative הֲא, but context typically resolves these ambiguities. For example, Genesis 17:17 reads הַלְּבֶן מֵאָה־שָׁנָה יִוָּלֵד; this must clearly be translated as a question, "Could [a child] be born to a hundred-year-old [man]?" The second change concerns words that begin with gutturals (but not with ר)—here too, the interrogative הֲא is vocalized as הַ. This may be seen in 2 Samuel 5:19, הַאֶעֱלֶה אֶל־פְּלִשְׁתִּים, "Should I go up [to fight] against the Philistines?" But before a guttural opening with a קָמֵץ, the interrogative הֲ is vocalized הֲ, as in הֶחָכָם יִהְיֶה אוֹ סָכָל, "Will he be a wise man or a fool?" in Qohelet (Ecclesiastes) 2:19.

The following chart summarizes the main rules of the interrogative הֲא.

Vocalization of the Interrogative הֲא

- Typically הֲ, as in הֲהִתְחַתֵּן.
- Before a שְׁוָא (or a compound שְׁוָא): הַ.
- Before a guttural (but not ר): הַ.
- Before a guttural opening with a קָמֶץ: הֶ.
- (Rarely and unpredictably, vocalized with a פַּתַח followed by a דָּגֵשׁ חָזָק.)

Other Interrogative Pronouns

The primary, independent interrogative pronouns in BH are מִי, "who[m]?," and מַה, "what?" The vocalization of מה is similar to that of the definite article: before nongutturals, it is vocalized as מַה, followed by a מַקֵּף and a דָּגֵשׁ חָזָק in the following word. Before gutturals, however, there is usually virtual doubling, though sometimes there is compensatory lengthening of פַּתַח to קָמֶץ, yielding מָה. On occasion, mostly before gutturals, מה may be vocalized as מֶה. The following examples illustrate the vocalization of מה:

Genesis 32:28,	מַה־שְּׁמֶךָ,	"What is your name?"
Genesis 31:36,	מַה חַטָּאתִי,	"What is my sin?"
Genesis 31:32,	מָה עִמָּדִי,	"What is with me?"
1 Kings 19:20,	מֶה־עָשִׂיתִי לָךְ׃	"What have I done to you?"

מה may also be preceded by a לָמֶד, in which case it means "why?" Usually, it is vocalized לְמָה, though before the gutturals א, ה, and ע it is vocalized לָמָה. "Why?" can also be expressed with מַדּוּעַ.

The vocalization of the other interrogatives is not affected by the words that follow them. These words include אֵיךְ, "how"; אַיֵּה and אֵיפֹה, "where"; אָנָה, "to where"; מֵאַיִן, "from where"; and מָתַי, "when." (These words and forms will not be repeated in the vocabulary below, and should be learned at this point.)

Vocabulary for chapter 8

אֹזֶן	ear
אַחֵר	(an)other, different (feminine אַחֶרֶת; plural אֲחֵרִים and אֲחֵרוֹת)
חוֹמָה	wall
חוּץ	outside (plural חוּצוֹת, streets)
חֵמָה	anger
חָצֵר	courtyard
יֶתֶר	remainder
כָּנָף	wing (dual, כְּנָפַיִם "hands," pl. כְּנָפוֹת, "end, corner")
כַּף	palm (plural כַּפּוֹת)
מִגְרָשׁ	open land
מַרְאֶה	appearance, vision
נֶגֶב	south, Southern Israel
נַחַל	stream, wadi
נָשִׂיא	chief (not president, as in MIH)
עֵדָה	congregation
פְּרִי	fruit
צָפוֹן	north
רֹב	multitude, greatness
רָעָב	famine
תָּמִיד	continually

In addition, learn the interrogatives taught in this chapter.

Exercises for chapter 8

1. Write the following words in biblical Hebrew; be sure to vocalize the words properly and to include other signs (דְּגֵשִׁים, marks for penultimate stress) as appropriate:

the instruction	the priest
the sword	the wilderness
the city	the master
the kindness	the festival
the chief	the anger
the Ark	the messenger
the nation	the gold
the land	the purification offering
the mountain	the night
the day	the tree
the nose	the Sabbath
the daybreak	the power
the wisdom	the sister
the firstborn	the document
the congregation	the open land
the courtyard	the ear
the elder	the generation
the name	

2. Using the interrogative הֲ, vocalize the following questions and translate them:

הֲטוֹבָה הָאָרֶץ	הֲרַע הָעֶבֶד
הֶחָכָם הָאִישׁ	הַזְּקֵנִים הַכֹּהֲנִים
	הֲזָקֵן הַגִּבּוֹר

3. Translate the following words, noting whether the initial הא is interrogative, the definite article, or ambiguous.

הֶחָכָם	הַטּוֹב
הַגְּבוּל	הָרַע
הַשָּׂפָה	הַמִּצְוָה
הָעֲבוֹדָה	הַנַּעַר
הֶעָוֹן	הֶעָפָר
הֶעָפָר	הַנַּעֲרָה
הַחַיִּים	הָעָם
הַקּוֹל	הַתּוֹרָה
הַנְאֻם	הַנְאֻם
הָעֹלָה	הָרַע
הַבְּהֵמָה	הָרָעָב
הָעוֹלָם	הָאוֹר
הָאוֹר	הַחֶסֶד
הַחֶרֶב	הַמִּלְחָמָה

9 The Vocalization of the Prepositions בּ, כּ, ל, and מִן; the Conjunction ו

The Prepositions בּ, כּ, ל, and מִן

Hebrew has two types of prepositions: those that are connected to a noun as part of the same word, and those that appear separately. The first type is called bound, or inseparable, while the second type is called unbound, or independent. The three bound prepositions are בּ, "in," כּ, "like," and ל, "to." (These prepositions may also be translated in other ways; their meaning is determined by the particular verbs with which they are used.) When attached to a word, they are vocalized in the same manner.

The most frequent vocalization is with a שְׁוָא, as in בְּדֶרֶךְ, "on a road" (note how the ד of דֶּרֶךְ has lost its דָּגֵשׁ קַל because it is neither at the beginning of the word nor following a closed syllable), כְּקוֹל, "like a voice," or לְמֶלֶךְ, "to a king." This vocalization is not possible if the word to which the preposition is attached begins with a שְׁוָא (including a חֲטָף), because the result would then be a word that begins with two שְׁוָאִים—for example, *לְשְׁלֹמֹה, "to Solomon." In such cases, the law of the שְׁוָא applies (see p. 42): initial Cĕ + Cĕ > CiC. In this case, *לְשְׁלֹמֹה becomes לִשְׁלֹמֹה. Similarly, we would have בִּשְׁלֹמֹה, "in Solomon," or כִּשְׁלֹמֹה, "like Solomon." The specialized case of the law of the שְׁוָא with gutturals also applies—that is, the initial vowel under the proclitic preposition is a full vowel of the same quality as the ultrashort vowel that follows it. Using this principle, for "to humanity," from אֱנוֹשׁ, we get לֶאֱנוֹשׁ (*לְאֱנוֹשׁ > לֶאֱנוֹשׁ). Similarly, we would get בָּאֲדָמָה for "in earth," or כָּאֳנִיָּה, "like a boat."

A subcase of the application of the law of the שְׁוָא occurs when the word to which the preposition is to be prefixed begins with a י vocalized with a שְׁוָא, as in the proper name

יְהוּדָה, "Judah/Judea." In these cases, the expected initial syllables *běyě*, *kěyě*, and *lěyě* become *bî*, *kî* and *lî*. Thus *בְּיְהוּדָה > *בִּיהוּדָה > בִּיהוּדָה; *כְּיְהוּדָה > כִּיהוּדָה; and *לְיְהוּדָה > לִיהוּדָה. Note that in each of these cases, there is no vowel under the י; instead, the preposition is vocalized with an extra-long vowel.

A final case involves one of these prepositions prefixed to a word with the definite article. As we have seen (p. 47), intervocalic ה is unstable and tends to get elided, with the result that its vowel is thrown backward. Thus from מָקוֹם, "place," we get הַמָּקוֹם, "the place" and לַמָּקוֹם, "to the place" (< *לְהַמָּקוֹם). Similarly, from חֶרֶב, "sword," we get הַחֶרֶב, "the sword" and בַּחֶרֶב, "by the sword" (< *בְּהַחֶרֶב). "Like the tent" would be expressed as כָּאֹהֶל (< *כְּהָאֹהֶל). Thus, the definite article is hidden when a definite word is joined to one of the prepositions בּ, כּ, or לּ.

It is therefore important to pay close attention to the vowel of the preposition, so that the word in question is translated properly as definite or indefinite. כְּשֵׁם, for example, would be "like a name," while כַּשֵּׁם would be "like the name." Similarly, לְאָח is translated "to a brother," in contrast to לָאָח, "to the brother." Certain cases, however, are ambiguous. For example, the word for "fifty" is חֲמִשִּׁים, and the form בַּחֲמִשִּׁים could mean either "in fifty" or "in the fifty." This ambiguity arises because "in fifty" would be vocalized בַּחֲמִשִּׁים (< *בְּחֲמִשִּׁים), according to the law of the שְׁוָא as it applies to gutturals. Yet when the definite article is prefixed to a ח, there is virtual doubling rather than compensatory lengthening, so "the fifty" would be expressed as הַחֲמִשִּׁים, and thus "in the fifty" would be בַּחֲמִשִּׁים (< *בְּהַחֲמִשִּׁים). Context will almost always determine in such cases whether the noun in question is definite.

Before divine names, the following forms are found. With יְהוָה, we get בַּיהוָה, "in YHWH," כַּיהוָה, "like YHWH," and לַיהוָה, "to YHWH." With אֱלֹהִים, we get בֵּאלֹהִים, "in God," כֵּאלֹהִים, "like God," and לֵאלֹהִים, "to God."

The following chart summarizes the vocalization of these bound prepositions.

> ### Vocalization of the Bound Prepositions בּ, כּ, and ל
>
> - Typically בּ, כּ, and ל are vocalized with a שְׁוָא.
> - Before an initial שְׁוָא, the prepositions בּ, כּ, and ל are vocalized with a חִירֶק.
> - Before a guttural beginning with a compound שְׁוָא, the prepositions בּ, כּ, and ל take the full vowel of the compound שְׁוָא.
> - Before a יוֹד vocalized with a שְׁוָא, the prepositions בּ, כּ, and ל take a חִירֶק, and the יוֹד loses its שְׁוָא.
> - The הָא of the definite article is elided before these prepositions, and the vowel of the הָא moves under the בּ, כּ, or ל.
> - Before divine names, we get get לֵאלֹהִים, כֵּאלֹהִים, בֵּאלֹהִים, לַיהוָה, כַּיהוָה, בַּיהוָה, and לַיהוָה.

The Conjunction ו

The vocalization of the conjunction "and" (ו) before a noun is similar to the vocalization of the letters בּ, כּ, and ל. (The use and vocalization of the ו before verbs is a more complex matter and will be dealt with in chapter 18.) Its typical form is וְ, as in וְאִשָּׁה, "and (a) woman." (If the word following the ו opened with a דָּגֵשׁ קַל, this is dropped, because the letter containing the דָּגֵשׁ is no longer word-initial, nor does it follow a closed syllable. Thus we have כַּף, "palm," but וְכַף, "and a palm.") The difficulties arise when the word begins with a שְׁוָא, because Hebrew will not tolerate two initial שְׁוָאִים. In such cases (in contrast to בכל), the initial ו becomes a וּ. Thus we express "and things" (with דְּבָרִים) as וּדְבָרִים (note the absence of the דָּגֵשׁ in the ד). In contrast to כִּשְׁלֹמֹה, "like Solomon," we get וּשְׁלֹמֹה, "and Solomon." If the word begins with a חֲטָף, the conjunctive ו is vocalized with the corresponding full vowel; this is the same rule that applies to בּ, כּ, and ל. For example, just as we have בָּאֲדָמָה, "in earth," we would have וַאֲדָמָה, "and earth." Before an initial י, we get וִי (with no vowel under the יוֹד—it is a long-i vowel), as in וִיסוֹד, "and foundation," from יְסוֹד, "foundation." Additionally, if the conjunctive ו precedes another labial (ב, ו, מ, and פ), the conjunction is vocalized וּ through dissimilation, as in וּבַת, "and a daughter"; וּמַיִם, "and water"; and וּפָנִים, "and (a) face." In contrast to בּ, כּ, and ל, the הָא of the definite article is not elided when it is preceded by the conjunctive וְ. Thus from יַיִן, "wine," we get וְהַיַּיִן, "and the wine," and from חֹק, "ordinance," we get וְהַחֹק, "and the ordinance."

In several instances, the expected וְ is lengthened to a וָ. This happens most often when the two words joined with the וְ form a logical pair or are frequently joined together, *and* if the syllable following the conjunctive ו is accented. This explains, for example, the form תֹ֙הוּ֙ וָבֹ֔הוּ, "unformed and void" in Genesis 1:2. A useful illustration of this principle may be found in the various pairs narrated in Genesis 8:22, עֹ֖ד כָּל־יְמֵ֣י הָאָ֑רֶץ זֶ֡רַע וְ֠קָצִיר וְקֹ֨ר וָחֹ֜ם וְקַ֧יִץ וָחֹ֛רֶף וְי֥וֹם וָלַ֖יְלָה לֹ֥א יִשְׁבֹּֽתוּ׃ "for as long as the earth will exist, planting and harvesting, cold and hot, summer and winter, day and night will not cease," where the pairs וְקַ֧יִץ וָחֹ֛רֶף, וְי֥וֹם וָלַ֖יְלָה, and וְקֹ֨ר וָחֹ֜ם contain a וָ. This vocalization with a קָמֶץ occurs because these are pairs of words that belong together, and the second word in each pair has either one syllable or penultimate stress. (Note the placement of the cantillation marks that also serve as accent markers.) In contrast, we find a וְ in זֶ֡רַע וְ֠קָצִיר, where the stress of וְ֠קָצִיר is ultimate (the cantillation mark ֠ is prepositive; see p. 21), and we also find a וְ in the words וְקֹ֨ר, וְקַ֧יִץ, and וְי֥וֹם, which are not closely affiliated with the previous words. Finally, when the conjunctive וְ precedes the word for God or gods, אֱלֹהִים, this word takes the form וֵאלֹהִים. With יְהוָה we get וַיהוָה, "and YHWH."

The forms of the conjunctive וְ are summarized below.

Vocalization of the Conjunctive וְ

- Typically וְ.

- Before an initial שְׁוָא: וּ.

- Before a compound שְׁוָא: ו with the full vowel of the compound שְׁוָא.

- Before יְ: וִי.

- Before a labial (בומפ): וּ.

- Before an accented syllable in a word pair: וָ.

- (The הַ of the definite article is not elided after the conjunctive וְ.)

- Before divine names we get וֵאלֹהִים and וַיהוָה.

The Preposition מִן

The vocalization of מִן is different from the vocalization of בכל and ו, because מִן, unlike the others, is a closed syllable and ends with a נ. As noted in the discussion of phonology (pp. 45–46), $C_1Vn+C_2V(C_3) > C_1VC_2+C_2V(C_3)$. For this reason, it is relatively unusual to find the word written as מִן in the Hebrew Bible; more typically, the final נ of that word is assimilated into the following word. So, for example, for "from a king," instead of the expected מִן־מֶלֶךְ* we have מִמֶּלֶךְ. (Note the דָּגֵשׁ חָזָק in the מ of מֶּלֶךְ, which indicates the assimilated נ of the preposition מִן.) The full form of the preposition may be seen before the definite article, as in Genesis 3:12, הִוא נָתְנָה־לִּי מִן־הָעֵץ, "she gave me from the tree." (In this verse, as is typical of the Torah, the pronoun "she" is spelled הוא, though it is pronounced הִיא; see p. 28). In such cases, the word מִן does not have its own accent but is almost without exception written מִן־, with a מַקֵּף indicating that it is attached to the following word. Through compensatory lengthening, however, the form מֵ is found as well, sometimes before the definite article, and typically before the gutturals and ר, which cannot be doubled. Thus "from a wind" is מֵרוּחַ, rather than מִן־רוּחַ* or מִרּוּחַ*. Compensatory lengthening is found irrespective of the consonant that begins the word to which מִן is appended (in contrast to the addition of the article, which results in compensatory lengthening with particular gutturals and virtual doubling with others). But in a handful of cases virtual doubling is found (for example, מִחוּץ). The behavior of מִן before an initial י is similar to the vocalization of י after the prepositions ב, כ, and ל; just as we find לִיהוּדָה for "to Judah," "from Judah" is expressed as מִיהוּדָה rather than the expected מִיְהוּדָה*. (Again, note the absence of the שְׁוָא underneath the י.)

The vocalization of מִן is summarized below.

The Vocalization of the Preposition מִן

- Typically (bound) מִ, followed by a דָּגֵשׁ חָזָק.
- Before the definite article: typically מִן־. (A מַקֵּף indicates that it is attached to the following word.)
- Before the gutturals and ר: מֵ (less often מִ).
- Before י: מִי.

Vocabulary for chapter 9

The vocabulary words in this unit are mostly prepositions. Although these are defined in the lexica, there is often not a clear one-to-one correspondence between Hebrew and English prepositions. The meaning of the preposition is often sensitive to the verb with which it is used. Nevertheless, this list provides the more common BH prepositions and their most common meanings; in most cases, the meanings of prepositions have not changed radically between BH and MIH, though several prepositions that are used in BH tend not to be used in MIH. Many of these prepositions are typically connected to the following word with a מַקֵּף; see the list on p. 27.

אַחֲרֵי, אַחַר	after
אֶל־	to, toward
אֵצֶל	beside
אֵת, אֶת־	with (typically denoting proximity; אֶת־ (or אֵת) is also used as a marker of the definite direct object)
בְּ	in (bound preposition)
בֵּין	between
יַעַן	because of
כְּ	like, as (bound preposition)
כִּי	because
לְ	to (bound preposition)
לְמַעַן	so that
לִקְרַאת	toward
מוּל	opposite
מִן־	from
נֶגֶד	opposite
עַד־	until, up to
עַל־	on
עִם־	with (typically denoting fellowship or companionship)
תַּחַת	under, instead of

Exercises for chapter 9

1. Write in Hebrew:

like a person	in the cultivable land
and the cereal offering	from a gate
from the king	and a mouth
to a stream	to the wall
like a house	to the neighbor
like the time	in the head
like a cubit	to humanity
and a face	and a fruit
and the blood	and a seat
and a nation	in a vessel
in justice	from the mother
like work	and glory
and here	from the sky
and bronze	to a wing
in silver	and an utterance
at (in) the new moon	the word
and a messenger	like a word

2. Write the BH word formed as a result of combining these various elements. Explain the phonological principles involved. Translate the resulting word into English:

מִן + שָׁנָה	
מִן + הַצֹּאן	
וְ + מַיִם	
בְּ + ה + אֹהֶל	
מִן + אִישׁ	
כְּ + בָשָׂר	
וְ + גְּבוּל	
לְ + גָּדוֹל	
לְ + יְרוּשָׁלַם	

3. Write the following prepositional phrases in Hebrew:

around the altar	opposite the place
beside the family	with the woman (write both ways)
to the tribe	between the south and the north
until the entrance	under the stone
on the lamb	opposite the Tabernacle (write both ways)
toward the army	

10 The Morphology of the Noun and the Adjective

In BH, as in all Semitic languages, it is traditional to speak of roots that are used as the consonantal basis for most words in the language, especially nouns, adjectives, and verbs. This description is largely correct, although we must realize that the concept of a root (Hebrew שֹׁרֶשׁ) is a medieval abstraction, and it is unclear how native speakers of BH might have comprehended the concept that we call a root. Most words derive from three-lettered (triliteral) roots. Most nouns are formed by putting these roots into particular patterns, sometimes supplementing them with prefixes or suffixes, mostly from the letters א, ה, ו, י, מ, נ, and ת (הֶאֱמַנְתִּיו—"I believed him"—is a useful mnemonic). From the root שמר, "to guard," for example, we have מִשְׁמָר, "prison," with a prefix מ; similarly, from the root אבד, "to perish," we have אֲבַדּוֹן, "place of destruction" (that is, "the underworld"), with a suffixed וֹן. Although the vast majority of biblical roots are triliteral, a significant number of common Hebrew words are biliteral (two-letter). These include: יָד, "hand," בֵּן, "son," עֵץ, "tree," and שֵׁם, "name."

In English, few words function as both nouns and adjectives; *beautiful* is an adjective, while *beauty* is a noun. It is therefore often useful in English to distinguish between a noun, "a word designating or naming a person, living being, object, or thing," and an adjective, "a word used to describe, qualify, or modify a noun," because in English the same word will not typically function as both noun and adjective. This is not, however, the case in Hebrew; note, for example, the word קָטָן (also vocalized קָטֹן), which may be translated either as an adjective meaning "little" or "young" or as a noun meaning "a little one" or "a young one." Context determines whether it functions as a noun or adjective; so, for example, in Genesis 27:42, where it is said of Rebecca, וַתִּקְרָא לְיַעֲקֹב בְּנָהּ הַקָּטָן, "she called Jacob, her young(er) son," הַקָּטָן is modifying or describing בְּנָהּ, and is therefore translated as an adjective. In Isaiah 60:22, on the other hand, הַקָּטֹן יִהְיֶה לָאֶלֶף, "the small(est) shall become one thousand [or 'a clan']," הַקָּטֹן is interpreted as a noun. Thus in terms of morphology it is useful to treat Hebrew nouns and adjectives together as a class. (In some grammars, the terms *noun* and *nominal* are used to describe this broader class, while the word *substantive* is used to distinguish what we typically call a noun.)

The form of Hebrew nouns may be distinguished along the three axes of number, gender, and definiteness. Thus we have singular vs. plural (vs. dual); masculine vs. feminine; unbound vs. bound (or construct). These distinctions are typically marked; it is particularly important to pay attention to how the form is marked, because that often determines an important nuance of the word's meaning.

In addition to these modifications of the noun, Hebrew nouns come in various forms or patterns (מִשְׁקָלִים). This is true of modern as well as biblical Hebrew, though few grammars of MIH emphasize this fact. These patterns are important because they help to explain why particular nouns get modified in unexpected ways—for example, why from עֶבֶד, "slave," we get עַבְדְּךָ, "your slave," from which all of the *segol*s of the base form have disappeared. These nominal patterns, like verbal patterns, are determined by the presence of vowel patterns, prefixes, and suffixes to a root. So from the root קדש, for example, we have the biblical noun קֹדֶשׁ, "sacredness," the adjective קָדוֹשׁ, "holy," and the noun מִקְדָּשׁ, "sanctuary" or "temple." The first two are distinguished by particular patterns of vowels (קֹדֶשׁ has the pattern □ֹ□ֶ□ [with penultimate stress], while קָדוֹשׁ has the pattern □ָ□וֹ□), whereas the latter has both a prefix מ and a particular pattern of vowels (מִ□ְ□ָ□).¹ These patterns recur with other roots as well. It thus makes sense to speak of a pattern *qṓṭel*, seen in such words as קֹדֶשׁ and בֹּקֶר, "morning" or "daybreak"; *qāṭôl*, seen in קָדוֹשׁ and גָּדוֹל, "big"; and *miqṭāl*, seen in מִקְדָּשׁ and מִשְׁפָּט, "justice."² In some cases, the particular patterning is of semantic significance. The pattern *qāṭôl*, for example, is typically used for forms that are primarily adjectives, like קָדוֹשׁ and גָּדוֹל. The nominal pattern *qiṭṭēl* is typically used to indicate what would be a disability from the biblical perspective, so we have, for example, עִוֵּר, "blind," גִּבֵּן, "hunchback," and (with compensatory lengthening) חֵרֵשׁ, "deaf" (< חִרֵּשׁ*). This particular nominal pattern is indicated not only by an initial חִירֶק and a final צֵרֵי in a closed syllable but by a doubled middle consonant (note the דָּגֵשׁ חָזָק). The pattern *qiṭṭēl* is relatively unusual in biblical Hebrew in that it typifies a semantic class of words. Although noun patterns are not as significant in terms of meaning as verbal patterns (the בִּנְיָנִים or derived conjugations), a schematic survey of noun types is important for understanding the various forms that a noun might take in different situations (for example, in the plural or construct, or with a suffix).

---

1. Throughout this textbook, I use □ to represent any Hebrew letter.
2. The letters *qtl* (קטל) are used by scholarly convention to represent the typical three root letters of Semitic languages.

The lexical form—that is, the form of the noun or adjective constituting the dictionary (lexicon) entry form—is typically the simple singular unbound form. The other forms of the noun or adjective are typically viewed in relation to this form. For the adjective *good*, for example, we find טוֹב, the masculine singular form listed in the lexicon, from which we derive טוֹבָה in the feminine singular, טוֹבִים (also spelled טֹבִים) in the masculine plural, and טוֹבוֹת (also spelled טֹבוֹת and טֹבֹת) in the feminine plural.[3] Similarly, we have פַּר, "bull," פָּרָה, "cow," פָּרִים, "bulls," and פָּרוֹת, "cows." We may say either that the masculine singular form has no suffix or that the suffix of the lexical form, the masculine singular, is ∅ (zero).

Masculine and Feminine

All nouns in Hebrew have grammatical gender, either masculine or feminine (there is no grammatical neuter, as in German or Greek). Some obviously feminine nouns, such as אֵם, "mother," are construed as grammatically feminine. A large number of objects (for example, אֶבֶן, "rock") are not obviously masculine or feminine in terms of their referent. We can tell whether a noun is construed by the language as masculine or feminine, however, by checking its gender agreement with other parts of speech. For example, we can see whether it is used in conjunction with a masculine or feminine adjective (for example, אָב זָקֵן, "an old father," where זָקֵן is unambiguously masculine so אָב must be masculine, vs. אֵם זְקֵנָה, "an old mother," where זְקֵנָה is unambiguously feminine, so אֵם must be feminine); whether it is the subject of a masculine or feminine verb (for example, וַיֵּרֶד הָאָב, "the father descended [masculine]," vs. וַתֵּרֶד הָאֵם, "the mother descended [feminine]"); or whether a masculine or feminine numeral is used with it (for example, אָב אֶחָד, "one father," vs. אֵם אַחַת, "one mother"). In some cases, the masculine and feminine forms of the "same" entity are not etymologically related; for example, for *parent*, we have אֵם for *mother* (that is, female parent) and אָב for *father* (male parent). Many nouns have no need for corresponding masculine and feminine forms; thus there is no feminine form for אֱנוֹשׁ, the generic word for humanity, nor is there a feminine form for כִּסֵּא, "chair." Usually, we can determine the gender of the noun by its ending: nouns that end in a ה or in an accented הָ are typically feminine, while all others (those that are unmarked) are masculine. Many of the exceptions to the principle are common words (for example, אֵם). Other unmarked words that are feminine include אֶבֶן, "rock"; אֶרֶץ, "earth" or "land"; בְּאֵר, "well"; חֶרֶב, "sword"; כּוֹס, "cup"; נֶפֶשׁ, "life-force"

---

3. Such variations in the spelling of a word, resulting from inconsistencies in the use of the *matres lectionis* (see p. 15), are a fundamental part of BH, and, in the future, will not generally be noted.

or "person"; עִיר, "city"; שְׁאוֹל, "the underworld"; תֵּבֵל, "inhabited world"; and usually אֵשׁ, "fire," רוּחַ, "wind," and שֶׁמֶשׁ, "sun." In addition, names of countries and cities, even though they are unmarked, are construed as feminine, as may be seen in Lamentations 1:3, גָּלְתָה יְהוּדָה . . . הִיא, "Judah was exiled (feminine singular) . . . she" or (Psalm 122:3) יְרוּשָׁלַםִ הַבְּנוּיָה, "Jerusalem built up" (feminine singular). Paired body parts are also typically feminine (for example, יָד, "hand/arm" and רֶגֶל, "foot/leg"). In addition, there are several words that Hebrew construes as either masculine or feminine; the most common of these is דֶּרֶךְ, path, way.

We know from other Semitic languages that the typical ָה form for the feminine is a secondary development from an accented -*aṯ*. Thus it should not be surprising when a feminine singular form that is best known in its singular unbound form (for example, שָׁנָה) appears with a ת instead, as in שְׁנָתוֹ, "his year," or שְׁנַת הָרָעָב, "the year of the famine." Based on historical Semitic linguistics, we know that the ָת form is a common feminine form; it is only when the feminine *-aṯ* is word-final and accented that in Hebrew it becomes an *āh* (ָה). This typically happens when the feminine word is not closely connected to another word or group of letters—that is, when it is not in construct or has no suffix attached to it.

The suffix ָה is typically added to masculine nouns or adjectives to produce feminine words. In many cases, this does not involve any further changes to the noun itself, as may be seen in the pair הַפָּר הַטּוֹב, "the good bull" vs. הַפָּרָה הַטּוֹבָה, "the good cow." In two situations, however, predictable changes occur.

In the first such case, the various types of vowel reductions, most especially propretonic reduction of the קָמֵץ, transpire as the result of the addition of an extra syllable to the word. The feminine of גָּדוֹל, big, for example, is גְּדוֹלָה (<*גָּדוֹלָה, with propretonic reduction of the initial ָ to a ְ). Similarly, a female prophet, related to the masculine נָבִיא, is נְבִיאָה. A wise man is אִישׁ חָכָם, while a wise woman is אִשָּׁה חֲכָמָה. (Note that the ח is vocalized ֲ because it is a guttural; see p. 34.)

The second situation is more complicated and concerns a class of nouns that are vocalized as bisyllabic with penultimate stress, like מֶלֶךְ. Various pieces of evidence converge to suggest that these words historically were monosyllabic and that their current vocalization pattern in the masculine singular is a result of helping vowels that were inserted, probably to facilitate their pronunciation. In fact, it is typically suggested that these words with penultimate stress represent earlier words of the following three categories: *qaṭl*, *qiṭl*, and *quṭl*. To some extent, the differences between these forms are masked in the masculine singular, where the consonant cluster is often broken up with the help of a short-e vowel (ֶ) between the second and third consonant. When suffixes (feminine, plural, or pronominal) are added to these words, however, their older form expresses itself. Because the most common form of these nouns parallels מֶלֶךְ—that is, they have a double סֶגוֹל—these forms are typically called segholates.

As noted, the segholates reflect three earlier forms. In Hebrew, in the unbound masculine singular, the form *qaṭl is generally represented by CéCeC, as in מֶלֶךְ; *qiṭl is reflected through either CéCeC or CéCeC (as in קֶבֶר, "grave," or סֵפֶר, "book"), and *quṭl is represented by CóCeC, as in קֹדֶשׁ, "holy." Of these forms, the only one frequently encountered as a feminine of a typically masculine noun is from *qaṭl. Thus, related to *king*, מֶלֶךְ, we find *queen*, מַלְכָּה. (In general, feminine nouns of the pattern מַ◌ְ◌ָה, where the first consonant is most often vocalized with the vowel ◌ַ, are feminine segholates.) Once the general historical principle of the segholates is understood, it is clear that מַלְכָּה is not somehow exceptionally derived from מֶלֶךְ; if anything, מֶלֶךְ is the exception in that its original *a* vowel is lost, and instead we find a double סֶגוֹל. An infrequent case of a feminine *qiṭl may be seen in the pair עֵגֶל, calf, and עֶגְלָה, heifer. (For a feminine singular *quṭl segholate with no corresponding masculine form, see, for example, חָרְבָה, "desolation"; note the קָמֵץ קָטָן, a short-u vowel, under the ח.)

Plurals

In general, the plural of a masculine noun or adjective is formed by adding ◌ִים, as in טוֹבִים, "good," or עֵצִים, "trees." The plural of feminine nouns is formed by adding וֹת (often spelled defectively, ◌ֹת), as in טוֹבוֹת, "good," or מִלְחָמוֹת, "wars." If the word ends in ◌ָה (masculine), the plural suffix is added to the part of the noun that precedes, as in קָשֶׁה, "difficult," which has קָשִׁים as its masculine plural, or שָׂדֶה, "field," which has שָׂדוֹת as its plural. A significant number of masculine nouns, however, take וֹת in the plural; these include אָבוֹת, "fathers"; דֹּרוֹת, "generations"; לֵילוֹת, "nights"; מַחֲנוֹת, "camps"; מַטּוֹת, "staffs"; שָׂדוֹת, "fields"; and שָׁבֻעוֹת, "weeks."[4] In addition, several feminine nouns take masculine suffixes; these include אֲבָנִים, "rocks"; חִטִּים, "sheaves of wheat"; רְחֵלִים, "ewes"; and שָׁנִים, "years." The fact that a particular noun takes the unexpected plural suffix, however, does not change the gender of that noun; in other words, despite its ◌ִים plural ending, the word שָׁנִים is feminine, following the gender of the singular שָׁנָה. Additionally, as in English, there are several words that are collectives—that is, words such as English *sheep*, which are singular in form but potentially

---

4. לַיְלָה is masculine, because its final ◌ָה is unaccented.

plural in referent; in BH these include צֹאן, "small cattle," and בָּקָר, "large cattle," as well as טַף, "little children"; יֶרֶק, "vegetation"; עוֹף, "birds"; and רֶמֶשׂ, "creeping things."

In terms of marking nouns and adjectives for number, Hebrew by and large distinguishes only between one object (unmarked in masculine) and many objects (marked with ים in the masculine singular). Some other Semitic languages routinely mark a triple distinction between one, two, and three or more. The form with two is called the dual and exists in Hebrew in a limited number of words. It is marked with יִם, as in "(two) hands," יָדַיִם. The largest category of duals is paired body parts, such as יָדַיִם, "hands, arms"; רַגְלַיִם, "feet, legs"; and שִׁנַּיִם, "teeth."[5] (These paired body parts are all feminine with the exception of שָׁדַיִם, "[female] breasts.") Other duals include שְׁנַיִם, "two," and מֹאזְנַיִם, "(two-part) scale."

As we have seen, the feminine suffix ָה is found only accented; in other situations, the older feminine ת is retained because the addition of the suffix prevented it from dropping away. Thus it is not surprising that the dual form of מֵאָה, "one hundred," is מָאתַיִם, "two hundred," and the dual of שָׂפָה, "lip," is שְׂפָתַיִם, "lips."

The type of propretonic reduction that we saw in the feminine is also present in the plural. For example, through propretonic reduction, from דָּבָר we get דְּבָרִים, "things," and from מָקוֹם we get מְקוֹמוֹת, "places" (masculine). The segholates form their plurals in a special way. Those of the form *qaṭl* and *qiṭl* form their plurals as ◌ְ◌ָ◌ִים—for example, מְלָכִים, "kings," קְבָרִים, "graves," and סְפָרִים, "books." The feminine segholates are comparable; thus *queens* is מְלָכוֹת. The plural of the *quṭl* form is ◌ֳ◌ָ◌ִים, as in קֳדָשִׁים, "holy (things)."

A final common change is seen in the plurals (and in some feminine nouns and adjectives). There is a class of biconsonantal Hebrew nouns that are really of the form *C_1V[short]C_2C_2; they are actually triconsonantal, ending with a doubled final consonant that cannot express itself in the masculine singular, because a word generally cannot end with a דָּגֵשׁ חָזָק.[6] When given the opportunity, however, as when a suffix is added, this doubling will express itself. There are not many such words, but some of them are common, including עַם, "nation," and רַב, "many." The plural of עַם is עַמִּים, and the plural of רַב is רַבִּים—with the addition of the suffix the doubling can (re)assert itself. (Similarly, the feminine singular of רַב is רַבָּה.) This same process can transpire in the dual; we thus have כַּפַּיִם, "palms," from the singular כַּף. Sometimes the doubling of the final consonant cannot be expressed because the final consonant is a guttural; in some cases, we see compensatory lengthening in the plural. This explains, for example, why we have שַׂר, "officer," but שָׂרִים (from *שַׂרִּים), "officers," as well as הָרִים from הַר, "mountain" and רֵעִים from רֵעַ.

---

5. Teeth were viewed as paired in ancient Israel (see Song of Songs 4:2; 6:7).

6. The common words אַתְּ, "you" (feminine singular), and נָתַתְּ, "you [feminine singular] gave," are exceptions to this principle.

The main suffixes for the masculine and feminine, both singular and plural, may be summarized by the following diagram.

Forms of Nouns and Adjectives

	Masculine	Feminine
Singular	∅	הָ◌ or ת◌ or תֶ◌ֶ
Plural	◌ִים	(וֹ)ת

This chart does not reflect the possible changes to the base form of the noun or the adjective. The most common changes are propretonic reduction, the return of the segholates to their older forms, and the return of nouns and adjectives with originally doubled final consonants to their older forms.

Vocabulary for chapter 10

אוֹת	sign
אָמָה	female slave, concubine
בֵּן	son (irregular plural בָּנִים)
בַּעַל	owner, husband, Baal (a Canaanite deity)
בַּת	daughter (irregular plural בָּנוֹת)
גֶּבֶר	man
דַּעַת	knowledge
דֶּרֶךְ	path, manner (both masculine and feminine)
זְרוֹעַ	arm (feminine; paired body part)
חֲמוֹר	donkey
חֵץ	arrow (plural חִצִּים)
חֹשֶׁךְ	darkness
טוֹב	good
יוֹמָם	by day (the ָם suffix is an adverbial suffix)
יַחְדָּו / יַחַד	together
יָמִין	right
כֹּחַ	strength
כְּסִיל	fool
מִקְנֶה	cattle
מִשְׁקָל	weight
נֶפֶשׁ	life-force, breath, person (feminine)
עוֹף	birds (collective)
עֶצֶם	bone (feminine; paired body part)
רַב	numerous (plural רַבִּים)
שְׂמֹאל	left
שִׁפְחָה	maid-servant
שֶׁקֶל	Shekel (a weight, approximately 11–13 grams)

Exercises for chapter 10

1. Translate the following words and explain the phonetic rules responsible for the vocalic changes exhibited in the changes from the singular to the plural:

גָּדוֹל גְּדוֹלִים
בֶּגֶד בְּגָדִים
רַב רַבִּים
אֶרֶץ אֲרָצוֹת
נָבִיא נְבִיאִים
שִׁפְחָה שְׁפָחוֹת
קֹדֶשׁ קָדָשִׁים
שַׂר שָׂרִים
חָדָשׁ חֲדָשִׁים
רֶגֶל רַגְלַיִם
מִנְחָה מְנָחוֹת

רוּחַ רוּחוֹת	
שֵׁבֶט שְׁבָטִים	

2. Translate into Hebrew:

numerous fields	big eyes
the righteous sons[7]	a straight path
a big stone	a good young girl
the righteous man	the wise daughters
the big houses	the holy land
many horses	good ordinances
a holy altar	a different bird
the bad land	straight arrows
a straight foot	the large camp
the large inheritance	the small family
the good fields	great kingdoms
great strength	the righteous nations
the many fools	the holy places
different donkeys	the wise and righteous prophet
a different owner	bad years
the straight river	the small city
the good oil	the wicked chiefs
the righteous maid-servant	good laws
the small mountains	

7. Note: In such cases, the definite article appears before both the noun and the adjective (for example, הָאִישׁ הַגָּדוֹל for "the big man"), as will be explained in more detail in the following chapter.

11 The Syntax of the Noun and the Adjective

Attributive and Predicative Adjectives

In English adjectives are used in two main ways: they may modify a noun directly (for example, "the good book"—an attributive use) or the adjective may be separated from the noun by a form of *is,* which is called a copula, or the verb of being (for example, "the book is good"—a predicative use). Hebrew also uses adjectives in these two ways. In the phrase הַסֵּפֶר הַטּוֹב, "the good book," the adjective טוֹב is being used attributively, vs. הַסֵּפֶר טוֹב, "the book is good," where the adjective טוֹב is being used predicatively. In its attributive use, the adjective and noun form a phrase that is part of a larger sentence (for example, וָאֶמְצָא אֶת־הַסֵּפֶר הַטּוֹב בְּבֵית הַמֶּלֶךְ, "I found the good book in the house of the king [palace]"), while in its predicative use, the adjective and noun form a sentence.

In its attributive use, the adjective must follow the noun, and the noun and adjective must agree in three ways: (1) number, (2) gender, and (3) definiteness. In the example used above, both הַטּוֹב and הַסֵּפֶר are singular, masculine, and definite (by means of the definite article). For example, the sentence could be modified to וָאֶמְצָא סְפָרִים טוֹבִים בְּבֵית הַמֶּלֶךְ, "I found good books in the house of the king (palace)," in which case both טוֹבִים and סְפָרִים are (1) plural, (2) masculine, and (3) indefinite. Similarly, וַתֹּאכַל הָאִשָּׁה הַצַּדִּיקָה אֶת הַלֶּחֶם, "The righteous woman ate the bread (or food)," is acceptable because, in the phrase הָאִשָּׁה הַצַּדִּיקָה, the noun and adjective are both (1) singular, (2) feminine, and (3) definite.[1] In this connection, it is important to remember that personal and geographical names, words in construct with definite nouns, and nouns with suffixes are always definite, even though they do not have definite articles prefixed to them, and that geographical names are construed as defi-

---

1. In the first sentence cited, the word אֵת precedes the definite direct object; see page 66.

THE SYNTAX OF THE NOUN AND THE ADJECTIVE

nite feminines, even if they are not marked as such (see p. 54). For this reason, in the phrase יְרוּשָׁלַ͏ִם הַבְּנוּיָה, "built (up) Jerusalem" (Psalms 122:3), where Jerusalem is a (proper) noun and "built (up)" is functioning adjectivally, both יְרוּשָׁלַ͏ִם and הַבְּנוּיָה are (1) singular, (2) feminine, and (3) definite.

Unlike in English, not all Hebrew sentences need a verb.[2] Thus the sentence הַסֵּפֶר טוֹב, in contrast to the English "The book good," is perfectly acceptable. Such Hebrew sentences that lack verbs are called nominal (from *noun*) sentences. In nominal sentences, predicate adjectives—that is, adjectives that serve as the predicate to the noun that serves as the sentence's subject—are typical.

The predicative use of the adjective differs from its attributive use in two fundamental ways: the noun may precede or may follow the adjective, and the predicate adjective is always unbound, thus the noun and adjective need not agree in the three ways in which attributive adjectives agree. Thus while the phrase הַסֵּפֶר הַטּוֹב is acceptable and *הַטּוֹב הַסֵּפֶר is not, "The book is good" may be expressed as either הַסֵּפֶר טוֹב or טוֹב הַסֵּפֶר.[3] In terms of agreement, the predicate adjective must agree in number and gender, but the predicate adjective is always indefinite, even if the noun is definite. Thus the following are acceptable as sentences using predicate adjectives:

טוֹב הַסֵּפֶר or הַסֵּפֶר טוֹב (The book is good.)
טוֹבִים הַסְּפָרִים or הַסְּפָרִים טוֹבִים (The books are good.)
גְּדוֹלָה הַמִּנְחָה or הַמִּנְחָה גְּדוֹלָה (The offering [or gift] is big.)
גְּדוֹלוֹת הַמְּנָחוֹת or הַמְּנָחוֹת גְּדוֹלוֹת (The offerings [or gifts] are big.)

סֵפֶר טוֹב ("A book is good") and מִנְחָה גְּדוֹלָה ("An offering is large") are also acceptable nominal sentences using predicate adjectives. In these cases, the noun does precede the adjective, and the noun and the adjectives do agree in number, gender, and definiteness; thus the adjective might be an attributive adjective ("a good book" or "a big offering"). Context always resolves possible ambiguities about whether an adjective is attributive or predicative; it is always possible to see whether the two words are a nominal sentence or a phrase that is part of the larger sentence.

Sentences or phrases may use more than one predicate or attributive adjective as long as each use follows the rules outlined above. Thus the phrase "the good tall prophet" would be expressed as הַנָּבִיא הַטּוֹב וְהַגָּדוֹל, while the sentence "The prophet is good and tall" would be הַנָּבִיא טוֹב וְגָדוֹל.

---

2. Some scholars would debate whether "is" in sentences like "The book is good." is really a verb, but this need not concern us here.
3. There is some debate about whether these two sentences are different, and it is possible that the second sentence, with the adjective (predicate) first, is emphasizing the predicate to some degree.

Hebrew may also use a personal pronoun of the appropriate gender and number (see p. 120) in nominal sentences, such as those consisting of a noun and a predicate adjective. Thus in addition to הַנָּבִיא טוֹב we could find הַנָּבִיא הוּא טוֹב; similarly we may find הַמִּנְחָה הִיא טוֹבָה. In this use such a pronoun is called a copula; it may appear in various places in the sentence and likely has an emphatic function. It is found, for example, in 1 Samuel 17:14, וְדָוִד הוּא הַקָּטָן, "*David* was the youngest."

The following chart presents the main differences between attributive and predicative adjectives.

Distinguishing Between Attributive and Predicative Adjectives

	Attributive	Predicative
Word order	noun-adjective only	noun-adj. or adj.-noun
Agreement	number, gender, definiteness	number, gender
Definiteness	adj. agrees with noun	adj. always indefinite
Copula	never used	used optionally

Comparatives and Superlatives

Many English adjectives come in three forms: a standard form, a comparative, and a superlative. For example, we have in English "mean" (unmarked), "meaner" (comparative), "meanest" (superlative), or "good" (unmarked), "better" (comparative), "best" (superlative). With the exception of some common words (like *good*), the comparative and superlative are generally formed from an adjective by adding -er and -est. Hebrew, unlike English, does not modify its adjectives in a similar way to form comparatives and superlatives.

Comparatives are formed with the preposition מִן, as in the sentence טוֹב דָּוִד מִשָּׁאוּל (or, less frequently, דָּוִד טוֹב מִשָּׁאוּל), "David is better than Saul." The two elements compared need to be separated by מִן, and the adjective may either precede or follow the first element of comparison. In this use, the adjective acts like a predicative adjective: it must agree with the first noun in number and gender, but it is always indefinite. For example, Qohelet 4:9 expresses "(The) two are better than (the) one" as טוֹבִים הַשְּׁנַיִם מִן־הָאֶחָד. This use of מִן as a comparative is not confined to adjectives; a class of verbs called stative verbs (see p. 112) may be used similarly, as in 1 Samuel 10:23, which says of Saul: וַיִּגְבַּהּ מִכָּל־הָעָם, "He was taller than the entire nation." The comparative use of מִן is relatively common in the Bible, and sentences using this construction should not be translated over-literally. For example, a sentence like like רַב הַזָּהָב מִן־הַכֶּסֶף, should be rendered "the gold was greater than the silver" or "there was more gold than silver" and not "the gold was great from the silver." Proverbs 8:11, כִּי־טוֹבָה חָכְמָה מִפְּנִינִים, for example, should be translated as "for wisdom is better than rubies," and Song of Songs 1:2, כִּי־טוֹבִים דֹּדֶיךָ מִיָּיִן: should be rendered "because your love is better than wine."

Unlike the comparative that uses מִן, there is no one, typical way of expressing the superlative in biblical Hebrew. The definite article may be used to indicate the superlative, as in 1 Samuel 17:14, וְדָוִד הוּא הַקָּטָן, "and David was the youngest (son)"; only context determines that the article here should be translated as a superlative. Song of Songs 1:8, 5:9, and 6:1, where the man calls his lover הַיָּפָה בַּנָּשִׁים, "the most beautiful among the women," are similar. When a noun in the singular is in construct with its plural, the phrase is usually a superlative, as in שִׁיר הַשִּׁירִים, "the song of songs" or "the finest [or the most sublime] song." In addition, to indicate a superlative an adjective may be modified either by the divine name or by the expression עַד־מָוֶת, "to the point of death." Both of these uses may be found in the Book of Jonah. In 3:3, the city of Nineveh is called עִיר־גְּדוֹלָה לֵאלֹהִים, literally "a great city to God" but better translated "the biggest city." In the following chapter (4:9), Jonah says to God, חָרָה־לִי עַד־מָוֶת, literally "I am angry to the point of death," which really means "I am as angry as I possibly can be." Context often determines whether the divine name or the expression עַד־מָוֶת is being used as a superlative or in its more literal sense.

Vocabulary for chapter 11

אַלְמָנָה	widow
בָּמָה	high place (for worship)
חִטָּה	wheat
חֲלוֹם	dream
טָהוֹר	ritually pure
טָמֵא	ritually impure
יֶלֶד	child, boy
מְאֹד	very (placed after an adjective or verb)
מִגְדָּל	tower
מָוֶת	death
מִזְמוֹר	psalm
מָחָר	tomorrow
עֵד	witness
עוֹד	still, again
עָנָן	cloud
קֶבֶר	grave
קְטֹרֶת	incense
קָרְבָּן	sacrifice (the initial קָמֶץ is a קָמֶץ קָטָן)
רֵאשִׁית	beginning of
שִׂמְחָה	happiness
שְׁאוֹל	Sheol, the biblical underworld
שִׁיר	song
שְׁמָמָה	desolation
תְּפִלָּה	prayer

THE SYNTAX OF THE NOUN AND THE ADJECTIVE

TRANSLATION TIP #2:

Do not be too literal; often words are used metaphorically, and should be translated thus.

Psalm 80:5: יְהוָה אֱלֹהִים צְבָאוֹת עַד־מָתַי עָשַׁנְתָּ בִּתְפִלַּת עַמֶּךְ׃

Although the literal meaning of עשׁן is "to smoke," it is often used metaphorically, typically as "to be angry." Thus this verse should be translated: "YHWH, God of Hosts; for how long will you be angry during the prayer of your nation?" not "YHWH, God of Hosts; for how long will you smoke during the prayer of your nation?"

Exercises for chapter 11

1. Note whether each of the following noun-adjective combinations is a sentence, a phrase, or an impossible combination. If it is grammatical, translate it:

קְטֹרֶת טוֹבָה		
אֱלֹהִים גְּדוֹלִים		
הַנָּשִׁים חֲכָמוֹת		
אֲבָנִים גְּדוֹלִים		
הַקֶּבֶר הַגָּדוֹל		
הַשִּׁיר טוֹב		
עִיר קָטֹן		
מַלְאָכִים רַבִּים		
קָרְבָּן טָמֵא		
הַבָּתִּים רָעִים		
הַזֶּבַח הַטְּהוֹרָה		
עֲבָדִים הַצַּדִּיקִים		
הַנְּבִיאוֹת רַבּוֹת		
הֶעָנָן גָּדוֹל		
רַגְלַיִם יְשָׁרוֹת		
הַשִּׁפְחָה רַע		
שִׂמְחָה גְּדוֹלָה מְאֹד		
אַלְמָנָה יְשָׁרָה		
בָּמָה קָטֹן		
אוֹתוֹת טוֹבוֹת		
הַנֶּפֶשׁ טוֹב		
פֵּרוֹת קְדֹשִׁים		
הַחֲלוֹם רַע		

THE SYNTAX OF THE NOUN AND THE ADJECTIVE

עֵד חָכָם מְאֹד		
חֲכָמִים רָעִים		
תְּפִלָּה קְטַנָּה		
חַג גָּדוֹל		
מַמְלְכוֹת רְשָׁעִים		
נַחֲלָה טוֹבָה		
לֶחֶם טוֹב		
אַיִל רָעָה		
בְּרִית חָדָשׁ		
הַפָּר טָמֵא		
שֶׁמֶשׁ חֲדָשָׁה		
מִלְחָמוֹת רַבּוֹת		
אָמָה צַדִּיקָה		
הַבַּעַל יָשָׁר		
הַזְּקֵנִים רְשָׁעִים		

2. Write the following phrases or sentences in Hebrew; be sure to vocalize correctly:

Happiness is good.	
The congregation is wicked.	
the great walls	
the many streams	
the new wheat	
holy land	
a righteous nation	
a good sacrifice	
the straight towers	
a new chest	
the many chariots	
impure lambs	
righteous warriors	
The incense is impure.	
the beautiful (= good) clouds	
bad servants	
pure rams	
The cattle are here.	
a small house	
many wars	
great noises (= voices)	
The garment is holy.	
the living prophet	
many graves	
great joy	

The prayers are good.	
The maid-servant is righteous.	
The chief is there.	
Darkness is bad.	
The children are good.	
the straight paths	
a small stone	
much blood	

3. Write the following sentences in BH; be sure to vocalize properly:

   God is in the Tabernacle.
   The cattle are behind (= after) the big city.
   The righteous prophet and the evil priest are in Sheol.
   Many messengers are opposite the mountain.
   Much wine and much grain are beside the altar.
   The holy man is with the righteous (= straight) woman.
   The large cattle are around the small house.
   The small sword is under the new throne.
   There is no righteousness in the land.

4. Translate the following phrases from the Bible and indicate whether the adjectives used are attributive or predicative. In this and all following chapters, your translation should be in good English but should also reflect an understanding of the syntax of the Hebrew. Words that you may not know are glossed:

Genesis 2:7

וַיְהִי הָאָדָם לְנֶפֶשׁ חַיָּה׃

The idiom וַיְהִי ... לְ means "became"

Genesis 29:2

וְהָאֶבֶן גְּדֹלָה

Exodus 1:8

וַיָּ֥קָם (arose) מֶֽלֶךְ־חָדָ֖שׁ עַל־מִצְרָ֑יִם (Egypt)

Numbers 19:9

מִח֤וּץ לַֽמַּחֲנֶה֙ בְּמָק֣וֹם טָה֔וֹר

Numbers 20:11

וַיֵּצְאוּ֙ (came out) מַ֣יִם רַבִּ֔ים

Numbers 20:15

וַנֵּ֥שֶׁב (We resided) בְּמִצְרַ֖יִם (Egypt) יָמִ֣ים רַבִּ֑ים

Deuteronomy 2:10

עַ֥ם גָּד֖וֹל וְרַ֥ב

Deuteronomy 28:38

זֶ֥רַע רַ֖ב תּוֹצִ֣יא (will bring forth, produce) הַשָּׂדֶ֑ה

Deuteronomy 28:64

אֱלֹהִ֣ים אֲחֵרִ֔ים ... עֵ֥ץ וָאָֽבֶן׃

Joshua 10:2

וַיִּֽירְא֣וּ (They were afraid) מְאֹ֔ד כִּ֣י עִ֤יר גְּדוֹלָה֙ גִּבְע֔וֹן (Gibeon)

1 Samuel 20:2

דָּבָ֥ר גָּד֖וֹל א֥וֹ דָּבָ֥ר קָטֹ֑ן

2 Samuel 20:16

וַתִּקְרָ֛א (called out) אִשָּׁ֥ה חֲכָמָ֖ה מִן־הָעִ֑יר

2 Kings 2:23

וּנְעָרִ֤ים קְטַנִּים֙ יָצְא֣וּ (departed) מִן־הָעִ֔יר

Psalm 51:12

לֵב טָהוֹר בְּרָא־לִי אֱלֹהִים (create [imperative] for me)

Psalm 96:1

שִׁירוּ לַיהוָה שִׁיר חָדָשׁ שִׁירוּ לַיהוָה כָּל־הָאָרֶץ: (Sing! [imperative])

Proverbs 10:1

בֵּן חָכָם יְשַׂמַּח־אָב (will gladden a father)

Daniel 11:3

וְעָמַד מֶלֶךְ גִּבּוֹר (will arise)

12 The Bound Form (Construct)
Morphology and Syntax

The Morphology of the Construct

In contrast to modern Hebrew, which typically expresses the relation of one noun belonging to another with the separate word שֶׁל, biblical Hebrew uses the construct form (סְמִיכוּת) to express belonging.[1] Thus, whereas modern Hebrew would say "the thing of the man," as הַדָּבָר שֶׁל הָאִישׁ, biblical Hebrew would say דְּבַר הָאִישׁ. In such constructions, the first word is said to be in construct (or bound) form (or state). In modern Hebrew, it is the נִסְמָךְ ("leaning"), while הָאִישׁ would be the סוֹמֵךְ ("supporting"). (The plain, unbound form—for example, דָּבָר—is called נִפְרָד, "separate" or "detached.") When a word is in the construct form, its vowel patterns may change, as in the change of דָּבָר to דְּבַר. These changes follow predictable rules; the first element in the construct chain acts as if it has lost its accent, and various vocalic reductions may take place. Indeed, there is often a מַקֵּף joining the noun in construct to the following noun, and the cantillation note that marks the accent is found on the following noun. In some grammars, the construct is called the genitive.

The construct form is not always different from the unbound form; for example, the segholates do not change in the construct (for example, סֵפֶר, "a book," and סֵפֶר־הָאִישׁ, "the man's book"). Changes of vocalization occur in many nouns. The following six rules are responsible for most of the changes seen in the construct:

[1]. This particle has biblical origins—it is a combination of the bound preposition לְ preceded by the rare biblical form of the (bound) relative pronoun שֶׁ. It may be seen, for example, in Song of Songs 3:7: שֶׁלִּשְׁלֹמֹה, "of Solomon." In the Bible, שֶׁל has not yet emerged as a separate ("independent" or "unbound") word. Indeed, in good Mishnah manuscripts, שֶׁל is still written at the beginning of the word to which it is attached ("proclitically")—for example, שֶׁלְּשַׁחֲרִית, "of the morning"; it is only in the middle ages that שֶׁל breaks off from the word that it precedes, becoming independent.

THE BOUND FORM (CONSTRUCT)

1. The קָמֵץ in a closed final syllable of the word in the construct reduces to a פַּתַח, as in the common expression בְּיַד־מֹשֶׁה, "via (literally 'by the hand of') Moses," where יַד is the construct form of יָד, "hand." This happens because the קָמֵץ is often found in closed, *accented* syllables, but, as a long vowel it is not usually found in closed, *unaccented* syllables. Because the קָמֵץ is now in a closed, unaccented syllable, it reduces to a פַּתַח.

2. The קָמֵץ and צֵרֵי in open syllables are subject to propretonic reduction. Thus from מָקוֹם, place, we have in Genesis 12:6 מְקוֹם שְׁכֶם, "the place of (the city) Shechem." The קָמֵץ of the word מָקוֹם, which was pretonic, is reduced because the construct always *acts as if* it has lost its primary accent, even in cases like this one, where it has its own accent and is *not* connected to the following word with a מַקֵּף. The צֵרֵי in the first syllable of segholates does not reduce.

    These two rules often combine. This can be seen in the common noun pattern ◻ָ◻ָ◻, as in the word דָּבָר, "word" or "thing." In construct, this changes to דְּבַר, with the קָמֵץ in the open, propretonic syllable reducing to a שְׁוָא (rule 2), and the קָמֵץ in the final closed syllable reducing to a פַּתַח (rule 1). Thus from the unbound form דָּבָר we get the common expression דְּבַר־יהוה, "the word of YHWH."

3. Feminine words that end in ◻ָה in the unbound form take ◻ַת in the construct, as noted above (p. 73). So, for example, the construct of תּוֹרָה is תּוֹרַת, as in Malachai 3:22, זִכְרוּ תּוֹרַת מֹשֶׁה עַבְדִּי, "Remember the teaching of my servant Moses." This rule may combine with the previous rule; thus מֵאָה changes to מְאַת, as in the expression מְאַת־שָׁנָה, "one hundred years."

4. In the masculine plural (or dual), final ◻ִים (or ◻ַ֫ יִם) is replaced by ◻ֵי, as in the change of יָמִים to יְמֵי—seen, for example, in Genesis 3:14, וְעָפָר תֹּאכַל כָּל־יְמֵי חַיֶּיךָ, "You shall eat dust all the days of your life." This change of suffix may combine with the previous rules. So, for example, from יָדַיִם we get יְדֵי, as in the famous Genesis 27:22, הַקֹּל קוֹל יַעֲקֹב וְהַיָּדַיִם יְדֵי עֵשָׂו, "The voice is the voice of Jacob, but the hands are the hands of Esau." (Note that קוֹל is in construct, but it undergoes no phonetic changes; its unbound and bound forms are identical, and context alone suggests that it must be a construct.) It is not unusual to see the rule of the שְׁוָא affect the vocalization of the noun in the plural; for example, from דְּבָרִים we get דִּבְרֵי; the קָמֵץ under the בּ is reduced because the word acts as if it has lost its stress (propretonic reduction). We are then left with *דְּבְרֵי, a form that begins with two שְׁוָאִים. Because this is impermissible in biblical Hebrew, the first שְׁוָא becomes a חִירֶק (דְּבָרִים > *דְּבְרֵי > *דִּבְרֵי > דִּבְרֵי; see p. 42).

5. The segholates (pp. 73–74) revert to their older form in the construct *plural*. Thus from מֶלֶךְ we get the plural מְלָכִים (see p. 75). But the plural construct is מַלְכֵי (note the כ rather than כּ), as the original *a* vowel of the older *qaṭl* form *returns*.[2] Similarly, from סֵפֶר, originally a *qiṭl*, we get סִפְרֵי, and from קֹדֶשׁ, a *quṭl*, we get קָדְשֵׁי (with a קָמֵץ קָטָן). If the second root letter is a guttural, the שְׁוָא, which should have closed the syllable, becomes a חֲטַף פַּתַח, secondarily opening up the syllable. We would have expected the plural construct of נַעַר, "lad," for example, to be *נַעְרֵי, by analogy to מַלְכֵי. The form *נַעְרֵי is acceptable in theory, because the שְׁוָא is a שְׁוָא נָח, and therefore closes the syllable (see p. 31). In many such instances, however, Hebrew prefers to open the syllable with the guttural, yielding the form נַעֲרֵי.

6. The feminine plural forms in the construct retain the plural form וֹת or ֹת, and the word itself is subject to various vowel changes noted above. For example, the construct of שֵׁמוֹת is שְׁמוֹת (rule 2), of מִשְׁפָּחוֹת is מִשְׁפְּחוֹת (rule 2), and of חֲרָבוֹת is חַרְבוֹת (rule 5). As in the masculine, the rule of the שְׁוָא will sometimes take effect; this is apparent in the plural מְנָחוֹת, "offerings" or "gifts," which becomes מִנְחוֹת (< *מְנְחוֹת). Of course, as in the masculine singular, in many cases the word itself will remain unchanged, either because of the syllabic structure of the unbound form, which was not open to syllabic change (for example, חֻקּוֹת), or because the changes occurred already when the singular form was pluralized (for example, the propretonic reduction from מָקוֹם to מְקוֹמוֹת, which is also the construct form [masculine, with feminine plural]).

In addition, other nouns are affected by the following principles:

1. Final צֵרִי in a closed syllable *may* change to פַּתַח. This may be seen in the construct of מִזְבֵּחַ (note that the final פַּתַח is a furtive פַּתַח and is not an integral part of the word's structure—see p. 12), which is מִזְבַּח, as in the expression מִזְבַּח־יהוה, "the altar of YHWH."

2. The two common words אָב and אָח generally have irregular constructs אֲבִי and אֲחִי. בֵּן also has an irregular construct, בֶּן־ (rarely בִּן־).

---

2. In contrast, "my king" is vocalized מַלְכִּי, with a כּ. This variation has caused extensive debate about the nature of the שְׁוָא of מַלְכֵי and the proper syllabification of the word (*mal kê* vs. *ma lĕkê*; the first is preferable). Some have even resolved the problem by suggesting that there is a third type of שְׁוָא, called a medium (or medial) שְׁוָא or a שְׁוָא מְרַחֵף. More likely, historical forces, related to vowels that have been lost, are responsible for the lack of דָּגֵשׁ in words like מַלְכֵי.

3. A final הֶ becomes הֵ, as in שְׂדֵה־הָאִשָּׁה, "the women's field" (from unbound שָׂדֶה).

4. Two-syllable words with penultimate stress of the pattern ַ֙יִם and ָ֙וֶם are reduced to single-syllable words, as in בַּ֫יִת > בֵּית־, "house" and מָ֫וֶת > מוֹת־, "death."

The chart below summarizes the main rules involved in the changes that the noun in the construct undergoes.

Changes in Form of the Noun in the Construct

- קָמֵץ in a closed final syllable reduces to a פַּתַח.
- קָמֵץ and צֵרִי in open syllables are subject to propretonic reduction.
- Final הָ returns to תָ.
- Final ִים (or ִ֫ים) is expressed as ֵי. There is no corresponding change in the feminine plural ending.
- Segholates revert to their older form.
- Final צֵרִי in a closed syllable *may* change to פַּתַח.
- אָב and אָח generally have the constructs אֲבִי and אֲחִי.
- בֵּן has the construct, בֶּן־ (rarely בֶּן).
- Final הֶ > הֵ.
- ַיִם > ֵי and ָוֶם > וֹם־.

The Syntax of the Construct

More than one noun may be in construct in a construct chain. So, for example, in Genesis 47:9 Jacob speaks of יְמֵי שְׁנֵי חַיֵּי אֲבֹתַי—literally, "the days (unbound = יָמִים) of the years (unbound = שָׁנִים) of the lives (unbound = חַיִּים) of my ancestors." The construct may appear once before a pair of nouns, as in Genesis 14:19, where אֵל עֶלְיוֹן, "God most high," is invoked as קֹנֵה שָׁמַיִם וָאָרֶץ׃, "creator of heaven and earth." (On the vocalization of the conjunctive וְ here, see p. 64.) Alternatively, the construct may be repeated, as in Genesis 24:3, בַּיהוָה֙ אֱלֹהֵ֣י הַשָּׁמַ֔יִם וֵֽאלֹהֵ֖י הָאָ֑רֶץ, "in YHWH, God of the heavens and the earth."

In contrast to the agreement of nouns modified by adjectives, the gender and number of each word in the construct chain need not agree. For example, נֶ֫פֶשׁ הָאִישׁ, "the life force (feminine) of the man" (masculine), or מִלְחֲמוֹת הָעָם, "the wars (feminine plural) of the nation" (masculine singular) is permissible. The נִסְמָךְ (the initial, dependent word[s] of the construct chain) can *never* be preceded by the direct object, however, and its status as definite or indefinite completely depends on whether the סוֹמֵךְ (the final word of the chain) is definite. דְּבַר נָבִיא, for example, is "*a* word of *a* prophet" while דְּבַר הַנָּבִיא is "*the* word of *the* prophet." Similarly, יַד יֶ֫לֶד is "a hand of a child," while יַד הַיֶּ֫לֶד is "the hand of the child." The forms הַדְּבַר נָבִיא and הַדְּבַר הַנָּבִיא are totally unacceptable. Obviously, this raises the problem of how one could say "the X of (a) Y" in biblical Hebrew. This locution cannot be achieved using the construct, for both the סוֹמֵךְ and נִסְמָךְ must agree in terms of definiteness. To express "the X of (a) Y," it is therefore necessary to paraphrase or "circumlocute" (to get around) the construct, typically by using the possessive pronoun לְ or the particle אֲשֶׁר. This strategy may be seen, for example, in the frequent psalm superscription מִזְמוֹר לְדָוִד, "a psalm of David." Personal names are by their nature definite (see p. 54), so מִזְמוֹר דָּוִד would mean "the psalm of David." To express "*a* psalm [indefinite] of David [definite]," it is necessary to use the possessive לְ. In general, no pronouns or other words may disrupt the connection between the words in a true construct chain.

Adjectives follow the entire construct chain. In 2 Samuel 17:14, "the good advice of Ahithophel" is expressed by עֲצַת אֲחִיתֹ֫פֶל הַטּוֹבָה, and in Exodus 23:13 we have וְשֵׁם אֱלֹהִים אֲחֵרִים, "name of other gods." This type of construction may create ambiguities. For example, סֵ֫פֶר הַמֶּ֫לֶךְ הַטּוֹב may be construed as either "the scroll of the good king" or "the good scroll of the king." (Note that סֵ֫פֶר is definite, for it is in construct with a definite noun.) Context usually resolves such ambiguities. In any case, that phrase, in which the descriptive adjective is being used, should not be confused with the sentence using a predicative adjective, סֵ֫פֶר הַמֶּ֫לֶךְ טוֹב, "the book of the king is good."

The illustrative cases above have typically translated the construct with "of." Although the possessive is the most frequent use of the construct, the construct may be used to express many relations between nouns. For this reason, although the flexible English "of" usually works well as a translation of the construct, it is not always suitable. In addition "of" can be ambiguous in certain cases; for example, the phrase אֵימַת מֶ֫לֶךְ could be translated as "fear of a king," but this is unclear—is the king the subject of the fear (subjective genitive), or is מֶ֫לֶךְ the object of the fear (objective genitive)? In such cases, the context may clarify whether the construct is the subject or object, and it should be translated appropriately. For example, the beginning of Proverbs 20:2, נַ֣הַם כַּ֭כְּפִיר אֵ֣ימַת מֶ֑לֶךְ, should be translated "like the roar of the lion is the fear one has for a king," to make it clear that the king is the object, not the subject of the fear (אֵימָה). Another case in which "of" would lead to an awkward translation is the phrase חַֽלְלֵי־חֶ֔רֶב, "pierced (or killed) *by* sword." Do not automatically insert the possessive "of" or an apostrophe and *s* when translating the construct.

Vocabulary for chapter 12

אָב	father (irregular plural אָבוֹת)
אָח	brother
אַחֲרוֹן	last
אַרְיֵה, אֲרִי	lion
בּוֹר	pit, cistern (irregular plural בֹּרוֹת)
בֶּטֶן	stomach, uterus
בְּיַד	by, via
בְּרָכָה	blessing
גְּבוּרָה	might
גֶּפֶן	vine
דֶּלֶת	door
זָכָר	male
זָר	foreigner
כֶּרֶם	vineyard
לְפִי	according to (לְ plus construct of פֶּה)
לִפְנֵי	before (לְ plus construct of פָּנִים)
מַלְכוּת	kingdom, kingship, reign
מִפְּנֵי	because (מִן plus construct of פָּנִים)
נְקֵבָה	female
קִיר	wall (irregular plural קִירוֹת)
רְחוֹב	plaza (contrast MIH "street"; irregular plural רְחוֹבוֹת)
רִיב	fight, dispute, lawsuit
שׁוֹר	ox
תָּוֶךְ	middle
תּוֹךְ	middle of (construct of תָּוֶךְ)

Exercises for chapter 12

1. Listed below are seven nouns in the unbound singular. Following the example below, write each noun in the singular construct, the unbound plural, and the plural construct. Explain the phonetic changes that take place in each of these forms.

   Example: דָּבָר

   דָּבָר; construct singular דְּבַר־: the initial קָמֶץ is reduced by propretonic reduction, and the final קָמֶץ is reduced because it is now in a closed *unaccented* syllable; plural unbound דְּבָרִים: the initial קָמֶץ is subject to propretonic reduction; plural construct דִּבְרֵי־: the קָמֶץ is reduced to a שְׁוָא, which leaves two consecutive שְׁוָאִים, and by the law of the שְׁוָא, the first שְׁוָא becomes a חִירֶק.

אַיִל

חֵץ

שֶׁמֶשׁ

בְּרָכָה

זָהָב

שִׁפְחָה	
דֶּרֶךְ	

2. Give the constructs of the following words and translate:

מַלְאָךְ		תּוֹרָה	
כָּבוֹד		בַּיִת	
זָהָב		מִזְבֵּחַ	
צָבָא		מִנְחָה	
חַיִל		עָוֺן	
אוֹר		זָקֵן	
עָפָר		חֵמָה	
מַרְאֶה		עֵדָה	
כֹּחַ		חַג	

3. Give the following words in the construct plural and translate:

מִנְחָה		שַׁעַר	
בֶּגֶד		תְּפִלָּה	
בְּרָכָה		חָכָם	
מַמְלָכָה		תּוֹעֵבָה	
כִּסֵּא		נָהָר	
שֵׁבֶט		חֲמוֹר	

THE BOUND FORM (CONSTRUCT)

שִׂמְחָה	מִגְדָּל
כֶּרֶם	גְּבוּרָה

4. Write the following construct chains in Hebrew:

the ox of the elder	
the plaza of the city	
the vineyards of Jerusalem	
the recesses (stomach) of the underworld	
the kingdom of YHWH	
a hand of the woman	
the right of YHWH	
the door of the house	
the appearance of the cloud	
a stone altar	
the multitude of the cattle	
the palm of the elder	
via (= by the hand of) the prophet	
the father of the young girl	
the weight of the silver	
according to the man of the big city	
the last of the prophets	
the brother of the young boy	
a blessing of a priest	
knowledge of God	
the breadth of the land	

the cistern of the good woman	
the length of the field	
a bone of an ox	
a shekel of gold	
the sons of the warrior	
the cattle of the impure man	
the death of the righteous woman	
the heart of the sea	
knowledge of the wise man	
the remainder of the donkeys	
the abomination of the wicked concubine	
the walls of the big house	
the good servant of the master	
the arm of the warrior	
the middle of the house	
all the gold of the king	
the number of cities	
the blood of the bull	
a deed of a prophet	
in the midst of the clan	
the tongue of the wise man	
outside the wall	
the beginning of wisdom	

5. Translate the following phrases from the Bible. Note which nouns are in the construct (or bound) form, and which are unbound. If the noun has undergone phonetic changes as a result of being bound to the following word, explain these changes:

Genesis 1:2

וְרוּחַ אֱלֹהִים מְרַחֶפֶת (was hovering) עַל־פְּנֵי הַמָּֽיִם:

Genesis 3:2

וַתֹּאמֶר (said) הָאִשָּׁה אֶל־הַנָּחָשׁ (the snake) מִפְּרִי עֵץ־הַגָּן נֹאכֵֽל (we may eat):

Genesis 3:24

דֶּרֶךְ עֵץ הַחַיִּֽים:

Genesis 11:9

וּמִשָּׁם הֱפִיצָם (scattered them) יְהוָה עַל־פְּנֵי כָּל־הָאָֽרֶץ:

Genesis 22:6

וַיִּקַּח (took) אַבְרָהָם אֶת־עֲצֵי הָעֹלָה

(Note: the אֵת in such cases is not translated; it indicates the following definite direct object [here עֲצֵי הָעֹלָה].)

Genesis 24:3

וְאַשְׁבִּיעֲךָ (I will adjure you) בַּיהוָה אֱלֹהֵי הַשָּׁמַיִם וֵאלֹהֵי הָאָרֶץ

Genesis 31:11

וַיֹּאמֶר אֵלַי (said to me) מַלְאַךְ הָאֱלֹהִים בַּחֲלוֹם יַעֲקֹב

Genesis 39:11

וְאֵין (there was no) אִישׁ מֵאַנְשֵׁי הַבַּיִת שָׁם בַּבָּֽיִת:

Exodus 3:22

כְּלֵי־כֶסֶף וּכְלֵי זָהָב

Exodus 14:22

וַיָּבֹאוּ (came) בְנֵי־יִשְׂרָאֵל בְּתוֹךְ הַיָּם

Exodus 19:9

וַיַּגֵּד (told) מֹשֶׁה אֶת־דִּבְרֵי הָעָם אֶל־יְהוָה׃

Proverbs 16:15

בְּאוֹר־פְּנֵי־מֶלֶךְ חַיִּים

13 The Participle

The modern Hebrew present tense (הֹוֶה) form is called the active participle in grammars of BH.¹ In MIH the present is part of the *verbal* system, while in biblical Hebrew, it is construed as, and typically should be seen as, a noun (or adjective) form. This is obvious in terms of the form's morphology (form): in verbs, for example, the first-person singular is undifferentiated in terms of gender (for example, כָּתַבְתִּי, "I wrote," or אֶכְתֹּב, "I will write," are masculine or feminine), while the participle distinguishes between "I [masculine] am writing," כֹּתֵב, and "I [feminine] am writing," כֹּתֶבֶת or כֹּתְבָה. Also, verbs generally have different forms for first, second, and third persons (for example, אֶכְתֹּב, "I will write"; תִּכְתֹּב, "you [masculine singular] will write"; and יִכְתֹּב, "he will write"), while participles do not (כֹּתֵב, for example, could be "I [masculine] am writing," "you [masculine singular] are writing," or "he is writing"). The definite article cannot be appended to verbs (you cannot say הַכָּתַבְתִּי*, "the I wrote," while you can say הַכֹּתֵב, "the writer"). Finally, BH verbs are typically negated by לֹא (for example, Genesis 2:17, לֹא תֹאכַל מִמֶּנּוּ, "do not eat from it"), while nouns are generally negated by אֵין (for example, Genesis 37:24, וְהַבּוֹר רֵק אֵין בּוֹ מָיִם:, "the pit/cistern was empty; there was no water in it"). Here, too, the participle generally follows the noun pattern, as in the participle in Psalm 72:12, וְאֵין־עֹזֵר לוֹ:, "and there was no helper for him." This evidence suggests that formally, the participle is a noun rather than a verb. Although the morphology of the participle suggests that it is a noun/adjective, its use in various types of phrases (syntax) suggests that it may be construed as either a noun or a verb. Context determines this issue, which will be discussed in the second part of this chapter.

   1. This chapter is concerned with the active participle; on the passive participle, see p. 175.

THE PARTICIPLE

The participle follows the forms of biblical adjectives. In the masculine singular, its ending is ∅ (zero); in the feminine singular it is הָ or ת; in the masculine plural, םִי; and in the masculine plural, ת(וֹ) (see the chart on p. 76). The קַל participle from healthy verbs takes the following forms:[2]

	Masculine	Feminine	
Singular	☐וֹ☐ֵ☐	☐וֹ☐ֶ☐ֶת	(less frequently ☐וֹ☐ְ☐ָה)
Plural	☐וֹ☐ְ☐ִים	☐וֹ☐ְ☐וֹת[3]	

For example, from the root כתב, "to write," we would have

	Masculine	Feminine	
Singular	כֹּתֵב	כֹּתֶבֶת	(less frequently כֹּתְבָה)
Plural	כֹּתְבִים	כֹּתְבוֹת	

These forms may be seen as adding appropriate gender and number suffixes to the masculine singular, with pretonic reduction of the צֵרִי to a שְׁוָא נָע. Thus כֹּתְבָה (< *כֹּתֵבָה) is syllabified and pronounced kō ṯĕḇah, with a שְׁוָא נָע, because it is reduced from another vowel; had it been a שְׁוָא נָח, the ב would have opened a syllable and become בּ.

There is a שְׁוָא נָע in the feminine singular and in all plural forms; these become modified to a חֲטָף פַּתַח if the preceding consonant is a guttural (see p. 31). For example, from the second guttural root שאל, "to ask," we would get:

---

2. This book assumes some knowledge of the meaning of the קַל from MIH. As will become clear later in this chapter, by "healthy verb" I mean a verb that is truly triliteral and has no gutturals. In that sense, it differs from the standard term "strong verb," which can include gutturals.

3. Reminder: there is substantial variation in the spelling of biblical Hebrew, so this form may also be vocalized as ☐ֹ☐ְ☐ת or ☐ֹ☐וֹ☐וֹת.

THE PARTICIPLE

	Masculine	Feminine	
Singular	שֹׁאֵל	שֹׁאֶלֶת	(less frequently שֹׁאֲלָה)
Plural	שֹׁאֲלִים	שֹׁאֲלוֹת	

From third guttural שמע, "to hear," we would get:

	Masculine	Feminine	
Singular	שֹׁמֵעַ	שֹׁמַעַת	(less frequently שֹׁמְעָה)
Plural	שֹׁמְעִים	שֹׁמְעוֹת	

Note how a helping vowel, the furtive *pátaḥ* (פַּתָח גְּנוּבָה; see p. 12), is inserted in the masculine singular under the final guttural; and note how the feminine singular form is vocalized with a final double פַּתָח instead of the expected סֶגוֹל, due to partial assimilation of each vowel to the guttural (p. 46).

Verbs that have an אָלֶף as their third root letter, such as מצא, "to find," are vocalized slightly differently in the feminine singular:

	Masculine	Feminine	
Singular	מֹצֵא	מֹצֵאת	(less frequently מֹצְאָה)
Plural	מֹצְאִים	מֹצְאוֹת	

These verbs are also called לא verbs. Hebrew verbs are named using the root פעל ("action" or "verb"), so that verbs that have an אָלֶף as their last root letter are designated לא verbs. (If the אָלֶף were in the first position, like אמר, it would be called a פא verb.) The form מֹצֵאת, rather than the expected מֹצֶאת*, illustrates the rule that Ceʾe > Cēʾ.

First gutturals are no different from healthy verbs; for example, from אמר, "to say," we would get:

	Masculine	Feminine	
Singular	אֹמֵר	אֹמֶרֶת	(less frequently אֹמְרָה)
Plural	אֹמְרִים	אֹמְרוֹת	

More difficult to explain are such verbs as בָּנֶה, "I [masculine], you [masculine singular], he build[s]/[am/are/is] building/[am/are/is] a builder." These forms are inaccurately called ל״ה verbs in many grammars. The designation ל״ה should be reserved for verbs like גָּבַהּ, was high, in which the הֵא is consonantal (see p. 26) and which would appear in the participle as גָּבֵהַּ, written with a הֵא מַפִּיק. In contrast, as we know from other Semitic languages, the true third radical of verbs like בָּנֶה is a יוֹד. Hence these verbs should be called ל״י verbs. Many grammars call them ל״ה because of the הֵא that appears in the קַל, third masculine singular perfect, e.g. בָּנָה.[4] This הֵא, however, is only a vowel letter (see pp. 14–15) and is not consonantal. Therefore, the designation ל״ה is imprecise and should be avoided.

ל״י verbs take the following forms in the קַל active participle:

	Masculine	Feminine	
Singular	בֹּנֶה	בֹּנָה	(rarely בֹּנִיָּה)
Plural	בֹּנִים	בֹּנוֹת[5]	

Although most Hebrew verbal roots are visibly triliteral—that is, composed of three root letters, there is a small but important class of verbs in BH that are biliteral; these typically comprise two consonants separated by a long vowel and are therefore called hollow verbs.

4. On the term *perfect,* see Chapter 18; meanwhile, it is sufficient to realize that it is the equivalent form of the modern Hebrew past (עָבָר).
5. Other spellings of the plural forms are common because of the irregular use of vowel letters in BH. Thus alongside בֹּנִים we find בָּנִים, and along with forms like בֹּנוֹת, we have בּוֹנוֹת.

These include some common verbs like קָם, "he got up, arose," and שָׂם, "he placed, put." In the third-person masculine singular imperfect (MIH future), these forms are יָקוּם and יָשִׂים; for this reason, traditional grammars call these types of verbs ע״ו (middle וָו) and ע״י (middle יוֹד), respectively. Neither the יוֹד nor the וָו is consonantal, however, because these letters are serving as *matres lectionis* (אִמּוֹת קְרִיאָה); the term *hollow* is thus more appropriate. The form of these hollow verbs in the קַל active participle is identical for both the hollow verbs with an *i* vowel and those with a *u* vowel. They are illustrated using ק(ו)ם and שׂ(י)ם :

	Masc.	Fem.	Masc.	Fem.
Singular	קָם	שָׂם	קָמָה	שָׂמָה
Plural	קָמִים	שָׂמִים	קָמוֹת	שָׂמוֹת

All of these forms of the participle of the hollow verb have ultimate (מִלְרַע) stress.

The following chart illustrates the various forms of the קַל active participle of the various verb types.

The קַל Active Participle

Healthy verbs

	Masculine	Feminine
Singular	כֹּתֵב	כֹּתֶבֶת (כֹּתְבָה)
Plural	כֹּתְבִים	כֹּתְבוֹת

First guttural verbs

	Masculine	Feminine
Singular	אֹמֵר	אֹמֶרֶת (אֹמְרָה)
Plural	אֹמְרִים	אֹמְרוֹת

(chart continues)

The קַל Active Participle (*Continued*)

Second guttural verbs

	Masculine	Feminine	
Singular	שֹׁאֵל	שֹׁאֶלֶת	(שֹׁאֲלָה)
Plural	שֹׁאֲלִים	שֹׁאֲלוֹת	

Third guttural verbs

	Masculine	Feminine	
Singular	שֹׁמֵעַ	שֹׁמַעַת	(שֹׁמְעָה)
Plural	שֹׁמְעִים	שֹׁמְעוֹת	

לא verbs

	Masculine	Feminine	
Singular	מֹצֵא	מֹצֵאת	(מֹצְאָה)
Plural	מֹצְאִים	מֹצְאוֹת	

לי verbs

	Masculine	Feminine	
Singular	בֹּנֶה	בֹּנָה	(rarely בֹּנִיָה)
Plural	בּוֹנִים	בֹּנוֹת	

Hollow verbs

	Masc.	Fem.	Masc.	Fem.
Singular	קָם	שָׂם	קָמָה	שָׂמָה
Plural	קָמִים	שָׂמִים	קָמוֹת	שָׂמוֹת

The Use of the Active Participle

The participle, like the adjective, may function attributively (for example, הַכֹּהֵן הָעוֹלֶה, "the ascending priest"), or as a predicate (for example, הַכֹּהֵן עוֹלֶה, "the priest is ascending"). In its attributive use, the participle is typically translated as an adjective (note how the form הַכֹּהֵן הָעוֹלֶה is parallel to הַכֹּהֵן הַזָּקֵן, "the old priest"), while as a predicate, it is usually translated as a verb (note how הַכֹּהֵן עוֹלֶה is similar to הַכֹּהֵן עָלָה, "the priest ascended"). In contrast to MIH the participle need not be translated as a present, though this is most often the case. Instead, the participle gains its temporal sense from the context. As a form related to an adjective, the participle is typically durative (rather than punctual) in sense—that is, it refers to an activity that continues over time.

As a nominal form, the participle will frequently be in the construct, and all of the normal rules for construct formation apply to it. For example, Exodus 18:21 refers to "those who fear God" as יִרְאֵי אֱלֹהִים, where יִרְאֵי is the construct of יְרֵאִים (יְרֵאִי* > יִרְאֵי* > יִרְאֵי), and several times we find the land of Israel called אֶרֶץ זָבַת חָלָב וּדְבָשׁ, "a land flowing with milk and honey" (Exodus 3:8 and elsewhere), where זָבַת is the construct of זָבָה, the קַל feminine singular participle ז(ו)ב, "to flow." (Note how the construct here is translated "with" rather than "of"; this is determined by context.)

BH is similar to MIH in its use of the particles יֵשׁ and אֵין ("there is/are" or "there is/are not") with nouns. This may be seen, for example, in Genesis 18:24, יֵשׁ חֲמִשִּׁים צַדִּיקִם, "there are fifty righteous people," or Genesis 39:11, וְאֵין אִישׁ מֵאַנְשֵׁי הַבַּיִת שָׁם בַּבָּיִת, "and there was no person from the household there at home." The same use extends to the active participles in their nominal use, as may be seen in Ruth 3:12, יֵשׁ גֹּאֵל, "there is a redeemer," or Psalm 72:12, וְאֵין־עֹזֵר לוֹ, "and there was no one to help him" (literally, "there was no helper to him"). The use of the participle in conjunction with both of these particles is an additional indication of the participle's nominal nature.

As a verb, the participle may even be followed by the particle אֵת / אֶת־, the typical marker of the definite direct object in BH. This may be seen in the single verse, Genesis 25:28, that contains the verb אהב twice, once in a finite verbal form, and once as a participle: וַיֶּאֱהַב יִצְחָק אֶת־עֵשָׂו כִּי־צַיִד בְּפִיו וְרִבְקָה אֹהֶבֶת אֶת־יַעֲקֹב, "Isaac loved Esau because there was game in his mouth, but Rebecca loved Jacob." (Reminder: personal [and geographical] names are definite in BH [see p. 54], and thus we have the definite direct object marker אֶת־ before the personal names in this verse.)

The participle's tense is determined from context. For example, it may be translated as a past, as in I Kings 14:17, הִיא בָאָה בְסַף־הַבָּיִת, "she came to the threshold of the house";

as a present, as in Genesis 3:5, כִּי יֹדֵעַ אֱלֹהִים, "for God knows"; or as a future, as in 1 Samuel 3:11, הִנֵּה אָנֹכִי עֹשֶׂה דָבָר בְּיִשְׂרָאֵל, "I will do something in Israel." Some cases, however, are ambiguous, and the verse may be translated in several different tenses.

Not all BH verbs have active participles. There is a class of BH verbs, called stative verbs, which describe a state of being rather than an action. These include verbs like כבד, "to be heavy." Such verbs are found in the perfect (for example, כָּבֵד, "he was heavy") or in the imperfect (יִכְבַּד, "he will be heavy"), but there is no participle כֹּבֵד*. Instead, such verbs typically have adjectives associated with them; these are often called verbal adjectives. In the case of כבד the form of the adjective is כָּבֵד, and it may serve in some ways as parallel to the participle. Just as we have הָאִישׁ אֹכֵל, "the man is eating," for example, we have הָאִישׁ כָּבֵד, "the man is heavy." The (verbal) adjectives, however, are not used transitively and thus do not take direct objects.

THE PARTICIPLE

Vocabulary for chapter 13

Note: Until chapter 24, all verbs will be defined in the קַל only. לֹ"י verbs are listed as לֹ"י, though most lexica list them as לֹ"ה verbs. (In other words, בָּנָה would be found in the lexica under בנה, even though its real root is בני.) Hollow verbs are listed with the *mater lectionis* that they show in parentheses; in the lexica, they would be found with this יוֹד or וָו as a middle vowel letter. All roots are listed without final letters and without דְּגֵשִׁים—as roots, neither of these is appropriate. In addition, after the verb's definition, its forms will be illustrated (right to left) in the 3ms perfect, participle, imperfect, and imperative.[6]

אכל	to eat (אָכַל אֹכֵל יֹאכַל אֱכֹל)
אמר	to say (אָמַר אֹמֵר יֹאמַר אֱמֹר)
ב(ו)א	to come (בָּא בָּא יָבֹא בֹּא)
הלך/(ילכ)	to walk, go (הָלַךְ הֹלֵךְ יֵלֵךְ לֵךְ)
ידע	to know (יָדַע יֹדֵעַ יֵדַע דַּע)
ילד	to give birth (יָלַד יֹלֵד יֵלֵד לֵד)
יצא	to leave (יָצָא יֹצֵא יֵצֵא צֵא)
ישב	to sit, dwell (יָשַׁב יֹשֵׁב יֵשֵׁב שֵׁב)
לקח	to take (לָקַח לֹקֵחַ יִקַּח קַח)
נשא	to carry (נָשָׂא נֹשֵׂא יִשָּׂא שָׂא)
נתן	to give (נָתַן נֹתֵן יִתֵּן תֵּן)
עלי	to go up (עָלָה עֹלֶה יַעֲלֶה עֲלֵה)
עשׂי	to do (עָשָׂה עֹשֶׂה יַעֲשֶׂה עֲשֵׂה)
קרא	to call, read (קָרָא קֹרֵא יִקְרָא קְרָא)
ראי	to see (רָאָה רֹאֶה יִרְאֶה רְאֵה)
שׂ(י)מ	to place (שָׂם שָׂם יָשִׂים שִׂים)
שאל	to ask (שָׁאַל שֹׁאֵל יִשְׁאַל שְׁאַל)
ש(ו)ב	to return (שָׁב שָׁב יָשׁוּב שׁוּב)
שלח	to send (שָׁלַח שֹׁלֵחַ יִשְׁלַח שְׁלַח)
שמע	to hear, heed (שָׁמַע שֹׁמֵעַ יִשְׁמַע שְׁמַע)

---

6. Note the introduction here of the shorthand system that will be used henceforth. In this shorthand, 1 is first person (I, we), 2 is second person (you, singular), and 3 is third person (he, she, they). M is masculine, f is feminine, and c is common (either masculine or feminine). S is singular, and p is plural. Thus, 3ms is third person, masculine, singular, or "he."

Special Vocabulary Note

The conjunction כִּי is one of the most frequent words in BH and has a wide variety of uses. Often it is translated "because." This use should not be confused with the expression of purpose or intended desired result, which is typically expressed through לְמַעַן, "in order that." When preceding a verb, כִּי often has a temporal sense and is rendered "when"; it may also express prerequisite conditions and be translated "if." It also often has the sense of "that," as reflected in the refrain in Genesis 1, וַיַּרְא אֱלֹהִים כִּי־טוֹב:, "God saw *that* it was good." These senses, along with others, will be illustrated through biblical excerpts in the following chapters.

THE PARTICIPLE

Exercises for chapter 13

1. Fully conjugate these verbs in the קַל active participle:

ms	fs	fs	mp	fp	root
					שׁמע
					שׁ(ו)ב
					שׁאל
					שׂ(י)מ
					ראי
					נשׂא
					אמר

(Example: for כתב: ms כֹּתֵב; fs כֹּתֶבֶת or כֹּתְבָה; mp כֹּתְבִים; fp כֹּתְבוֹת.)

2. Write the following in BH:

he is eating	you (ms) are placing
you (fp) are listening	she is sending
I (f) am saying	you (fs) are leaving
we (f) are seeing	they (m) are asking
you (fs) came	you (fp) are walking
she is giving birth	I (f) know
he is carrying	they (m) are taking
you (mp) are dwelling	they (f) are going up
he is returning	you (ms) are reading
they (m) are doing	I (m) am giving

3. Write the following in vocalized BH; you might have recourse to the following personal names (PNs) as you translate these passages: אַבְרָהָם, Abraham; שָׂרָה, Sarah; יַעֲקֹב, Jacob; רָחֵל, Rachel; מֹשֶׁה, Moses; חַנָּה, Hannah; שְׁמוּאֵל, Samuel; דָּוִד, David; תָּמָר, Tamar; שְׁלֹמֹה, Solomon; אֵלִיָּהוּ, Elijah.

David is hearing the word of the good prophet in the evening.

The prophet is always saying, "There is no peace for the wicked."

Tamar is leaving the big city and is going to the field of the wise foreigner.

The family of Jacob is coming by day from the straight river.

The children are saying, "Tomorrow, Hannah is taking the offering to the Tabernacle."

Moses knows that (כִּי) the instruction of YHWH is good.

The women are asking, "Do David and Solomon see the evil messenger (who is) near the big vineyard of the priest?"

The righteous women are going up together to the top (head) of the mountain and are reading David's psalm.

God does great deeds for the nation and gives the nation food because (כִּי) the nation heeds the ordinances.

THE PARTICIPLE

The woman who (אֲשֶׁר) is dwelling in the big house near the straight path is giving birth to a child.

Sarah is returning and is sending much wheat to Abraham, who is placing the wheat in the chest.

The big lion is eating the male and the female (people) because they (הֵם) are evil before YHWH.

4. Translate the following phrases from the Bible. In these exercises and those in the following chapters, personal names are indicated by PN and geographical names are indicated by GN. Note all participles in these verses, and parse them:

Genesis 3:5

וִהְיִיתֶם (You will become) כֵּאלֹהִים יֹדְעֵי טוֹב וָרָע׃

Genesis 7:16

וְהַבָּאִים זָכָר וּנְקֵבָה מִכָּל־בָּשָׂר בָּאוּ (came)

Genesis 13:5

וְגַם (And also) ־לְלוֹט הַהֹלֵךְ אֶת־אַבְרָם (PN) הָיָה צֹאן־וּבָקָר וְאֹהָלִים׃

The idiom הָיָה לְ means "belonged to."

Genesis 46:26

כָּל־הַנֶּפֶשׁ הַבָּאָה לְיַעֲקֹב מִצְרַיְמָה (to Egypt) יֹצְאֵי יְרֵכוֹ (his loins) מִלְּבַד נְשֵׁי בְנֵי־יַעֲקֹב

Exodus 24:17

וּמַרְאֵה כְּבוֹד יְהוָה כְּאֵשׁ אֹכֶלֶת בְּרֹאשׁ הָהָר לְעֵינֵי בְּנֵי יִשְׂרָאֵל׃

Leviticus 12:7

זֹאת (This is) תּוֹרַת הַיֹּלֶדֶת לַזָּכָר אוֹ לַנְּקֵבָה׃

Numbers 32:13

כָּל־הַדּוֹר הָעֹשֶׂה הָרַע בְּעֵינֵי יְהוָה:

Deuteronomy 4:21

הָאָרֶץ הַטּוֹבָה אֲשֶׁר יְהוָה אֱלֹהֶיךָ (your God) נֹתֵן לְךָ נַחֲלָה:

The last word of the sentence is being used adverbially; translate "as נַחֲלָה."

Deuteronomy 10:12

וְעַתָּה (And now) יִשְׂרָאֵל (PN) מָה יְהוָה אֱלֹהֶיךָ שֹׁאֵל מֵעִמָּךְ (from you)

Joshua 2:15

כִּי בֵיתָהּ (בָּיִת) בְּקִיר (in the wall of) הַחוֹמָה וּבַחוֹמָה הִיא יוֹשָׁבֶת:

Note: the final word יוֹשָׁבֶת is the pausal form of יוֹשֶׁבֶת.

Joshua 3:8

הַכֹּהֲנִים נֹשְׂאֵי אֲרוֹן־הַבְּרִית

Isaiah 40:3

קוֹל קוֹרֵא בַּמִּדְבָּר פַּנּוּ (prepare [imperative]) דֶּרֶךְ יְהוָה

Jeremiah 12:11

כִּי אֵין אִישׁ שָׂם עַל־לֵב:

Ezekiel 8:12

כִּי אֹמְרִים אֵין יְהוָה רֹאֶה אֹתָנוּ (us)

Psalm 1:6

כִּי־יוֹדֵעַ יְהוָה דֶּרֶךְ צַדִּיקִים וְדֶרֶךְ רְשָׁעִים תֹּאבֵד (will perish):

THE PARTICIPLE

Psalm 65:3

שֹׁמֵעַ תְּפִלָּה עָדֶיךָ (before you) כָּל־בָּשָׂר יָבֹאוּ (will/may come):

Psalm 98:9

לִפְנֵי־יְהוָה כִּי בָא לִשְׁפֹּט (to judge) הָאָרֶץ

Song of Songs 3:6

מִי זֹאת (is this [fs]) עֹלָה מִן־הַמִּדְבָּר

Ecclesiastes 1:7

כָּל־הַנְּחָלִים הֹלְכִים אֶל־הַיָּם וְהַיָּם אֵינֶנּוּ מָלֵא (does not become full)

14 The Independent, Demonstrative, and Relative Pronouns

Biblical pronouns are similar, but not always identical, in form and use to modern Hebrew pronouns. This chapter outlines independent pronouns—namely, those that are not joined to other words (for example, הוּא, "he"), and the following two chapters outline pronouns that are affixed to other words (for example, סִפְרוֹ, "his book," אֵלָיו, "to him").

The following paradigm lists the more common forms of the independent subjective personal pronoun; forms in parentheses indicate pausal forms. When more than one form is listed, the more common form is to the left. It is noteworthy that the (predominant) plural 2f, 3m, and 3f forms differ from those used in MIH.

The Independent Subjective Personal Pronoun		
	Singular	*Plural*
1c[1]	אֲנִי (אָֽנִי) אָנֹכִי (אָנֹֽכִי)	אֲנַ֫חְנוּ (אֲנָֽחְנוּ)
2m	אַתָּה (אָֽתָּה, אָֽתָּה)	אַתֶּם
2f	אַתְּ (אָֽתְּ)	אַתֵּן אַתֵּ֫נָה
3m	הוּא	הֵ֫מָּה הֵם
3f	הִיא [הוּא: כְּתִיב Pentateuch]	הֵ֫נָּה

---

1. c is an abbreviation for "common"—in other words, a form used for both masculine (m) and feminine (f).

As in MIH, these pronouns may be used in nominal sentences in place of a noun—for example, מַלְאָךְ הוּא or הוּא מַלְאָךְ, "he is a messenger/divine messenger," or הֵנָּה נָשִׁים צַדִּיקוֹת or נָשִׁים צַדִּיקוֹת הֵנָּה, "they are righteous women." (The order with the pronoun first is preferred.) In this respect, the active participle acts like a noun/adjective, so one may also say הוּא כֹּתֵב or כֹּתֵב הוּא, "he is writing/is a writer." Given that the participle כֹּתֵב could be used for first, second, or third person singular, the inclusion of the independent pronoun clarifies the subject of the sentence. By contrast, with finite verbs in the imperfect (modern future tense) and perfect (modern past tense), the personal independent pronouns are generally not used, because these verbal forms are highly differentiated by person (for example, 3ms כָּתַב, 2ms כָּתַבְתָּ, 1cs כָּתַבְתִּי), and the independent personal pronoun is not needed to clarify the subject of the verb. In other words, in MIH, for "he wrote the matter" one might say הוּא כָּתַב אֶת־הַדָּבָר, while BH would usually say כָּתַב אֶת־הַדָּבָר (or וַיִּכְתֹּב), omitting the personal pronoun הוּא. Scholars have suggested that in BH when the pronoun is unnecessarily present, it has an emphatic purpose, as in Genesis 44:27, אַתֶּם יְדַעְתֶּם, "you really know."

The demonstrative pronoun is used to point to a person or object; in English, something near is referred to with the demonstrative "this" or "these," while something far is referred to using "that" or "those." Hebrew distinguishes as well between the near and the far, and further differentiates between objects based on gender. Thus for near objects we have זֶה (m), זֹאת (f), and אֵלֶּה (cp). For far objects ("that," "those") the paradigm is identical to the personal pronouns, so we have הוּא (ms), הִיא (fs), הֵם, and much less frequently, הֵמָּה (mp) and הֵנָּה (fp). Syntactically, these pronouns are like adjectives: they may be used attributively or as a predicate. In the former use, they must follow the noun and must agree with it in number, gender, and definition. Because the use of these pronouns points to a particular noun, both the noun and the pronoun must be definite in such cases. Examples of attributive uses are: בַּדּוֹר הַזֶּה, "in this generation" (Genesis 7:1; note that בַּדּוֹר is definite, because there is a פַּתָח under the ב [< *בְּהַדּוֹר]), הָאָרֶץ הַזֹּאת, "this land" (Genesis 12:7; reminder: אֶרֶץ is feminine), and בַּיָּמִים הָהֵם, "in those days" (Genesis 6:4 and elsewhere). Note the vocalization of the article in הָהֵם; this vocalization, with compensatory lengthening, is always found (rather than the expected *הַהֵם) with the definite plural demonstrative pronoun. (We thus have הַהוּא, הַהִיא, but הָהֵם, הָהֵמָּה, and הָהֵנָּה.) In the attributive use, both the noun and the demonstrative pronoun must be definite; "this generation" is הַדּוֹר הַזֶּה, while דּוֹר זֶה is unacceptable. When used as a predicate (translated with English "is"), the demonstrative pronoun precedes the noun, as in אַתָּה הָאִישׁ, "you are the man" (2 Samuel 12:7); הֲזֹאת נָעֳמִי, "Is this Naomi?" (Ruth 1:19); or הֵמָּה הַגִּבֹּרִים, "those were the warriors" (Genesis 6:4). In addition to these uses, זֶה or זֹאת is sometimes added after an interrogative, as in God's question to the woman in Genesis 3:13: מַה־זֹּאת עָשִׂית, "What have you done?" (literally: "What is this you have done?") There is no clear difference in meaning between questions that append the demonstrative to the interrogative and those that do not.

A relative pronoun connects a dependent clause to a main clause and refers back to a constituent in the main clause. In English these include "that," "which," and "who(m)," as in the sentence "I saw the king *who* sat on the throne." In modern Hebrew, שׁ (followed by a דָּגֵשׁ חָזָק) fills this function. The form שׁ is found infrequently in BH, typically in some early, northern, and late texts; the far more frequent form of the relative pronoun is אֲשֶׁר, as in Genesis 13:15, כָּל־הָאָרֶץ אֲשֶׁר־אַתָּה רֹאֶה, "all the land that you see," or Genesis 39:17, הָעֶבֶד הָעִבְרִי אֲשֶׁר־הֵבֵאתָ לָּנוּ, "the Hebrew slave whom you brought to us." Hebrew can omit אֲשֶׁר where it might be expected before a dependent clause, as in Genesis 15:13, בְּאֶרֶץ לֹא לָהֶם, "in a land that is not theirs."

Vocabulary for chapter 14

גדל	to grow up, be great	(גָּדַל יִגְדַּל גָּדֹל lacking)
דרש	to inquire, seek	(דָּרַשׁ דֹּרֵשׁ יִדְרֹשׁ דָּרֹשׁ)
זכר	to remember	(זָכַר זֹכֵר יִזְכֹּר זָכֹר)
כבד	to be heavy	(כָּבֵד יִכְבַּד כָּבֹד lacking)
כרת	to cut (used often with the noun בְּרִית in the sense of making a covenant) (כָּרַת כֹּרֵת יִכְרֹת כָּרֹת)	
כתב	to write	(כָּתַב כֹּתֵב יִכְתֹּב כָּתֹב)
לבש	put on a garment	(לָבַשׁ יִלְבַּשׁ לָבֹשׁ lacking)
מלך	to reign	(מָלַךְ מֹלֵךְ יִמְלֹךְ מָלֹךְ)
ספר	to count	(סָפַר סֹפֵר יִסְפֹּר סָפֹר)
פקד	to remember, visit, count	(פָּקַד פֹּקֵד פָּקֹד יִפְקֹד)
קבר	to bury	(קָבַר קֹבֵר יִקְבֹּר קָבֹר)
קרב	to approach	(קָרַב יִקְרַב קָרֹב lacking)
רדפ	to chase	(רָדַף רֹדֵף יִרְדֹּף רָדֹף)
שרפ	to burn	(שָׂרַף שֹׂרֵף יִשְׂרֹף שָׂרֹף)
שבר	to break	(שָׁבַר שֹׁבֵר יִשְׁבֹּר שָׁבֹר)
שכנ	to dwell	(שָׁכַן שֹׁכֵן יִשְׁכֹּן שָׁכֹן)
שמר	to guard, observe	(שָׁמַר שֹׁמֵר יִשְׁמֹר שָׁמֹר)
שפכ	to pour out	(שָׁפַךְ שֹׁפֵךְ יִשְׁפֹּךְ שָׁפֹךְ)

Exercises for chapter 14

1. Give the BH forms for the following independent subjective personal pronouns:

you (fs)	you (ms)
she	we
they (m)	you (mp)
you (fp)	I
he	they (f)

2. Write the following short sentences in BH:

    He is guarding the messengers.

    You (ms) are counting the sheep.

    I (f) am reigning on the throne of kingship.

    We (m) are pouring out the oil.

    You (fp) are breaking the wall.

    They (m) are putting on a new garment.

    You (mp) are cutting down the trees.

    They (f) are inquiring of (use the direct object marker) Baal.

    She remembers the covenant with YHWH.

    You (fs) are writing the big book.

    He is visiting Sarah in the field of Abraham.

    I (m) am chasing after the evil people.

    We are burning the house because the house is impure.

    He dwells in the big house that is on the hill.

3. Write these phrases in BH:

that desolation	this lawsuit
that work	this time
those young men	this land
that glory	those seats
These are the large cattle.	that night
this place	those clouds
those concubines	that wilderness
You are the messenger.	this vision
these festivals	this border
These are the paths.	these kingdoms
this anger	She is the maidservant.
We are gods.	that darkness
these high places	that joy
These are the courtyards.	those prayers
those pits	this foreigner
these bulls	

4. Write in BH:

They (m) are burying the bones of the prophet whom the lion devoured (= ate אָכַל).

That righteous man who is walking toward the city gate is eating the fruit of the vine.

They are coming to the plaza so that (לְמַ֫עַן) they will hear (יִשְׁמְעוּ) the teachings of that priest.

I am pouring the water on the altar of YHWH that is in the house of YHWH.

That man is not eating bread because there is a great famine in that land.

David is making a covenant with the warriors who are going out to war.

The courtyard of the chief is smaller than this plaza.

The anger of YHWH is great because they are not (אֵין הֵם = אֵינָם) observing the law and listening to the words of that righteous prophet.

That fool is not taking arrows to that war because he is not (אֵין הוּא = אֵינֶנּוּ) smart.

She is the woman who is leaving the city on the donkey and is going to the vineyard.

5. Translate the following phrases from the Bible:

Genesis 3:14

אָרוּר (cursed) אַתָּה מִכָּל־הַבְּהֵמָה וּמִכֹּל

חַיַּת (construct of חַיָּה, [wild] animal) הַשָּׂדֶה

(Note: In this verse, אָרוּר ... מִן is being used as a comparative.)

Genesis 2:12

וּזְהַב הָאָרֶץ הַהִוא טוֹב

Genesis 3:19

כִּי־עָפָר אַתָּה וְאֶל־עָפָר תָּשׁוּב (you will return):

THE INDEPENDENT, DEMONSTRATIVE, AND RELATIVE PRONOUNS 127

Genesis 3:20

כִּי הִוא הָיְתָה (was) אֵם כָּל־חָי׃

Genesis 4:9

הֲשֹׁמֵר אָחִי (אָח my) אָנֹכִי׃

Genesis 6:2

וַיִּרְאוּ (saw) בְנֵי־הָאֱלֹהִים אֶת־בְּנוֹת הָאָדָם כִּי טֹבֹת הֵנָּה

Genesis 9:12

זֹאת אוֹת־הַבְּרִית אֲשֶׁר־אֲנִי נֹתֵן בֵּינִי וּבֵינֵיכֶם (between me and between you)
וּבֵין כָּל־נֶפֶשׁ חַיָּה אֲשֶׁר אִתְּכֶם (with you) לְדֹרֹת עוֹלָם׃

Genesis 13:15

כִּי אֶת־כָּל־הָאָרֶץ אֲשֶׁר־אַתָּה רֹאֶה

Genesis 15:18

בַּיּוֹם הַהוּא כָּרַת יְהוָה אֶת־אַבְרָם (PN) בְּרִית

Genesis 20:11

אֵין־יִרְאַת (יִרְאָה, fear, construct of) אֱלֹהִים בַּמָּקוֹם הַזֶּה

Genesis 21:10

לֹא יִירַשׁ (will not inherit) בֶּן־הָאָמָה הַזֹּאת עִם־בְּנִי עִם־יִצְחָק (PN)

Genesis 24:23

בַּת־מִי אַתְּ

Genesis 25:7

וְאֵלֶּה יְמֵי שְׁנֵי־חַיֵּי אַבְרָהָם (PN) אֲשֶׁר־חָי (he lived)

Genesis 26:24

וַיֵּרָ֨א אֵלָ֜יו (appeared to him) יְהוָה֙ בַּלַּ֣יְלָה הַה֔וּא

וַיֹּ֕אמֶר (he said) אָנֹכִ֕י אֱלֹהֵ֖י אַבְרָהָ֣ם (PN) אָבִ֑יךָ (your)

Genesis 29:26

כִּ֚י מִן־הַבְּאֵ֣ר הַה֔וּא יַשְׁק֖וּ הָעֲדָרִ֑ים (they would give the flocks drink)

וְהָאֶ֥בֶן גְּדֹלָ֖ה עַל־פִּ֥י הַבְּאֵֽר׃

Exodus 1:1

וְאֵ֗לֶּה שְׁמוֹת֙ בְּנֵ֣י יִשְׂרָאֵ֔ל (PN) הַבָּאִ֖ים מִצְרָ֑יְמָה אֵ֣ת יַעֲקֹ֔ב אִ֥ישׁ

וּבֵית֖וֹ (and his house[hold]) בָּֽאוּ׃

Exodus 3:5

כִּ֚י הַמָּק֗וֹם אֲשֶׁ֤ר אַתָּה֙ עוֹמֵ֣ד (from the root עמד, to stand)

עָלָ֔יו (on it) אַדְמַת־קֹ֖דֶשׁ הֽוּא׃

Exodus 13:4

הַיּ֖וֹם אַתֶּ֣ם יֹצְאִ֑ים בְּחֹ֖דֶשׁ הָאָבִֽיב׃ (Aviv—the name of a month)

Numbers 9:7

וַ֠יֹּאמְרוּ (said) הָאֲנָשִׁ֤ים הָהֵ֨מָּה֙ אֵלָ֔יו (to him) אֲנַ֥חְנוּ טְמֵאִ֖ים לְנֶ֣פֶשׁ אָדָ֑ם

Ezekiel 2:3

בֶּן־אָדָ֞ם שׁוֹלֵ֨חַ אֲנִ֤י אֽוֹתְךָ֙ (you) אֶל־בְּנֵ֣י יִשְׂרָאֵ֔ל

Joel 3:2

וְגַ֥ם (even) עַל־הָֽעֲבָדִ֖ים וְעַל־הַשְּׁפָח֑וֹת בַּיָּמִ֣ים הָהֵ֔מָּה

אֶשְׁפּ֖וֹךְ (I will pour out) אֶת־רוּחִֽי׃

15 The Possessive Pronominal Suffixes
The Singular

Possessive pronominal suffixes may be added to nouns (for example, סִפְרִי, "my book"), prepositions (לְךָ, "to you" [ms]), the direct object marker אֵת (אֹתָהּ, "her"), and verbs (יְדָעוּךָ, "they knew you"). These suffixes fall into two main patterns that may be seen in the contrast between the forms לִי, "to me," and עָלַי, "upon me," or between סִפְרִי, "my book," and סְפָרַי, "my books." There is one pattern for nouns in the singular, the prepositions בְּ, "in"; לְ, "to"; כְּ, "like"; מִן, "from"; עִם, "with"; אֵת, "with"; the words אֵין (a negative particle); עוֹד, "still"; and הִנֵּה (often translated in Bible English as "behold"; see the vocabulary list at the end of this chapter), as well as the direct object marker אֵת; these are examined in this chapter. The next chapter deals with the other pattern, comprising suffixes to the noun in the plural as well as the remaining prepositions. The direct object suffixes to verbs are explained in chapter 23.

The suffixes attached to these prepositions and to singular nouns are almost identical. But the prepositions do not, by and large, change when the pronouns are added to them, while most nouns go through changes that are connected to the shifts in tone resulting from the added suffix to the word. The following chart shows the forms of לְ, אֵין, סוּס, דָּבָר, and מִנְחָה with suffixes; it introduces the basics concerning the pronominal suffixes added to the singular; a more complete list appears at the conclusion of the chapter.

Pronominal Suffixes Added to the Singular

	לְ	אֵין	סוּס	דָּבָר	מִנְחָה
1cs	לִי	אֵינֶנִּי	סוּסִי	דְּבָרִי	מִנְחָתִי
2ms	לְךָ	אֵינְךָ	סוּסְךָ	דְּבָרְךָ	מִנְחָתְךָ
2fs	לָךְ	אֵינֵךְ	סוּסֵךְ	דְּבָרֵךְ	מִנְחָתֵךְ
3ms	לוֹ	אֵינֶנּוּ	סוּסוֹ	דְּבָרוֹ	מִנְחָתוֹ
3fs	לָהּ	אֵינֶנָּה	סוּסָהּ	דְּבָרָהּ	מִנְחָתָהּ
1cp	לָנוּ	אֵינֶנּוּ	סוּסֵנוּ	דְּבָרֵנוּ	מִנְחָתֵנוּ
2mp	לָכֶם	אֵינְכֶם	סוּסְכֶם	דְּבַרְכֶם	מִנְחַתְכֶם
2fp	לָכֶן		סוּסְכֶן	דְּבַרְכֶן	מִנְחַתְכֶן
3mp	לָהֶם	אֵינָם	סוּסָם	דְּבָרָם	מִנְחָתָם
3fp	לָהֶן		סוּסָן	דְּבָרָן	מִנְחָתָן

The relative uniformity of the suffixes is obvious from reading across any column. Some minor variation in the pronouns, however, is also evident; in the 2fs, for example, we have לְךָ, with a קָמֵץ, but אֵינֵךְ, with a צֵרִי. In the 3ms, we have לוֹ, but אֵינֶנּוּ. These variations need to be memorized. There is consistency in the suffixes with nouns, however, where we have a paradigm of 1cs ◌ִי-, 2ms ◌ְךָ-, 2fs ◌ֵךְ-, 3ms וֹ◌-, 3fs ◌ָהּ-, 1cp ◌ֵנוּ-, 2mp כֶם-, 2fp כֶן-, 3mp ◌ָם-, 3fp ◌ָן-. In the 1cp, the accent is on the penultimate syllable. In all other cases, it is on the ultimate syllable, namely on the added pronominal suffix. The 2m and f plural suffixes כֶם and כֶן, which are closed and always accented, are called heavy suffixes. The others are light suffixes.

Some of these suffixes change slightly at major disjunctive accents (see p. 47). Most significant is the change of the 2ms suffix to ◌ָךְ, which is identical to the usual form of the 2fs with many of the pronouns. This means that the form לָךְ could be "to you," feminine singular or masculine singular pausal. In Genesis 23:11, for example, הַשָּׂדֶה נָתַתִּי לָךְ, "I am giving/selling the field to you," לָךְ has Abraham as its referent and is *masculine* singular (pausal). Context clarifies whether the intended referent of the pronoun is masculine or feminine.

THE POSSESSIVE PRONOMINAL SUFFIXES: THE SINGULAR

Biblical lexica list some forms that each noun takes when a pronominal suffix is added to it; nevertheless, it is useful to understand the more common forms of nominal patterns and the changes that they undergo when these suffixes are added to them.

Adding suffixes to a word with a syllable structure like סוּס, a monosyllabic word with an unchangeable vowel, is quite straightforward, but such words, which do not change at all when suffixes are added, are not common. The changes in words like דָּבָר are quite predictable: in all cases except the second plural, we have propretonic reduction of the קָמֶץ to a שְׁוָא because the tone has moved two syllables away from the initial דּ. The בָ stays in these cases, because it is stable as a קָמֶץ, a long vowel, in an open pretonic syllable. (In this connection, note that the proper syllabification of דְּבָרְךָ, "your [ms] word," is děbā rěkā—the קָמֶץ there is a קָמֶץ גָּדוֹל, and the שְׁוָא is a שְׁוָא נָע.) In the second person plural, however, the heavy suffix begins a syllable, and the ר ends a syllable, so the קָמֶץ is shortened to a פַּתַח because it is now in a closed, unaccented syllable.

In דָּבָר the בָר is accented, while in דְּבַרְכֶם, "your [mp] word," and דְּבַרְכֶן, "your [fp] word," as a result of the addition of the heavy suffix, בַר is no longer accented. The status of the שְׁוָא under this ר is unclear. On the one hand, the ר seems to close the syllable, and thus is responsible for the change of the קָמֶץ to the פַּתַח. On the other hand, the following כ does not take a דָּגֵשׁ קַל. The medieval grammarians made up a separate category of medium שְׁוָא for such a vowel (see p. 94, n. 2), but this analysis is disputed. In any case, the noun דָּבָר takes two different forms before a suffix: in the 2p it is דְּבַר־, while in all the other forms it is דְּבָר־. This is typical; for this reason, it is usually necessary to learn only two forms of the noun to which the suffix is added: the 2p form (the heavy suffix form) and all others.

Certain nouns do not change when the pronominal suffixes are added. These include monosyllabic words with vowels whose vowel quality is not subject to changes, like סוּס (unchangeable long וּ), שִׁיר (unchangeable long ִי) and קוֹל (unchangeable long וֹ).[1] Certain longer nouns are also stable; these include words like רְכוּשׁ and חֲלוֹם (the initial שְׁוָא or חֲטָף and the later שׁוּרֶק or חוֹלֶם are unchangeable), as well as two-syllable nouns like צַדִּיק, which are stable because they begin with a short vowel in a closed syllable and end with an unchangeable long vowel (in this case, unchangeable long ִי).

Monosyllabic nouns such as עַם, whose root really is ʿamm, will express themselves disyllabically when the pronominal suffixes are added, just as they did in the plural. (Similarly, remember that the plural of עַם is עַמִּים; see p. 75.) "My nation" for example, is עַמִּי, and

---

1. These words may at times be spelled defectively, especially when suffixes are added to them; for example, קוֹל is on occasion spelled קֹל, and we find, for example, קֹלְךָ and קֹלִי. The vowel is "unchangeable" in the sense that it is not reduced to a שְׁוָא.

"your (ms) nation" is עַמְּךָ. From אֵם, "mother," we get אִמִּי, "my mother," and (mp) אִמְּכֶם, "your [mp] mother." The common monosyllabic noun יָד, "hand," yields some irregular forms: we have the expected יָדִי, "my hand," but in the 2p, we have יֶדְכֶם, "your [mp] hand."

Nouns with penultimate stress like בַּיִת and מָוֶת (but not typical segholates like סֵפֶר) use their construct forms as their base before all of the suffixes. Thus "my house" is בֵּיתִי, "your (mp) house" is בֵּיתְךָ, "my death" is מוֹתִי, and "your (ms) death" is מוֹתְךָ.

In disyllabic words the types of changes seen in the two קְמָצִים of דָּבָר are quite common. Thus from מָקוֹם, with an initial (reducible) קָמֵץ and an unchangeable long חוֹלֶם, we have propretonic reduction throughout, yielding the forms מְקוֹמִי, "my place," and מְקוֹמְכֶם, "your [mp] place." נָבִיא is similar, except that the guttural א cannot be vocalized with a שְׁוָא נָע; we therefore have the form נְבִיאִי, "my prophet," but נְבִיאֲכֶם, "your [mp] prophet." Words like כּוֹכָב are the opposite of מָקוֹם in that they have an unchangeable long חוֹלֶם in their first syllable but a (reducible) קָמֵץ in their final syllable. As seen above with דָּבָר, this קָמֵץ reduces only before the heavy suffixes of the 2p. Thus we have כּוֹכָבִי, "my star," but in the 2mp כּוֹכַבְכֶם, "your [mp] star."

There are other less common forms that nouns will take before a pronominal suffix; these may be found in biblical lexica under the listing of each noun, or may be seen in "A Classified List of Nouns" in Thomas O. Lambdin's *Introduction to Biblical Hebrew*, 285–301.

Segholates usually return to their original forms (see p. 73) when pronominal suffixes are added to them. From מֶלֶךְ (*qaṭl), we get מַלְכִּי, "my king," and מַלְכְּכֶם, "your [mp] king"; from קֶבֶר (*qiṭl), we get קִבְרִי, "my grave," and קִבְרְכֶם, "your [mp] grave;" from סֵפֶר (also *qiṭl), we get סִפְרִי, "my book," and סִפְרְכֶם, "your [mp] book"; and from קֹדֶשׁ (*quṭl), we get קָדְשִׁי, "my holiness," and קָדְשְׁכֶם, "your [mp] holiness." (The קָמֵץ in these words originates in a u-class vowel and is thus a קָמֵץ קָטָן.) These forms present few difficulties; it is noteworthy only that the base of the 2p forms is identical to the other forms, and that the first syllable ends with a שְׁוָא נָח and is therefore closed, so we have a דָּגֵשׁ קַל at the beginning of the second syllable in forms like מַלְכְּכֶם. (Contrast the plural, מַלְכֵי.)

If one of the root letters of a segholate is a guttural, these patterns are sometimes modified. If the noun is first guttural, and the segholate is of the *qiṭl type with an initial צֵרִי as in עֵדֶר, the base becomes עֶדְרִ־, as in עֶדְרִי, "my flock," and עֶדְרְכֶם, "your [mp] flock." If the noun is second guttural, the first vowel will be a short vowel related to the original short vowel, while the vowel under the second consonant will be either the same short vowel or the corresponding semivowel (חֲטָף). For example, from נַעַר, we get נַעֲרִי, "my lad," נַעַרְךָ, "your [ms] lad," and נַעַרְכֶם, "your [mp] lad." When the suffix is preceded by a שְׁוָא, the full vowel is present (for example, נַעְרְךָ and נַעְרְכֶם), whereas when the suffix begins with a vowel other than a שְׁוָא, we have a semivowel (for example, נַעֲרִי and נַעֲרוֹ). תֹּאַר, "appearance," a *quṭl* like קֹדֶשׁ, is formed similarly to נַעַר, by using the short vowel קָמֵץ קָטָן. We thus have תָּאֳרִי, "my appearance"; תָּאֳרוֹ, "his appearance"; תָּאָרְךָ, "your [ms] appearance"; and תָּאָרְכֶם, "your [mp] appearance." Segholates with gutturals in the third root letter follow predictable patterns: they are vocalized like nongutturals, with the exception that the second of two consecutive consonants that would be vocalized with a שְׁוָא (which is by definition a נָע שְׁוָא) becomes a חֲטַף פַּתַח because it is a guttural and cannot be vocalized with a שְׁוָא נָע. For example, from זֶרַע, "seed" or "descendent," we get זַרְעִי, "my seed"|| מַלְכִּי and זַרְעוֹ, "his seed"|| מַלְכּוֹ, but זַרְעֲךָ, "your [ms] seed"|| מַלְכְּךָ, and זַרְעֲכֶם, "your [mp] seed"|| מַלְכְּכֶם. Similarly, from אֹרַח, "path," we have אָרְחִי, "my path"|| קָדְשִׁי; אָרְחוֹ, "his path"|| קָדְשׁוֹ; אָרְחֲךָ, "your [ms] path"|| קָדְשְׁךָ; and אָרְחֲכֶם, "your [mp] path"|| קָדְשְׁכֶם.

Feminine nouns follow predictable rules, including the return of the original -*at* (see p. 73). From מִנְחָה, the base form to which the pronominal suffixes are added is מִנְחַת־, except before the heavy 2p suffixes, where it is מִנְחַת־. Because the first syllable is a closed syllable with a short vowel, it remains unchanged. In other cases we have propretonic reduction; for example, from שָׁנָה we get שְׁנָתִי, my year, and שְׁנַתְכֶם, your [mp] year, while from עֵצָה we get עֲצָתִי, my advice, and עֲצַתְכֶם, your [mp] advice (note the חֲטַף פַּתַח replacing the initial שְׁוָא נָע; see p. 34). In other cases the rule of the שְׁוָא becomes operative (see p. 42). This explains why from בְּרָכָה we get בִּרְכָתִי, my blessing (< בְּרָכָתִי* with propretonic reduction), and בִּרְכַתְכֶם, your [mp] blessing.

Below is a complete chart of the suffixes to singular nouns and the related pronouns and particles. The suffixes to two forms deserve special attention: מִן and כְּ, both of which are supplemented when the pronominal suffixes are added. The word מִן is doubled in all but the 2p and 3p forms, resulting in a base מִמֶּנּ־ (מִנְמֶנּ־*); כְּ is supplemented in all but the 2p and 3p forms by the syllable מוֹ, which is related to the word מָה, but is here used as a filler.

The chart is from Paul Joüon and T. Muraoka, *A Grammar of Biblical Hebrew* (Rome: Pontifical Biblical Institute, 1994), one of the standard reference grammars of biblical Hebrew. The pronouns and nouns that concern the plurals (*Pl.* and *plur.*) are the subject of the following chapter.

Paradigm 20. Suffixes of nouns (§ 94)

Sing.		1st c.	2nd m.	2nd f.	3rd m.	3rd f.
Sg.m.	סוּס	סוּסִי	סוּסְךָ(־ְ)	סוּסֵךְ	סוּסוֹ	סוּסָהּ
Sg.f.	סוּסָה	סוּסָתִי	סוּסָתְךָ(־ְ)	סוּסָתֵךְ	סוּסָתוֹ	סוּסָתָהּ
Pl.m.	סוּסִים	סוּסַי(־ְ)	סוּסֶיךָ	סוּסַיִךְ(־ְ)	סוּסָיו	סוּסֶיהָ
Pl.f.	סוּסוֹת	סוּסוֹתַי(־ְ)	סוּסוֹתֶיךָ	סוּסוֹתַיִךְ(־ְ)	סוּסוֹתָיו	סוּסוֹתֶיהָ
Sg.m. § 96Bf	שָׂדֶה	שָׂדִי	שָׂדְךָ(־ְ)	שָׂדֵךְ	שָׂדֵהוּ(וֹ)	שָׂדֶהָ(־ֶהָ)
בְּ § 103 f		בִּי	בְּךָ(בָּךְ)	בָּךְ	בּוֹ	בָּהּ
לְ § 103 f		לִי	לְךָ(לָךְ)	לָךְ	לוֹ	לָהּ
כְּ § 103 g		כָּמוֹנִי	כָּמוֹךָ		כָּמוֹהוּ	כָּמוֹהָ
מִן § 103 h		[d]מִמֶּנִּי	[h]מִמְּךָ	מִמֵּךְ	מִמֶּנּוּ	מִמֶּנָּה
עִם § 103 i		[e]עִמִּי	עִמְּךָ(־ְ)	עִמָּךְ	עִמּוֹ	עִמָּהּ
[a]אֵת § 103 j		אִתִּי	אִתְּךָ(־ְ)	אִתָּךְ	אִתּוֹ	אִתָּהּ
[b]אֵת § 103 k		אֹתִי	אֹתְךָ(־ְ)	אֹתָךְ	אֹתוֹ	אֹתָהּ
אֵין § 102 k		אֵינֶנִּי	אֵינְךָ	אֵינֵךְ	אֵינֶנּוּ	אֵינֶנָּה
עוֹד § 102 k		[f]עוֹדֶנִּי	עוֹדְךָ	עוֹדָךְ(×1)	עוֹדֶנּוּ	עוֹדֶנָּה[l]
הִנֵּה § 102 k		[g]הִנְנִי	הִנְּךָ[i]	הִנָּךְ	הִנּוֹ	
[c]בֵּין § 103 n		בֵּינִי	בֵּינְךָ(־ְ)	בֵּינֵךְ	בֵּינוֹ[k]	

Suffixes of the plur. noun

עַל § 103 m		עָלַי(־ְ)	עָלֶיךָ	עָלַיִךְ(־ְ)	עָלָיו	עָלֶיהָ
עַד § 103 m		עָדַי	עָדֶיךָ		עָדָיו	עָדֶיהָ
אֶל § 103 m		אֵלַי(־ְ)	אֵלֶיךָ	אֵלַיִךְ(־ְ)	אֵלָיו	אֵלֶיהָ

[a] with [b] sign of the accusative [c] בֵּין with sg. suf. like a sg. noun, and with pl. suf. like a pl. noun
[d] poet. (מֶ)מִנִּי [e] עִמָּדִי [f] עוֹדִי 4× [g] הִנֶּנִּי 2×; הִנְנִי [h] מִמֶּךָ [i] הִנֶּךְ 1× [j] poet. לָמוֹ 2×
[k] בֵּינָיו [l] עוֹדָהּ

THE POSSESSIVE PRONOMIAL SUFFIXES: THE SINGULAR
and of particles (§ 102–103)

Plur	1st c.	2nd m.	2nd f.	3rd m.	3rd f.
Sg.m.	סוּסֵ֫נוּ	סוּסְכֶם	סוּסְכֶן	סוּסָם	סוּסָן
Sg.f.	סוּסָתֵ֫נוּ	סוּסַתְכֶם	סוּסַתְכֶן	סוּסָתָם	סוּסָתָן
Pl.m.	סוּסֵ֫ינוּ	סוּסֵיכֶם	סוּסֵיכֶן	סוּסֵיהֶם	סוּסֵיהֶן
Pl.f.	סוּסוֹתֵ֫ינוּ	סוּסוֹתֵיכֶם	סוּסוֹתֵיכֶן	סוּסוֹתֵיהֶם	סוּסוֹתֵיהֶן
Sg.m.	שָׂדֵ֫נוּ	(שָׂדְכֶם)	(שָׂדְכֶן)	שָׂדָם	שָׂדָן

	בָּ֫נוּ	בָּכֶם		בָּהֶם, בָּם[e]	בָּהֵן[l]
	לָ֫נוּ	לָכֶם	(לָכֶן)[d]	לָהֶם[f]	לָהֵן[m]
	כָּמֹ֫ונוּ	כָּכֶם[c]		כָּהֶם[g]	כָּהֵ֫נָּה[n]
	מִמֶּ֫נּוּ	מִכֶּם	מִכֶּן	מֵהֶם[h]	מֵהֵ֫נָּה[o]
	עִמָּ֫נוּ	עִמָּכֶם		עִמָּם[i]	
	אִתָּ֫נוּ	אִתְּכֶם		אִתָּם	
	אוֹתָ֫נוּ	אֶתְכֶם		אֹתָם[j]	אֶתְהֶן[p]
	אֵינֶ֫נּוּ	אֵינְכֶם		אֵינָם	
				עוֹדָם	
	הִנֶּ֫נּוּ[a]	הִנְּכֶם		הִנָּם	
	בֵּינֵ֫ינוּ[b]	בֵּינֵיכֶם		בֵּינֵיהֶם[k]	

Suffixes of the plur. noun

	עָלֵ֫ינוּ	עֲלֵיכֶם		עֲלֵיהֶם	עֲלֵיהֶן
		עֲדֵיכֶם			
	אֵלֵ֫ינוּ	אֲלֵיכֶם		אֲלֵיהֶם	אֲלֵיהֶן

---

[a] הִנֶּ֫נּוּ; הִנְנוּ   [b] בֵּינוֹתֵ֫ינוּ   [c] poet. כְּמוֹכֶם   [d] 1 × לָכֵ֫נָה   [e] 3 × בָּהֵ֫מָּה   [f] poet. לָמוֹ; 1 × לָהֵ֫מָּה
[g] ṣerê; 1 × כָּהֵם, 1 × כָּהֵ֫מָּה   [h] 2 × מֵהֵ֫מָּה   [i] more freq. than עִמָּהֶם   [j] more freq. than אֶתְהֶם
[k] בֵּינוֹתָם   [l] 3 × בָּהֵ֫נָּה, 3 × בָּהֵן   [m] 4 × לָהֵ֫נָּה   [n] 1 × כָּהֵן   [o] 2 × מֵהֵן   [p] more freq. than אֹתָן

Vocabulary for chapter 15

אֶבְיוֹן	poor person
אוֹצָר	treasure, storehouse (irregular plural אוֹצָרוֹת)
אֵשׁ	fire
גִּבְעָה	hill
גֵּר	sojourner
הֵיכָל	temple, palace
הִנֵּה	This word is a presentative particle; i.e., it presents information that is new from the perspective of the narrator or one of the characters. It need not always be translated. When translated, it should be rendered in a contextually appropriate way (for example, "see," "wow," "indeed"); older translations mechanically translate it "behold," which is no longer idiomatic English.
חָמָס	violence
חֵן	favor (with suffix, חִנּוֹ)
יַעַר	forest
יְשׁוּעָה	salvation
מִקְדָּשׁ	sanctuary, Temple
עֹז	strength (with suffixes, typically as in עָזִּי or עֻזִּי)
עֶלְיוֹן	highest, supreme
עָנִי	poor, humble
עֵצָה	advice, counsel
צַר	enemy, straits, narrow (these are homonyms)
צָרָה	straits, distress
קָהָל	assembly
קֵץ	end (with suffixes, e.g., קִצּוֹ)
קֶשֶׁת	bow, rainbow
תָּמִים	complete, faultless

Exercises for chapter 15

1. Write from memory the complete paradigms of the following prepositions and nouns with suffixes:

3fp	3mp	2fp	2mp	1cp	3fs	3ms	2fs	2ms	1cs	
										בְּ
										אֵת (= with)
										אֵת (= direct object marker)
										קוֹל
										בָּשָׂר
										כֶּרֶם
										בְּרָכָה

2. Write the following prepositions and particles with suffixes in BH: (Forms with "with" should be written in two ways.)

to me	in it (fs)
from us	like you (ms)
with you (mp)	with her
you (ms) are not	he still
here I am	with you (ms)
they (m) are still	between him
from you (fs)	you (ms) are not
here they (m) are	from them (fp)
like her	to us
with him	us (direct object marker)
to him	from you (fp)

3. Write the following nouns with singular suffixes in BH; be sure that you understand any changes that the noun goes through:

my left	his forest
your (ms) poor person	their (m) bow
your (fp) distress	her treasure
your (fp) sacrifice	her blood
their (fp) family	our purification offering
their (f) sanctuary	my wisdom
my wine	her work
their (m) word	his hill
your (mp) sojourner	your (ms) strength
your (mp) assembly	my servant
your (fp) small cattle	your (ms) death
their (m) tribe	the violence against her (= her violence)
their (fp) kindness	our tower
my house	your (ms) gold
his anger	its (f) weight
her land	your (fp) palace
their (mp) garment	our distress
their (m) salvation	your (fp) inheritance
her advice	your (mp) end
his favor	

4. Write the following sentences in BH:

The wicked man is spilling the blood of the faultless humble man because he is observing the words of that book.

I am putting it (m) on the highest chest because there is something holy in it (m).

The enemy is breaking it (feminine) because they are saying, "There is gold and silver in it."

All of a sudden (הִנֵּה) he is not in his house because he has gone (הָלַךְ) to the house of the wise man who dwells beside my vineyard.

They are still coming to the city because there is a famine and they have no bread.

I am writing all the words of the prophet on a scroll and sending it to them because they are very wicked.

I am asking you (fs) for (= asking from you) small and large cattle for an offering at the Temple. Are you giving it to me?

Is his prayer better than our prayer? Is his sacrifice better than our incense?

Why is your son going up there? Is he chasing that great warrior who is eating there?

I am giving it (f) to them (m) because they are better than you (mp).

5. Translate the following phrases from the Bible. When the phrase contains a noun with a suffix, note the form of the noun without the suffix (e.g. if it has the word דְּבָרוֹ, write דָּבָר). Be sure that you understand why the form of the noun has changed.

Genesis 7:7

וַיָּבֹא נֹחַ (PN) וּבָנָיו וְאִשְׁתּוֹ וּנְשֵׁי־בָנָיו אִתּוֹ אֶל־הַתֵּבָה (the ark)

Genesis 9:12

וַיֹּאמֶר אֱלֹהִים זֹאת אוֹת־הַבְּרִית אֲשֶׁר־אֲנִי נֹתֵן בֵּינִי וּבֵינֵיכֶם
וּבֵין כָּל־נֶפֶשׁ חַיָּה אֲשֶׁר אִתְּכֶם לְדֹרֹת עוֹלָם:

Genesis 13:15

כִּי אֶת־כָּל־הָאָרֶץ אֲשֶׁר־אַתָּה רֹאֶה לְךָ אֶתְּנֶנָּה (I will give it)
וּלְזַרְעֲךָ עַד־עוֹלָם:

Genesis 17:19

וַיֹּאמֶר אֱלֹהִים אֲבָל (indeed) שָׂרָה (PN) אִשְׁתְּךָ יֹלֶדֶת לְךָ בֵּן

Genesis 21:22

אֱלֹהִים עִמְּךָ בְּכֹל אֲשֶׁר־אַתָּה עֹשֶׂה:

Genesis 22:7

וַיֹּאמֶר (said) יִצְחָק (PN) אֶל־אַבְרָהָם (PN) אָבִיו וַיֹּאמֶר אָבִי
וַיֹּאמֶר הִנֶּנִּי בְנִי וַיֹּאמֶר הִנֵּה הָאֵשׁ (fire) וְהָעֵצִים וְאַיֵּה הַשֶּׂה לְעֹלָה:

Genesis 23:18

לְעֵינֵי בְנֵי־חֵת (the Hittites) בְּכֹל בָּאֵי שַׁעַר־עִירוֹ:

Genesis 24:37

לֹא־תִקַּח (take) אִשָּׁה לִבְנִי מִבְּנוֹת הַכְּנַעֲנִי (the Canaanites)
אֲשֶׁר אָנֹכִי יֹשֵׁב בְּאַרְצוֹ:

Genesis 32:2

וְיַעֲקֹ֖ב (PN) הָלַ֣ךְ (went) לְדַרְכּ֑וֹ וַיִּפְגְּעוּ־ב֖וֹ מַלְאֲכֵ֥י אֱלֹהִֽים׃

Genesis 33:9

וַיֹּ֥אמֶר עֵשָׂ֖ו (PN) יֶשׁ־לִ֣י רָ֑ב אָחִ֕י יְהִ֥י לְךָ֖ (may you have) אֲשֶׁר־לָֽךְ׃

Genesis 34:24

וַֽיִּשְׁמְע֤וּ אֶל־חֲמוֹר֙ (PN) וְאֶל־שְׁכֶ֣ם (PN) בְּנ֔וֹ כָּל־יֹצְאֵ֖י שַׁ֣עַר עִיר֑וֹ

Genesis 41:39

אֵין־נָב֥וֹן (intelligent) וְחָכָ֖ם כָּמֽוֹךָ׃

Genesis 43:7

הַע֨וֹד אֲבִיכֶ֥ם חַ֛י הֲיֵ֥שׁ לָכֶ֖ם אָ֑ח

Exodus 15:11

מִֽי־כָמֹ֤כָה בָּֽאֵלִם֙ יְהוָ֔ה

Deuteronomy 1:10

יְהוָ֥ה אֱלֹהֵיכֶ֖ם הִרְבָּ֣ה (multiplied) אֶתְכֶ֑ם וְהִנְּכֶ֣ם הַיּ֔וֹם כְּכוֹכְבֵ֥י (כּוֹכָב = star) הַשָּׁמַ֖יִם לָרֹֽב׃

Deuteronomy 5:5

אָ֠נֹכִי עֹמֵ֨ד בֵּין־יְהוָ֤ה וּבֵֽינֵיכֶם֙ בָּעֵ֣ת הַהִ֔וא

Deuteronomy 19:1

כִּֽי־יַכְרִ֞ית (destroy) יְהוָ֤ה אֱלֹהֶ֙יךָ֙ אֶת־הַגּוֹיִ֔ם אֲשֶׁר֙ יְהוָ֣ה אֱלֹהֶ֔יךָ נֹתֵ֥ן לְךָ֖ אֶת־אַרְצָ֑ם

Joshua 9:25

וְעַתָּ֖ה הִנְנ֣וּ בְיָדֶ֑ךָ כַּטּ֨וֹב וְכַיָּשָׁ֧ר בְּעֵינֶ֛יךָ לַעֲשׂ֥וֹת (to do) לָ֖נוּ עֲשֵֽׂה (do)׃

Judges 11:34

אֵין־לוֹ מִמֶּנּוּ בֵּן אוֹ־בַת׃

Micah 7:18

מִי־אֵל כָּמוֹךָ נֹשֵׂא עָוֺן

16 The Possessive Pronominal Suffixes
The Plural

The possessive prepositions עַל, "on," עַד, "until," אֶל, "to," אַחַר, "after," תַּחַת, and "under," as well as all plural nouns, have a set of pronominal suffixes that differ from those noted in the previous chapter. The pronouns all follow the paradigms of masculine *plural* nouns, which, in contrast to masculine singular nouns with pronominal suffixes, are characterized by the presence of a יוֹד between the noun or pronoun of the suffix (for example, עָלֶיךָ, סוּסֵיהֶן). In the case of the noun plurals, this יוֹד might be related to the יוֹד of the plural suffix ◌ִים. With the prepositions עַל, עַד, and אֶל, it is possible that the יוֹד is present because the poetic forms of these prepositions (עֲלֵי, עֲדֵי, and אֱלֵי), all of which contain a יוֹד, are used as a base. The יוֹד of the 3ms suffix ◌ָיו is not pronounced.

Pronominal Suffixes Added to the Plural

	עַל	עַד	אֶל	סוּס[1]	דָּבָר	מִנְחָה
1cs	עָלַי	עָדַי	אֵלַי	סוּסַי	דְּבָרַי	מִנְחוֹתַי
2ms	עָלֶיךָ	עָדֶיךָ	אֵלֶיךָ	סוּסֶיךָ	דְּבָרֶיךָ	מִנְחוֹתֶיךָ
2fs	עָלַיִךְ		אֵלַיִךְ	סוּסַיִךְ	דְּבָרַיִךְ	מִנְחוֹתַיִךְ
3ms	עָלָיו	עָדָיו	אֵלָיו	סוּסָיו	דְּבָרָיו	מִנְחוֹתָיו
3fs	עָלֶיהָ	עָדֶיהָ	אֵלֶיהָ	סוּסֶיהָ	דְּבָרֶיהָ	מִנְחוֹתֶיהָ
1cp	עָלֵינוּ		אֵלֵינוּ	סוּסֵינוּ	דְּבָרֵינוּ	מִנְחוֹתֵינוּ
2mp	עֲלֵיכֶם	עֲדֵיכֶם	אֲלֵיכֶם	סוּסֵיכֶם	דִּבְרֵיכֶם	מִנְחוֹתֵיכֶם
2fp	עֲלֵיכֶן			סוּסֵיכֶן	דִּבְרֵיכֶן	מִנְחוֹתֵיכֶן
3mp	עֲלֵיהֶם		אֲלֵיהֶם	סוּסֵיהֶם	דִּבְרֵיהֶם	מִנְחוֹתֵיהֶם
3fp	עֲלֵיהֶן		אֲלֵיהֶן	סוּסֵיהֶן	דִּבְרֵיהֶן	מִנְחוֹתֵיהֶן

It is noteworthy that in contrast to the pronominal suffixes added to the plural, there are four heavy (penultimately accented) syllables: 2mp, 2fp, 3mp, and 3fp. To the extent that different forms appear before particular (heavy) suffixes in the plural, it is then the second- and third-person plurals that should be contrasted to other forms, which take light suffixes. For example, the plural of דָּבָר is דְּבָרִים. In most forms, the base for the plural suffixes is דְּבָרֵי־, which is shortened from דְּבָרִים; in these forms, such as דְּבָרֶיךָ, "your [ms] things," the קָמֵץ under the בֵּית is pretonic, so it is reduced. Before the heavy suffixes, however, the expected form would have been *דְּבָרֵיכֶם, where the בָּ syllable is now propretonic. It therefore reduces to a שְׁוָא, and following the law of the שְׁוָא, the first שְׁוָא (דְּ) is replaced by a חִירֶק (see p. 42), resulting in the form דִּבְרֵיכֶם, "your [mp] things." The feminine plural always uses the feminine construct form as its base, while the pronouns אַחַר and תַּחַת consistently use אַחֲרֵי־ and תַּחְתֵּי־ as their base. The third-person plural form is sometimes shortened; thus we often find forms like מִנְחוֹתָם, "their [m] offerings," in addition to מִנְחוֹתֵיהֶם, "their [m] offerings."

---

1. Some of the forms of these particular plural nouns with suffixes are not attested, but may be reconstructed with certainty from nouns of similar מִשְׁקָלִים.

In the case of segholates there are also typically two forms to which the suffixes may be added. The light suffix is added to shortened unbound plural (for example, מְלָכִים; the base to which the suffix is added is מְלָכ־), while the heavy suffix is added to the plural construct (for example, מַלְכֵי; the base to which the suffix is added is מַלְכֵי־). Thus "my kings" would be מְלָכַי, and "their kings" would be מַלְכֵיהֶם.

In some cases the suffixed forms in the singular and plural are quite similar and may have been pronounced identically (for example, סוּסֵנוּ, "our horse," and סוּסֵינוּ, "our horses"), though they are distinguished in writing. The suffixed forms of several singular and plural nouns are listed below in adjacent columns to highlight these differences.

Comparison of Pronominal Suffixes Added to Singular and Plural

	singular	plural	singular	plural	singular	plural
1cs	סוּסִי	סוּסַי	דְּבָרִי	דְּבָרַי	מִנְחָתִי	מִנְחוֹתַי
2ms	סוּסְךָ	סוּסֶיךָ	דְּבָרְךָ	דְּבָרֶיךָ	מִנְחָתְךָ	מִנְחוֹתֶיךָ
2fs	סוּסֵךְ	סוּסַיִךְ	דְּבָרֵךְ	דְּבָרַיִךְ	מִנְחָתֵךְ	מִנְחוֹתַיִךְ
3ms	סוּסוֹ	סוּסָיו	דְּבָרוֹ	דְּבָרָיו	מִנְחָתוֹ	מִנְחוֹתָיו
3fs	סוּסָהּ	סוּסֶיהָ	דְּבָרָהּ	דְּבָרֶיהָ	מִנְחָתָהּ	מִנְחוֹתֶיהָ
1cp	סוּסֵנוּ	סוּסֵינוּ	דְּבָרֵנוּ	דְּבָרֵינוּ	מִנְחָתֵנוּ	מִנְחוֹתֵינוּ
2mp	סוּסְכֶם	סוּסֵיכֶם	דְּבַרְכֶם	דִּבְרֵיכֶם	מִנְחַתְכֶם	מִנְחוֹתֵיכֶם
2fp	סוּסְכֶן	סוּסֵיכֶן	דְּבַרְכֶן	דִּבְרֵיכֶן	מִנְחַתְכֶן	מִנְחוֹתֵיכֶן
3mp	סוּסָם	סוּסֵיהֶם	דְּבָרָם	דִּבְרֵיהֶם	מִנְחָתָם	מִנְחוֹתֵיהֶם
3fp	סוּסָן	סוּסֵיהֶן	דְּבָרָן	דִּבְרֵיהֶן	מִנְחָתָן	מִנְחוֹתֵיהֶן

The chapter thus far has outlined the most common noun forms; a more complete list, reproduced from Joüon-Muraoka, *A Grammar of Biblical Hebrew,* is reproduced on the following pages.

Paradigm 17. Inflexion of the noun:

	1. qatl	2. qitl	3. qutl	4. qatl gutt.	5. qutl gutt.
	§ Ac *king*	§ Ae *book*	§ Ag *holiness*	§ Ai *lad*	§ Aj *work*
Sg.abs.	מֶ֫לֶךְ ᵃ	סֵ֫פֶר	קֹ֫דֶשׁ	נַ֫עַר(ְ)	פֹּ֫עַל
cst.	מֶ֫לֶךְ	סֵ֫פֶר	קֹ֫דֶשׁ	נַ֫עַר	פֹּ֫עַל
light suf.	מַלְכִּי ᵇ	סִפְרִי ᵉ	קָדְשִׁי ᶠ	נַעֲרִי	פָּעֳלִי
heavy suf.	מַלְכְּכֶם	סִפְרְכֶם	קָדְשְׁכֶם	נַעַרְכֶם	פָּעָלְכֶם
Pl.abs.	מְלָכִים	סְפָרִים	קָדָשִׁים(קֳ)	נְעָרִים	פְּעָלִים
cst.	מַלְכֵי ᶜ	סִפְרֵי	קָדְשֵׁי	נַעֲרֵי	פָּעֳלֵי
light suf.	מְלָכַי	סְפָרַי	קָדָשַׁי(קֳ)	נְעָרַי	פְּעָלַי
heavy suf	מַלְכֵיכֶם			נַעֲרֵיכֶם	פָּעֳלֵיכֶם
Du. abs.	רַגְלַ֫יִם ᵈ		מָתְנַ֫יִם	נַעֲלַ֫יִם	
cst.	רַגְלֵי		מָתְנֵי	נַעֲלֵי	
suffixes	רַגְלַי		מָתְנַי	נַעֲלַי	

ᵃ כֶּ֫רֶם   ᵇ בִּטְנִי, נֶגְדִּי   ᶜ נִסְכֵּי   ᵈ בִּרְכַּ֫יִם   ᵉ חֶלְקִי   ᶠ גָּדְלוֹ

	12. qatal	13. qatil	14. qata(i)l ל״ה	15. qātal	16. qātil
	§ Bb *word*	§ Bd *old*	§ Bf *field*	§ Cb *aeon*	§ Cc *enemy*
Sg.abs.	דָּבָר	זָקֵן, כָּתֵף ᵇ	שָׂדֶה	עוֹלָם	אוֹיֵב
cst.	דְּבַר	זְקַן, כֶּ֫תֶף	שְׂדֵה	עוֹלַם	אוֹיֵב(יְ)
light suf.	דְּבָרִי	זְקֵנִי	שָׂדִי	עוֹלָמִי	אוֹיְבִי
	דְּבָרְךָ		שָׂדְךָ	עוֹלָמְךָ	אוֹיִבְךָ(יְ)
heavy suf.	דְּבַרְכֶם		(שְׂדֵכֶם)	עוֹלַמְכֶם	אוֹיִבְכֶם(יְ)
Pl.abs.	דְּבָרִים	זְקֵנִים	פָּנִים ᵈ	עוֹלָמִים	אוֹיְבִים
cst.	דִּבְרֵי	זִקְנֵי	פְּנֵי	עוֹלְמֵי	אוֹיְבֵי
light suf.	דְּבָרַי	זְקֵנַי	פָּנַי	עוֹלָמַי	אוֹיְבַי
heavy suf.	דִּבְרֵיכֶם	זִקְנֵיכֶם	פְּנֵיכֶם	עוֹלְמֵיכֶם	אוֹיְבֵיכֶם
Du.abs.	כְּנָפַ֫יִם ᵃ	יְרֵכַ֫יִם ᶜ		מֶלְקָחַ֫יִם ᵉ	מֹאזְנַ֫יִם ᶠ
cst.	כַּנְפֵי				
light suf.	כְּנָפַי	יְרֵכַי			
heavy suf.	כַּנְפֵיכֶם				

ᵃ כָּנָף *wing*   ᵇ כָּתֵף *shoulder*   ᶜ יָרֵךְ *thigh*   ᵈ *face*   ᵉ *tongs*   ᶠ *scales*

Masculine, § 96

6. qatl ע"ו § Al death	7. qatl ע"י § Am olive	8. qatl ע"ע § An people	9. qitl ע"ע § Ao goat	10. qutl ע"ע § Ap law	11. qatl ל"ה § Aq fruit
מָ֫וֶתa	זַ֫יִתb	עַם(עָם)	עֵזc	חֹק	פְּרִי(פֶּ֫רִי)
מוֹת	זֵית	עַם	עֵז	חָק, חֹק	פְּרִי
מוֹתִי	זֵיתִי	עַמִּי	עִזִּי	חֻקִּי	פִּרְיִי
מוֹתְכֶם	זֵיתְכֶם	עַמְּכֶם	עֻזְּכֶם	(חֻקְּכֶם)d	פֶּרְיְכֶם
שׁוֹטִים	זֵיתִים	עַמִּים	עִזִּים	חֻקִּים	גְּדָיִיםe
שׁוֹטֵי	זֵיתֵי	עַמֵּי	עִזֵּי	חֻקֵּי	גְּדָיֵי
שׁוֹטַי	זֵיתַי	עַמַּי	עִזַּי	חֻקַּי	
שׁוֹטֵיכֶם	זֵיתֵיכֶם	עַמֵּיכֶם	עִזֵּיכֶם	חֻקֵּיכֶם	
		כַּפַּ֫יִם	שְׁנַ֫יִם		
		כַּפֵּי	שְׁנֵי		
		כַּפַּי	שְׁנַי		

a שׁוֹט whip   b חֵיק bosom   c אֵם mother, pl. אִמּוֹת; שֵׁן tooth   d חָקְכֶם   e גְּדִי kid

17. qāti(a)l ל"ה § Ce seer	18. qatīl § Db official in charge	19. qatīl ל"ה § Dc afflicted	20. qi(u)tāl § Dd writing
חֹזֶה	פָּקִיד	עָנִי	כְּתָב
חֹזֵה	פְּקִיד	עֲנִי	כְּתָב
חֹזִי	פְּקִידִי	כְּתָבִי	
חֹזְךָ	פְּקִידְךָ	כְּתָבְךָ	
חֹזְכֶם	פְּקִידְכֶם	כְּתָבְכֶם	
חֹזִים	פְּקִידִים	עֲנִיִּים	מְצָדוֹתa
חֹזֵי	פְּקִידֵי	עֲנִיֵּי	מְצָדוֹת
חֹזַי	פְּקִידַי		
חֹזֵיכֶם	פְּקִידֵיכֶם	עֲנִיֵּיכֶם	

a מְצָד fortification

Paradigm 18. Inflexion of the noun: Feminine, § 97

	21. qatl § A b queen	22. qatal § B b justice	23. qatal § E b year	24. [final segholate] § F b shoot
Sg.abs.	מַלְכָּה[a]	צְדָקָה	שָׁנָה	יוֹנֶקֶת
cst.	מַלְכַּת	צִדְקַת	שְׁנַת	יוֹנֶקֶת
light suf.	מַלְכָּתִי	צִדְקָתִי	שְׁנָתִי	יוֹנַקְתִּי
heavy suf.	מַלְכַּתְכֶם	צִדְקַתְכֶם	שְׁנַתְכֶם	יוֹנַקְתְּכֶם
Pl.abs.	מְלָכוֹת	צְדָקוֹת	שָׁנוֹת[b]	יוֹנְקוֹת
cst.	מַלְכוֹת	צִדְקוֹת	שְׁנוֹת	יוֹנְקוֹת
suf.	מַלְכוֹתַי	צִדְקוֹתַי	שְׁנוֹתַי	יוֹנְקוֹתַי
Du.abs.			שְׂפָתַיִם[c]	
cst.			שִׂפְתֵי	
light suf.			שְׂפָתַי	
heavy suf.			שִׂפְתֵיכֶם	

[a] כִּבְשָׂה *lamb*   [b] *poetic, § 90 b; ordinary plural* שָׁנִים   [c] *lips*

Paradigm 19. Irregular nouns §§ 98–99[a]

	1 (§ 98b) father	2 (§ 98b) brother	4 (§ 98c) son	5 (§ 98d) daughter	7 (§ 98d) sister
Sg.abs.	אָב	אָח	בֵּן	בַּת	אָחוֹת
cst.	אֲבִי	אֲחִי	בֶּן־[f]	בַּת	אֲחוֹת
Suf.Sg.1 c	אָבִי	אָחִי	בְּנִי	בִּתִּי	אֲחֹתִי
2 m.	אָבִיךָ	אָחִיךָ	בִּנְךָ[g]	בִּתְּךָ[h]	אֲחוֹתְךָ
2 f.	אָבִיךְ	אָחִיךְ	בְּנֵךְ		אֲחוֹתֵךְ
3 m.	אָבִיו[b]	אָחִיו[d]	בְּנוֹ	בִּתּוֹ	אֲחֹתוֹ
3 f.	אָבִיהָ	אָחִיהָ	בְּנָהּ	בִּתָּהּ	אֲחֹתָהּ
Pl. 1 c.	אָבִינוּ	אָחִינוּ	בְּנֵנוּ		אֲחֹתֵנוּ
2 m.	אֲבִיכֶם	אֲחִיכֶם		בִּתְּכֶם	
3 m.	אֲבִיהֶם	אֲחִיהֶם			אֲחֹתָם
Pl.abs.	אָבוֹת	אַחִים	בָּנִים	בָּנוֹת	אֲחָיוֹת*
cst.	אֲבוֹת	אֲחֵי	בְּנֵי	בְּנוֹת	אַחְיוֹת*
Suf.Sg.1 c	אֲבֹתַי	אַחַי[e]	בָּנַי	בְּנֹתַי	אַחְיוֹתַי
2 m.	אֲבֹתֶיךָ	אַחֶיךָ	בָּנֶיךָ	בְּנֹתֶיךָ	
2 f.		אַחַיִךְ	בָּנַיִךְ	בְּנֹתַיִךְ	אֲחוֹתַיִךְ
3 m.	אֲבֹתָיו	אֶחָיו	בָּנָיו	בְּנֹתָיו	אַחְיוֹתָיו
3 f.		אַחֶיהָ	בָּנֶיהָ	בְּנֹתֶיהָ	
Pl. 1 c.	אֲבֹתֵינוּ	אַחֵינוּ	בָּנֵינוּ	בְּנֹתֵינוּ	
2 m.	אֲבֹתֵיכֶם	אֲחֵיכֶם	בְּנֵיכֶם	בְּנֹתֵיכֶם	אַחְיוֹתֵיכֶם
3 m.	אֲבֹתָם[c]	אֲחֵיהֶם	בְּנֵיהֶם	בְּנֹתֵיהֶם	אַחְיוֹתֵיהֶם

[a] We have omitted the forms with *pl. fem. suffixes*. [b] אֲבִיהוּ [c] more frequent than אֲבֹתֵיהֶם. § 94 g [d] אֲחִיהוּ

[e] אֶחָי [f] בֶּן [g] בְּנְךָ [h] בִּתֵּךָ

All nouns (singular and plural) with suffixes are considered to be definite, just like nouns with the definite article (for example, הָאִישׁ), nouns in construct with a definite noun (דְּבַר הָאִישׁ), and personal and geographical names. Thus, nouns with suffixes never take the definite article—that is, you cannot say *הַדְּבָרֵיכֶם or *הַסּוּסָה. Additionally, attributive adjectives that modify these nouns must be definite. Thus we must say דִּבְרֵיכֶם הַטּוֹבִים, "your good words/things"; in contrast, דִּבְרֵיכֶם טוֹבִים would have the structure of a nominal sentence using a predicate adjective and would be translated as "your words/things are good." Finally, the definite direct object marker אֵת (also spelled אֶת־) is typically used before nouns with suffixes. This may be seen in Genesis 3:10, וַיֹּאמֶר אֶת־קֹלְךָ שָׁמַעְתִּי בַּגָּן, "he said, 'I heard your voice in the garden,'" and 30:13, וַתִּקְרָא אֶת־שְׁמוֹ אָשֵׁר׃, "she named him (literally, 'she called his name') Asher." A more complex example is found in Amos 7:10, where Amaziah, priest of Bethel, having accused Amos, sends a message to King Jeroboam (II): לֹא־תוּכַל הָאָרֶץ לְהָכִיל אֶת־כָּל־דְּבָרָיו׃, "the land cannot endure all of his words." In this sentence, כָּל־ is in construct with דְּבָרָיו; because דְּבָרָיו is definite (it is a noun with a pronominal suffix), the entire nominal phrase is thereby definite, and the direct object marker אֶת־ is present.

Vocabulary for chapter 16

בּוֹשׁ(ו)	to be ashamed	(בּוֹשׁ בּוֹשׁ יֵבוֹשׁ בּוֹשׁ)
בִּין(י)	to understand	(בָּן יָבִין בִּין lacking)
בכי	to cry	(בָּכָה בֹּכֶה יִבְכֶּה בְּכֹה)
גּוּר(ו)	to sojourn	(גָּר גָּר יָגוּר גּוּר)
גלי	to uncover, exile	(גָּלָה גֹּלֶה יִגְלֶה גְּלֹה)
טהר	to be pure	(טָהֵר יִטְהַר טָהֹר lacking)
טמא	to be impure	(טָמֵא lacking יִטְמָא lacking)
מצא	to find	(מָצָא מֹצֵא יִמְצָא מְצֹא)
נגשׁ	to approach	(יִגַּשׁ גַּשׁ lacking lacking)
סוּר(ו)	turn aside	(סָר סָר יָסוּר סוּר)
עמד	to stand	(עָמַד עֹמֵד יַעֲמֹד עֲמֹד)
פני	to turn	(פָּנָה פֹּנֶה יִפְנֶה פְּנֵה)
קבץ	to assemble	(קָבַץ קֹבֵץ יִקְבֹּץ קְבֹץ)
קדשׁ	to be holy	(קָדֹשׁ lacking יִקְדַּשׁ lacking)
קוּם(ו)	to rise (also used with other verbs to indicate beginning an action) (קָם קָם יָקוּם קוּם)	
רבי	to become great or numerous	(רָבָה יִרְבֶּה רְבֵה lacking)
רוּם(ו)	to become high	(רָם רָם יָרוּם רוּם)
רוּץ(ו)	to run	(רָץ רָץ יָרוּץ רוּץ)
שׁלם	to be whole	(שָׁלֵם lacking יִשְׁלַם lacking)
שׁפט	to judge	(שָׁפַט שֹׁפֵט יִשְׁפֹּט שְׁפֹט)
שׁתי	to drink	(שָׁתָה שֹׁתֶה יִשְׁתֶּה שְׁתֵה)

Exercises for chapter 16

1. Write from memory the complete paradigms of the following prepositions and nouns with suffixes:

3fp	3mp	2fp	2mp	1cp	3fs	3ms	2fs	2ms	1cs	
										עַל
										עַד
										אֶל
										שִׁירִים
										מִגְדָּלִים
										חֲכָמִים
										כְּבָשִׂים
										תְּפִלּוֹת
										בְּרָכוֹת

2. Write the following prepositions and particles with suffixes in BH:

to you (mp)	on me
until you (ms)	after him
under us	to them (f)
until her	on them (m)

3. Write the following prepositions and particles with suffixes in BH:

to (לְ) me	on me
from you (ms)	to (אֶל) you (ms)
her (direct object marker)	after her
with us	under us
from you (mp)	after you (mp)
like them (f)	to (אֶל) them (f)

4. Write the following nouns with plural suffixes in BH:

my kings	his face
your (ms) poor people	their (m) bows
your (fp) priests	her treasures
your (fp) sacrifices	her houses
their (fp) families	our purification offerings
their (f) sanctuaries	my altars
my gates	her deeds (= works)
their (m) words	his rams
your (mp) sojourners	your (ms) Sabbaths
your (mp) abominations	my servants
your (ms) commandments	their (m) tribes
her domesticated animals	their (fp) openings
our towers	my ordinances
your (ms) maidservants	his donkeys

its (f) walls	her dreams
your (fp) palaces	their (mp) garments
our straits	their (m) songs
your (fp) high places	its (m) clouds
your (mp) blessings	his bows

5. Write the following pairs of nouns with suffixes in BH; be sure that you can distinguish between the singular and plural suffixes and that you understand why these words are transformed in the way that they are:

my temple	my temples
your (ms) vineyard	your (mp) vineyards
your (ms) high place	your (ms) high places
his maidservant	his maidservants
her pit	her pits
our donkey	our donkeys
your (mp) concubine	your (mp) concubines
your (fs) wall	your (fp) walls
their (m) generation	their (m) generations
their (f) family	their (f) families

6. Write in BH:

That man and this woman are drinking the water of the big stream that is across from my house.

The nation is crying because they are not finding their gold in their fields.

The righteous woman is getting up, is turning to the right, and is standing behind (= after) him.

Your sojourners who sojourn in your midst are turning aside from my teachings.

The children of the poor man are running to the field toward my slave and are asking him for food.

The judge is judging them because they are burning your houses with the fire.

My king is exalted (= his heart is high) because God is giving him a great victory in the war.

7. Translate the following phrases from the Bible. When the phrase contains a noun with a suffix, note the form of the noun without the suffix (for example, if it has the word דְּבָרָיו, write דְּבָרִים). Be sure that you understand why the form of the noun has changed.

Genesis 3:14

וְעָפָר תֹּאכַל (you will eat) כָּל־יְמֵי חַיֶּיךָ:

Genesis 10:20

אֵלֶּה בְנֵי־חָם (Ham) לְמִשְׁפְּחֹתָם לִלְשֹׁנֹתָם בְּאַרְצֹתָם בְּגוֹיֵהֶם:

Genesis 15:7

וַיֹּאמֶר (He said) אֵלָיו אֲנִי יְהוָה אֲשֶׁר הוֹצֵאתִיךָ (brought you out) מֵאוּר כַּשְׂדִּים (Ur of the Chaldees) לָתֶת (to give) לְךָ אֶת־הָאָרֶץ הַזֹּאת לְרִשְׁתָּהּ (to inherit it):

Genesis 17:7

וַהֲקִמֹתִי (I will fulfill) אֶת־בְּרִיתִי בֵּינִי וּבֵינֶךָ וּבֵין זַרְעֲךָ אַחֲרֶיךָ
לְדֹרֹתָם לִבְרִית עוֹלָם לִהְיוֹת (to be) לְךָ לֵאלֹהִים וּלְזַרְעֲךָ אַחֲרֶיךָ׃

Genesis 18:8

וְהוּא־עֹמֵד עֲלֵיהֶם תַּחַת הָעֵץ

Genesis 19:31

אָבִינוּ זָקֵן וְאִישׁ אֵין בָּאָרֶץ לָבוֹא (to come) עָלֵינוּ כְּדֶרֶךְ כָּל־הָאָרֶץ׃

Genesis 22:11

וַיִּקְרָא (called) אֵלָיו מַלְאַךְ יְהוָה מִן־הַשָּׁמַיִם וַיֹּאמֶר אַבְרָהָם ׀ אַבְרָהָם
וַיֹּאמֶר הִנֵּנִי׃

Genesis 28:13

וְהִנֵּה יְהוָה נִצָּב (was standing) עָלָיו וַיֹּאמַר (and He said) אֲנִי יְהוָה
אֱלֹהֵי אַבְרָהָם (PN) אָבִיךָ וֵאלֹהֵי יִצְחָק (PN) הָאָרֶץ אֲשֶׁר אַתָּה
שֹׁכֵב (שכב = to lie down) עָלֶיהָ לְךָ אֶתְּנֶנָּה (I will give it) וּלְזַרְעֶךָ׃

Genesis 36:6

וַיִּקַּח עֵשָׂו (PN) אֶת־נָשָׁיו וְאֶת־בָּנָיו וְאֶת־בְּנֹתָיו וְאֶת־כָּל־נַפְשׁוֹת בֵּיתוֹ
וְאֶת־מִקְנֵהוּ וְאֶת־כָּל־בְּהֶמְתּוֹ

Exodus 17:12

וִידֵי מֹשֶׁה (PN) כְּבֵדִים וַיִּקְחוּ (they took) אֶבֶן
וַיָּשִׂימוּ (and they placed) תַחְתָּיו וַיֵּשֶׁב (and he sat) עָלֶיהָ

Leviticus 8:30

וַיְקַדֵּשׁ (He sanctified) אֶת־אַהֲרֹן (PN) אֶת־בְּגָדָיו וְאֶת־בָּנָיו
וְאֶת־בִּגְדֵי בָנָיו אִתּוֹ:

Deuteronomy 4:36

וְעַל־הָאָרֶץ הֶרְאֲךָ (he showed you) אֶת־אִשּׁוֹ הַגְּדוֹלָה
וּדְבָרָיו שָׁמַעְתָּ (you heard) מִתּוֹךְ הָאֵשׁ:

Deuteronomy 11:1

וְאָהַבְתָּ (you should love) אֵת יְהוָה אֱלֹהֶיךָ וְשָׁמַרְתָּ (and should observe)
מִשְׁמַרְתּוֹ (his injunctions) וְחֻקֹּתָיו וּמִשְׁפָּטָיו וּמִצְוֺתָיו כָּל־הַיָּמִים:

Deuteronomy 12:5

הַמָּקוֹם אֲשֶׁר־יִבְחַר (will choose) יְהוָה אֱלֹהֵיכֶם
מִכָּל־שִׁבְטֵיכֶם לָשׂוּם (to place) אֶת־שְׁמוֹ שָׁם

1 Samuel 8:16

וְאֶת־עַבְדֵיכֶם וְאֶת־שִׁפְחוֹתֵיכֶם וְאֶת־בַּחוּרֵיכֶם (בָּחוּר = young man)
הַטּוֹבִים וְאֶת־חֲמוֹרֵיכֶם יִקָּח (he will take)

1 Kings 11:43

וַיִּשְׁכַּב (lay) שְׁלֹמֹה (PN) עִם־אֲבֹתָיו וַיִּקָּבֵר (and he was buried)
בְּעִיר דָּוִד אָבִיו וַיִּמְלֹךְ (reigned) רְחַבְעָם (PN) בְּנוֹ תַּחְתָּיו:

Jeremiah 2:1

וַיְהִי (was) דְבַר־יְהוָה אֵלַי לֵאמֹר:

Jeremiah 44:17

אֲנַ֗חְנוּ וַאֲבֹתֵ֨ינוּ֙ מְלָכֵ֣ינוּ וְשָׂרֵ֔ינוּ בְּעָרֵ֖י יְהוּדָ֑ה
וּבְחֻצ֖וֹת (streets) יְרוּשָׁלָ֑͏ִם

Amos 4:8

וְלֹא־שַׁבְתֶּ֥ם (you did not return) עָדַ֖י נְאֻם־יְהוָֽה׃

Psalm 65:3

שֹׁמֵ֥עַ תְּפִלָּ֑ה עָדֶ֖יךָ כָּל־בָּשָׂ֣ר יָבֹֽאוּ (will come)׃

17 The Numerals

As in English and modern Hebrew, it is important to distinguish between the cardinal numbers (one, two, and so on; שְׁנַיִם, אֶחָד) and the ordinal numbers (first, second, and so on; רִאשׁוֹן, שֵׁנִי). The ordinals, which are dealt with at the end of the chapter, are always adjectives. The cardinals are more complex; sometimes cardinals are adjectives, while at other times they are nouns in the narrow sense.

Charts follow for the numerals one through nineteen. The numbers one through ten appear in four forms: masculine unbound (for example, פָּרִים שְׁנַיִם, "two cows"), masculine bound (that is, construct; for example, שְׁנֵי פָּרִים), feminine unbound (פָּרוֹת שְׁתַּיִם), and feminine bound (construct; שְׁתֵּי פָרוֹת). The second part of this chapter explains when particular forms are used. In addition, the vocalization of several of the numerals changes slightly at major pauses.

The Numerals 1–10

	m. unbound	m construct (bound)	f unbound	f construct (bound)
1	אֶחָד	אַחַד	אַחַת	אַחַת
2	שְׁנַיִם	שְׁנֵי	שְׁתַּיִם[1]	שְׁתֵּי
3	שְׁלֹשָׁה	שְׁלֹשֶׁת	שָׁלֹשׁ	שְׁלֹשׁ
4	אַרְבָּעָה	אַרְבַּעַת	אַרְבַּע	אַרְבַּע
5	חֲמִשָּׁה	חֲמֵשֶׁת	חָמֵשׁ	חֲמֵשׁ
6	שִׁשָּׁה	שֵׁשֶׁת	שֵׁשׁ	שֵׁשׁ
7	שִׁבְעָה	שִׁבְעַת	שֶׁבַע	שְׁבַע
8	שְׁמֹנָה	שְׁמֹנַת	שְׁמֹנֶה	שְׁמֹנֶה
9	תִּשְׁעָה	תִּשְׁעַת	תֵּשַׁע	תְּשַׁע
10	עֲשָׂרָה	עֲשֶׂרֶת	עֶשֶׂר	עֶשֶׂר

Once we move beyond ten, there is no distinction between the bound and unbound forms, so it is necessary only to learn one form for the masculine and one for the feminine.

---

1. The דָּגֵשׁ in שְׁתַּיִם and שְׁתֵּי is anomalous but correct.

The Numerals 11–19

	masculine	feminine
11	אַחַד עָשָׂר	אַחַת עֶשְׂרֵה
alternate form	עַשְׁתֵּי עָשָׂר	עַשְׁתֵּי עֶשְׂרֵה
12	שְׁנֵים עָשָׂר	שְׁתֵּים עֶשְׂרֵה
13	שְׁלֹשָׁה עָשָׂר	שְׁלֹשׁ עֶשְׂרֵה
14	אַרְבָּעָה עָשָׂר	אַרְבַּע עֶשְׂרֵה
15	חֲמִשָּׁה עָשָׂר	חֲמֵשׁ עֶשְׂרֵה
16	שִׁשָּׁה עָשָׂר	שֵׁשׁ עֶשְׂרֵה
17	שִׁבְעָה עָשָׂר	שְׁבַע עֶשְׂרֵה
18	שְׁמֹנָה עָשָׂר	שְׁמֹנֶה עֶשְׂרֵה
19	תִּשְׁעָה עָשָׂר	תְּשַׁע עֶשְׂרֵה

Multiples of ten do not differentiate between masculine and feminine. Twenty is expressed as עֶשְׂרִים, while the other decades are expressed as plurals of the corresponding digits—that is, שְׁלֹשִׁים (thirty), אַרְבָּעִים (forty), חֲמִשִּׁים (fifty), שִׁשִּׁים (sixty), שִׁבְעִים (seventy), שְׁמֹנִים (eighty) and תִּשְׁעִים (ninety). Numbers not divisible by ten are written as a combination of the decade plus the smaller numeral; either numeral may precede. Thus fifty-seven (masculine) may be expressed as חֲמִשִּׁים וְשִׁבְעָה or שִׁבְעָה וַחֲמִשִּׁים.

Larger multiples of ten are illustrated below.

The Numerals 100, 1,000, and 10,000

	unbound	const.	dual	plural	pl. construct
100	מֵאָה	מְאַת	מָאתַיִם (200)	מֵאוֹת	מְאוֹת
1,000	אֶלֶף	אֶלֶף	אַלְפַּיִם (2,000)	אֲלָפִים	אַלְפֵי
10,000	רִבּוֹ, רִבּוֹא, רְבָבָה		רִבֹּתַיִם (20,000)	רִבּ(וֹ)אוֹת	

In the unbound form, the cardinal number one is a full-fledged adjective following the noun that it modifies and agreeing with it in terms of number, gender, and definiteness. Thus we have Genesis 1:9, מָקוֹם אֶחָד, "one place," and 11:1, שָׂפָה אֶחָת, "one language." (Note the pausal form אֶחָת for אַחַת at the major disjunctive accent.) In the construct, it is a noun, in the sense of "one of," as in Genesis 22:2, אַחַד הֶהָרִים, "one of the mountains." The forms that end with ד are masculine, while those ending with a ת are feminine, as expected. The words for "two" take the form of the dual; those with an internal תַּ are feminine. There is a wide variability in how 2X may be expressed. The following forms may all be used and seem to be identical in meaning: שְׁתַּיִם בָּנוֹת, בָּנוֹת שְׁתַּיִם, and שְׁתֵּי בָנוֹת, "two daughters." The form שְׁתֵּי בָנוֹת is the most frequent; although it uses the construct שְׁתֵּי, it should *not* be translated as "two of daughters." (This would be expressed with the preposition מִן, as שְׁתַּיִם מִבְּנֹתָיו.)

The numbers between three and ten are all of the unexpected gender; like all Semitic numbers, those marked by typically feminine suffixes (הָ֯; תֹ֯ in construct) are masculine, while those unmarked, and expected to be masculine, are feminine. Like the number two, these may follow or precede the noun, and if they precede, they may appear in the unbound or the construct form. The noun that they modify may either be in the plural (for example, חֲמִשָּׁה שְׁקָלִים, "five shekels" in Leviticus 27:6) or be a collective (עֲשָׂרָה בָקָר בְּרִאִים in 1 Kings 5:3). (In the last example, note how the adjective בְּרִאִים, "fat," follows the numeral and noun, and is in the plural, agreeing with the plurality of the referent, the collective noun בָּקָר. This is called logical, rather than grammatical agreement.)

The cardinals eleven through ninety-nine precede the noun that they modify, and this noun is typically in the plural form. Certain common nouns may appear in the singular, however, even in cases where they are not typically used as collectives, as in Deuteronomy 1:2, אַחַד עָשָׂר יוֹם, "eleven days." The cardinals eleven through nineteen are formed by placing the numbers one through nine in construct with ten (עָשָׂר for masculine, עֶשְׂרֵה for feminine; the expected genders have returned, as illustrated on p. 161). Larger numbers are formed by combining their constituent elements, usually in descending order; for example, according to Numbers 1:46, the people of Israel numbered 603,550: שֵׁשׁ־מֵאוֹת אֶלֶף וּשְׁלֹשֶׁת אֲלָפִים וַחֲמֵשׁ מֵאוֹת וַחֲמִשִּׁים. Ascending numbers are also found. In Numbers 1:39 the tribe of Dan numbered 62,700: שְׁנַיִם וְשִׁשִּׁים אֶלֶף וּשְׁבַע מֵאוֹת. (Note that seven hundred is expressed as שְׁבַע מֵאוֹת, by having שְׁבַע in construct with the following *hundred*.) Sometimes the item counted may be enumerated between each part of the number, as in Genesis 23:1, of Sarah's 127-year lifespan: מֵאָה שָׁנָה וְעֶשְׂרִים שָׁנָה וְשֶׁבַע שָׁנִים. Finally, the numeral itself does not typically take the definite article; when a noun is not present with the numeral, however, the numeral itself may be definite, as in the expression "the X (people)" in Abraham's bargaining with God over the inhabitants of Sodom in Genesis 18. Thus, in Genesis 18:31, God responds: לֹא אַשְׁחִית בַּעֲבוּר הָעֶשְׂרִים, "I will not destroy (it) for the sake of the/those twenty (righteous people)."

The fraction חֲצִי (sometimes חֵצִי in the unbound form), "one-half," (much less frequently, "middle") is also well-attested in BH. It precedes the noun that it is modifying; in Exodus 24:6, for example, we have וַיִּקַּח מֹשֶׁה חֲצִי הַדָּם, "Moses took half of the blood," and in Numbers 12:12 we have חֲצִי בְשָׂרוֹ, "half of its flesh." If חֲצִי is part of a larger number, it is found after that number, as in the frequent measurement in the construction of the Tabernacle, אַמָּתַיִם וָחֵצִי, "two and a half cubits" (for example, Exodus 25:10; אַמָּתַיִם is a dual from אַמָּה).

Ordinal forms (first, second, and so on) exist in biblical Hebrew only for the numbers one through ten. As noted at the beginning of the chapter, these are full-fledged adjectives; they follow the noun and agree with it in terms of gender and definition. For numbers larger than ten, there are no special ordinal forms, and the cardinals are used as ordinals. In addition, cardinals sometimes replace ordinals with no apparent difference in meaning, even in cases when the ordinals might have been used, as in Genesis 1:5, וַיְהִי־עֶרֶב וַיְהִי־בֹקֶר יוֹם אֶחָד׃, "There was dusk and dawn of a first day." There יוֹם אֶחָד parallels the ordinal numbers used elsewhere in the chapter (for example, verse 13, יוֹם שְׁלִישִׁי, "a third day"). A chart of the ordinals follows; from two through ten they are constructed from the cardinals, and from three through ten most follow the pattern סְסִי in the masculine and סְסִית in the feminine. The ordinals have the expected grammatical endings for masculine and feminine adjectives.

The Ordinal Numbers 1–10

	masculine	feminine		masculine	feminine
1	רִאשׁוֹן	רִאשׁוֹנָה	6	שִׁשִּׁי	שִׁשִּׁית
2	שֵׁנִי	שֵׁנִית	7	שְׁבִיעִי	שְׁבִיעִית
3	שְׁלִישִׁי	שְׁלִישִׁית	8	שְׁמִינִי	שְׁמִינִית
4	רְבִיעִי	רְבִיעִית	9	תְּשִׁיעִי	תְּשִׁיעִית
5	חֲמִישִׁי	חֲמִישִׁית	10	עֲשִׂירִי	עֲשִׂירִית

Vocabulary for chapter 17

בער	to burn	(בָּעַר בֹּעֵר יִבְעַר lacking)
דבק	to cling to	(דָּבַק lacking יִדְבַּק lacking)
זרע	to plant, to sow	(זָרַע זֹרֵעַ יִזְרַע זֶרַע)
חלק	to divide	(חָלַק חֹלֵק יַחֲלֹק חֵלֶק)
יבש	to be dry	(יָבֵשׁ lacking יִיבַשׁ lacking)
לכד	to capture	(לָכַד לֹכֵד יִלְכֹּד לֶכֶד)
למד	to learn	(לָמַד לֹמֵד יִלְמַד לֶמֶד)
מדד	to measure	(מָדַד lacking יָמֹוד lacking)
משל	to rule	(מָשַׁל מֹשֵׁל יִמְשֹׁל מְשָׁל)
סגר	to close	(סָגַר סֹגֵר יִסְגֹּר סְגֹר)
עזר	to help	(עָזַר עֹזֵר יַעֲזֹר עֵזֶר)
פעל	to do	(פָּעַל פֹּעֵל יִפְעַל lacking)
רחק	to be far	(רָחַק lacking יִרְחַק רְחַק)
רכב	to ride	(רָכַב רֹכֵב יִרְכַּב רְכַב)
שנא	to hate	(שָׂנֵא שֹׂנֵא יִשְׂנָא שְׂנָא)
שבת	to cease, to rest	(שָׁבַת lacking יִשְׁבֹּת lacking)
שחט	to slaughter	(שָׁחַט שֹׁחֵט יִשְׁחַט שְׁחַט)
שכב	to lie down, to have sex with	(שָׁכַב שֹׁכֵב יִשְׁכַּב שְׁכַב)
תפש	to capture	(תָּפַשׂ תֹּפֵשׂ יִתְפֹּשׂ תְּפֹשׂ)
תקע	strike, blow (a horn)	(תָּקַע תֹּקֵעַ יִתְקַע תְּקַע)

Exercises for chapter 17

1. Write the following in BH. When there is more than one option, write them all:

one time	
one thing	
two temples	
two hills	
three treasures	
three pieces of advice	
four straits	
four temples	
five bows	
five fathers	
six blessings	
six pits	
seven doors	
seven foreigners	
eight vineyards	
eight prayers	
nine songs	
nine cities	
ten high places	
ten psalms	
eleven widows	
eleven boys	
twelve shekels	

twelve maidservants	
thirteen bones	
thirteen fools	
fourteen arrows	
fourteen paths	
fifteen daughters	
fifteen sons	
sixteen signs	
sixteen sacrifices	
seventeen walls	
seventeen courtyards	
eighteen scrolls	
eighteen abominations	
nineteen rivers	
nineteen times	
twenty lambs	
twenty Sabbaths	
thirty cubits	
forty descendants	
fifty garments	
sixty rams	
seventy swords	
eighty offerings	
ninety young girls	
one hundred wicked people	
the hundred wicked women	

fifty-four houses	
eighty-two priests	
ninety-five days	
sixty-eight and a half nights	
thirty-nine messengers	
ten thousand fools	
2,531 sheep	
1,216 people	

2. Write the following in BH:

the first place	the second woman
the third man	the fourth nation
the fifth slave	the sixth holy man
the seventh prophet of YHWH	the eighth month
the ninth burnt offering	the tenth pilgrimage
the fourteenth tribe	the fifty-third horse

3. Translate the following passages from the Bible; be sure that you understand the syntax of each large number. The words from these verses that might not be known to you are glossed below:

Genesis 5:5

וַיִּהְיוּ (were) כָּל־יְמֵי אָדָם֙ (PN) אֲשֶׁר־חַ֔י (he lived)
תְּשַׁע מֵאוֹת֙ שָׁנָ֔ה וּשְׁלֹשִׁ֖ים שָׁנָ֑ה וַיָּמֹֽת (and he died):

Genesis 5:23

וַיְהִ֞י (were) כָּל־יְמֵ֣י חֲנ֑וֹךְ (PN) חָמֵ֤שׁ וְשִׁשִּׁים֙ שָׁנָ֔ה וּשְׁלֹ֥שׁ מֵא֖וֹת שָׁנָֽה:

Exodus 38:26

מִבֶּ֨ן עֶשְׂרִ֤ים שָׁנָה֙ וָמַ֔עְלָה (and above) לְשֵׁשׁ־מֵא֥וֹת אֶ֖לֶף וּשְׁלֹ֣שֶׁת אֲלָפִ֑ים וַחֲמֵ֥שׁ מֵא֖וֹת וַחֲמִשִּֽׁים׃

Exodus 38:28

הָאֶ֕לֶף וּשְׁבַ֨ע הַמֵּא֜וֹת וַחֲמִשָּׁ֣ה וְשִׁבְעִ֗ים

1 Kings 10:26

וַיְהִי־ל֗וֹ (he had) אֶ֚לֶף וְאַרְבַּע־מֵא֣וֹת רֶ֔כֶב וּשְׁנֵים־עָשָׂ֥ר אֶ֖לֶף פָּרָשִׁ֑ים (horsemen)

Jeremiah 52:30

בִּשְׁנַ֨ת שָׁלֹ֣שׁ וְעֶשְׂרִים֮ לִנְבוּכַדְרֶאצַּר֒ (ל + PN) הֶגְלָ֗ה (exiled, deported) נְבֽוּזַרְאֲדָן֙ (PN) רַב־טַבָּחִ֔ים (chief of the guards) יְהוּדִ֕ים (Judeans) נֶ֕פֶשׁ שְׁבַ֥ע מֵא֖וֹת אַרְבָּעִ֣ים וַחֲמִשָּׁ֑ה כָּל־נֶ֕פֶשׁ אַרְבַּ֥עַת אֲלָפִ֖ים וְשֵׁ֥שׁ מֵאֽוֹת׃

Ezra 2:3–4

3 בְּנֵ֣י פַרְעֹ֔שׁ (PN) אַלְפַּ֕יִם מֵאָ֖ה שִׁבְעִ֥ים וּשְׁנָֽיִם׃

4 בְּנֵ֣י שְׁפַטְיָ֔ה (PN) שְׁלֹ֥שׁ מֵא֖וֹת שִׁבְעִ֥ים וּשְׁנָֽיִם׃

(The form שְׁנָֽיִם and several forms in the text below are pausal.)

Ezra 2:64–67

64 כָּל־הַקָּהָ֖ל כְּאֶחָ֑ד אַרְבַּ֣ע רִבּ֔וֹא אַלְפַּ֖יִם שְׁלֹשׁ־מֵא֥וֹת שִׁשִּֽׁים׃

65 מִ֠לְּבַד (aside from) עַבְדֵיהֶ֤ם וְאַמְהֹֽתֵיהֶם֙ אֵ֔לֶּה שִׁבְעַ֣ת אֲלָפִ֔ים שְׁלֹ֥שׁ מֵא֖וֹת שְׁלֹשִׁ֣ים וְשִׁבְעָ֑ה וְלָהֶ֛ם מְשֹׁרְרִ֥ים וּמְשֹׁרְרֽוֹת (male and female singers) מָאתָֽיִם׃

66 סוּסֵיהֶ֕ם שְׁבַ֥ע מֵא֖וֹת שְׁלֹשִׁ֣ים וְשִׁשָּׁ֑ה פִּרְדֵיהֶ֕ם (פֶּרֶד = mule) מָאתַ֖יִם אַרְבָּעִ֥ים וַחֲמִשָּֽׁה׃

67 גְּמַ֨לֵּיהֶ֔ם (גָּמָל = camel) אַרְבַּ֥ע מֵא֖וֹת שְׁלֹשִׁ֣ים וַחֲמִשָּׁ֑ה חֲמֹרִ֕ים שֵׁ֣שֶׁת אֲלָפִ֔ים שְׁבַ֥ע מֵא֖וֹת וְעֶשְׂרִֽים׃

18 Introduction to the Verb

The most difficult aspect of BH is the verbal system, which differs radically from that of MIH. These differences are outlined in this chapter and are illustrated in greater detail in the following chapters. In some cases, the forms referring to the same (grammatical) person are different. For example, the 3fp imperfect/future in BH is תִּכְתֹּבְנָה, "they will write," while in MIH, most people would say תִּכְתְּבוּ.[1] In some cases, the placement of stress has changed, and this has affected the vocalization, as in the change from BH כְּתַבְתֶּם, "you wrote," to modern spoken כָּתַבְתֶּם. Certain forms have dropped out, except in certain standard phrases ("frozen forms"). These include the cohortative, which is used in BH to express a wish or desire in the first person ("let's . . ." or "may we . . . ," as in the story of the tower of Babel, when God says הָבָה נֵרְדָה, "Come, let us go down" [Genesis 11:7]). The cohortative is found in modern Hebrew as a frozen form—for example, in the song הָבָה נָגִילָה, "let's rejoice." The jussive, a comparable third-person form that is ubiquitous in the Bible (for example, Genesis 1:3, יְהִי אוֹר, "let there be light"), is also not productive in MIH; it is found only in such places as the song and the expression יְהִי לוֹ, "let it be." Modern Israeli Hebrew is a three-tense system, with past (כָּתַב), present (כֹּתֵב) and future (יִכְתֹּב); as we saw in connection to the participle, BH does not have a present tense. Furthermore, as we shall see, BH probably does not view the world in terms of "tenses" at all—that is, as actions transpiring at specific times; thus terms like *past* and *present* have been avoided in favor of terms like *perfect* or *imperfect*. Instead of tenses, many scholars speak of the (verbal) "aspects" of BH.

The greatest difference between the MIH and BH verbal system is in the use by BH of what some have called converted tenses. These are forms like וַיִּכְתֹּב, with a prefixed וַ,

---

1. The terms *imperfect* and *perfect* are explained later in this chapter; in the meantime, they should be seen as similar to *future* and *past*, respectively.

which seem to be identical in meaning to כָּתַב, or וְכָתַב, which in turn seems to mean the same as יִכְתֹּב. In the Aqedah, the story of the binding of Isaac, for example, we find וַיִּקַּח אַבְרָהָם אֶת־עֲצֵי הָעֹלָה וַיָּשֶׂם עַל־יִצְחָק בְּנוֹ וַיִּקַּח בְּיָדוֹ אֶת־הָאֵשׁ וְאֶת־הַמַּאֲכֶלֶת, "Abraham took the wood for the burnt offering, and placed it on Isaac, his son; and he took in his hand the fire(stone) and the knife" (Genesis 22:6). The same sentence would be expressed in modern Hebrew as . . . אַבְרָהָם לָקַח . . .וְשָׂם (אֹתָם) . . . וְהוּא לָקַח. The popular understanding is that this וַ converts tenses from past to future and vice versa; this is reflected in the imprecise names of "the conversive וַ," or וָו הַהִפּוּך or וָו הַמְהַפֶּכֶת. A more satisfactory English term is the *waw*-consecutive. MIH no longer uses these verbal forms with וַ prefixes, and their function is frequently misunderstood by speakers of MIH.

The rest of the chapter outlines the fundamental structure of the BH verbal system, highlighting the differences between it and MIH. The emphasis will be on the special terminology that is used for BH and the syntactic features that set BH apart from later levels of Hebrew.

Scholars continue to debate whether BH has a true tense system. Many suggest that instead of viewing the world in terms of past and present, BH focuses on the action connected to the verb, and whether that situation is complete or incomplete. "Perfect" verbs are used for complete actions, and "imperfect" verbs are used for incomplete actions. Given that complete actions are generally in the past, while incomplete actions are generally in the future, there is a substantial overlap between the MIH past and the BH perfect and between the MIH future and the BH imperfect. The terms *perfect* and *imperfect*, are typically used in the standard biblical grammars and lexica.[2]

The perfect is typified by suffixes that are added to the verbal root, as in כָּתַבְתִּי, "I wrote." In contrast, the imperfect is characterized by prefixes, as in אֶכְתֹּב, "I will write." For this reason, some grammars refer to the perfect as the suffix tense, while the imperfect is called the prefix tense. Some also name the tenses on the basis of the form of the root קטל in the 3ms קל; thus they contrast the יִקְטֹל ("imperfect") to the קָטַל ("perfect").

In addition to the perfect and imperfect, BH has forms that express desires or commands. In the second person it has the imperative that is like the MIH command (צִוּוּי) in form and meaning (for example, Genesis 22:2, קַח־נָא אֶת־בִּנְךָ, "take your son," a singular קל imperative from לקח). As we have seen, in the first person BH has the cohortative. The cohortative is formed from the imperfect; הָ is added to the first-person imperfect verb.

---

2. There is now considerable debate on this issue. Some scholars suggest that BH does express tenses, and prefer using *past* and *future*. I here retain the terms *perfect* and *imperfect*, which are used in most grammars and lexica.

(Some phonetic changes may result.) In Genesis 37:17, for example, we find נֵלְכָה דֹּתָיְנָה, "Let's go to Dothan." (The word דֹּתָיְנָה, translated "to Dothan" is an example of a "directive." The directive is formed by adding a הָ suffix and penultimate stress to a place name, and is translated "to . . . .") In that sentence, we find נֵלְכָה, "let us go," instead of the imperfect נֵלֵךְ, "we shall go." An additional example may be found in Exodus 20:19, where, after hearing the Decalogue, the people say to Moses דַּבֵּר־אַתָּה עִמָּנוּ וְנִשְׁמָעָה, "Speak to us so we may hear." (וְנִשְׁמָעָה is pausal; otherwise, the form would have been נִשְׁמְעָה. These forms are both related to the 1p imperfect נִשְׁמַע, "we shall hear.")

The jussive similarly conveys volition—namely, the notion of "let" or "may." It is typically found with the third person and is related in form to the imperfect. It is often identical to the imperfect, in which case context alone determines that we have a jussive rather than an imperfect, though in several classes of "unhealthy" verbs the jussive is a shortened form of the imperfect. This may be seen, for example, in Genesis 1:3, יְהִי אוֹר, "Let there be light," where יְהִי is a jussive related to the longer imperfect יִהְיֶה. Similarly, after Hannah's vow in 1 Samuel 1, her husband, Elkanah, wishes that God will fulfill His word; this is expressed through the jussive יָקֵם, a הִפְעִיל from the hollow root ק(ו)ם, in the phrase אַךְ יָקֵם יְהוָה אֶת־דְּבָרוֹ, "may YHWH fulfill his word (promise)" (verse 23). The form יָקֵם, "may he fulfill," is a shortened form of the corresponding imperfect יָקִים, "he will fulfill." By definition, a second-person jussive follows the negative particle אַל to express a prohibition (the negation of an imperative), as in Genesis 22:12, אַל־תִּשְׁלַח יָדְךָ אֶל־הַנַּעַר, "Do not send forth your hand against the boy." (Here, as is often the case, the imperfect and jussive are identical in form.)

As we have seen, BH tends to use the perfect and imperfect in conjunction with the *waw*-consecutive. After certain short words, however, including לֹא, "not," מִי, "who[m]," מַה, "what," כִּי, "because," אֲשֶׁר, "which" or "that," and אָז, "then," the verb is no longer clause-initial, so the forms without וְ appear as in the following examples.

Genesis 2:17, לֹא תֹאכַל מִמֶּנּוּ, "You may not eat from it." תֹאכַל is a קַל 2ms imperfect from אכל. (Note that the ת of תֹאכַל has no קַל דָּגֵשׁ because it is preceded by a word with a conjunctive accent that ends with a vowel [לֹא]; see p. 33.)

Genesis 3:11, מִי הִגִּיד לְךָ, "Who told you." הִגִּיד is a הִפְעִיל 3ms perfect from נגד.

Genesis 3:13, מַה־זֹּאת עָשִׂית, "What have you done?" עָשִׂית is a קַל 2fs perfect from עשׂי. (On the root of עָשִׂית as עשׂי, and on ל״י verbs in general, see p. 225.)

Genesis 3:14, כִּי עָשִׂיתָ זֹּאת, "because you did this." עָשִׂיתָ is a קַל 3ms perfect from עשׂי.

Genesis 2:22, הַצֵּלָע אֲשֶׁר לָקַח מִן־הָאָדָם, "the rib (or 'side') that he took from the person." לָקַח is a קַל 3ms perfect from לקח.

Exodus 15:1, אָ֣ז יָשִֽׁיר־מֹשֶׁ֩ה וּבְנֵ֨י יִשְׂרָאֵ֜ל, "Moses and Israel then sang." יָשִׁיר is a 3ms imperfect from the hollow root שׁ(י)ר. (The verb is in the singular because it is agreeing with מֹשֶׁה, the first element of the compound subject, rather than with the entire phrase מֹשֶׁה וּבְנֵי יִשְׂרָאֵל. Note that this imperfect is translated in the past; the adverb אָז is typically followed by an imperfect, even if the action is completed.)

In most cases, however, BH prefers to use "converted tenses"—that is, verbs are typically introduced with the *waw*-consecutive. Thus instead of the perfect (for example, כָּתַבְתִּי), it uses the converted imperfect (for example, וָאֶכְתֹּב), and instead of the imperfect (אֶכְתֹּב), it uses the converted perfect (וְכָתַבְתִּי; note the shift to an ultimate accent and the loss of the דָּגֵשׁ in the כ because it no longer opens the word or follows a closed syllable). The converted perfect is formed by prefixing וְ to the perfect; in some cases (1cs and 2ms), there is a change in stress as well (for example, כָּתַבְתִּי, but וְכָתַבְתִּי; similarly, כָּתַבְתָּ, but וְכָתַבְתָּ). The converted imperfect is formed by prefixing וַ followed by a דָּגֵשׁ חָזָק to the jussive. In the first-person imperfect, which has a prefix א and thus cannot be doubled (that is, take a דָּגֵשׁ חָזָק), we have compensatory lengthening, and the prefix becomes וָ. In some cases, the accent is moved from the ultima to penultima and there is a change in or loss of the final vowel. Genesis 22:6, cited above, shows typical forms of the imperfect, which include וַיִּקַּח (the קַל 3ms jussive of לקח is יִקַּח) and וַיָּ֫שֶׂם (the קַל 3ms imperfect of שׂ[י]ם is יָשִׂים; the corresponding jussive is יָשֵׂם, which with penultimate stress becomes יָּ֫שֶׂם).[3]

In most cases, the converted imperfect is identical in meaning to the perfect, and the converted perfect is identical in meaning to the imperfect. Furthermore, it is crucial to remember that even though the converted imperfect resembles the jussive in form, it must *not* be translated as a jussive ("may . . ."); rather it should be translated as a perfect.

The perfect and the converted imperfect are most often used for actions that are complete—namely, actions that transpired in the past. In these cases, this may be reflected with an English past or pluperfect (for example, "have loved"). Sometimes the past action continues into the present, and an English present is a suitable translation. With stative verbs, which describe a state of being (as opposed to active verbs, which describe an action), the perfect may be translated as "have become" ("ingressive"). The following examples illustrate these uses. In addition, the perfect and converted imperfect are used in many other ways. Some of these are described below; others may be seen in biblical reference grammars.

---

3. Note the double cantillation mark on וַיָּ֫שֶׂם. The cantillation mark on the word is a פַּשְׁטָא, which is postpositive; to show that the true accent on the word is penultimate, that accent is repeated on the accented syllable itself (֫); see p. 22.

> ### Translation of the Perfect and the Converted Imperfect
>
> Genesis 37:3, וְיִשְׂרָאֵל אָהַב אֶת־יוֹסֵף מִכָּל־בָּנָיו, "But Israel loved Joseph more than all his other children" (simple past).
>
> Genesis 25:28, וַיֶּאֱהַב יִצְחָק אֶת־עֵשָׂו, "Isaac loved Esau" (simple past).
>
> Exodus 21:5, אָהַבְתִּי אֶת־אֲדֹנִי, "I love my master" (present).
>
> Amos 3:2, רַק אֶתְכֶם יָדַעְתִּי, "only you have I known/singled out" (past perfect).
>
> 2 Samuel 15:10, מָלַךְ אַבְשָׁלוֹם בְּחֶבְרוֹן, "Absalom has become king in Hebron" (ingressive).

Usually context makes it clear in what sense the perfect/converted imperfect is being used. Translators should feel comfortable adding such phrases as "has become." Additionally, the וְ of the converted imperfect must not be slavishly translated as "and"; it is often best left untranslated.

The main use of the imperfect/converted perfect is to indicate an incomplete or future action or to express moods, such as "could," "can," "should," "would," "may," and "might." It is often difficult to decide whether the imperfect/converted perfect is being used in a future or modal sense; even if it is modal, deciding just what modal sense is being used can be tricky. These ambiguities are often of interpretive significance. The imperfect/converted perfect are also used for repeated or habitual actions. The examples below illustrate these main uses.

> ### Translation of the Imperfect and the Converted Perfect
>
> Genesis 18:29, לֹא אֶעֱשֶׂה בַּעֲבוּר הָאַרְבָּעִים, "I will not do (it) for the sake of the forty" (future).
>
> Genesis 39:9, וְאֵיךְ אֶעֱשֶׂה הָרָעָה הַגְּדֹלָה הַזֹּאת, "And how could I do this great evil?" (modal—"could").
>
> Exodus 30:1, וְעָשִׂיתָ מִזְבֵּחַ מִקְטַר קְטֹרֶת, "You should make an altar for the offering of incense" (modal—"should").
>
> Job 1:5, כָּכָה יַעֲשֶׂה אִיּוֹב כָּל־הַיָּמִים, "That is what Job always used to do all of the days/time" ("habitual").

It is much more frequent to encounter BH verbs in their converted forms, because the language prefers what has been called narrative sequence. Such a sequence consists of a chain of verbs, where each verb begins with a וְ. This describes a sequence in which each situation is subsequent to the previous situation. For example, in describing the binding of Isaac (the Aqedah), Abraham goes through a sequence of actions that are all described in the converted imperfect (Genesis 22:9–10). The verbs in the converted imperfect are underlined.

9 וַיָּבֹ֗אוּ אֶֽל־הַמָּקוֹם֮ אֲשֶׁ֣ר אָֽמַר־ל֣וֹ הָאֱלֹהִים֒ וַיִּ֨בֶן שָׁ֤ם אַבְרָהָם֙ אֶת־הַמִּזְבֵּ֔חַ וַֽיַּעֲרֹ֖ךְ אֶת־הָעֵצִ֑ים וַֽיַּעֲקֹד֙ אֶת־יִצְחָ֣ק בְּנ֔וֹ וַיָּ֤שֶׂם אֹתוֹ֙ עַל־הַמִּזְבֵּ֔חַ מִמַּ֖עַל לָעֵצִֽים׃ 10 וַיִּשְׁלַ֤ח אַבְרָהָם֙ אֶת־יָד֔וֹ וַיִּקַּ֖ח אֶת־הַֽמַּאֲכֶ֑לֶת לִשְׁחֹ֖ט אֶת־בְּנֽוֹ׃

"They came to the place that God had told him; Abraham built the altar there and set up the wood and bound Isaac his son; he placed him on the altar above the wood. Abraham sent out his hand and took the knife to slaughter his son." Thus this series of seven converted imperfects in two verses indicates a consecutive set of actions transpiring in the past. As the translation indicates, it is not usually necessary to indicate this by a word like "then," which explicitly notes that each action follows the preceding one, nor is it a good idea to translate each וְ as "and," because the וְ is part of the narrative structure and not simply the conjunction "and."

Because converted perfects and converted imperfects (rather than imperfects and perfects) are the norm, the "unconverted" terms are sometimes used for special reasons and must be looked at closely. As we have seen, certain words like לֹא and כִּי require the unconverted forms (p. 171). Additionally, the normal word order in BH is verb followed by noun, as seen, for example, in Genesis 22:10, וַיִּשְׁלַ֤ח אַבְרָהָם֙ אֶת־יָד֔וֹ, "Abraham sent out his hand." In cases where the noun precedes the verb, perhaps for emphasis or contrast, the regular perfect or imperfect is used, as in 1 Samuel 15:34, וְשָׁא֛וּל עָלָ֥ה אֶל־בֵּית֖וֹ, "but Saul went up to his house." Additionally, the plain perfect is often used in the sense of a pluperfect—namely, to indicate that the action described precedes the previous verb. For example, Jonah 1:5, וְיוֹנָ֗ה יָרַד֙ אֶל־יַרְכְּתֵ֣י הַסְּפִינָ֔ה, should be translated "Jonah had gone down to the bowels of the ship," which indicates that the action narrated in this verse precedes that of verse 4; had it said וַיֵּ֣רֶד יוֹנָ֔ה, using a converted imperfect, then Jonah's descent to the bowels of the ship would be subsequent to verse 4.

The uses of narrative sequences should not be confused with cases in which a וְ vocalized with a שְׁוָא precedes an imperfect. This use of a וְ vocalized with a שְׁוָא plus imperfect, in contrast to וְ with a פַּתַח followed by doubling, introduces purpose clauses that should typically be translated with "so" or "in order." For example, Jonah 1:11,

מַה־נַּעֲשֶׂה לְךָ וְיִשְׁתֹּק הַיָּם, should be translated as "What should we do to you so that the sea will be quiet?" In contrast, מַה־נַּעֲשֶׂה לְךָ וַיִּשְׁתֹּק הַיָּם, would be "What should we do to you? The sea was quiet." This use of the וְ vocalized with a שְׁוָא followed by an imperfect to introduce a purpose clause ("so that") is most often found when the imperfect plus וְ is preceded by a volitional form (an imperative, jussive, or cohortative).

The perfect, imperfect, converted perfect, converted imperfect, imperative, cohortative, and jussive are not the only forms that are related to the verb in BH, though these are the only finite verbal forms. We already saw that the קַל active participle (for example, כֹּתֵב) is always nominal in form, and often functions as a noun; in addition, there is a passive participle (for example, כָּתוּב, "is written") that is a noun as well. (Note its various forms, כָּתוּב, כְּתוּבָה, כְּתוּבִים, and כְּתוּבוֹת, and the fact that these forms may take a definite article, as in הַדָּבָר הַכָּתוּב, "the matter that is/was/will be written.")

In contrast to MIH, where we speak of *the* infinitive (מָקוֹר), BH has two types of infinitives: an infinitive construct (מָקוֹר נָטוּי) and an infinitive absolute (מָקוֹר מֻחְלָט). The infinitive construct is similar in form and meaning to the MIH infinitive, though in contrast to its modern counterpart, it need not be preceded by the preposition לְ. The קַל infinitive of כתב, for example, is כְּתֹב, which would usually be translated "to write," or "writing." Additionally, unlike MIH, pronominal suffixes are often added to the BH infinitive, and the word undergoes predictable changes, which are discussed in the next chapter, as in כָּתְבִי (with a קָמֵץ קָטָן), "my writing." The addition of this type of pronominal suffix is an indication of the nominal status of the infinitive construct. In BH the infinitive construct is often preceded by the prepositions בְּ or כְּ, as in בִּכְתֹב, "in writing," or כְּכָתְבִי, "when I wrote."

The infinitive absolute is typically used to strengthen a verb, but sometimes it functions as a pseudoimperative. Its form in the קַל is ☐(וֹ)☐ָ☐; this is quite similar to the imperative ms ☐☐☐ and should not be confused with it. It is found, for example, in the phrase שָׁמוֹר תִּשְׁמְרוּן אֶת־מִצְוֹת יְהוָה אֱלֹהֵיכֶם (Deuteronomy 6:17), in the sense of "you shall certainly/completely observe the commandments of YHWH your God." (The final נון of תִּשְׁמְרוּן is often called energic or paragogic; its function, however, is unclear, and it is best left untranslated.) It is also found, for example, in Deuteronomy 11:13, וְהָיָה אִם־שָׁמֹעַ תִּשְׁמְעוּ אֶל־מִצְוֹתַי, "if you completely heed my commandments." (Note the פַּתָח גְּנוּבָה of שָׁמֹעַ, which is secondary and does not affect the fact that the structure of שָׁמֹעַ is ☐☐ָ☐; see p. 12.) The most famous use of the infinitive absolute as a pseudoimperative is in the Sabbath commandment in the Decalogue. Exodus 20:8, for example, reads: זָכוֹר אֶת־יוֹם הַשַּׁבָּת לְקַדְּשׁוֹ, "Remember the Sabbath day to keep it holy." It is as if the text said... זָכוֹר תִּזְכֹּר, "you should certainly remember..."; this explains how the infinitive absolute by itself functions as a pseudoimperative.

Each of these forms such as the perfect, cohortative, or infinitive absolute changes as the verb appears in particular בִּנְיָנִים or derived conjugations. For example, the *Qal* infinitive absolute from נתן, נָתֹן, "certainly give," is distinct in form and meaning from the *Nifal* infinitive absolute הִנָּתֹן, "certainly be given." Most of the examples in this chapter are in the *Qal* (קַל), the simple or light conjugation, where the verbal root is not augmented. The other בִּנְיָנִים are marked either by a prefix and/or an infix, such as doubling. When a verb appears in these בִּנְיָנִים, its meaning is almost always different from the קַל.

Classical BH grammars usually enumerate seven major בִּנְיָנִים: (1) קַל or פָּעַל, (2) נִפְעַל, (3) פִּעֵל, (4) פֻּעַל, (5) הִפְעִיל, (6) הָפְעַל and (7) הִתְפַּעֵל. This is not quite accurate; there are really five major בִּנְיָנִים: (1) קַל or פָּעַל, (2) נִפְעַל, (3) פִּעֵל and its passive, פֻּעַל, (4) הִפְעִיל, and its passive, הָפְעַל and (5) הִתְפַּעֵל. Each of the בִּנְיָנִים has particular morphological characteristics: קַל is not augmented; נִפְעַל has a prefix נוּן (that may be assimilated); פִּעֵל and פֻּעַל are characterized by doubling of the middle root letter (for example, דִּבֶּר); הִפְעִיל and הָפְעַל both have a prefix הֵא (which may be elided); and הִתְפַּעֵל has a prefix הִת and doubling of the middle root letter (for example, יִתְפַּלֵל). A more complete explanation of the morphology of these בִּנְיָנִים, as well as a discussion of their function, is found in chapters 24–25.

Vocabulary for chapter 18

בגד	to deal or act treacherously (lacking	בָּגַד בָּגֹד יִבְגֹּד)
בקע	to split, cleave	(בָּקַע בֹּקֵעַ בָּקְעַ יִבְקַע)
ברח	to flee	(בָּרַח בֹּרֵחַ יִבְרַח בָּרֹחַ)
גרש	to chase out (lacking rare גֵּרֵשׁ lacking)	
הפך	to turn, overturn	(הָפַךְ הֹפֵךְ יַהֲפֹךְ הָפֹךְ)
הרי	to conceive, to become pregnant (lacking	יַהֲרֶה lacking הָרָה)
זעק	to scream	(זָעַק יִזְעַק זְעֹק)
טמנ	to hide (lacking	יִטְמֹן lacking טָמַן)
כרע	to kneel, to bow down (lacking	כָּרַע כֹּרֵעַ יִכְרַע)
כשל	to stumble (lacking	כָּשַׁל כֹּשֵׁל יִכְשַׁל)
מאס	to reject, to spurn, to despise (lacking	מָאַס מֹאֵס יִמְאַס)
מכר	to sell	(מָכַר מֹכֵר יִמְכֹּר מָכֹר)
סלח	to forgive	(סָלַח סֹלֵחַ יִסְלַח סָלֹחַ)
פדי	to redeem	(פָּדָה פֹּדֶה יִפְדֶּה פָּדֹה)
פרש	to spread out (lacking	פָּרַשׂ פֹּרֵשׂ יִפְרֹשׂ)
צמח	to sprout (lacking	צָמַח צֹמֵחַ יִצְמַח)
קצר	to be short, reap (rare	קָצַר קֹצֵר יִקְצֹר)
קרע	to rip	(קָרַע קֹרֵעַ יִקְרַע קָרֹעַ)
קשי	to be hard (lacking	יִקְשֶׁה lacking קָשָׁה)
רחצ	to wash	(רָחַץ רֹחֵץ יִרְחַץ רָחֹץ)
שבע	to be sated	(שָׂבַע יִשְׂבַּע שָׂבֹעַ lacking)
שדד	to devastate (lacking	שָׁדַד שֹׁדֵד יָשׁוּד)

There are no formal exercises for this chapter. Because this chapter is the foundation for the following chapters, be sure to read it several times.

19 The קַל of Healthy Verbs

The student who understands the rules of phonology and knows all of the paradigms for the healthy verb in the קַל will have few problems with any BH verb. This is thus *the* fundamental chapter for understanding the morphology of the Hebrew verb; the forms that it surveys must be memorized with care.

The Perfect and the Converted Perfect

As we have seen, Hebrew verbs can be categorized as active or stative (p. 112). This difference is important in conjugating verbs, because these types of verbs typically have different conjugations: active verbs, like כתב, "to write," appear as כָּתַב in the קַל 3ms perfect, while stative verbs, like כבד, "to be heavy," typically appear as כָּבֵד in the קַל 3ms perfect. Additionally, there is a small class of stative verbs that have an *o* vowel, such as קָטֹן, "he was small."

The conjugation of these three classes of verbs follows.

Healthy Verbs in the Perfect

	כתב	כבד	קטן
3ms	כָּתַב	כָּבֵד	קָטֹן
3fs	כָּתְבָה	כָּבְדָה	קָטְנָה
2ms	כָּתַבְתָּ	כָּבַדְתָּ	קָטֹנְתָּ
2fs	כָּתַבְתְּ	כָּבַדְתְּ	קָטֹנְתְּ
1cs	כָּתַבְתִּי	כָּבַדְתִּי	קָטֹנְתִּי
3cp	כָּתְבוּ	כָּבְדוּ	קָטְנוּ
2mp	כְּתַבְתֶּם	כְּבַדְתֶּם	קְטָנְתֶּם
2fp	כְּתַבְתֶּן	כְּבַדְתֶּן	קְטָנְתֶּן
1cp	כָּתַבְנוּ	כָּבַדְנוּ	קָטֹנּוּ (< *קָטֹנְנוּ)

The suffixes of the perfect are the same throughout; the only difference is in the theme vowel—that is, the vowel under the middle radical (עַיִן הַפֹּעַל). In all types of verbs, the initial קָמֵץ is propretonic, and therefore reduced in the second-person plural forms, which have heavy (closed, accented) suffixes; in the other cases, the קָמֵץ is pretonic, and thus remains. The theme vowel of the verb is prone to pretonic reduction; it is lost in the 3fs (for example, *כָּתַבָה > כָּתְבָה) and in the 3p (e.g. *כָּתַבוּ > כָּתְבוּ), because retaining it would have meant having a short vowel in an open, unaccented syllable; it remains in the closed syllables in the second-person forms (for example, כְּבַדְתֶּם or כְּבַדְתֶּן). In a-class verbs, the *a* remains in all places except for the 3fs and 3p, where it is pretonic, and therefore reduced. In i-class verbs, however, the theme vowel remains only in the 3ms; this is because at a certain point in history, *i* in closed accented syllables became *a*. (This phenomenon is called Philippi's law.) In o-class verbs, the theme vowel *o* remains except for cases where pretonic reduction is seen. This means that the קָמֵץ in the words קְטָנְתֶּם and קְטָנְתֶּן is a קָמֵץ קָטָן—that is, an o-class vowel (see p. 13). This is the form that an *o* vowel frequently takes in a closed unaccented syllable. It is also clear that the קָמֶץ is a קָמֶץ קָטָן because it appears in a closed, unaccented syllable—the syllable must be closed because of the דָּגֵשׁ קַל in the תּ of the following syllable (קָטְנָ תֶּן).

Converted perfects are, with minor exceptions, perfects with a prefixed וְ. If the perfect began with a דָּגֵשׁ קַל, the דָּגֵשׁ is dropped (for example, וְכָתְבָה, "she will write"), because the letters ב, ג, ד, כ, פ, and ת are no longer at the beginning of a word or following a closed syllable. In addition, the stress of the 2ms and 1cs changes from penultimate to ultimate, so in the converted perfect, we have the forms וְכָתַבְתָּ (not וְכָתַבְתָּ*), וְקָטָנְתָּ, וְכָבַדְתָּ, וְכָתַבְתִּי, and וְקָטֹנְתִּי (note the change of vocalization to a קָמֶץ קָטָן since the syllable is now unaccented).

Unfortunately, it is not always possible to know the theme vowel of a verb by its meaning; some verbs which are active in function are conjugated as stative verbs, and vice versa. Most biblical Hebrew verbs are active in form; the following is a list of relatively common, healthy stative verbs. They are listed in their 3ms perfect forms, so the appropriate theme vowel is obvious: קָטֹן, "to be small"; שָׁפֵל, "to be low"; כָּבֵד, "to be heavy"; טָהֵר, "to be pure"; and יָכֹל, "to be able."

The Imperfect and the Converted Imperfect

Although the perfect has three possible theme vowels, only two are found in the imperfect: *o* for active verbs (for example, יִכְתֹּב) and *a* for stative verbs (יִכְבַּד). The paradigm for these two verb types follows.

THE קַל OF HEALTHY VERBS

	כתב	כבד
	Healthy Verbs in the Imperfect	
3ms	יִכְתֹּב	יִכְבַּד
3fs	תִּכְתֹּב	תִּכְבַּד
2ms	תִּכְתֹּב	תִּכְבַּד
2fs	תִּכְתְּבִי	תִּכְבְּדִי
1cs	אֶכְתֹּב	אֶכְבַּד
3mp	יִכְתְּבוּ	יִכְבְּדוּ
3fp	תִּכְתֹּבְנָה	תִּכְבַּדְנָה
2mp	תִּכְתְּבוּ	תִּכְבְּדוּ
2fp	תִּכְתֹּבְנָה	תִּכְבַּדְנָה
1cp	נִכְתֹּב	נִכְבַּד

The behavior of the imperfect is more regular than that of the perfect. It is necessary only to observe that in both active and stative verbs, the theme vowel reduces when it is not accented (pretonic reduction), as in the forms יִכְבְּדוּ, יִכְתְּבוּ, תִּכְבְּדִי, תִּכְתְּבִי (< *תִּכְתֹּבִי), תִּכְבְּדוּ, and תִּכְתְּבוּ. At the pause, however, the accent on these forms is retracted and becomes penultimate, and the theme vowel returns, as in Leviticus 19:30, אֶת־שַׁבְּתֹתַי תִּשְׁמֹרוּ, "You must observe my Sabbaths." Finally, it is not unusual for a נוּן to be added to the 2 and 3 mp forms, as we saw above in Deuteronomy 6:17, שָׁמוֹר תִּשְׁמְרוּן אֶת־מִצְוֹת יְהוָה אֱלֹהֵיכֶם. This נוּן is called a paragogic (that is, added) נוּן, and its function is unclear, so it is best left untranslated.

The converted imperfect for healthy קַל verbs is formed by adding a וַ followed by a דָּגֵשׁ חָזָק before the imperfect (for example, from יִכְתֹּב, "he will write," we get וַיִּכְתֹּב, "he wrote"). The only exception is before the 1cs form that begins with א and thus cannot be doubled. Here we find compensatory lengthening; thus we have וָאֶכְתֹּב. Converted imperfects from the root כתב include וַיִּכְתֹּב, "he wrote"; וַתִּכְבַּד, "she/you [ms] were heavy"; וַתִּכְתְּבִי, "you [fs] wrote"; וַיִּכְבְּדוּ, "they [m] were heavy"; וַתִּכְתֹּבְנָה, "you [fp] /they [f] wrote"; וָאֶכְתֹּב, "I wrote"; and וַנִּכְתֹּב, "we wrote."

Some verbs, such as כבד, are conjugated as stative in both the perfect and imperfect. A small number of verbs are conjugated as active in the perfect, with an a-theme vowel, and as stative in the imperfect, with an a-theme vowel (for example, לָמַד, יִלְמַד). Among verbs in the vocabulary so far, these include גדל, דבק, למד, קרב, רכב, and שׁכב; the vocalization of verbs or all types is noted in the vocabulary lists.

The Jussive, the Imperative, and the Cohortative

In these verbs, the jussive looks identical in form with the imperfect. Thus jussives may be identified as such when they are preceded by אַל (see p. 171), or when the sense demands "may/let he/him/she/her/it . . ."—for example, Psalm 96:11, יִרְעַם הַיָּם וּמְלֹאוֹ, "let the sea and everything in it thunder."

The imperative קל in all cases may be viewed as derived from the imperfect but without a prefix, as shown below.

Imperatives of Healthy Verbs as Derived from Imperfects

	Imperfect	Imperative		Imperfect	Imperative	
2ms	תִּכְתֹּב	כְּתֹב		תִּכְבַּד	כְּבַד	
2fs	תִּכְתְּבִי	כִּתְבִי	(<*כְּתְבִי)[1]	תִּכְבְּדִי	כִּבְדִי	(<*כְּבְדִי)
2mp	תִּכְתְּבוּ	כִּתְבוּ	(<*כְּתְבוּ)	תִּכְבְּדוּ	כִּבְדוּ	(<*כְּבְדוּ)
2fp	תִּכְתֹּבְנָה	כְּתֹבְנָה		תִּכְבַּדְנָה	כְּבַדְנָה	

It is noteworthy that in cases where the second root letter has a דָּגֵשׁ קַל in the imperfect (for example, תִּכְבְּדוּ), the דָּגֵשׁ is not present in the imperative (כִּבְדוּ) because the second root letter no longer follows a closed syllable.

The ms imperative is sometimes found with a suffix ־ָה, as in Psalm 25:20, שָׁמְרָה נַפְשִׁי, "save my life" (literally "guard my life-force"). The addition of the suffix changes

---

1. Note how the rule of the שְׁוָא is operative here and in the mp.

THE קַל OF HEALTHY VERBS

the vocalization somewhat; שָׁמְרָה* < שָׁמְרָה (with a קָמֵץ קָטָן; the o-class vowel is thrown backward, and because it is now found in a closed, unaccented syllable, it is represented by a קָמֵץ קָטָן). These forms are called elongated imperatives.

The cohortative, the first-person volitional form, is formed by adding an accented הָ. As a result of the shift of the accent, pretonic reduction takes place, yielding the forms אֶכְתְּבָה (<*אֶכְתֳּבָה), "may I write," and אֶכְבְּדָה (<*אֶכְבַּדָה), "may I be heavy." At the pause, however, the stress retracts, so the theme vowel is retained, as in Psalm 59:10, אֶשְׁמֹ֫רָה, "may I guard."

The Participles

The קַל active participle has been discussed (pp. 105–112); to review, the active participle is really a noun and therefore has four endings, depending on whether the form is masculine or feminine, singular or plural. The forms of the (active) participle of כתב are noted below.

The Active Participle of Healthy Verbs	
ms	כֹּתֵב
fs	כֹּתֶ֫בֶת (כֹּתְבָה)
mp	כֹּתְבִים
fp	כֹּתְבוֹת

Stative verbs, by their nature, typically do not form active participles; when they do, they are identical in form to active verbs.

The passive participle is an adjective as well, and therefore is not conjugated. Its masculine singular form is כָּתוּב; the other forms are derived from this, as may be seen below.

The Passive Participle of Healthy Verbs	
ms	כָּתוּב
fs	כְּתוּבָה
mp	כְּתוּבִים
fp	כְּתוּבוֹת

All of these would typically be translated as "written." The fs and p forms are all derived from the ms כָּתוּב; note the propretonic reduction of the קָמֵץ in these forms.

The Infinitives

The theme vowels of the imperfect are also used in the infinitive construct; thus we have the infinitive constructs כְּתֹב and שְׁכַב. (The infinitive construct is often identical to the imperative ms; context distinguishes between these two forms.) In contrast to MIH, in BH the prefix לְ need not precede the infinitive, as may be seen by comparing translations of "I did not know how to write": MIH לֹא יָדַעְתִּי לִכְתֹּב; BH לֹא יָדַעְתִּי כְּתֹב. The biblical infinitive construct is often used with pronominal suffixes, as in Psalm 91:11, לִשְׁמָרְךָ בְּכָל־דְּרָכֶיךָ, "to watch you [literally: to your watching] in all of your paths"; these forms are illustrated below. With these suffixes, the infinitive of both active (*o* verbs, for example, יִכְתֹּב) and stative (*a* verbs, for example יִכְבַּד) have an *o* vowel; because the vowel is in a closed, unaccented syllable, it is written as a קָמֵץ קָטָן. This vowel typically moves backward, to the first syllable of the word ("vowel retraction").

The Infinitive Construct of Healthy Verbs with Suffixes		
	Singular	Plural
1c	כָּתְבִי	כָּתְבֵנוּ
2m	כָּתְבְךָ (or כָּתְבָךְ)	כָּתְבְכֶם
2f	כָּתְבֵךְ	כָּתְבְכֶן
3m	כָּתְבוֹ	כָּתְבָם
3f	כָּתְבָהּ	כָּתְבָן

The infinitive construct, with and without pronominal suffixes, is used frequently in a wide variety of ways. The following offer some examples of its range of use:

Genesis 3:24, לִשְׁמֹר אֶת־דֶּרֶךְ עֵץ הַחַיִּים, "*to guard* the path of/to the tree of life."

2 Samuel 11:16, וַיְהִי בִּשְׁמוֹר יוֹאָב אֶל־הָעִיר, "when Joab *was guarding* the city." (The use of infinitive constructs after וַיְהִי, the common converted imperfect form of היי, is quite common. Typically, the preposition ב or כ follows the verb היי and precedes the infinitive.)

Psalm 91:11, לִשְׁמָרְךָ בְּכָל־דְּרָכֶיךָ, "to guard you in all of your paths." (Note that this form לִשְׁמָרְךָ, with no vowel retraction, is sometimes found rather than the expected לִשְׁמָרְךָ.)

2 Kings 14:22, אַחֲרֵי שְׁכַב־הַמֶּלֶךְ עִם־אֲבֹתָיו, "after the king lay with his fathers."

Deuteronomy 6:7, וּבְשָׁכְבְּךָ וּבְקוּמֶךָ, "and when you lie down and when you wake up."

As in the construct, there can be some confusion about whether the infinitive is the subject or the object of an action involved. In וַיְהִי בַּהֲרֹג אִישׁ, for example, the noun אִישׁ could be the subject ("when a man killed") or a direct object ("when a man was killed"). The same ambiguity exists in forms like בְּהָרְגִי, which could be "when I killed" or "when I was killed." These ambiguities are typically resolved by the nature of the verb (בְּכָתְבִי, for example, can be only "when I wrote," not "when I was written") or by context. When the direct object is definite, we typically would have וַיְהִי בַּהֲרֹג אֶת הָאִישׁ, "when the man was killed," which is not ambiguous due to the אֶת.

There is also a small group of words that forms its infinitive construct in the feminine gender. The most common of these are יִרְאָה (from ירא) and אַהֲבָה (from אהב). These forms are identical with abstract nouns of the same meaning (abstract nouns frequently end with ־ָה, as in חָכְמָה, "wisdom"); context alone determines whether these forms are infinitives or nouns. The use of the feminine infinitive may be seen twice in Deuteronomy 10:12:

וְעַתָּה יִשְׂרָאֵל מָה יְהוָה אֱלֹהֶיךָ שֹׁאֵל מֵעִמָּךְ כִּי אִם־לְיִרְאָה
אֶת־יְהוָה אֱלֹהֶיךָ לָלֶכֶת בְּכָל־דְּרָכָיו וּלְאַהֲבָה אֹתוֹ וְלַעֲבֹד אֶת־
יְהוָה אֱלֹהֶיךָ בְּכָל־לְבָבְךָ וּבְכָל־נַפְשֶׁךָ:

"Now, O Israel, what does YHWH your God ask of you? Only to fear YHWH your God, to follow all his ways and to love him, and to worship YHWH your God with all of your heart and your soul." (Note how לְיִרְאָה and וּלְאַהֲבָה, the feminine infinitives, take direct objects [they are followed by אֶת־ and אֹתוֹ] and are syntactically parallel to the infinitives לָלֶכֶת and וְלַעֲבֹד.)

The infinitive construct is negated by לְבִלְתִּי, as in Deuteronomy 8:11, לְבִלְתִּי שְׁמֹר מִצְוֹתָיו, "not observing his commandments."

The infinitive absolute appears in the קַל as קָטוֹל. For example, from כתב we get כָּתוֹב. Its use may be seen in Genesis 50:24, וַיֹּאמֶר יוֹסֵף אֶל־אֶחָיו אָנֹכִי מֵת וֵאלֹהִים פָּקֹד יִפְקֹד אֶתְכֶם, "Joseph said to his brothers, 'I am about to die; God will certainly remember you.'" This form may not be preceded by a preposition and is never connected to a pronominal suffix. It is important not to confuse the infinitive absolute (for example, כָּתוֹב) with the ms passive participle (כָּתוּב), which is similar in form, though not in meaning.

Vocabulary for chapter 19

אבל	mourn	(lacking אָבַל יֶאֱבַל lacking)
בחן	test, examine	(בָּחַן בֹּחֵן יִבְחַן בְּחַן)
גנב	to steal	(lacking גָּנַב גֹּנֵב יִגְנֹב)
זקן	to be old	(lacking זָקֵן יִזְקַן lacking)
חבש	to bind	(חָבַשׁ חֹבֵשׁ יַחֲבֹשׁ חֲבֹשׁ)
חכם	to be wise	(חָכַם יֶחְכַּם חֲכַם lacking)
ינק	to nurse	(lacking יָנַק יֹנֵק יִינַק)
נאף	to commit adultery	(lacking נָאַף נֹאֵף יִנְאַף)
נטש	to abandon	(נָטַשׁ יִטֹּשׁ נְטוֹשׁ lacking)
פגע	to meet	(פָּגַע יִפְגַּע פְּגַע lacking)
פחד	to fear	(lacking פָּחַד יִפְחַד lacking)
פשע	to rebel, sin	(פָּשַׁע פֹּשֵׁעַ יִפְשַׁע פְּשַׁע)
צדק	to be right	(lacking צָדַק יִצְדַּק lacking)
קשר	to tie, conspire	(lacking קָשַׁר קֹשֵׁר יִקְשֹׁר)
רעש	to shake	(lacking רָעַשׁ רֹעֵשׁ יִרְעַשׁ)
רצח	to murder	(lacking רָצַח רֹצֵחַ יִרְצַח)
שחק	to laugh	(lacking שָׂחַק יִשְׂחַק lacking)
שקט	to be quiet, undisturbed	(lacking שָׁקַט שֹׁקֵט יִשְׁקֹט)
תעה	to wander, to err	(lacking תָּעָה תֹּעֶה יִתְעֶה)

TRANSLATION TIP #3:

Vowels matter. In particular, be sure to use vowel patterns to distinguish between verbs and nouns. A typical nominal pattern consists of two קָמֵצִים, while verbs in the קַל perfect 3ms have a קָמֵץ followed by a פַּתַח.

Psalm 13:6, אָשִׁירָה לַיהוָה כִּי גָמַל עָלָי

גָּמָל is the noun "camel," while the verb גמל means "to deal fairly" or "to reward." The vocalization here suggest that the form is a verb, thus we should translate: "Let me sing to YHWH because he has rewarded me," rather than "Let me sing to YHWH because a camel is on me."

Exercises for chapter 19

1. Identify the forms in each pair, translate them and explain the phonological process that caused the vocalization of the second word in the pair to differ from the first:

גָּנַב-גְּנַבְתֶּם
כָּבֵד-כָּבַדְתְּ
כְּתֹב-כִּתְבִי
כָּתוּב-כְּתוּבוֹת
יִכְתֹּב-יִכְתְּבוּ
כֹּתֶב-כֹּתְבוֹת

2. Write out the following conjugations; for the perfect and imperfect, be sure to start with the 3ms form:

In the perfect: קטן כבד ספר

In the imperfect: למד שׁכן (Reminder: למד is conjugated as a stative in the imperfect and as an active verb in the perfect.)

In the imperative: למד שׁכן

In the infinitive with suffixes (begin with 1cs), and the infinitive absolute: זכר

In the active and passive participle: קבר

3. Using the chart below, parse (analyze) the following verbs; be sure to indicate ambiguities:

Verb	Root	"Tense"	Person	Gender	Number	Other	Translation
שָׁקְטָה							
קְשֹׁר							
וָאֶגְנֹב							
יִזְקַן							
פִּרְשִׂי							
שִׁפְכִי							
מָכוֹר							
סָגוּר							
אֲגָרְשָׁה							
טָמֶנֶת							
רְחוּמוֹת							
וּמָשַׁל							
תִּקְצֹרְנָה							
תִּפְשְׁתֶן							
רְכֹב							
לִכְדוּ							
כָּרְתָן							
קְבוֹר							
וַיִּשְׁבֹּת							
וְדָבְקָה							
נִרְכְּבָה							
יִשְׁמְרוּ							
דְּבַקְתֶּם							
בֹּגְדִים							
שָׁכְנָה							

4. Write in BH; for forms that are perfect or imperfect, give both the nonconverted and converted forms (for "I grew up," for example, write both גָּדַלְתִּי and וָאֶגְדַּל):

I grew old		
you (fs) inquired		
to be quiet		
you (ms) were right		
she will deal treacherously		
you (ms) cut		
they (f) chased out		
it (ms) is hidden		
let us sell		
spread out! (mp)		
she approached		
you (fp) reaped		
he will certainly capture		
let's break		
my ceasing		
you (mp) rode		
it (fp) is closed		
they are ruling		
he grew up		
we will learn		
capture! (fp)		
may he cling		

5. Translate the following biblical passages; parse all verbs and verb-related forms:

Genesis 35:22

וַיֵּ֣לֶךְ (went) רְאוּבֵ֔ן וַיִּשְׁכַּב֙ אֶת־בִּלְהָה֙ פִּילֶ֣גֶשׁ אָבִ֔יו
וַיִּשְׁמַ֖ע יִשְׂרָאֵ֑ל

Exodus 21:37

כִּ֤י יִגְנֹֽב־אִישׁ֙ שׁ֣וֹר אוֹ־שֶׂ֔ה... חֲמִשָּׁ֣ה בָקָ֗ר
יְשַׁלֵּם֙ (he must pay) תַּ֣חַת הַשּׁ֔וֹר וְאַרְבַּע־צֹ֖אן תַּ֥חַת הַשֶּֽׂה׃

Deuteronomy 24:9

זָכ֕וֹר אֵ֧ת אֲשֶׁר־עָשָׂ֛ה יְהוָ֥ה אֱלֹהֶ֖יךָ לְמִרְיָ֑ם בַּדֶּ֖רֶךְ
בְּצֵאתְכֶ֥ם (in your leaving = as you left) מִמִּצְרָֽיִם׃

Joshua 22:5

רַ֣ק ׀ (only, indeed) שִׁמְר֤וּ מְאֹד֙ לַעֲשׂ֣וֹת (infin. construct of עשׂי)
אֶת־הַמִּצְוָ֣ה וְאֶת־הַתּוֹרָ֗ה אֲשֶׁ֨ר צִוָּ֥ה (commanded) אֶתְכֶ֜ם מֹשֶׁ֣ה עֶֽבֶד־יְהוָ֗ה
לְ֠אַהֲבָה אֶת־יְהוָ֨ה אֱלֹהֵיכֶ֜ם וְלָלֶ֧כֶת (infin. construct of הלך) בְּכָל־דְּרָכָ֛יו
וְלִשְׁמֹ֥ר מִצְוֺתָ֖יו וּלְדָבְקָה־ב֑וֹ וּלְעָבְד֕וֹ בְּכָל־לְבַבְכֶ֖ם וּבְכָל־נַפְשְׁכֶֽם׃

1 Samuel 8:5

וַיֹּאמְר֣וּ (converted imperfect of אמר) אֵלָ֗יו הִנֵּה֙ אַתָּ֣ה זָקַ֔נְתָּ
וּבָנֶ֕יךָ לֹ֥א הָלְכ֖וּ בִּדְרָכֶ֑יךָ עַתָּ֗ה (now) שִֽׂימָה־לָּ֥נוּ (elongated imperative of שׂ[י]ם)
מֶ֛לֶךְ לְשָׁפְטֵ֖נוּ (from שפט, "to judge, lead") כְּכָל־הַגּוֹיִֽם׃

1 Samuel 23:17b–18

וְאַתָּה֙ תִּמְלֹךְ֙ עַל־יִשְׂרָאֵ֔ל... וְגַם־ (also, indeed) שָׁא֣וּל (PN)
אָבִ֔י יֹדֵ֖עַ כֵּֽן (thus): 18 וַיִּכְרְת֧וּ שְׁנֵיהֶ֛ם בְּרִ֖ית לִפְנֵ֣י יְהוָ֑ה
וַיֵּ֤שֶׁב (converted imperfect of ישׁב) דָּוִד֙ בַּחֹ֔רְשָׁה (GN) וִיהוֹנָתָ֖ן הָלַ֥ךְ לְבֵיתֽוֹ׃

THE קַל OF HEALTHY VERBS

1 Kings 16:27–30

27 וְיֶ֛תֶר (remainder) דִּבְרֵ֥י עָמְרִי֙ (PN) אֲשֶׁ֣ר עָשָׂ֔ה וּגְבוּרָת֖וֹ
אֲשֶׁ֣ר עָשָׂ֑ה הֲלֹֽא־הֵ֣ם כְּתוּבִ֗ים עַל־סֵ֛פֶר דִּבְרֵ֥י הַיָּמִ֖ים לְמַלְכֵ֥י יִשְׂרָאֵֽל׃
28 וַיִּשְׁכַּ֤ב עָמְרִי֙ עִם־אֲבֹתָ֔יו וַיִּקָּבֵ֖ר (was buried) בְּשֹׁמְר֑וֹן (GN)
וַיִּמְלֹ֛ךְ אַחְאָ֥ב (PN) בְּנ֖וֹ תַּחְתָּֽיו׃ פ
29 וְאַחְאָ֣ב בֶּן־עָמְרִ֗י מָלַךְ֙ עַל־יִשְׂרָאֵ֔ל בִּשְׁנַ֛ת שְׁלֹשִׁ֥ים וּשְׁמֹנֶ֖ה
שָׁנָ֑ה לְאָסָ֣א (PN) מֶ֣לֶךְ יְהוּדָ֑ה וַ֠יִּמְלֹךְ אַחְאָ֨ב בֶּן־עָמְרִ֤י עַל־יִשְׂרָאֵל֙
בְּשֹׁ֣מְר֔וֹן עֶשְׂרִ֥ים וּשְׁתַּ֖יִם שָׁנָֽה׃ 30 וַיַּ֨עַשׂ (converted imperfect of עשׂי)
אַחְאָ֤ב בֶּן־עָמְרִי֙ הָרַ֔ע בְּעֵינֵ֥י יְהוָ֖ה מִכֹּ֥ל אֲשֶׁ֥ר לְפָנָֽיו׃

1 Kings 22:7

וַיֹּ֙אמֶר֙ יְה֣וֹשָׁפָ֔ט (PN) הַאֵ֨ין פֹּ֥ה נָבִ֛יא לַיהוָ֖ה ע֑וֹד (still)
וְנִדְרְשָׁ֖ה מֵאוֹתֽוֹ׃

20 The קַל of Verbs with Gutturals

This chapter does not outline all guttural verbs; verbs that have an אָלֶף in the final position (לא״), as well as some verbs that have an אָלֶף in the initial (פ״א) position, do not follow the patterns of the typical guttural (החע) verbs. These will be surveyed in the next two chapters. The conjugation of קַל verbs with the gutturals החע in any position, and ע״א verbs, is quite predictable, as long as the following rules are remembered (see p. 34):

1. The gutturals החע cannot take a שְׁוָא נָע. The expected שְׁוָא נָע is replaced by a חֲטָף פַּתַח (ֲ).
2. In some cases, these gutturals prefer not to be vocalized with a שְׁוָא נָח, and are vocalized with a חֲטָף פַּתַח instead.
3. In cases where applying either of these two rules results in a חֲטָף followed by a שְׁוָא, the law of the שְׁוָא (p. 42) is applied.

The Perfect and the Converted Perfect

The paradigms for verbs with gutturals in each of the three root letters are below. Note that in the perfect, gutturals typically have *a* as their theme vowel; only חפצ is conjugated as a stative (for example, חָפֵץ, "he desired"). I have set the various verbs next to the paradigm for the healthy כתב and have marked all differences with a ✸ so that they are easily noticed.

The קַל of Verbs with Gutturals

Gutturals in the Perfect				
	Healthy	*First guttural*	*Second guttural*	*Third guttural*
	כתב	עמד	שחט	שלח
3ms	כָּתַב	עָמַד	שָׁחַט	שָׁלַח
3fs	כָּתְבָה	עָמְדָה	✲ שָׁחֲטָה	שָׁלְחָה
2ms	כָּתַ֫בְתָּ	עָמַ֫דְתָּ	שָׁחַ֫טְתָּ	שָׁלַ֫חְתָּ
2fs	כָּתַבְתְּ	עָמַדְתְּ	שָׁחַטְתְּ	✲ שָׁלַחַתְּ
1cs	כָּתַ֫בְתִּי	עָמַ֫דְתִּי	שָׁחַ֫טְתִּי	שָׁלַ֫חְתִּי
3mp	כָּתְבוּ	עָמְדוּ	✲ שָׁחֲטוּ	שָׁלְחוּ
3fp	כָּתְבוּ	עָמְדוּ	✲ שָׁחֲטוּ	שָׁלְחוּ
2mp	כְּתַבְתֶּם	✲ עֲמַדְתֶּם	שְׁחַטְתֶּם	שְׁלַחְתֶּם
2fp	כְּתַבְתֶּן	✲ עֲמַדְתֶּן	שְׁחַטְתֶּן	שְׁלַחְתֶּן
1cp	כָּתַ֫בְנוּ	עָמַ֫דְנוּ	שָׁחַ֫טְנוּ	שָׁלַ֫חְנוּ

The converted perfect is as expected; the same shifts in accent occur in these verbs as in healthy verbs. The only unusual form is the 2fs of third gutturals—for example, שָׁלַחַתְּ. This may be a combination of the forms שָׁלַ֫חְתְּ* and שָׁלַחַתְּ*.

The Imperfect and the Converted Imperfect

Unlike the perfect, the imperfect of first gutturals distinguishes between active and stative verbs, because the guttural is distant from the theme vowel. This distinction, however, is kept only in first guttural verbs; second and third gutturals are characterized by the preferred a-vowel (see p. 46), so all of these verbs look stative. Stative first guttural verbs include חזק, "to be strong," אהב, "to love," אשם, "to be guilty," and חסר, "to lack." Notwithstanding the paradigm below, there is a certain amount of inconsistency concerning the vocalization of gutturals that would have closed a syllable created by the addition of the prefix of the imperfect. Forms like יֶחֱזַק predominate, where the guttural that should have closed the syllable opens it (יֶחֱזַק > *יִחְזַק). Forms like יֶחְסַר, where the guttural closes the syllable, are also attested, but are less frequent. I have set the various verbs next to the paradigm for the healthy כתב and כבד, so the effects of the gutturals may be apparent.

Gutturals in the Imperfect

	Healthy active	Stative	First guttural	First guttural stative	Second guttural	Third guttural
	כתב	כבד	עמד	חזק	שחט	שלח
3ms	יִכְתֹּב	יִכְבַּד	יַעֲמֹד	יֶחֱזַק	יִשְׁחַט	יִשְׁלַח
3fs	תִּכְתֹּב	תִּכְבַּד	תַּעֲמֹד	תֶּחֱזַק	תִּשְׁחַט	תִּשְׁלַח
2ms	תִּכְתֹּב	תִּכְבַּד	תַּעֲמֹד	תֶּחֱזַק	תִּשְׁחַט	תִּשְׁלַח
2fs	תִּכְתְּבִי	תִּכְבְּדִי	תַּעַמְדִי	תֶּחֶזְקִי	תִּשְׁחֲטִי	תִּשְׁלְחִי
1cs	אֶכְתֹּב	אֶכְבַּד	אֶעֱמֹד	אֶחֱזַק	אֶשְׁחַט	אֶשְׁלַח
3mp	יִכְתְּבוּ	יִכְבְּדוּ	יַעַמְדוּ	יֶחֶזְקוּ	יִשְׁחֲטוּ	יִשְׁלְחוּ
3fp	תִּכְתֹּבְנָה	תִּכְבַּדְנָה	תַּעֲמֹדְנָה	תֶּחֱזַקְנָה	תִּשְׁחַטְנָה	תִּשְׁלַחְנָה
2mp	תִּכְתְּבוּ	תִּכְבְּדוּ	תַּעַמְדוּ	תֶּחֶזְקוּ	תִּשְׁחֲטוּ	תִּשְׁלְחוּ
2fp	תִּכְתֹּבְנָה	תִּכְבַּדְנָה	תַּעֲמֹדְנָה	תֶּחֱזַקְנָה	תִּשְׁחַטְנָה	תִּשְׁלַחְנָה
1cp	נִכְתֹּב	נִכְבַּד	נַעֲמֹד	נֶחֱזַק	נִשְׁחַט	נִשְׁלַח

These paradigms are relatively straightforward and self-explanatory. Only the first gutturals are somewhat difficult. The initial guttural changes to the expected prefix vowel of חִירֶק (for example, תִּכְתְּבוּ) to a פַּתַח in the case of active verbs, and a סְגוֹל for statives. The first root letter, which in healthy verbs closed the first syllable, may open the second syllable (תִּ חֱ זַק נָה || תִּכְ בַּדְ נָה). Forms like תַּעַמְדוּ and תֶּחֶזְקוּ are the result of the application of the law of the שְׁוָא to gutturals (pp. 46–47): תַּעַמְדוּ > *תַּעְמְדוּ > *תַעֲמְדוּ and תֶּחֶזְקוּ > *תֶּחְזְקוּ > *תֶחֱזְקוּ.

The converted imperfect is formed exactly as expected; unless there is another weakness in the root, these verbs are not shortened in the converted imperfect.

The Jussive, the Imperative, and the Cohortative

The jussive is identical to the imperfect—there is no shortening. The cohortative, as expected, adds the suffix הָ‎, and some slight modifications result; we find, for example, נִשְׁחֲטָה (‏*נִשְׁחַטָה>‏*נִשְׁחֲטָה), נַעַמְדָה (‏*נַעֲמֹדָה>‏*נַעַמְדָה), and נִשְׁלְחָה. (No cohortatives of stative type first gutturals are attested.)

The imperative in all cases may be viewed as derived from the imperfect, but without a prefix. Thus we get the following forms:

Gutturals in the Imperative

	Active healthy	Active first guttural	Stative first guttural	Second guttural	Third guttural	Stative healthy
	כתב	עמד	חזק	שחט	שלח	כבד
2ms	כְּתֹב	עֲמֹד	חֲזַק	שְׁחַט	שְׁלַח	כְּבַד
2fs	כִּתְבִי	עִמְדִי	חִזְקִי	שַׁחֲטִי	שִׁלְחִי	כִּבְדִי
2mp	כִּתְבוּ	עִמְדוּ	חִזְקוּ	שַׁחֲטוּ	שִׁלְחוּ	כִּבְדוּ
2fp	כְּתֹבְנָה	עֲמֹדְנָה	חֲזַקְנָה	שְׁחַטְנָה	שְׁלַחְנָה	כְּבַדְנָה

It is best to study the imperative of these gutturals in relation to healthy verbs rather than in relation to the imperfects of gutturals in which there are many secondary forms. In the case of first gutturals, the שְׁוָא נָע is replaced by a חֲטָף פַּתַח. In the middle gutturals, in addition to the שְׁוָא נָע being replaced by a חֲטָף פַּתַח, the law of the שְׁוָא with gutturals applies (p. 44), so the first vowel is a פַּתַח. The third gutturals are completely straightforward; they are all similar to healthy stative verbs.

The ms imperative is sometimes found as an elongated imperative, with a suffix הָ‎, as in Genesis 43:8, שִׁלְחָה הַנַּעַר אִתִּי, "send the lad with me." (Note how the form is changed from ‏*שְׁלָחָה by pretonic reduction and then application of the law of the שְׁוָא: ‏*שְׁלָחָה > ‏*שְׁלְחָה > שִׁלְחָה.)

The Participles

The active participles are predictable, as noted in the following chart.

Active Participles of Gutturals

	Healthy	First guttural	Second guttural	Third guttural
	כתב	עמד	שחט	שלח
ms	כֹּתֵב	עֹמֵד	שֹׁחֵט	שֹׁלֵחַ
fs	כֹּתֶבֶת	עֹמֶדֶת	שֹׁחֶטֶת	שֹׁלַחַת
	כֹּתְבָה	עֹמְדָה	שֹׁחֲטָה	שֹׁלְחָה
mp	כֹּתְבִים	עֹמְדִים	שֹׁחֲטִים	שֹׁלְחִים
fp	כֹּתְבוֹת	עֹמְדוֹת	שֹׁחֲטוֹת	שֹׁלְחוֹת

The only form that is not as expected is the fs of third gutturals, where we find שֹׁלַחַת instead of *שֹׁלֶחֶת; the change to פַּתַח occurs as a result of the influence of the final guttural.

The passive participle is fully predictable.

Passive Participles of Gutturals

	Healthy	First guttural	Second guttural	Third guttural
	כתב	עמד	שחט	שלח
ms	כָּתוּב	עָמוּד	שָׁחוּט	שָׁלוּחַ
fs	כְּתוּבָה	עֲמוּדָה	שְׁחוּטָה	שְׁלוּחָה
mp	כְּתוּבִים	עֲמוּדִים	שְׁחוּטִים	שְׁלוּחִים
fp	כְּתוּבוֹת	עֲמוּדוֹת	שְׁחוּטוֹת	שְׁלוּחוֹת

The Infinitives

The infinitive construct of עמד is עֲמֹד. There are several words, however, most beginning with חִית, that act like regular healthy verbs when they follow the preposition לָמֶד, as in לַחְשֹׁב. (Note that the preposition is vocalized with a פַּתַח before the guttural, as expected.) From שחט we get שְׁחֹט, and from שלח, שְׁלֹחַ. It is noteworthy that the infinitive constructs of these gutturals all have an o-vowel, rather than the a-vowel that often typifies gutturals. The first gutturals are regular when pronominal suffixes are added to the infinitive construct, as in 2ms, עָמְדְךָ (|| כָּתְבְךָ), or 3mp, בְּעָמְדָם (|| בְּכָתְבָם). On the other hand, second gutturals take a פַּתַח, as in the form וּבְשַׁחֲטָם. The third gutturals are also regular, as in Numbers 32:8, בְּשָׁלְחִי אֹתָם מִקָּדֵשׁ בַּרְנֵעַ, "when I sent them from Kadesh Barnea."

The infinitive absolute is regular; the forms are שָׁלוֹחַ, שָׁחוֹט, עָמוֹד. The פַּתַח גְּנוּבָה (see p. 12) is found in the third gutturals; it is seen, for example, in the idiom וְהָיָה אִם־שָׁמֹעַ תִּשְׁמְעוּ, "if you fully heed" (Deuteronomy 11:13 and elsewhere).

THE קַל OF VERBS WITH GUTTURALS

Vocabulary for chapter 20

בחר	to choose	(בָּחַר בֹּחַר יִבְחַר בְּחַר)
בטח	to trust	(בָּטַח בֹּטֵחַ יִבְטַח בְּטַח)
בלע	to swallow	(בָּלַע lacking יִבְלַע lacking)
גאל	to redeem	(גָּאַל גֹּאֵל יִגְאַל גְּאַל)
גבה	to be high	(גָּבַהּ lacking יִגְבַּהּ lacking)
הרג	to kill	(הָרַג הֹרֵג יַהֲרֹג הֲרֹג)
זבח	to sacrifice	(זָבַח זֹבֵחַ יִזְבַּח זְבַח)
חדל	to cease (= MIH הִפְסִיק)	(חָדַל lacking יֶחְדַּל חֲדַל)
חזק	to be strong	(חָזַק יֶחֱזַק lacking חֲזַק)
חפץ	to delight in	(חָפֵץ lacking יַחְפֹּץ lacking)
חרש	to plow, engrave	(חָרַשׁ חֹרֵשׁ יַחֲרֹשׁ lacking)
חשב	to think	(חָשַׁב חֹשֵׁב יַחְשֹׁב lacking)
כעס	to be angry	(כָּעַס lacking יִכְעַס lacking)
משח	to anoint	(מָשַׁח מֹשֵׁחַ יִמְשַׁח מְשַׁח)
נחל	to inherit, possess	(נָחַל lacking יִנְחַל lacking)
עבד	to work, serve	(עָבַד עֹבֵד יַעֲבֹד עֲבֹד)
עבר	to pass	(עָבַר עֹבֵר יַעֲבֹר עֲבֹר)
עזב	to leave, abandon	(עָזַב עֹזֵב יַעֲזֹב עֲזֹב)
ערך	to arrange	(עָרַךְ עֹרֵךְ יַעֲרֹךְ עֲרֹךְ)
צעק	to cry out (similar to זעק, which is very similar phonetically; (צָעַק צֹעֵק יִצְעַק צְעַק)
שמח	to be happy	(שָׂמַח יִשְׂמַח lacking שְׂמַח)
שכח	to forget	(שָׁכַח שֹׁכֵחַ יִשְׁכַּח שְׁכַח)

Exercises for chapter 20

1. Identify the forms in each pair, translate them and explain the phonological process that causes the vocalization of the second word in the pair to differ from the first.

שָׁמְעָה-צָעֲקָה
יִסְגֹּר-יַעֲזֹר
תִּמְלֹךְ-תִּשְׂמַח
רְכַבְתֶּם-אֲמַרְתֶּם
יִכְרֹת-יִבְעַר
פְּקֹדְנָה-גְּאַלְנָה
זְכוּרָה-חֲבוּשָׁה

לִשְׁאֹל-לִפְגֹּעַ
טָמְנָם-זַעֲקָם

2. Write out the following conjugations; for the perfect and imperfect, be sure to start with the 3ms form:

   In the perfect: כרע פחד עבד

   In the imperfect: זרע נאף חזק עבר

   In the imperative: ברח מאס ערך חזק

   In the infinitive with suffixes (begin with 1cs), and the infinitive absolute: צעק

   In the active and passive participle: ידע שאל

THE קַל OF VERBS WITH GUTTURALS

3. Using the chart below, parse the following verbs; be sure to indicate ambiguities:

Verb	Root	"Tense"	Person	Gender	Number	Other	Translation
שָׁכַח							
שְׁבַעְתֶּן							
רָחֲצָה							
וַיֶּחְכַּם							
תִּנְאַף							
וּפָעַלְנוּ							
וַיִּרְחַק							
וְאָבְלוּ							
רִצְחִי							
עָזְבִי							
יִכְעֲסוּ							
וָאֶשְׂחַק							
סְלַח							
גָּבַהְתִּי							
וַנַּחֲרֹשׁ							
הֲפֹךְ							
בֹּקֵעַ							
מֹשַׁחַת							
וְנַחֲלוּ							
מָאֲסוּ							
זְבַח							
חֲשֹׁבְנָה							
נָאֲפוּ							
קָרוֹעַ							
נִבְחֲנָה							

4. Write in BH; for translations that may be expressed by the perfect or imperfect, give both the nonconverted and converted forms (for example, for "I grew up," write both וָאֶגְדַּל and גָּדַלְתִּי):

he divided		
may I work		
you (ms) trust		
they (m) slaughtered		
it (fs) is sprouting		
stumblers		
they (f) are taking		
don't sin		
they (f) are making noise		
you (mp) desired (= took delight in)		
cease! (ms)		
he is swallowing		
you (fs) heard		
to choose		
choosing her (= her choosing)		
let's scream		

THE קַל OF VERBS WITH GUTTURALS

5. Translate the following biblical passages, parse all verbs and analyze all nouns with suffixes. Here, and in the following chapters, each passage is followed by short explanatory glosses:

Genesis 18:9–11

9 וַיֹּאמְרוּ אֵלָיו אַיֵּה שָׂרָה אִשְׁתֶּךָ וַיֹּאמֶר הִנֵּה בָאֹהֶל:

10 וַיֹּאמֶר שׁוֹב אָשׁוּב אֵלֶיךָ כָּעֵת חַיָּה וְהִנֵּה־בֵן לְשָׂרָה אִשְׁתֶּךָ וְשָׂרָה שֹׁמַעַת פֶּתַח הָאֹהֶל וְהוּא אַחֲרָיו:

11 וְאַבְרָהָם וְשָׂרָה זְקֵנִים בָּאִים בַּיָּמִים

V. 9 וַיֹּאמְרוּ converted imperfect of אמר.
The meaning of the dots on top of אֵלָיו is disputed; they may reflect a tradition that the word is to be deleted.

V. 10 שׁוֹב אָשׁוּב infinitive absolute plus converted imperfect of שׁו(ב).
עֵת חַיָּה idiomatic for "next year."
Note how the second part of the verse uses a nonconverted tense (וְשָׂרָה שֹׁמַעַת) to show that the actions narrated are simultaneous.

Genesis 43:7

וַיֹּאמְרוּ שָׁאוֹל שָׁאַל־הָאִישׁ לָנוּ וּלְמוֹלַדְתֵּנוּ לֵאמֹר הַעוֹד אֲבִיכֶם חַי הֲיֵשׁ לָכֶם אָח

מוֹלַדְתֵּנוּ = מוֹלֶדֶת (kindred, family) +1cp suffix.

Exodus 22:22–23

צָעֹק יִצְעַק אֵלַי שָׁמֹעַ אֶשְׁמַע צַעֲקָתוֹ: 23 וְחָרָה אַפִּי וְהָרַגְתִּי אֶתְכֶם בֶּחָרֶב וְהָיוּ נְשֵׁיכֶם אַלְמָנוֹת וּבְנֵיכֶם יְתֹמִים:

V. 22 צַעֲקָתוֹ is a feminine abstract noun with suffix, related to the verb צעק.

V. 23 וְחָרָה אַפִּי literally, "my nose will burn" (converted perfect of חרי), idiomatic for "I will be angry."

Deuteronomy 12:12

וּשְׂמַחְתֶּ֞ם לִפְנֵ֣י ׀ יְהוָ֣ה אֱלֹהֵיכֶ֗ם אַתֶּ֨ם וּבְנֵיכֶ֤ם וּבְנֹֽתֵיכֶם֙ וְעַבְדֵיכֶ֣ם וְאַמְהֹתֵיכֶ֔ם וְהַלֵּוִי֙ אֲשֶׁ֣ר בְּשַֽׁעֲרֵיכֶ֔ם כִּ֣י אֵ֥ין ל֛וֹ חֵ֥לֶק וְנַחֲלָ֖ה אִתְּכֶֽם׃

חֵ֥לֶק וְנַחֲלָ֖ה   these two terms are used together in what some would call a hendiadys in the sense of "tribal allotment."

2 Samuel 5:3–5

3 וַ֠יָּבֹאוּ כָּל־זִקְנֵ֨י יִשְׂרָאֵ֤ל אֶל־הַמֶּ֙לֶךְ֙ חֶבְר֔וֹנָה וַיִּכְרֹ֨ת לָהֶ֥ם הַמֶּ֥לֶךְ דָּוִ֛ד בְּרִ֛ית בְּחֶבְר֖וֹן לִפְנֵ֣י יְהוָ֑ה וַיִּמְשְׁח֧וּ אֶת־דָּוִ֛ד לְמֶ֖לֶךְ עַל־יִשְׂרָאֵֽל׃ פ 4 בֶּן־שְׁלֹשִׁ֥ים שָׁנָ֛ה דָּוִ֖ד בְּמָלְכ֑וֹ אַרְבָּעִ֥ים שָׁנָ֖ה מָלָֽךְ׃ 5 בְּחֶבְר֗וֹן מָלַךְ֙ עַל־יְהוּדָ֔ה שֶׁ֥בַע שָׁנִ֖ים וְשִׁשָּׁ֣ה חֳדָשִׁ֑ים וּבִירוּשָׁלִַ֣ם מָלַ֗ךְ שְׁלֹשִׁ֤ים וְשָׁלֹשׁ֙ שָׁנָ֔ה עַ֥ל כָּל־יִשְׂרָאֵ֖ל וִיהוּדָֽה׃

V. 3   וַיָּבֹ֖אוּ a converted imperfect from ב(ו)א.

חֶבְר֔וֹנָה a directive, thus "to Hebron."

1 Kings 11:31–32

31 וַיֹּ֙אמֶר֙ לְיָרָבְעָ֔ם קַח־לְךָ֖ עֲשָׂרָ֣ה קְרָעִ֑ים כִּ֣י כֹ֤ה אָמַר֙ יְהוָ֜ה אֱלֹהֵ֣י יִשְׂרָאֵ֗ל הִנְנִ֨י קֹרֵ֤עַ אֶת־הַמַּמְלָכָה֙ מִיַּ֣ד שְׁלֹמֹ֔ה וְנָתַתִּ֣י לְךָ֔ אֵ֖ת עֲשָׂרָ֥ה הַשְּׁבָטִֽים׃ 32 וְהַשֵּׁ֥בֶט הָאֶחָ֖ד יִֽהְיֶה־לּ֑וֹ לְמַ֣עַן ׀ עַבְדִּ֣י דָוִ֗ד וּלְמַ֙עַן֙ יְר֣וּשָׁלִַ֔ם הָעִיר֙ אֲשֶׁ֣ר בָּחַ֣רְתִּי בָ֔הּ מִכֹּ֖ל שִׁבְטֵ֥י יִשְׂרָאֵֽל׃

V. 31   וַיֹּ֙אמֶר֙ converted imperfect of אמר.

קַח irregular imperative from לקח (see next chapter).

קְרָעִ֑ים from קֶרַע, "torn pieces."

כֹה "thus," very frequently in the prophetic phrase כֹּה אָמַר יְהוָה.

V. 32   הָעִיר֙ אֲשֶׁ֣ר בָּחַ֣רְתִּי בָ֔הּ The pronoun בָּהּ refers back to יְרוּשָׁלִַם (3fs); this is good Hebrew style, but it should not be reflected in the translation (that is, translate "the city that I chose," not "the city that I chose it").

Isaiah 1:11

לָמָּה־לִּי רֹב־זִבְחֵיכֶם֙ יֹאמַ֣ר יְהוָ֔ה
שָׂבַ֛עְתִּי עֹל֥וֹת אֵילִ֖ים וְחֵ֣לֶב מְרִיאִ֑ים
וְדַ֨ם פָּרִ֧ים וּכְבָשִׂ֛ים וְעַתּוּדִ֖ים לֹ֥א חָפָֽצְתִּי׃

יֹאמַר   imperfect of אמר, here "says."

חֵלֶב מְרִיאִים   "fat of fatlings."

עַתּוּדִים   "he-goats."

Jeremiah 5:18–19

18 וְגַ֛ם בַּיָּמִ֥ים הָהֵ֖מָּה נְאֻם־יְהוָ֑ה לֹֽא־אֶעֱשֶׂ֥ה אִתְּכֶ֖ם כָּלָֽה׃ 19 וְהָיָ֗ה
כִּ֤י תֹאמְרוּ֙ תַּ֣חַת מֶ֗ה עָשָׂ֨ה יְהוָ֧ה אֱלֹהֵ֛ינוּ לָ֖נוּ אֶת־כָּל־אֵ֑לֶּה וְאָמַרְתָּ֣
אֲלֵיהֶ֔ם כַּאֲשֶׁ֤ר עֲזַבְתֶּם֙ אוֹתִ֔י וַתַּעַבְד֛וּ אֱלֹהֵ֥י נֵכָ֖ר בְּאַרְצְכֶ֑ם כֵּ֚ן
תַּעַבְד֣וּ זָרִ֔ים בְּאֶ֕רֶץ לֹ֥א לָכֶֽם׃

V. 18   אֶעֱשֶׂה imperfect of עשׂי.

כָּלָה   "annihilation."

V. 19   תֹאמְרוּ imperfect of אמר.

תַּחַת מֶה   literally "under, in exchange for what," idiomatic for "because of what."

נֵכָר   "foreignness."

Note: The important syntactic elements in this verse are כַּאֲשֶׁר . . . כֵּן; this should be translated idiomatically as "because" or "since . . . so."

Ezekiel 5:16–17

וְשָׁבַרְתִּי לָכֶם מַטֵּה־לָחֶם:
17 וְשִׁלַּחְתִּי עֲלֵיכֶם רָעָב וְחַיָּה רָעָה וְשִׁכְּלֻךְ וְדֶבֶר
וָדָם יַעֲבָר־בָּךְ וְחֶרֶב אָבִיא עָלַיִךְ אֲנִי יְהוָה דִּבַּרְתִּי:

V. 17   וְשִׁלַּחְתִּי שלח in the פִּעֵל, "let loose."

חַיָּה "(wild) animal."

וְשִׁכְּלֻךְ "and they will make you childless."

אָבִיא הִפְעִיל of בו(א), "I will bring."

דִּבַּרְתִּי פִּעֵל of דבר, "to speak."

Psalm 119:109

נַפְשִׁי בְכַפִּי תָמִיד וְתוֹרָתְךָ לֹא שָׁכָחְתִּי:

תָּמִיד "always."

Note: Some traditions assume a reading of בְּכַפְּךָ for our בְכַפִּי; how would that be translated?

21 The קַל of פ״נ, פ״י, and פ״א Verbs

These three classes of verbs all have initial letters that cause certain changes in the paradigm of healthy verbs. These exceptions are of different types and are largely predictable based on phonological rules. In the case of פ״נ verbs, the initial נוּן is typically assimilated when it is immediately followed by a nonguttural consonant ($C_1Vn+C_2V[C_3] > C_1VC_2+C_2V[C_3]$; see pp. 45–46). Additionally, in certain cases that would not have been anticipated, the נוּן is dropped.

פ״י verbs are more complex. Hebrew words that begin with יוֹד have two possible origins: some originally began with יוֹד, while most others, based on historical and comparative evidence, began with וָו. In Hebrew, however, an initial וָו almost always changed to יוֹד; this explains, for example, why there is only a single biblical word that begins with וָו (וָו, "hook"). The different origins of פ״י verbs explain why there are two classes of these verbs: those that were originally פ״י, and those that are historically פ״ו. In the case of the first class, the weak יוֹד affects the conjugation, especially in the imperfect and related forms, while in the second, the original וָו was retained in certain בִּנְיָנִים and forms.

פ״א verbs also belong to two main classes: many are conjugated like first guttural verbs (for example, from אנף, "to be angry," we get יֶחֱזַק || יֶאֱנַף). In the five common verbs אכל, "to eat," אבד, "to stray," אמר, "to say," אבי, "to be willing," and אפי, "to bake," the initial אָלֶף is particularly weak, especially in the imperfect (for example, יִכְבַּד || יֶאֱנַף || יֹאמַר).

The Perfect and the Converted Perfect

I have not offered paradigms for these verbs in the perfect because their behavior is fully predictable. In the case of פ״נ verbs, we have both active and stative verbs—for example, נָפַל, "he fell," like כָּתַב, and נָבֵל, "he/it withers," like כָּבֵד. Both types of פ״י verbs take both active and stative forms in the perfect. We have, for example, יָשַׁב, "he sat" (which is historically a פ״ו), and יָבֵשׁ, "he/it is dry" (this is a true פ״י). All of the special פ״א verbs are active and thus follow the paradigm for active first gutturals (for example, עָמַד ‖ אָמַר and עֲמַדְתֶּם ‖ אֲבַדְתֶּם).

The converted perfect presents no problems; the וְ is added, and the expected changes in accent in the 1cs and 2ms transpire. The imperfect and the converted imperfect are more complex and are outlined below.

The Imperfect and Converted Perfect of פ״ו, פ״י, and פ״א Verbs

	Active	Stative[1]	Active פ״נ	Stative פ״נ	Active פ״ו	Stative פ״ו	Stative פ״י	פ״א
	כתב	כבד	נפל	נגשׁ	ישׁב	ירשׁ	יטב	אכל
3ms	יִכְתֹּב	יִכְבַּד	יִפֹּל	יִגַּשׁ	יֵשֵׁב	יִירַשׁ	יִיטַב	יֹאכַל
3fs	תִּכְתֹּב	תִּכְבַּד	תִּפֹּל	תִּגַּשׁ	תֵּשֵׁב	תִּירַשׁ	תִּיטַב	תֹּאכַל
2ms	תִּכְתֹּב	תִּכְבַּד	תִּפֹּל	תִּגַּשׁ	תֵּשֵׁב	תִּירַשׁ	תִּיטַב	תֹּאכַל
2fs	תִּכְתְּבִי	תִּכְבְּדִי	תִּפְּלִי	תִּגְּשִׁי	תֵּשְׁבִי	תִּירְשִׁי	תִּיטְבִי	תֹּאכְלִי
1cs	אֶכְתֹּב	אֶכְבַּד	אֶפֹּל	אֶגַּשׁ	אֵשֵׁב	אִירַשׁ	אִיטַב	אֹכַל
3mp	יִכְתְּבוּ	יִכְבְּדוּ	יִפְּלוּ	יִגְּשׁוּ	יֵשְׁבוּ	יִירְשׁוּ	יִיטְבוּ	יֹאכְלוּ
3fp	תִּכְתֹּבְנָה	תִּכְבַּדְנָה	תִּפֹּלְנָה	תִּגַּשְׁנָה	תֵּשַׁבְנָה		תִּיטַבְנָה	תֹּאכַלְנָה
2mp	תִּכְתְּבוּ	תִּכְבְּדוּ	תִּפְּלוּ	תִּגְּשׁוּ	תֵּשְׁבוּ	תִּירְשׁוּ	תִּיטְבוּ	תֹּאכְלוּ
2fp	תִּכְתֹּבְנָה	תִּכְבַּדְנָה						
1cp	נִכְתֹּב	נִכְבַּד	נִפֹּל	נִגַּשׁ	נֵשֵׁב	נִירַשׁ	נִיטַב	נֹאכַל

(Note: different verbs of the same class are used to fill in this paradigm. For example, ינק, a stative פ״י, may be used to determine how יטב is conjugated. The blank spaces in this paradigm represent forms that are not attested with any verb in BH. These forms could be guessed with relative certainty, but they are best left blank.)

---

1. Reminder: not all verbs conjugated as statives are semantically stative.

The conjugation of the פ״נ verbs in the imperfect is quite straightforward; the נוּן assimilates, leaving a דָּגֵשׁ חָזָק in the first root letter of the verb, as in יִגַּשׁ (*יִנְגַּשׁ>).² In parsing biblical verbs, it is therefore important to pay attention to דְּגֵשִׁים in verbs, for they might mask a lost נוּן root letter that must be identified so that the root can be recognized and translated properly. The regular stative and active categories are operative with the same standard theme vowels.

The פ״י (/ פ״ו) verbs belong to two main classes: stative verbs that have a יוֹד in addition to the prefix of the imperfect (for example, יִירַשׁ) and active verbs that have the prefix letter only, without the initial יוֹד of the root (for example, יֵשֵׁב). (Infrequently, the יוֹד of the root of the stative verb is omitted in the imperfect, but the vowel stays as חִירֶק.) The theme vowels of these verbs are different as well: active verbs have *e* as in יֵשֵׁב, while stative verbs have *a* as in יִירַשׁ. The verbs that are true פ״וs are conjugated as statives. Active פ״י verbs include ירד, "to descend"; יצא, "to go out"; ילך, "to go"; ילד, "to give birth"; and ידע, "to know," while stative פ״יs include: ירא, "to fear"; ישן, "to sleep"; יעץ, "to counsel"; יעף, "to be tired"; יכל, "to be able"; and יגר, "to be in dread."

The group of פ״א verbs is characterized by an o-vowel in the prefix and an a-vowel under the second root letter. In addition, the 1cs form is written with only a single אָלֶף, as in אֹכַל.

The converted imperfect is largely as expected, with a וָן followed by a דָּגֵשׁ חָזָק preceding the imperfect, as in (Genesis 28:16), וַיִּיקַץ יַעֲקֹב מִשְּׁנָתוֹ, "Jacob awoke from his sleep." Active פ״י verbs of the same type as ישב in the converted imperfect have penultimate accent in the second and third persons in cases where the last syllable is closed; compare the placement of the accents in 1 Samuel 5:7, לֹא־יֵשֵׁב אֲרוֹן אֱלֹהֵי יִשְׂרָאֵל עִמָּנוּ, "the ark of the God of Israel should not reside with us," and Genesis 22:19, וַיֵּשֶׁב אַבְרָהָם בִּבְאֵר שָׁבַע, "Abraham resided in Beersheba." (Note that the final long vowel of וַיֵּשֶׁב is shortened because the accent is no longer ultimate.)

The common verb אמר is irregular; in the converted imperfect it appears as וַיֹּאמֶר, but in pause as וַיֹּאמַר. The various forms of the very common 3ms form אמר may be seen in the following examples:

Deuteronomy 15:16, וְהָיָה כִּי־יֹאמַר אֵלֶיךָ, "if he says to you."
Genesis 1:3, וַיֹּאמֶר אֱלֹהִים יְהִי אוֹר, "God said, 'Let there be light.'"
Exodus 2:14, וַיִּירָא מֹשֶׁה וַיֹּאמַר, "Moses was afraid and said."

2. The נוּן does not assimilate before a guttural, thus יִנְחַל, "he will possess."

The Jussive, the Imperative, and the Cohortative

The jussives of all of these forms are identical with the imperfects. The cohortatives are also constructed as expected by adding an accented הָ (pretonic reduction usually results). Thus we find, for example, נִפְּלָה־נָּא בְיַד־יְהוָה, "let's fall into YHWH's hand" (2 Samuel 24:14, from נפל). The imperatives are more complex. They are introduced in the chart below and are explained afterward.

The Imperative of פ״נ, פ״י, and פ״א Verbs

	Active	Active	Stative	Active	Stative	פ״א
	כתב	נפל	נגשׁ	ישׁב	ירשׁ	אכל
2ms	כְּתֹב	נְפֹל	גַּשׁ	שֵׁב	רֵשׁ	אֱכֹל
2fs	כִּתְבִי	נִפְלִי	גְּשִׁי	שְׁבִי	רְשִׁי	אִכְלִי
2mp	כִּתְבוּ	נִפְלוּ	גְּשׁוּ	שְׁבוּ	רְשׁוּ	אִכְלוּ
2fp	כְּתֹבְנָה	נְפֹלְנָה	גַּשְׁנָה	שֵׁבְנָה	rare	

In the פ״נ verbs, the imperative is formed in two ways. In verbs that are stative and have an a-theme vowel, like נגשׁ, the initial נון is dropped (for example, גַּשׁ); whereas in verbs that are active and have an o-theme vowel, the נון is retained, just like healthy verbs (כְּתֹב ‖ נְפֹל). In the פ״י verbs, the initial יוֹד is always dropped; when the syllable following the vowel is accented, the theme vowel appears (for example, רַשׁ, שֵׁבְנָה); when the first syllable is unaccented, its vowel reduces to a שְׁוָא (רְשִׁי, רְשׁוּ). No imperatives are found of statives like יטב or יבשׁ. As a result of the dropping of the נון in stative verbs and of the יוֹד in stative פ״י verbs, the imperatives of these two may look almost identical (גַּשׁ from נגשׁ and רֵשׁ from ירשׁ).

Verbs that are פ״א have imperatives like first gutturals; the only difference is that the ms form is vocalized with an initial חֲטַף סֶגוֹל rather than a חֲטַף פַּתַח. This is because אָלֶף prefers a חֲטַף סֶגוֹל and its related forms, as seen in the prefix vowel of the regular imperfect אֶכְתֹּב. This initial חֲטַף סֶגוֹל is present in these special פ״א verbs as well as in regular פ״א verbs. From the root אסר, for example, we find the ms imperative אֱסֹר.

The Participles

The participles of these forms are fully regular; the initial letters are retained, and no unexpected vocalic changes transpire. For example, we would have the active participles נֹפֵל, יֹשֵׁב, and אֹכְלִים and the passive participles אָמוּר and יְדוּעִים.

The Infinitives

The infinitive constructs are not all regular; in several of them, the initial "weak" letter is dropped, and the infinitive appears with a feminine ending (a תָ). The word as a whole is then vocalized as a segholate, as □ֶ□ֶת. As a result of these processes, certain פ״נ and פ״י verbs have identical forms as □ֶ□ֶת in the infinitive construct. Thus in Psalm 133:1, הִנֵּה מַה־טּוֹב וּמַה־נָּעִים שֶׁבֶת אַחִים גַּם־יָחַד, "How good and pleasant it is that brothers dwell together," we know that שֶׁבֶת is from ישׁב because the root נשׁב, "to blow," does not make sense in this context. A chart of the infinitive constructs follows.

The Infinitive Construct of פ״נ, פ״י, and פ״א Verbs

	Active	Stative	Active	Stative	פ״א
root	נפל	נגשׁ	ישׁב	ירשׁ	אכל
infinitive construct	נְפֹל	גֶּשֶׁת	שֶׁבֶת	רֶשֶׁת	אֲכֹל (rarely אֱכֹל)

Contrary to expectations, the initial נוּן of infinitives like נְפֹל is not assimilated when a prepositional לָמֶד is prefixed, so the resulting form is לִנְפֹּל; the other bound prepositions act similarly, yielding בִּנְפֹל and כִּנְפֹל. (Note the inconsistency in whether the פ״א takes a דָּגֵשׁ קַל; after the preposition ל, the דָּגֵשׁ קַל is present, but after ב or כ, the דָּגֵשׁ קַל is absent.) Pronominal suffixes are typically added to נְפֹל and אֲכֹל according to the rules of healthy and first guttural roots; we thus have forms like: מִיּוֹם נָפְלוֹ עַד־הַיּוֹם הַזֶּה, "from the day he defected (fell) until this day" (1 Samuel 29:3; כָּתְבוֹ ‖ נָפְלוֹ), and בְּיוֹם אֲכָלְכֶם מִמֶּנּוּ, "on the day you eat from it" (Genesis 3:5; כָּתְבְכֶם ‖ אֲכָלְכֶם). The segholate forms are *qitl*s. We thus add suffixes to -□ֶ□ֶת, as in, אוֹ בְגִשְׁתָּם אֶל־הַמִּזְבֵּחַ, "or when they approach the altar" (Exodus 28:43), or יְהוָה אֱלֹהֵיכֶם נָתַן לָכֶם אֶת־הָאָרֶץ הַזֹּאת לְרִשְׁתָּהּ, "YHWH your God gave you this land to possess it" (Deuteronomy 3:18).

Special Forms

The following verbs that are פּ״נ or פּ״י are conjugated in unexpected ways: נתנ, לקח, verbs that are פּ״י and have a צָדִי as their second root letter (פּ״צ), and the verbs הלכ and יכל.

Several complications arise in conjugating נתנ, "to give," which has two נוּנִים and is a very common word. In the perfect, the second נ assimilates into the following suffix; we thus have forms like נָתַתִּי (< *נָתַנְתִּי|| כָּתַבְתִּי and שָׁכַנְתִּי).[3] The 2ms is frequently written with a final *mater lectionis* as נָתַתָּה; the vowel letter הֵא in the 2ms perfect is found less often with other verbs. The imperfect has forms like יִתֵּן (< *יִנְתֵּן); note the unusual צֵרִי as theme vowel. The infinitive construct, תֵּת, is also irregular, and, with suffixes, it appears as תִּתּ־, as in טוֹב תִּתִּי אֹתָהּ לָךְ מִתִּתִּי אֹתָהּ לְאִישׁ אַחֵר, "it is better for me to give her to you than [literally, 'my giving her to you is better than'] to give her to another man" (Genesis 29:19). The attested imperatives are תֵּן (ms), תֶּן־ (ms proclitic), תְּנָה (ms elongated), תְּנִי (fs), and תְּנוּ (mp).

The paradigm of לקח, "to take," is similar to נתנ, to which it is semantically related ("give" and "take"). This explains why in the imperfect, the initial לָמֶד, that is usually stable, has assimilated (for example, יִקַּח; contrast יִלְמַד). Its infinitive construct, קַחַת, is based on the segholate pattern of פּ״נ verbs, with the additional influence of the guttural. In most other forms, both נתנ and לקח are regular.

A paradigm for נתנ in the perfect and imperfect follows.

The Verb נתנ

	Perfect Singular	Imperfect Singular	Perfect Plural	Imperfect Plural
3m	נָתַן	יִתֵּן	נָתְנוּ	יִתְּנוּ
3f	נָתְנָה	תִּתֵּן	נָתְנוּ	תִּתֵּנָּה
2m	נָתַתָּה	תִּתֵּן	נְתַתֶּם	תִּתְּנוּ
2f	נָתַתְּ	תִּתְּנִי		
1c	נָתַתִּי	אֶתֵּן	נָתַנּוּ	נִתֵּן

---

3. Note that the נוּן of שָׁכַנְתִּי is not assimilated; in general, the נוּן of פּ״נ verbs is not assimilated before suffixes.

There are six biblical roots that are פ"י and have a צָדִי as their second root letter (פִי"צ); these include יצק, "to pour," and יצר, "to fashion." (The common יצא is not conjugated like these verbs.) The imperfect of these verbs is unusual: יִצֹּק and יִצֹּר; there is only a single יוֹד, and the middle צָדִי has been doubled. The consonant צָדִי is prone to doubling. As a result, there has been a type of exchange here: the expected long vowel in an open syllable (יִי) has been exchanged for a short vowel in a closed syllable (יִצ). The exchange is even—that is, an unaccented, closed syllable with a short vowel is equivalent to an unaccented, open syllable with a long vowel—allowing forms like יִצֹּר to develop.

The biblical verb "to go" is effectively derived from two roots: הלכ in the perfect, and ילכ in the imperfect and related forms. (This phenomenon is called suppletion.) In the perfect, הלכ follows the paradigm of first gutturals, as in הָלַךְ or הֲלַכְתֶּם. In the imperfect, ילכ is treated as a פ"י like יָשַׁב, yielding forms like יֵלֵךְ and תֵּלְכוּ. Forms like the infinitive construct and imperative are related to the imperfect, so for these too the root is ילכ, as in the imperative ms לֵךְ (elongated לְכָה) and the infinitive construct לֶכֶת.

There is some debate about why the conjugation of יכל is so unusual and whether or not it is truly a קַל. Nonetheless, it is a common word, and its forms are well attested. In the perfect, its base form is יָכֹל, with other forms including 3fs יָכְלָה and 3mp יָכְלוּ (pausal יָכֹלוּ). In the imperfect, it anomalously has a *u* prefix vowel; thus the 3ms is יוּכַל, and other forms are similar (for example, תּוּכַל, נוּכַל, and יוּכְלוּ [also spelled יָכֹלוּ]).

Vocabulary for chapter 21

אבד	to perish	(אָבַד אֹבֵד יֹאבַד אֲבֹד)
אחז	to grasp, hold	(אָחַז אֹחֵז יֹאחֵז אֲחֹז)
אסף	to gather	(אָסַף אֹסֵף יֶאֱסֹף אֱסֹף)
אסר	to bind	(אָסַר אֹסֵר יֶאֱסֹר אֱסֹר)
אשם	to be guilty	(אָשֵׁם and אָשֵׁם lacking יֶאְשַׁם lacking)
יגע	to work, to be tired	(lacking יָגֵעַ lacking יִיגַע)
יטב	to be good	(lacking יָטַב lacking יִיטַב lacking)
יכל	to be able	(יָכֹל lacking יוּכַל lacking)
יסד	to establish	(יָסַד lacking lacking יְסֹד)
יסף	to do more, do again	(יָסַף lacking lacking סַף)
יצק	to pour out	(יָצַק lacking צֹק and יְצֹק יִצֹק)
יצר	to fashion, form	(lacking יֹצֵר יִצֹּר יְצֹר)
ירא	to fear	(יָרֵא lacking יִירָא יְרָא)
ירד	to descend	(יָרַד יֹרֵד יֵרֵד רֵד)
ירש	to possess, inherit	(יָרַשׁ יֹרֵשׁ יִירַשׁ רֵשׁ)
נגף	to smite	(נָגַף נֹגֵף יִגֹּף lacking)
נדד	to wander	(נָדַד נֹדֵד יִדּוֹד lacking)
נדר	to vow	(נָדַר נֹדֵר יִדֹּר נְדֹר)
נפל	to fall	(נָפַל נֹפֵל יִפֹּל נְפֹל)
נצר	to watch, guard	(נָצַר נֹצֵר יִצֹּר נְצֹר)
נשק	to kiss	(נָשַׁק נֹשֵׁק יִשַּׁק שַׁק)

Exercises for chapter 21

1. Identify the forms in each pair, translate them, and explain the phonetic process that causes the vocalization of the second word in the pair to differ from the first.

יִכְבַּד-יִשַּׁק
תִּפְקְדִי-תִּתְּנִי
תִּשְׁמַע-תִּקַּח
אֶרְדֹּף- אֶצֹּר
גְּשִׁי-כִּרְתִי
רְשׁוּ-קִבְרוּ

2. Write out the following conjugations; for the perfect and imperfect, be sure to start with the 3ms form:

   In the perfect: יצר אחז

   In the imperfect and imperative: אסר אבד נדר נגף ירד יבש

   In the infinitive with suffixes (begin with 1cs), and the infinitive absolute: אסף ישב נגש

   In the active and passive participle: נגף יצר אמר

3. Using the chart below, parse the following verbs; be sure to indicate ambiguities:

Verb	Root	"Tense"	Person	Gender	Number	Other	Translation
וַתִּפֹּל							
רְדוּ							
וַיֵּיטַב							
נֵלֵךְ							
נָאֹף							
נָחֵל							
יָסֹף							
רְשָׁתָה							
שִׁבְתָּם							
נוּכַל							
וַיִּטֹּשׁ							
נָדֶרֶת							
יוֹסְדוֹת							
תֹּאשַׁם							
שֶׁבְנָה							
לְכָה							
קַח							
נִפְלָה							
יוֹנִקֵי							
וְיָבְשׁוּ							
גְּשׁוּ							
נָגְפוּ							
יָכְלוּ							
וַיֹּאמֶר							
רֶשֶׁת							

4. Write in BH; for translations that may be expressed by the perfect or imperfect, give both the nonconverted and converted forms (for example, for "I grew up," write both וָאֶגְדַּל and גָּדַלְתִּי):

she approached		
she is inheriting		
make a vow! (fs)		
you (ms) will gather		
his approaching		
they (f) will fall		
we will reside		
I inherited		
sit! (mp)		
you (fs) ate		
she will pour out		
he will kiss		
you (mp) will fall		
go down! (ms)		
she will grasp		
I will perish		
may we approach		
may he eat		
they (ms) are bound up		
her eating		
you (fp) will take		
they (m) went		

THE קַל OF פנ״, פי״, AND פא״ VERBS

5. Translate the following biblical passages, parse all verbs, and analyze all nouns with suffixes:

Genesis 3:2–3

2 וַתֹּאמֶר הָאִשָּׁה אֶל־הַנָּחָשׁ מִפְּרִי עֵץ־הַגָּן נֹאכֵל: 3 וּמִפְּרִי הָעֵץ אֲשֶׁר בְּתוֹךְ־הַגָּן אָמַר אֱלֹהִים לֹא תֹאכְלוּ מִמֶּנּוּ וְלֹא תִגְּעוּ בּוֹ פֶּן־תְּמֻתוּן:

V. 2   נָחָשׁ "snake."

V. 3   The nonconverted אָמַר is a pluperfect, "had said."

       פֶּן "lest," "or else."

       תְּמֻתוּן imperfect with an added (paragogic) נוּן from the root מ(ו)ת.

Genesis 17:17–19

17 וַיִּפֹּל אַבְרָהָם עַל־פָּנָיו וַיִּצְחָק וַיֹּאמֶר בְּלִבּוֹ הַלְּבֶן מֵאָה־שָׁנָה יִוָּלֵד וְאִם־שָׂרָה הֲבַת־תִּשְׁעִים שָׁנָה תֵּלֵד: 18 וַיֹּאמֶר אַבְרָהָם אֶל־הָאֱלֹהִים לוּ יִשְׁמָעֵאל יִחְיֶה לְפָנֶיךָ: 19 וַיֹּאמֶר אֱלֹהִים אֲבָל שָׂרָה אִשְׁתְּךָ יֹלֶדֶת לְךָ בֵּן וְקָרָאתָ אֶת־שְׁמוֹ יִצְחָק וַהֲקִמֹתִי אֶת־בְּרִיתִי אִתּוֹ לִבְרִית עוֹלָם לְזַרְעוֹ אַחֲרָיו:

V. 17   צחק "to laugh." (note pausal form of וַיִּצְחָק rather than וַיִּצְחַק.) יִוָּלֵד "to be born" (ילד of נִפְעַל).

V. 18   לוּ "if only."

        יִחְיֶה "will live."

V. 19   אֲבָל "indeed."

        וַהֲקִמֹתִי "and I will establish" (הִפְעִיל of ק[ו]מ).

Genesis 28:20–21

וַיִּדַּ֥ר יַעֲקֹ֖ב נֶ֣דֶר לֵאמֹ֑ר אִם־יִהְיֶ֨ה אֱלֹהִ֜ים עִמָּדִ֗י
וּשְׁמָרַ֙נִי֙ בַּדֶּ֤רֶךְ הַזֶּה֙ אֲשֶׁ֣ר אָנֹכִ֣י הוֹלֵ֔ךְ וְנָֽתַן־לִ֥י לֶ֛חֶם לֶאֱכֹ֖ל וּבֶ֥גֶד לִלְבֹּֽשׁ׃
21 וְשַׁבְתִּ֥י בְשָׁל֖וֹם אֶל־בֵּ֣ית אָבִ֑י וְהָיָ֧ה יְהוָ֛ה לִ֖י לֵאלֹהִֽים׃

The pattern וַיִּדַּר ... נֶדֶר, where the verb has a noun from the same root as its direct object, is called "the cognate accusative." This is a frequent pattern in BH, but it should not be reflected overliterally in translation.

וּשְׁמָרַנִי = וְשָׁמַר אֹתִי. (These direct object suffixes for verbs will be introduced in chapter 23.)

Genesis 41:37–38

37 וַיִּיטַ֥ב הַדָּבָ֖ר בְּעֵינֵ֣י פַרְעֹ֑ה וּבְעֵינֵ֖י כָּל־עֲבָדָֽיו׃
38 וַיֹּ֥אמֶר פַּרְעֹ֖ה אֶל־עֲבָדָ֑יו הֲנִמְצָ֣א כָזֶ֔ה אִ֕ישׁ אֲשֶׁ֛ר ר֥וּחַ אֱלֹהִ֖ים בּֽוֹ׃

V. 38 נִמְצָא "found" (נִפְעַל from מצא).

Exodus 2:7–8

7 וַתֹּ֤אמֶר אֲחֹתוֹ֙ אֶל־בַּת־פַּרְעֹ֔ה הַאֵלֵ֗ךְ וְקָרָ֤אתִי לָךְ֙ אִשָּׁ֣ה מֵינֶ֔קֶת מִ֖ן הָעִבְרִיֹּ֑ת וְתֵינִ֥ק לָ֖ךְ אֶת־הַיָּֽלֶד׃ 8 וַתֹּֽאמֶר־לָ֥הּ בַּת־פַּרְעֹ֖ה לֵ֑כִי וַתֵּ֙לֶךְ֙ הָֽעַלְמָ֔ה וַתִּקְרָ֖א אֶת־אֵ֥ם הַיָּֽלֶד׃

V. 7 וְקָרָאתִי a converted perfect from קרא, "to call." Hebrew may combine various phrases with a וְ, even where English uses prepositions or subordinate clauses; it is therefore proper to translate הַאֵלֵךְ וְקָרָאתִי as "should I go to call."

מֵינֶקֶת "nursing" (a הִפְעִיל fs participle from ינק, functioning as a noun). Note how Hebrew has two nouns, both unbound, side by side (אִשָּׁה מֵינֶקֶת). Such words are said to be in apposition. Typically, the word *namely* could be put between such words. Thus אִשָּׁה מֵינֶקֶת is literally "a woman, namely a nurse," but here it should be translated idiomatically as "a nursing woman, nursemaid."

הָעִבְרִיֹּת fp of עִבְרִי, "Hebrew." Words that end in ִי and indicate ethnic groups are called "gentilics." כְּנַעֲנִי, "a Canaanite," is another example of a gentilic.

עַלְמָה "young woman."

וְתֵינִק Note the nonconversive וְ that introduces a purpose clause ("so that").

THE קַל OF פ״נ, פ״י, AND פ״א VERBS

Deuteronomy 4:26a

הַעִידֹ֨תִי בָכֶ֜ם הַיּ֗וֹם אֶת־הַשָּׁמַ֙יִם֙ וְאֶת־הָאָ֔רֶץ כִּֽי־אָבֹ֣ד תֹּאבֵד֔וּן
מַהֵ֗ר מֵעַ֤ל הָאָ֙רֶץ֙ אֲשֶׁ֨ר אַתֶּ֜ם עֹבְרִ֧ים אֶת־הַיַּרְדֵּ֛ן שָׁ֖מָּה לְרִשְׁתָּ֑הּ

הַעִידֹ֨תִי בָכֶ֜ם   "I take as witnesses against you."

מַהֵ֗ר   "quickly."

Joshua 14:6–7

6 וַיִּגְּשׁ֨וּ בְנֵֽי־יְהוּדָ֤ה אֶל־יְהוֹשֻׁ֙עַ֙ בַּגִּלְגָּ֔ל וַיֹּ֣אמֶר אֵלָ֔יו כָּלֵ֥ב בֶּן־יְפֻנֶּ֖ה הַקְּנִזִּ֑י
אַתָּ֣ה יָדַ֗עְתָּ אֶֽת־הַדָּבָ֡ר אֲשֶׁר־דִּבֶּ֣ר יְהוָה֩ אֶל־מֹשֶׁ֨ה אִישׁ־הָאֱלֹהִ֜ים
עַל־אֹדוֹתַ֧י וְעַ֥ל אֹדוֹתֶ֖יךָ בְּקָדֵ֥שׁ בַּרְנֵֽעַ: 7 בֶּן־אַרְבָּעִ֨ים שָׁנָ֜ה אָנֹכִ֗י
בִּשְׁלֹ֨חַ מֹשֶׁ֤ה עֶֽבֶד־יְהוָה֙ אֹתִ֔י מִקָּדֵ֥שׁ בַּרְנֵ֖עַ לְרַגֵּ֣ל אֶת־הָאָ֑רֶץ וָאָשֵׁ֤ב
אֹתוֹ֙ דָּבָ֔ר כַּאֲשֶׁ֖ר עִם־לְבָבִֽי:

V. 6 בַּגִּלְגָּ֔ל is "at Gilgal." Place names and personal names do not take the definite article, except for certain geographical names that transparently derive from common nouns, like גִּלְגָּל, "round area," or הַיַּרְדֵּן, "that which descends."

הַקְּנִזִּי Another gentilic, "the Kenizite."

דִּבֶּר "spoke" (פִּעֵל of דבר).

אֹדוֹת "concerning."

V. 7 לְרַגֵּל "to spy" (פִּעֵל infinitive construct of רגל).

וָאָשֵׁב "I returned" (הִפְעִיל converted imperfect of ב[ו]ש).

2 Samuel 24:14

וַיֹּ֧אמֶר דָּוִ֛ד אֶל־גָּ֖ד צַר־לִ֣י מְאֹ֑ד נִפְּלָה־נָּ֣א בְיַד־יְהוָ֗ה
כִּֽי־רַבִּ֣ים רַחֲמ֔וֹ [רַחֲמָ֔יו] וּבְיַד־אָדָ֖ם אַל־אֶפֹּֽלָה:

The כְּתִיב is רַחֲמוֹ and the קְרֵי is רַחֲמָיו [רַחֲמָיו].

2 Kings 1:11–12

וַיַּ֨עַן אֵלִיָּ֤ה וַיְדַבֵּר֙ אֲלֵיהֶ֔ם 12 כֹּה־אָמַ֤ר הַמֶּ֙לֶךְ֙ מְהֵרָ֣ה רֵ֔דָה׃
אִם־אִ֤ישׁ הָאֱלֹהִים֙ אָ֔נִי תֵּ֤רֶד אֵשׁ֙ מִן־הַשָּׁמַ֔יִם וְתֹ֥אכַל
אֹתְךָ֖ וְאֶת־חֲמִשֶּׁ֑יךָ וַתֵּ֤רֶד אֵשׁ־אֱלֹהִים֙ מִן־הַשָּׁמַ֔יִם
וַתֹּ֥אכַל אֹת֖וֹ וְאֶת־חֲמִשָּֽׁיו׃

- V. 11   מְהֵרָה "hastily, quickly."
- V. 12   "he responded" (קל from עני).

    וַיְדַבֵּר a פֹּעַל of דבר.

Esther 1:1–3

וַיְהִ֖י בִּימֵ֣י אֲחַשְׁוֵר֑וֹשׁ ה֣וּא אֲחַשְׁוֵר֗וֹשׁ הַמֹּלֵךְ֙ מֵהֹ֣דּוּ וְעַד־
כּ֔וּשׁ שֶׁ֛בַע וְעֶשְׂרִ֥ים וּמֵאָ֖ה מְדִינָֽה׃ 2 בַּיָּמִ֖ים הָהֵ֑ם כְּשֶׁ֣בֶת ׀ הַמֶּ֣לֶךְ
אֲחַשְׁוֵר֗וֹשׁ עַ֚ל כִּסֵּ֣א מַלְכוּת֔וֹ אֲשֶׁ֖ר בְּשׁוּשַׁ֥ן הַבִּירָֽה׃ 3 בִּשְׁנַ֤ת שָׁלוֹשׁ֙
לְמָלְכ֔וֹ עָשָׂ֣ה מִשְׁתֶּ֔ה לְכָל־שָׂרָ֖יו וַעֲבָדָ֑יו

- V. 1   וַיְהִי "it was" (קל converted imperfect of היי). This very often should not be translated, because it merely indicates that the following narrative is transpiring in the past. וְהָיָה is used in a similar fashion for actions transpiring in the future.

    מְדִינָה "province" (contrast MIH "state"). This word, found only in LBH, is a loanword from Aramaic.

    בִּירָה "citadel" (contrast MIH "capital"). This word, found only in LBH, is a loanword from Akkadian, via Aramaic.

- V. 3   מִשְׁתֶּה "a party," where drinking takes place. (The root of מִשְׁתֶּה is שתי, "to drink.")

22 The קַל of Hollow Verbs, ל״א and ל״י Verbs, and Geminates

This chapter presents common defective verbs, whose paradigms must be memorized with care. Hollow verbs contain two consonants separated by one long vowel, typically marked with either a וָו (for example, יָקוּם, "he will arise") or a יֹוד (for example, יָשִׂים, "he will place"). These verbs are often called ע״ו and ע״י verbs, as if the middle consonant were וָו or יֹוד; this is not, however, accurate for BH—וָו and יֹוד appear as vowel letters for long vowels in the imperfect and related forms, including the imperative, cohortative, and jussive. (Several verbs are conjugated as both ע״ו and ע״י.) ל״א verbs are relatively straightforward; the main difference from the paradigm of healthy (or third guttural) verbs is that the final אָלֶף is usually silent, and thus the previous vowel may be lengthened because the final syllable is not closed (יִמְצָא || יִכְבַּד). ל״י verbs are more complex; the etymologically final יֹוד is usually not retained, and its loss results in dramatic changes to the verb. In many forms, including the 3ms perfect and imperfect, the final יֹוד is deleted and is replaced by the final vowel letter הָא (for example, בָּנָה and יִבְנֶה). For this reason, many grammars call these verbs ל״ה, but this, too, is imprecise.

Geminates are roots in which the second and third root letter are identical, like סבב. These are also called ע״ע, because עַיִן הַפֹּעַל is repeated. Depending on the form, both consonants may appear separately (for example, 3ms perfect, סָבַב), may coalesce and carry a דָּגֵשׁ חָזָק (for example, perfect 2ms, סַבּוֹתָ), or may be reduced to a single letter (for example, 3ms imperfect יָסֹב). Sometimes the first root letter rather than the second may be geminated (for example, another form of the 3ms imperfect of סבב is יִסֹּב), in which case the conjugated verb can be easily confused with a פ״נ verb.

The Perfect and the Converted Perfect

The conjugation of the perfect and converted perfect appears below; after the paradigms, individual forms are explained.

The Perfect of Hollow Verbs, לא״ and ל״י Verbs, and Geminates

	Hollow active (ע״ו)	Hollow stative (ע״ו)	Hollow (ע״י)	לא״ active	לא״ stative	ל״י all	Geminate active (ע״ע)	Geminate stative (ע״ע)
	ק(ו)ם	מ(ו)ת	ש(י)מ	מצא	מלא	בני	סבב	תמם
3ms	קָם	מֵת	שָׂם	מָצָא	מָלֵא	בָּנָה	סָבַב	תַּם
3fs	קָ֫מָה	מֵ֫תָה	שָׂ֫מָה	מָצְאָה	מָלְאָה	בָּנְתָה	סָבְבָה	תַּ֫מָּה
2ms	קַ֫מְתָּ	מַ֫תָּה¹	שַׂ֫מְתָּ	מָצָ֫אתָ	מָלֵ֫אתָ	בָּנִ֫יתָ	סַבּ֫וֹתָ	
2fs	קַמְתְּ		שַׂמְתְּ	מָצָאת	מָלֵאת	בָּנִית	סַבּוֹת	
1cs	קַ֫מְתִּי	מַ֫תִּי	שַׂ֫מְתִּי	מָצָ֫אתִי	מָלֵ֫אתִי	בָּנִ֫יתִי	סַבּ֫וֹתִי	
3p	קָ֫מוּ	מֵ֫תוּ	שָׂ֫מוּ	מָצְאוּ	מָלְאוּ	בָּנוּ	סָבְבוּ	תַּ֫מּוּ
2mp	קַמְתֶּם		שַׂמְתֶּם	מְצָאתֶם	מְלֵאתֶם	בְּנִיתֶם	סַבּוֹתֶם	
2fp						בְּנִיתֶן		
1cp	קַ֫מְנוּ	מַ֫תְנוּ	שַׂ֫מְנוּ	מָצָ֫אנוּ	מָלֵ֫אנוּ	בָּנִ֫ינוּ	סַבּ֫וֹנוּ	

In hollow verbs, the suffixes are the same as the typical perfect suffixes, but the base to which they are added is biliteral rather than triliteral. In active verbs, the base is either קָם, for the third person, or קַם, for the first and second person. In stative verbs, the base has a צֵרִי in the third person, which becomes a פַּתַח in the first and second person (contrast healthy verbs, 3ms כָּבֵד but 1cs כָּבַ֫דְתִּי). It is important to remember that in all cases except the 2p, when heavy suffixes are added, the accent is penultimate, as in קָ֫מָה, "she stood"; this is in contrast to the fs active participle קָמָה. Forms like קָם are ambiguous—context usually determines whether they should be parsed as 3ms perfects or as ms active participles.

---

1. In this form, as well as the following מַ֫תִּי, the תָּ has a דָּגֵשׁ חָזָק because it incorporates both the final root letter and the initial letter of the suffix (*מַתְתִּי > מַ֫תִּי).

The conjugation of the ל"א verbs is straightforward. They are identical to healthy verbs, with three exceptions:

(1) In both active and stative verbs, the syllable before the suffix is open, so if the suffix begins with a תָּ, it does not take a דָּגֵשׁ קַל (compare מָצָאתִי‖כָּתַבְתִּי).

(2) As a result of vocalic lengthening, active verbs have a קָמֵץ under the second root letter (for example, מָצָאנוּ—compensatory lengthening); in the 3fs and 3p, it is subject to pretonic reduction (מָצְאוּ > [כָּתְבוּ‖מָצָאוּ*]).

(3) Stative verbs retain their characteristic e-vowel throughout because it is in an open syllable (כָּבַדְתִּי‖מָלֵאתָ כָּבֵד‖מָלֵא); in the 3fs and 3p this צֵרִי is subject to pretonic reduction (מָלְאָה > מָלֵאָה*), as in regular verbs (כָּתְבָה > כָּתֵבָה*).[2]

It is impossible to understand the forms of ל"י verbs fully without a solid grounding in historical Hebrew grammar. All ל"י verbs, whether active or stative, are conjugated in the same way. In the first and second person, the typical verbal suffixes are added to the base בָּנִי־; the קָמֵץ is subject to propretonic reduction before the heavy suffixes in the 2p. The i- vowel in these forms is a remnant of the original final יוֹד; this יוֹד disappears in the third-person forms, בָּנָה (ms), בָּנְתָה (fs), and בָּנוּ (mp). The accent in these ל"י verbs is penultimate only in the 2ms, 1cs, and 1cp, as in the healthy verbs; otherwise, it is ultimate. Thus if a verb has the form קָ☐וּ and its accent is ultimate, it is a ל"י verb (for example, בָּנוּ, from בני), while if it has penultimate stress, it is a hollow verb (שָׁ֫מוּ, from שׂ[י]מ).

In active geminate verbs (like סבב), a distinction should be made between the third person and other forms. In the third person, the verb is typically conjugated like healthy verbs; its doubled letter is expressed twice. The initial vowel is קָמֵץ, as in healthy verbs (for example, כָּתַב). The only difference is in the 3fs and 3p. Instead of a שְׁוָא under the second root radical (כָּתְבָה), we often find a חֲטַף פַּתַח (סָבֲבָה); this may be a convention that tells the reader that the שְׁוָא is a שְׁוָא נָע, and therefore this חֲטַף פַּתַח should be pronounced as a שְׁוָא נָע rather than as a פַּ֫תַח. In the second and first persons, the doubling coalesces, and the base to which suffixes are added is סַבּוֹ־. This base is accented (for example, סַבּ֫וֹתָ) except when a heavy suffix is added (סַבּוֹתֶם). The first syllable is now closed, so it is vocalized with a פַּתַח, a short vowel. The חוֹלֶם (וֹ) that links the base (סַבּ) from the verbal suffixes is sometimes called a linking vowel because of its function.

As the chart indicates, stative geminate verbs (for example, תמם) are poorly attested in the perfect. The doubled consonant never expresses itself in this form with all three root letters appearing, and the base is תַמֹ־; in the 3ms, however, when the doubling (דָּגֵשׁ חָזָק) cannot be expressed because no vowel follows it, we have the form תַּם. The פַּ֫תַח of this form distinguishes it from the קָמֵץ of hollow verbs, like קָם. It is important to remember this dis-

---

2. Reminder: Philippi's law (p. 179) functions only in *closed* accented syllables.

tinction in order to look up verbs under the proper root. In other forms, it is important to notice the דָּגֵשׁ חָזָק because it signifies that the verb is a geminate; for example, קַלּוּ, with the דָּגֵשׁ חָזָק, would be looked up under קלל, while גָּלוּ has גלי as its root (though the lexica would list it under גלה, as a לה״ root).

Verbs in the converted perfect are constructed as expected, with the following main exception: the stress of 1cs and 2ms לא״ and ל״ה verbs often does not become ultimate; we thus have, for example, וְעָשִׂיתָ in contrast to וְכָתַבְתָּ. (This is because the accented syllable is open, so it retains the stress.)

The Imperfect and the Converted Imperfect

The conjugation of the various imperfects appears below; individual forms are explained after the paradigms.

The Imperfect of Hollow Verbs, ל״א and ל״ה Verbs, and Geminates

	Hollow (ע״ו)	Hollow (ע״י)	ל״א all	ל״ה all	Geminate active (ע״ע)		Geminate stative (ע״ע)
	ק(ו)מ	שׂ(י)מ	מצא	בני	סבב	סבב	קלל
3ms	יָקוּם	יָשִׂים	יִמְצָא	יִבְנֶה	יָסֹב	יִסֹּב	יֵקַל
3fs	תָּקוּם	תָּשִׂים	תִּמְצָא	תִּבְנֶה	תָּסֹב	תִּסֹּב	תֵּקַל
2ms	תָּקוּם	תָּשִׂים	תִּמְצָא	תִּבְנֶה	תָּסֹב	תִּסֹּב	תֵּקַל
2fs	תָּקוּמִי	תָּשִׂימִי	תִּמְצְאִי	תִּבְנִי	תָּסֹבִּי	תִּסֹּבִי	תֵּקַלִּי
1cs	אָקוּם	אָשִׂים	אֶמְצָא	אֶבְנֶה	אָסֹב	אֶסֹּב	אֵקַל
3mp	יָקוּמוּ	יָשִׂימוּ	יִמְצְאוּ	יִבְנוּ	יָסֹבּוּ	יִסֹּבוּ	יֵקַלּוּ
3fp	תְּקוּמֶינָה	תְּשִׂימֶנָה	תִּמְצֶאנָה	תִּבְנֶינָה		תְּסֻבֶּינָה	
2mp	תָּקוּמוּ	תָּשִׂימוּ	תִּמְצְאוּ	תִּבְנוּ	תָּסֹבּוּ	תִּסֹּבוּ	תֵּקַלּוּ
2fp	תְּקוּמֶינָה	תְּשִׂימֶנָה	תִּמְצֶאנָה	תִּבְנֶינָה			
1cp	נָקוּם	נָשִׂים	נִמְצָא	נִבְנֶה	נָסֹב	נִסֹּב	נֵקַל

Very few hollow verbs are conjugated as statives; the most common is בּ(וֹ)שׁ, as in יֵבוֹשׁ, "he will be ashamed." In most cases, it is immaterial whether the verb is active or stative; all that matters is its middle vowel. Thus the stative מ(וֹ)ת would be conjugated the same way as the active ק(וּ)ם. Verbs that are middle *u* often have a וָ as a *mater lectionis*, while those that are middle *i* often have a יוֹד as a *mater*. (The forms may also be written defectively—for example, as יָקֻם as well as יָקוּם.) The verbal prefix is a קָמֵץ, which becomes שְׁוָא in the first person through propretonic reduction. The expected suffixes are appended to the root. The only exception to this is the second person plural, where there is often a linking vowel (יִ֭) between the verbal root and the suffix, as in תְּקוּמֶ֫ינָה. Alongside forms like תְּקוּמֶ֫ינָה, however, we also find forms like תָּקֹ֫מְנָה that lack a linking vowel. (Note the slight change of vowel quality from *u* to *ō*.)

Active and stative לא״ verbs share a common conjugation, which is similar to the stative healthy verbs. But there are two exceptions: the vowel preceding the אָלֶף is lengthened to a קָמֵץ (יְכַבַּד || יִמְלָא, יִמְצָא) and the second-person forms are תִּמְצֶ֫אנָה and תִּמְלֶ֫אנָה. In contrast, the conjugation of ל״י is much less predictable and must be memorized.

Active geminates are conjugated in two ways:

(1) The geminated consonant is doubled only in cases where a vocalic suffix is added to it, as in the 2fs תָּסֹ֫בִּי. Otherwise, the gemination does not show, and the forms are similar to hollow verbs, with a קָמֵץ under the prefix; yet in contrast to the hollow verbs, the geminates have *o* as a theme vowel (for example, נָסֹב [from סבב]; compare נָקוּם [from ק(וּ)ם]).

(2) The gemination may be moved backward to the initial root letter, resulting in forms like תִּסֹּב. Stative verbs follow the vocalic pattern of יֵקַל rather than יָסֹב; they, too, may also be conjugated by moving the gemination backward.

Many of these imperfects change form when they appear as converted imperfects. The ל״א verbs and geminates are largely unchanged, but the hollow and ל״י verbs go through major changes in the 3ms, 3fs, and 2ms. The hollow verb's accent becomes penultimate and the middle vowel is reduced: in the case of o-class verbs, it is reduced to a קָמֵץ קָטָן, while in i-class verbs, it becomes a סֶגוֹל. (At pauses, the accent does not retract, so this reduction does not take place.) Thus we find forms like וַיָּ֫שָׁב (from שׁ(וּ)ב; compare יָשׁוּב) and וַתָּ֫קָם (from ק(וּ)ם; compare יָקוּם), both with a קָמֵץ קָטָן, and וַיָּ֫שֶׂם (from שׂ(י)ם; compare יָשִׂים). In the case of ל״י verbs, in the 3ms, 3fs, and 2ms, the final syllable (מַ֑ה) is dropped, which would result in difficult-to-pronounce forms like וַיִּ֫בְןְ*. These forms are like segholate (nouns) in that they (historically) ended with a doubled consonant. As we have seen with the segholates, helping vowels may be inserted to break up a consonant cluster. These vowels are not fully predictable, but the most common patterns are seen in וַיִּ֫בֶן and וַיֵּ֫שְׁתְּ. If the second vowel is a guttural, a double פַּתָח is inserted, as in the following common ל״ה second guttural verbs: וַיַּ֫עַשׂ (from עשׂי; compare יַעֲשֶׂה), וַיַּ֫עַל (from עלי; compare יַעֲלֶה), וַיַּ֫עַן (from עני; compare יַעֲנֶה), and וַתַּ֫הַר (from הרי). These converted imperfect forms are very common and should be memorized with care.

The Jussive, the Imperative, and the Cohortative

The jussive forms are similar to the converted imperfects without a prefixed וַ. In other words, with ל״א verbs and geminates the jussive is identical to the imperfect form, while, in hollow and ל״ה verbs, the verb is shortened. The jussive of ק(ו)ם is יָקֵם and of שׂ(י)ם is יָשֵׂם, as in 1 Samuel 2:20, יָשֵׂם֩ יְהוָ֨ה לְךָ֥ זֶ֛רַע מִן־הָאִשָּׁ֥ה הַזֹּ֖את, "May YHWH give you a descendent from this woman." In ל״ה verbs we encounter the same shortened (or "apocopated") forms that we have in the converted imperfect, as in יְכַל (from כלי, to "end" or "waste away"; the imperfect is יִכְלֶה), or יַ֫עַל as in Exodus 10:12, נְטֵ֨ה יָדְךָ֜ עַל־אֶ֤רֶץ מִצְרַ֨יִם֙ בָּֽאַרְבֶּ֔ה וְיַ֖עַל עַל־אֶ֣רֶץ מִצְרָ֑יִם, "Extend your hand over the land of Egypt for the locusts, so they may come up over the land of Egypt" (the imperfect is יַעֲלֶה), or Genesis 22:12, וְאַל־תַּ֥עַשׂ ל֖וֹ מְאֻ֑מָה, "Don't do anything to him." (Reminder: the jussive is used in conjunction with אַל to negate the imperative; this form is called the prohibitive.)

With the exception of ל״א and ל״ה roots, the cohortative is formed, as expected, through the addition of ָה. For example, from שׁ(ו)ב we have אָשׁ֫וּבָה (note the penultimate stress), and from שׂ(י)ם we have אָשִׂ֫ימָה, as in the famous verse in Deuteronomy 17:14, אָשִׂ֤ימָה עָלַי֙ מֶ֔לֶךְ כְּכָל־הַגּוֹיִ֖ם אֲשֶׁ֥ר סְבִיבֹתָֽי׃, "Let me place a king over me like all the nations that surround me." In ל״א and ל״ה roots no final ָה is added, so the cohortative is identical in form to the imperfect, and context alone determines whether a verb should be translated as a cohortative. For example, in Genesis 11:4, הָ֣בָה ׀ נִבְנֶה־לָּ֣נוּ עִ֗יר, "Come, let's build a city for ourselves," context suggests that נִבְנֶה should be translated as a cohortative, though its form is identical to the imperfect.

The imperatives may typically be seen as shortened forms of the imperfects, as the following chart notes.

	Hollow (ע״ו)	Hollow (ע״י)	ל״א all	ל״ה all	Geminate (ע״ע)
	ק(ו)מ	שׁ(י)מ	מצא	בני	סבב
2ms	קוּם	שִׂים	מְצָא	בְּנֵה	סֹב
2fs	קוּמִי	שִׂימִי	מִצְאִי	בְּנִי	סֹבִּי
2mp	קוּמוּ	שִׂימוּ	מִצְאוּ	בְּנוּ	סֹבּוּ
2fp	קְמֶנָה		מְצֶאנָה	בְּנֶינָה	

The Imperative of Hollow Verbs, ל״א and ל״ה Verbs, and Geminates

The only unexpected form is the ms imperative of ל״ה verbs, where we have בְּנֵה instead of the expected *בְּנֶה.

The Participles

The active participles are illustrated below.

Active Participles of Hollow Verbs, ל״א and ל״ה Verbs, and Geminates

	Hollow (ע״ו)	Hollow (ע״י)	ל״א all	ל״ה all	Geminate (ע״ע)
	ק(ו)מ	שׁ(י)מ	מצא	בני	סבב
ms	קָם	שָׂם	מֹצֵא	בֹּנֶה	סֹבֵב
fs	קָמָה[3]	שָׂמָה[4]	מֹצֵאת	בֹּנָה	סֹבֶבֶת
mp	קָמִים	שָׂמִים	מֹצְאִים	בֹּנִים	סֹבְבִים
fp	קָמוֹת	שָׂמוֹת	מֹצְאוֹת	בֹּנוֹת	סֹבְבוֹת

3. Contrast the perfect קָמָה.
4. Contrast the perfect שָׂמָה.

Passive participles of hollow verbs are rare. They are regular in ל״א and geminate verbs (for example, שָׁנוּא and בָּלוּל). In ל״י verbs, the etymologically original יוֹד is retained, yielding the following forms: בָּנוּי, בְּנוּיָה, בְּנוּיִם, and בְּנוּיוֹת.

The Infinitives

In the infinitive construct of hollow verbs, the long vowel is retained, so we have, for example, קוּם and שִׁית. (Exceptionally, the infinitive construct of שׂ[י]ם is שׂוּם.) These are identical to the ms imperative, but context will determine whether one of these forms is an imperative or an infinitive construct. (Likewise, in most other verbs too, the ms imperative and the infinitive construct are identical, and context must be used to distinguish between them.) When suffixes are added to these forms of the infinitive construct, the suffixes are accented; we thus have the opposition between קוּמִי, "my arising", an infinitive construct plus 1cs suffix, with ultimate stress, in contrast to קוּמִי, "arise!" a fs imperative, with penultimate stress.

The infinitive construct of ל״א verbs is regular (for example, מְצֹא); the vowel may be moved backward and be expressed with a קָמֶץ קָטָן when suffixes are added, as in מָצְאִי, "my finding." (Contrast the imperative מִצְאִי, "find!") ל״י verbs form the infinitive construct with the form ◌◌וֹת, as in בְּנוֹת, "building of"; this ending remains unchanged when suffixes are added (for example, בְּנוֹתִי, "my building" or "when I built" [|| כָּתְבִי]), or with a first guttural, עֲשׂוֹתָהּ, her doing). Geminates usually take the form ◌◌, as in Deuteronomy 2:14, עַד־תֹּם כָּל־הַדּוֹר, "until the perishing of the generation," literally "until the perishing of the entire generation," but better translated as "until the entire generation perished." With a suffix, the gemination reasserts itself, and the vowel is expressed as a קִבּוּץ, as in Deuteronomy 31:30, דִּבְרֵי הַשִּׁירָה הַזֹּאת עַד תֻּמָּם, "the words of this song until their end(ing)."

The infinitive absolute takes the following forms:

Hollow verbs: קוֹם and שׂוֹם, as in Deuteronomy 17:15, שׂוֹם תָּשִׂים עָלֶיךָ מֶלֶךְ, "You shall certainly place a king over you."
ל״א verbs: מָצוֹא (regular).
ל״י verbs: גָּלֹה as in Amos 5:5, כִּי הַגִּלְגָּל גָּלֹה יִגְלֶה, "for Gilgal will most certainly be exiled."
Geminate verbs: סָבוֹב (regular).

Vocabulary for chapter 22

בזז	plunder	(בָּזַז בֹּזֵז יָבֹז בֹּז)
בזי	despise	(בָּזָה בֹּזֶה יִבְזֶה lacking)
בני	to build	(בָּנָה בֹּנֶה יִבְנֶה בְּנֵה)
ברא	to create	(בָּרָא בֹּרֵא יִבְרָא בְּרָא)
ג(י)ל	to rejoice	(גָּל יָגִיל גִּיל lacking)
דמם	to be silent	(דַּם יִדֹּם דֹּם lacking)
זני	to be or act as a whore (also used metaphorically, of abandoning YHWH) (זָנָה זֹנֶה יִזְנֶה lacking)
ח(י)ל/ח(ו)ל	to writhe	(חָל יָחִיל חִיל rare)
חתת	to be shattered, dismayed	(חַת יֵחַת חֹת lacking)
כלי	to be finished, cease	(כָּלָה lacking יִכְלֶה lacking)
ל(י)נ/ל(ו)נ	to stay overnight	(לָן לָן יָלִין לִין)
מ(ו)ט	to totter	(מָט מָט יָמוּט lacking)
מ(ו)ת	to die	(מֵת מֵת יָמוּת מוֹת)
מלא	to be full	(מָלֵא מָלֵא יִמְלָא מְלָא)
נ(ו)ס	to flee	(נָס נָס יָנוּס נוּס)
סבב	to turn, to go around	(סָבַב סוֹבֵב יָסֹב סֹב or יָסֹב סֹב)
ע(ו)פ	to fly	(עָף עָף יָעוּף lacking)
פ(ו)צ	to be scattered	(יָפוּץ פּוּץ lacking lacking)
פרי	to be fruitful	(פָּרָה פֹּרֶה יִפְרֶה פְּרֵה)
צפי	to keep watch	(צָפָה יִצְפֶּה lacking lacking)
צרר	to show hostility toward	(צָרַר צֹרֵר יָצֹר lacking)
קלל	to be light	(קַל יֵקַל lacking lacking)
קני	to purchase	(קָנָה קֹנֶה יִקְנֶה קְנֵה)
ר(י)ב	to fight, engage in a legal battle	(רָב רָב יָרִיב רִיב)

רנן	to cry out (almost always in joy)	(רָן יָרֹן lacking lacking)
רעע	to be bad	(רַע lacking יֵרַע lacking)
רפא	to heal	(רָפָא רֹפֵא יִרְפָּא רְפֹא)
רצי	to be pleased (contrast MIH, want)	(רָצָה רֹצֶה יִרְצֶה רְצֵה)
שבי	to capture	(שָׁבָה שֹׁבֶה יִשְׁבֶּה שְׁבֵה)
ש(י)ר	to sing	(שָׁר שָׁר יָשִׁיר שִׁיר)
ש(י)ת	to place	(שָׁת יָשִׁית שִׁית lacking)
שמם	to be desolated, appalled	(שָׁמַם שׁוֹמֵם יִשֹּׁם שֹׁם)
תלי	to hang	(תָּלָה תֹּלֶה יִתְלֶה תְּלֵה)
תמם	to be complete	(lacking תֹּם יִתֹּם lacking)

TRANSLATION TIP #4

Be sure to distinguish between different classes of defective verbs.

Genesis 32:7 וַיָּשֻׁ֫בוּ הַמַּלְאָכִים אֶל־יַעֲקֹב

The initial verb וַיָּשֻׁ֫בוּ has as its root שׁ(ו)ב, not ישׁב. The initial יוֹד is the prefix of the imperfect, not a root letter. The spelling is *defective* (חָסֵר), but the o-class vowel of the hollow root is still visible (שֻׁ). The קַל converted imperfect from ישׁב would be וַיֵּשְׁבוּ. In addition, although biblical מַלְאָךְ may mean either a "(human) messenger" or a "divine messenger" ("angel"), in this case, context supports the former. Thus, this should be translated "The messengers returned to Jacob," not "The angels sat on Jacob."

THE קל OF HOLLOW VERBS, ל״א AND ל״י VERBS, AND GEMINATES

Exercises for chapter 22

1. Identify the forms in each pair, translate them, and explain the phonological process that causes the vocalization of the second word in the pair to differ from the first.

שָׁפַט-סָר
רְצָחָתֶם-בְּרָאתֶם
קִבּוּץ-קְנוֹת
מְשַׁחַת-סַבּוֹת
יִטְהַר-יִטְמָא
חֹשְׁבִים-צֹרְרִים

2. Write out the following conjugations; for the perfect and imperfect, be sure to start with the 3ms form:

In the perfect, imperfect, and imperative: קלל צפי מלא קרא שׁ(י)ר מ(ו)ת ר(ו)מ

In the active and passive participle, infinitive absolute, and infinitive construct:
דמם רפא שׁתי ר(י)ב נ(ו)ס

THE קל OF HOLLOW VERBS, לא AND לי VERBS, AND GEMINATES

3. Using the chart below, parse the following verbs; be sure to indicate ambiguities:

Verb	Root	"Tense"	Person	Gender	Number	Other	Translation
נָס							
יִדְמוּ							
רְבוּ							
רִיבוּ							
תַּמּוּ							
מַתִּי							
חֵפֶן							
וַיִּגֶל							
וַיֵּשֶׁב							
כְּסוּתֶךָ							
יָשֵׂם							
גִּילִי							
שִׁיתִי							
בְּנוֹתוֹ							
רָנִּי							
וַיִּזְנוּ							
תִּרְצוּ							
פֹּרָה							
וַתֹּאכַל							
פְּדוּיֵי							
בּוֹשׁ							
וּתְפוּצֶינָה							
חִילוּ							
וַיְבַקֵּשׁ							
בָּזוּ							

4. Write in BH; for translations that may be expressed by the perfect or imperfect, give both the non-converted and converted forms:

he hung		
you (fp) healed		
he will certainly fly		
it (f) will totter		
she is plundering		
to put		
their exile/ exiling them		
fearers (m) of		
she conceived		
she had difficulty in her giving birth (= bearing)		
hung (ms)		
she is running		
she ran		
to run		
she takes delight in		
she will sojourn		
he cried		
understand! (mp)		
I will be ashamed		
my arising		
fly! (fs)		
they (m) were silent		
you (fs) found		
it (fs) is wandering		
to act as a harlot		

5. Translate the following biblical passages, parse all verbs and analyze all nouns with suffixes:

Genesis 3:4–6

4 וַיֹּאמֶר הַנָּחָשׁ אֶל־הָאִשָּׁה לֹא־מוֹת תְּמֻתוּן: 5 כִּי יֹדֵעַ אֱלֹהִים כִּי בְּיוֹם אֲכָלְכֶם מִמֶּנּוּ וְנִפְקְחוּ עֵינֵיכֶם וִהְיִיתֶם כֵּאלֹהִים יֹדְעֵי טוֹב וָרָע: 6 וַתֵּרֶא הָאִשָּׁה כִּי טוֹב הָעֵץ לְמַאֲכָל וְכִי תַאֲוָה־הוּא לָעֵינַיִם וְנֶחְמָד הָעֵץ לְהַשְׂכִּיל וַתִּקַּח מִפִּרְיוֹ וַתֹּאכַל וַתִּתֵּן גַּם־לְאִישָׁהּ עִמָּהּ וַיֹּאכַל:

V. 5 וְנִפְקְחוּ "will be opened" (נִפְעַל of פקח).

V. 6 מַאֲכָל "eating."

תַאֲוָה "thing desired" (from אוי).

וְנֶחְמָד "desirable" (נִפְעַל participle of חמד).

לְהַשְׂכִּיל "to look at (?), to teach" (הִפְעִיל infinitive of שׂכל).

Genesis 13:15–18

15 כִּי אֶת־כָּל־הָאָרֶץ אֲשֶׁר־אַתָּה רֹאֶה לְךָ אֶתְּנֶנָּה וּלְזַרְעֲךָ עַד־עוֹלָם: 16 וְשַׂמְתִּי אֶת־זַרְעֲךָ כַּעֲפַר הָאָרֶץ אֲשֶׁר | אִם־יוּכַל אִישׁ לִמְנוֹת אֶת־עֲפַר הָאָרֶץ גַּם־זַרְעֲךָ יִמָּנֶה: 17 קוּם הִתְהַלֵּךְ בָּאָרֶץ לְאָרְכָּהּ וּלְרָחְבָּהּ כִּי לְךָ אֶתְּנֶנָּה: 18 וַיֶּאֱהַל אַבְרָם וַיָּבֹא וַיֵּשֶׁב בְּאֵלֹנֵי מַמְרֵא אֲשֶׁר בְּחֶבְרוֹן וַיִּבֶן־שָׁם מִזְבֵּחַ לַיהוָה: פ

V. 15 אֶתְּנֶנָּה = אֶתֵּן אֹתָהּ.

V. 16 לִמְנוֹת from מני, "to count."

יִמָּנֶה a נִפְעַל from מני; translate as a passive.

הִתְהַלֵּךְ a הִתְפָּעֵל imperative from הלכ, "to walk throughout."

רֹחַב "width."

V. 18 וַיֶּאֱהַל "move a tent from place to place."

Genesis 21:32–34

וַיִּכְרְתוּ בְרִית בִּבְאֵר שָׁבַע וַיָּקָם אֲבִימֶלֶךְ וּפִיכֹל֙ שַׂר־צְבָאוֹ וַיָּשֻׁבוּ אֶל־אֶרֶץ פְּלִשְׁתִּים: 33 וַיִּטַּע אֶשֶׁל בִּבְאֵר שָׁבַע וַיִּקְרָא־שָׁם בְּשֵׁם יְהוָה אֵל עוֹלָם: 34 וַיָּגָר אַבְרָהָם בְּאֶרֶץ פְּלִשְׁתִּים יָמִים רַבִּים: פ

V. 33 אֶשֶׁל "tamarisk tree."

Genesis 42:23–24

23 וְהֵם֙ לֹא יָדְעוּ כִּי שֹׁמֵעַ יוֹסֵף כִּי הַמֵּלִיץ בֵּינֹתָם: 24 וַיִּסֹּב מֵעֲלֵיהֶם וַיֵּבְךְּ וַיָּשָׁב אֲלֵהֶם וַיְדַבֵּר אֲלֵהֶם וַיִּקַּח מֵאִתָּם אֶת־שִׁמְעוֹן וַיֶּאֱסֹר אֹתוֹ לְעֵינֵיהֶם:

V. 23 מֵלִיץ "intermediary, interpreter" (הִפְעִיל participle of לי[ן]צ).

Exodus 3:3–5

3 וַיֹּאמֶר מֹשֶׁה אָסֻרָה־נָּא וְאֶרְאֶה אֶת־הַמַּרְאֶה הַגָּדֹל הַזֶּה מַדּוּעַ לֹא־יִבְעַר הַסְּנֶה: 4 וַיַּרְא יְהוָה כִּי סָר לִרְאוֹת וַיִּקְרָא אֵלָיו אֱלֹהִים מִתּוֹךְ הַסְּנֶה וַיֹּאמֶר מֹשֶׁה מֹשֶׁה וַיֹּאמֶר הִנֵּנִי: 5 וַיֹּאמֶר אַל־תִּקְרַב הֲלֹם שַׁל־נְעָלֶיךָ מֵעַל רַגְלֶיךָ כִּי הַמָּקוֹם אֲשֶׁר אַתָּה עוֹמֵד עָלָיו אַדְמַת־קֹדֶשׁ הוּא:

V. 3 נָא often follows a verb; it should not be translated "please" as in MIH. Its exact function is unclear.

מַרְאֶה "sight."

סְנֶה a type of bush; it is not the generic BH word for "bush."

V. 4 וַיַּרְא converted imperfect of ראי.

V. 5 הֲלֹם "to here."

שַׁל from נשל, "to slip off."

נְעָלֶיךָ from נַעַל, "shoe."

Deuteronomy 12:27–28

27 וְעָשִׂ֤יתָ עֹלֹתֶ֙יךָ֙ הַבָּשָׂ֣ר וְהַדָּ֔ם עַל־מִזְבַּ֖ח יְהוָ֣ה אֱלֹהֶ֑יךָ
וְדַם־זְבָחֶ֗יךָ יִשָּׁפֵךְ֙ עַל־מִזְבַּח֙ יְהוָ֣ה אֱלֹהֶ֔יךָ וְהַבָּשָׂ֖ר תֹּאכֵֽל׃
28 שְׁמֹ֣ר וְשָׁמַעְתָּ֗ אֵ֚ת כָּל־הַדְּבָרִ֣ים הָאֵ֔לֶּה אֲשֶׁ֥ר אָנֹכִ֖י מְצַוֶּ֑ךָּ לְמַעַן֩
יִיטַ֨ב לְךָ֜ וּלְבָנֶ֤יךָ אַחֲרֶ֙יךָ֙ עַד־עוֹלָ֔ם כִּ֤י תַעֲשֶׂה֙ הַטּ֣וֹב וְהַיָּשָׁ֔ר בְּעֵינֵ֖י
יְהוָ֥ה אֱלֹהֶֽיךָ׃ ס

V. 27 יִשָּׁפֵךְ "shall be spilled," a נִפְעַל of שׁפך.

V. 28 מְצַוֶּךָּ "am commanding you," a פִּעֵל participle of צוי with a 2ms suffix.

Deuteronomy 21:22–23

22 וְכִֽי־יִהְיֶ֣ה בְאִ֗ישׁ חֵ֛טְא מִשְׁפַּט־מָ֖וֶת וְהוּמָ֑ת וְתָלִ֥יתָ אֹת֖וֹ עַל־עֵֽץ׃ 23 לֹא־תָלִ֨ין
נִבְלָת֜וֹ עַל־הָעֵ֗ץ כִּֽי־קָב֤וֹר תִּקְבְּרֶ֙נּוּ֙ בַּיּ֣וֹם הַה֔וּא כִּֽי־קִלְלַ֥ת אֱלֹהִ֖ים תָּל֑וּי
וְלֹ֤א תְטַמֵּא֙ אֶת־אַדְמָ֣תְךָ֔ אֲשֶׁר֙ יְהוָ֣ה אֱלֹהֶ֔יךָ נֹתֵ֥ן לְךָ֖ נַחֲלָֽה׃ ס

V. 22 וְהוּמָת "and he is killed" a הָפְעַל, from מ(ו)ת.

V. 23 תִּקְבְּרֶנּוּ = תִּקְבֹּר אֹתוֹ.

קִלְלַת construct of קְלָלָה, "curse."

תְטַמֵּא a פִּעֵל of טמא in the sense of "make impure." (The קַל is stative, "to be impure.")

1 Samuel 14:45

45 וַיֹּ֨אמֶר הָעָ֜ם אֶל־שָׁא֗וּל הֲֽיוֹנָתָ֤ן ׀ יָמוּת֙ אֲשֶׁ֣ר עָ֠שָׂה הַיְשׁוּעָ֨ה הַגְּדוֹלָ֣ה
הַזֹּאת֮ בְּיִשְׂרָאֵל֒ חָלִ֗ילָה חַי־יְהוָה֙ אִם־יִפֹּ֞ל מִשַּׂעֲרַ֤ת רֹאשׁוֹ֙ אַ֔רְצָה כִּֽי־
עִם־אֱלֹהִ֖ים עָשָׂ֣ה הַיּ֣וֹם הַזֶּ֑ה וַיִּפְדּ֧וּ הָעָ֛ם אֶת־יוֹנָתָ֖ן וְלֹא־מֵֽת׃ ס

חָלִילָה "far be it!"

חַי־יְהוָה אִם an oath formula. The construct חַי־יְהוָה is "by YHWH's life," while אִם here functions as a negative, introducing the contents of the oath.

מִשַּׂעֲרַת from שַׂעֲרָה, "a single hair."

1 Kings 8:48

48 וְשָׁ֣בוּ אֵלֶ֗יךָ בְּכָל־לְבָבָם֙ וּבְכָל־נַפְשָׁ֔ם בְּאֶ֥רֶץ אֹיְבֵיהֶ֖ם אֲשֶׁר־שָׁב֣וּ אֹתָ֑ם
וְהִֽתְפַּלְל֣וּ אֵלֶ֗יךָ דֶּ֤רֶךְ אַרְצָם֙ אֲשֶׁ֣ר נָתַ֣תָּה לַאֲבוֹתָ֔ם הָעִיר֙ אֲשֶׁ֣ר בָּחַ֔רְתָּ
וְהַבַּ֖יִת אֲשֶׁר־בָּנִ֥יתָ [בָּנִ֖יתִי] לִשְׁמֶֽךָ׃

וְהִתְפַּלְלוּ a הִתְפָּעֵל of פלל, "to pray."

1 Kings 21:14–16

14 וַיִּשְׁלְח֖וּ אֶל־אִיזֶ֣בֶל לֵאמֹ֑ר סֻקַּ֥ל נָב֖וֹת וַיָּמֹֽת׃ 15 וַֽיְהִי֙ כִּשְׁמֹ֣עַ
אִיזֶ֔בֶל כִּֽי־סֻקַּ֥ל נָב֖וֹת וַיָּמֹ֑ת וַתֹּ֨אמֶר אִיזֶ֜בֶל אֶל־אַחְאָ֗ב ק֣וּם רֵ֞שׁ
אֶת־כֶּ֣רֶם ׀ נָב֣וֹת הַיִּזְרְעֵאלִ֗י אֲשֶׁ֤ר מֵאֵן֙ לָתֶת־לְךָ֣ בְכֶ֔סֶף כִּ֣י אֵ֥ין נָב֛וֹת
חַ֖י כִּי־מֵֽת׃ 16 וַיְהִ֛י כִּשְׁמֹ֥עַ אַחְאָ֖ב כִּ֣י מֵ֣ת נָב֑וֹת וַיָּ֣קָם אַחְאָ֗ב לָרֶ֛דֶת
אֶל־כֶּ֛רֶם נָב֥וֹת הַיִּזְרְעֵאלִ֖י לְרִשְׁתּֽוֹ׃

V.14   סֻקַּל "was stoned," a qal passive of סקל (see p. 270).

V.15   מֵאֵן "refused," a פִּעֵל perfect of מאן.

Jeremiah 32:8–9

8 וַיָּבֹ֣א אֵ֠לַי חֲנַמְאֵ֨ל בֶּן־דֹּדִ֜י כִּדְבַ֣ר יְהוָה֮
אֶל־חֲצַ֣ר הַמַּטָּרָה֒ וַיֹּ֣אמֶר אֵלַ֡י קְנֵ֣ה נָ֠א אֶת־שָׂדִ֨י אֲשֶׁר־בַּעֲנָת֜וֹת אֲשֶׁ֣ר ׀
בְּאֶ֣רֶץ בִּנְיָמִ֗ין כִּֽי־לְךָ֞ מִשְׁפַּ֧ט הַיְרֻשָּׁ֛ה וּלְךָ֥ הַגְּאֻלָּ֖ה קְנֵה־לָ֑ךְ וָאֵדַ֕ע
כִּ֥י דְבַר־יְהוָ֖ה הֽוּא׃ 9 וָאֶקְנֶה֙ אֶת־הַשָּׂדֶ֔ה מֵאֵ֛ת חֲנַמְאֵ֥ל בֶּן־דֹּדִ֖י אֲשֶׁ֣ר
בַּעֲנָת֑וֹת וָאֶשְׁקֲלָה־לּוֹ֙ אֶת־הַכֶּ֔סֶף שִׁבְעָ֥ה שְׁקָלִ֖ים וַעֲשָׂרָ֥ה הַכָּֽסֶף׃

V. 8   דּוֹד "uncle."

    מַטָּרָה "guard."

    יְרֻשָּׁה "inheritance."

    גְּאֻלָּה "redemption."

V. 9   וָאֶשְׁקֲלָה This is a cohortative form, but, in some cases—especially in LBH—cohortative forms are used where we expect imperfects, and should be translated as imperfects.

23 Combined Deficiencies and the קַל with Verbal Suffixes

Verbs with Combined Deficiencies

BH verbs, like their modern Hebrew counterparts, may be defective in more than one way. The verb עלי, for example, is first guttural as well as ל״י, ב(ו)א is both ל״א and hollow, and ידע is פ״י and third guttural. In fact, many of the most common Hebrew verbs are doubly defective or combine a deficiency with a guttural; these include: ב(ו)א, "to come"; הי״י, "to be"; ידע, "to know"; נשׂא, "to carry"; עלי, "to ascend"; עשׂי, "to do"; and ראי, "to see."

In most cases, these verbs share the characteristics of the two verb types that they belong to. The paradigm of נשׂא may be predicted, for example, by combining features of פ״נ and ל״א verbs. Thus in the imperfect 3ms it is יִשָּׂא—the final vowel is a קָמֶץ, as in ל״א verbs (compare יִמְצָא), while the initial נון is assimilated, as in פ״נ verbs (compare יִגַּשׁ). Similarly, its ms imperative is שָׂא—like stative פ״נ verbs, the initial נון of the root is absent (compare גַּשׁ), while like ל״א verbs, its final vowel is a קָמֶץ (compare מְצָא).

The same basic principle applies to verbs that are first guttural and ל״י like עלי and עשׂי. The 3ms imperfect is יַעֲלֶה, with the final סֶה of ל״י verbs (compare יִבְנֶה), and with the חֲטָף פַּתַח under the first root letter and the פַּתַח as the prefix vowels, as in first gutturals (compare יַעֲמֹד). The imperative is עֲלֵה, sharing its second half with בְּנֵה and its first half with עֲמֹד. The 2mp imperfect would be עֲשִׂיתֶם—the first syllable is similar to עֲמַדְתֶּם, while the second is like בְּנִיתֶם. The jussive and converted imperfect are shortened, like the ל״י verb יִבֶן; because gutturals prefer the פַּתַח, the jussive is יַעַשׂ, and the converted imperfect is וַיַּעַשׂ.

ידע is similar. The 3ms perfect is יָדַע, as expected, because both פ״י verbs and third gutturals are regular in the perfect (for example, שָׁלַח and יָרַד). The imperfect is יֵדַע, similar in its first syllable to יֵרֵד and in its second to יִשְׁלַח. The imperative is דַּע—it is monosyllabic like פ״נ verbs and vocalized with a פַּתַח like third gutturals. יצא follows ל״א verbs in the perfect (יָצָא || מָצָא), and in the imperfect it follows פ״י, so, for example, it has the 3ms imperfect of יֵצֵא (|| יֵרֵד). Its ms imperative is צֵא, and its infinitive construct is צֵאת (< *צֵאֶת).

The verb רא״י follows the ל״ה paradigms. In the 3ms perfect, for example, it is רָאָה (|| בָּנָה), and in the imperfect it is יִרְאֶה (|| יִבְנֶה). The converted imperfect forms are not entirely as expected; we typically have וָאֵרֶא, וַתֵּרֶא and וַיַּרְא.

The verb הי״י is irregular—it is first guttural, has a middle יוֹד (which is, however, consonantal—this is not a hollow verb), and is ל״ה. The verb חי״י is similar. Some of the perfect forms are as expected—for example, הָיָה || בָּנָה and הָיִינוּ || בָּנִינוּ. The 3ms of חי״י, however, is usually חַי, and the 2mp form of הי״י is הֱיִיתֶם (|| בְּנִיתֶם), but the שְׁוָא is replaced with a חֲטָף due to the guttural). The חֲטַף סֶגוֹל is also found in the masculine imperatives, where we have הֱיֵה and הֱיוּ (but חֲיִי) and in the infinitive construct, הֱיוֹת. In the imperfect, the guttural does not influence the quality of the initial vowels as expected, so we have, for example, יִהְיֶה (|| יִבְנֶה, in contrast to יַעֲמֹד). The jussive is יְהִי (as in Genesis 1:2, יְהִי אוֹר, "let there be light"); the converted imperfect takes an identical form, as in Genesis 1:2, וַיְהִי־אוֹר, "and there was light." (Note how the converted imperfect is not followed by a דָּגֵשׁ חָזָק; because the יוֹד is vocalized with a שְׁוָא; in these cases, the syllable וְיִ* is typically shortened to וַיְ. We saw this with the definite article as well; see p. 55.)

The קַל with Objective Pronominal Suffixes

Definite direct objects may be governed by verbs in three ways in BH:

(1) They may appear as nouns adjacent to the verbs, and are usually introduced with the particle אֵת, as in Deuteronomy 6:17, שָׁמוֹר תִּשְׁמְרוּן אֶת־מִצְוֺת יְהוָה אֱלֹהֵיכֶם, "you should certainly heed the commandments of YHWH your God."

(2) They may appear as objective pronominal suffixes attached directly to the verb, as in Proverbs 4:6, אַל־תַּעַזְבֶהָ וְתִשְׁמְרֶךָּ, "Do not abandon it (fs = wisdom) so it will guard you."

(3) This same notion might have also been expressed אַל תַּעֲזֹב אוֹתָהּ וְתִשְׁמֹר אוֹתְךָ, with a separate, declined pronoun. (This is similar to [1], above, with a pronoun replacing the noun.)

The pronoun referring to the same person may sometimes be directly attached to the verb and, at other times, appear as a separate element, as the following pair illustrates: וַיִּשְׁמֹר אֹתָנוּ, "he guarded us" (1 Samuel 30:23), and וַיִּשְׁמְרֵנוּ, "he guarded us" (Joshua 24:17). It is not clear whether there is a difference in meaning or style between these cases. The forms where the object suffix is directly attached to the verb are more common, and are particularly frequent in certain LBH texts.

There are special forms for object suffixes attached to verbs. These are related to, but not identical to, the forms of the pronominal suffixes attached to nouns and pronouns (see chapters 15 and 16). The object suffixes are used for verbs in the perfect, converted perfect, imperfect, converted imperfect, jussive, imperative, and cohortative; the infinitive construct and participle are nouns, and the nominal suffixes are typically added to them.

Four complications make it difficult to offer a simple paradigm for the forms of the suffixes:

(1) The forms of the suffixes are slightly different for the perfect and imperfect, as may be seen in the pair וּשְׁמָרַנִי, "he will guard me" (Genesis 28:20), with a suffix ־ַנִי, and יִשְׁמְרֵנִי, "he will guard me" (Job 29:2), with a suffix ־ֵנִי.

(2) The suffixes may also appear with an additional נוּן between the verb and the suffix, as in וְאֶשְּׁמְרֶנָּה, "so I may observe it (fs)" (Psalm 119:34). This נוּן is called the energic נוּן, and it is doubtful that the forms with the נוּן and those without it differ in meaning. The נוּן may become assimilated into the suffix, marked only by a דָּגֵשׁ חָזָק, as in Proverbs 4:6, וְתִשְׁמְרֶךָּ. (The נוּן in the first person suffix נִי is different and is not optional.)

(3) It is not sufficient to offer the forms of the suffixes alone, because their addition changes the tonic syllable and therefore affects the form of the verb to which they are attached, as may be seen by contrasting וְשָׁמַר, "he will watch," with וּשְׁמָרוֹ, "and he will watch over him" (Jeremiah 31:10). These changes are largely predictable. With the addition of the suffix ־וֹ, for example, שְׁמַרוֹ * > שְׁמָרוֹ. The initial קָמֵץ is lost by propretonic reduction, and the פַּתַח is elongated to the קָמֵץ because, as a result of the addition of the suffix, it is now found in an open unaccented syllable that prefers long vowels.

(4) The changes that transpire, and to some extent the forms of the suffixes, depend on what type of verb they are appended to. For example, the forms are quite different with ל״י verbs, as may be seen by contrasting the pair וּשְׁמָרוֹ, "and he will watch over him" (Jeremiah 31:10), and עָשָׂהוּ, "he fashioned him" (for example, Hosea 8:6).

For these reasons, three paradigms follow. The first, which offers the general forms of the suffix, is from the standard BH reference grammar, *Gesenius' Hebrew Grammar as Edited and Enlarged by the Late E. Kautzsch . . . Second English Edition . . . by A. E. Cowley* (Oxford: Oxford University Press, 1910). The second offers a chart of the "Strong Verb with Suffixes," and the third is of "Verbs ל״ה[1] with Suffixes"; these are both from Gesenius as well. Although these charts are initially difficult to use, they offer an introduction to these basic grammars.

The middle of the following chart illustrates the pronominal objective suffixes added to verbs. The personal pronouns and the possessive suffixes added to nouns are provided for comparison; this shows that the verbal object suffixes are sufficiently similar to the nominal suffixes for them to be recognized with ease.

---

1. Although these verbs are historically ל״י, and this grammar calls them ל״י verbs, most earlier grammars call them ל״ה verbs.

Pronominal Suffixes

Nominative of the Pronoun, or *Pronomen separatum*.	Accusative of the Pronoun,
	A. Simple form.
Sing. I. comm. אָנֹכִי, in pause אָנֹ֫כִי; אֲנִי, in pause אָ֫נִי *I*.	־ֵ֫נִי ; ־ֵ֫־ נִי *me*.
2. { m. אַתָּה (אַתְּ), in pause אָ֫תָּה / אַתָּה / f. אַתְּ (אַתִּי) } *thou*.	ךָ ; ךָ֫־, in pause ךָ֫־, ךָ־ / ךְ ; ךְ־ ; ךְ־, ךְ־ } *thee*.
3. { m. הוּא *he*. / f. הִיא *she*.	הוּ, וּ ; ־ֵ֫הוּ (ֹה), וֹ ; ־ֵ֫הוּ *him*. הָ ; הָ־ ; הָ־ *her (eam)*.
Plur. I. comm. אֲנַ֫חְנוּ (נַ֫חְנוּ), in pause אֲנָ֫חְנוּ (נָ֫חְנוּ) *we*.	נוּ ; ־ֵ֫נוּ ; ־ֵ֫נוּ *us*.
2. { m. אַתֶּם / f. אַתֵּ֫נָה, אַתֵּן } *you*.	כֶם ; כֶם־ / [־ֶ כֶן ; כֶן־] } *you*.
3. { m. הֵ֫מָּה, הֵם / f. הֵ֫נָּה } *they*.	(הֶם), ם ; ם־, ם־, ם־֫מוֹ* ; ם־, (ם־֫), מוֹ־֫* *them (eos)*. [הֶן], ן ; ן־,(ן־֫) ; [ן־] *them (eas)*.

COMBINED DEFICIENCIES AND THE קַל WITH VERBAL SUFFIXES

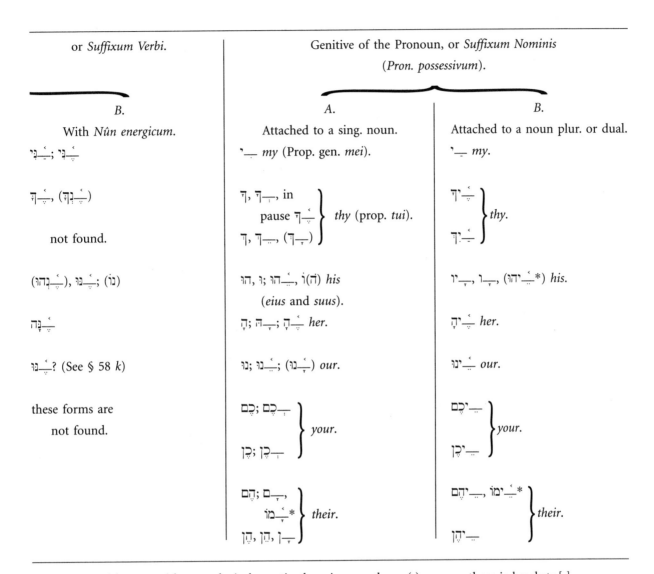

Note: Forms with an asterisk are exclusively poetic, those in parentheses ( ) are rare, those in brackets [ ] do not occur.

In the charts from Gesenius on the following pages, the person of the verb is read across and the person of the verbal suffix is read down. For example, "he killed her" is found by looking at the top line, marked *Perf. Qal* 3. *m.* [= "he"] and the fifth column over, marked "3 Sing *f.*" ["her"], namely קְטָלָהּ. "She killed him" would be found by looking at the second line, marked 3. *f.* [= "she"] and the fourth column over, marked 3 Sing. *m.* [= "him"], namely קְטָלַתּוּ or קְטָלָתְהוּ.

The Strong Verb

Suffixes		1 Sing.	2 Sing. m.	2 Sing. f.	3 Sing. m.
Perf. Qal	3. m.	{ קְטָלַ֫נִי / שְׁכָחַ֫נִי }	קְטָלְךָ	קְטָלֵךְ	{ קְטָלָ֫הוּ / קְטָלוֹ }
	3. f.	קְטָלַ֫תְנִי	קְטָלַ֫תְךָ	קְטָלַ֫תֶךְ	{ קְטָלַ֫תְהוּ / קְטָלָ֫תוּ }
	2. m.	קְטַלְתַּ֫נִי	—	—	{ קְטַלְתָּ֫הוּ / קְטַלְתּוֹ }
	2. f.	קְטַלְתִּ֫ינִי	—	—	קְטַלְתִּ֫יהוּ
	1. c.	—	קְטַלְתִּ֫יךָ	קְטַלְתִּ֫יךְ	{ קְטַלְתִּ֫יו / קְטַלְתִּ֫יהוּ }
Plur.	3. c.	קְטָל֫וּנִי	{ קְטָל֫וּךָ / אֲהֵב֫וּךָ }	קְטָל֫וּךְ	קְטָל֫וּהוּ
	2. m.	קְטַלְתּ֫וּנִי	—	—	קְטַלְתּ֫וּהוּ
	1. c.	—	קְטַלְנ֫וּךָ	קְטַלְנ֫וּךְ	קְטַלְנ֫וּהוּ
Inf. Qal		{ קָטְלִי / קָטְלֵ֫נִי }	{ כָּתְבְּךָ / קָטְלְךָ }	קָטְלֵךְ	קָטְלוֹ
Imp. Qal	2. (from an Imperf. in a)	קָטְלֵ֫נִי (שְׁמָע֫וּנִי, שְׁלָחֵ֫נִי)	—	—	קָטְלֵ֫הוּ
Impf. Qal	3. m.	{ יִקְטְלֵ֫נִי / יִלְבָּשֵׁ֫נִי }	יִקְטָלְךָ / יִלְבָּשְׁךָ	יִקְטָלֵךְ / יִלְבָּשֵׁךְ	יִקְטְלֵ֫הוּ / יִלְבָּשֵׁ֫הוּ
	3. m. with Nûn energ.	יִקְטְלֶ֫נִּי	יִקְטָלְךָ	—	יִקְטְלֶ֫נּוּ
	plur. 3. m.	יִקְטְל֫וּנִי	יִקְטְל֫וּךָ	יִקְטְל֫וּךְ	{ יִקְטְל֫וּהוּ / יִגְאָל֫וּהוּ }
Perf. Pi'ēl	3. m.	קִטְּלַ֫נִי	קִטֶּלְךָ	קִטְּלֵךְ	קִטְּלוֹ

with Suffixes

3 Sing. f.	1 plur.	2 plur. m.	2 plur. f.	3 plur. m.	3 plur. f.
קְטָלָה	קְטָלָנוּ	wanting.	wanting.	{ קְטָלָם / לְבֵשָׁם }	קְטָלָן
קְטָלַתָּה	קְטָלַתְנוּ	—	—	קְטָלָתַם	wanting.
קְטַלְתָּה	קְטַלְתָּנוּ	—	—	קְטַלְתָּם	wanting.
קְטַלְתִּיהָ	קְטַלְתִּינוּ	—	—	קְטַלְתִּים	wanting.
קְטַלְתִּיהָ	—	קְטַלְתִּיכֶם	wanting.	קְטַלְתִּים	קְטַלְתִּין
קְטָלוּהָ	קְטָלוּנוּ	wanting.	wanting.	קְטָלוּם	קְטָלוּן
wanting.	קְטַלְתּוּנוּ	—	—	wanting.	wanting.
קְטַלְנוּהָ	—	קְטַלְנוּכֶם	wanting.	קְטַלְנוּם	wanting.
קָטְלָה	קָטְלֵנוּ	{ כָּתְבְכֶם / קָטְלְכֶם }	wanting.	קָטְלָם	קָטְלָן
{ קָטְלָה / קָטְלָה }	קָטְלֵנוּ	—	—	קָטְלֵם	—
{ יִקְטְלָהּ / יִלְבָּשֶׁהָ / יִקְטְלָהּ }	{ יִקְטְלֵנוּ / יִלְבָּשֵׁנוּ }	יִקְטָלְכֶם	wanting.	יִקְטְלֵם	wanting.
יִקְטְלֶנָּה	יִקְטְלֶנּוּ	—	—	—	—
יִקְטְלוּהָ	יִקְטְלוּנוּ	יִקְטְלוּכֶם	wanting.	יִקְטְלוּם	wanting.
קָטְלָה	קָטְלֵנוּ	wanting.	wanting.	קָטְלֵם	קָטְלָן

ל״י Verbs

		1. Sing.	2. Sing. m.	2. Sing. f.
Perf. Qal.	3. m.	נָחַ֫נִי	רָאֲךָ, עָשְׂךָ	
		P. עָשָׂ֫נִי	P. קָנְךָ, עָנְךָ	
	3. f.	עָשַׂ֫תְנִי		
	2. m.	רְאִיתַ֫נִי		
		P. עֲנִיתַ֫נִי		
	2. f.	Pi. רִמִּיתִ֫נִי		
	1. c.		רְאִיתִ֫יךָ	עֲנִתִיךְ
Plur.	3. c.	עָשׂ֫וּנִי	רָא֫וּךָ	Pi. כִּסּוּךְ
	1. c.		Pi. קִוִּינ֫וּךָ	
Imper.	2. m.	נְחֵ֫נִי }		
		עֲנֵ֫נִי }		
	2. f.	Hiph. הַרְאִ֫ינִי		
Plur.	2. m.	Pi. כַּסּ֫וּנִי		
Impf.	3. m.	יִרְאֵ֫נִי	יִפְדְּךָ }	
			יַחְתְּךָ }	
	3. f.		תִּשְׁבֶּ֫ךָ	
	2. m.	תִּרְאֵ֫נִי		
	2. f.			
	1. c.		אֶרְאֶ֫ךָ	אֶעֱדֵךְ
			אֶעֱנְךָ	
Plur.	3. m.	יַעֲשׂ֫וּנִי	Pi. יִפְתּ֫וּךָ	
	2. m.	תְּצַוֻּ֫נִי		
	1. c.			

with Suffixes

3. Sing. m.	3. Sing. f.	1. Plur.	3. Plur. m.
עָשָׂהוּ	רָאָה	עָשָׂנוּ	עָשָׂם
Pi. כִּלָּהוּ	Pi. צִוַּתָּה		Hiph. הֶעֱלָתַם
Pi. כִּסִּיתוֹ	עָשִׂיתָהּ	Pi. דִּכִּיתָנוּ	עֲנִיתָם
עֲשִׂיתִיהוּ / רְאִיתִיו	רְאִיתִיהָ		רְאִיתִים
עֲשׂוּהוּ / Pi. קִוִּינֻהוּ	רָאוּהָ		שָׁבוּם
		Hiph. הֶרְאָנוּ	רְעֵם
תְּלוּהוּ			Hiph. הֲכוּם
יִרְאֵהוּ / יִלְוֵנוּ	יִרְאָהּ / יִרְאֶנָּה	Pi. יְצַוֵּנוּ	יַחְצֵם / יַעֲשֵׂם
Hiph. תַּשְׁקֵהוּ			
תַּעֲשֵׂנוּ	תַּעֲשֶׂהָ	Hiph. תַּתְעֵנוּ	תּוֹרֵם
			Pi. תְּכַסִּים
אֶרְאֶנּוּ / אֶעֱנֵהוּ	אֶעֱשֶׂנָּה		אֶפְדֵּם
Pi. יְפַתּוּהוּ	יַעֲשׂוּהָ	Pi. יְעַנּוּנוּ	
נִשָּׁקֶנּוּ	נַעֲשֶׂנָּה		תִּצּוּם

Vocabulary for chapter 23

אבי	to desire	(אָבָה אָבָה יֹאבֶה lacking)
אהב	to like, love	(אָהֵב אֹהֵב יֶאֱהַב אֱהֹב)
אפי	to bake	(אָפָה אֹפֶה יֹאפֶה אֲפֵה)
ארר	to curse	(אָרַר אֹרֵר יָאֹר אֹר)
הגי	to utter, groan, meditate	(הָגָה lacking יֶהְגֶּה lacking)
היי	to be	(הָיָה הֹוֶיה [rare] יִהְיֶה הֱיֵה)
חזה	to see, have a vision	(חָזָה חֹזֶה יֶחֱזֶה חֲזֵה)
חטא	to sin	(חָטָא חֹטֵא יֶחֱטָא lacking)
חיי	to be alive	(חַי יִחְיֶה חֲיֵה lacking)
חלי	to get/be sick	(חָלָה חֹלֶה lacking rare)
חני	to encamp	(חָנָה חֹנֶה יַחֲנֶה חֲנֵה)
חנן	to show favor	(חָנַן חֹנֵן יָחֹן חֹן)
חסי	to seek refuge	(חָסָה חֹסֶה יֶחְסֶה חֲסֵה)
חרי	to be angry	(חָרָה lacking יֶחֱרֶה lacking)
יעצ	to advise	(יָעַץ יוֹעֵץ יִיעַץ lacking)
ירי	to shoot	(יָרָה יֹרֶה יִרֶה rare)
נגע	to touch	(נָגַע נֹגֵעַ יִגַּע גַּע)
נ(ו)ח	to rest	(נָח lacking יָנוּחַ lacking)
נטי	to extend	(נָטָה נֹטֶה יִטֶּה נְטֵה)
נטע	to plant	(נָטַע נֹטֵעַ יִטַּע נְטַע)
נסע	to depart, journey	(נָסַע נֹסֵעַ יִסַּע סַע)
ע(ו)ר	to rouse oneself	(mostly imperative עוּר and participle עֵר)
עני	to answer	(עָנָה עֹנֶה יַעֲנֶה עֲנֵה)
רעי	to tend sheep	(רָעָה רֹעֶה יִרְעֶה רְעֵה)

//
Exercises for chapter 23

1. Using the chart below, parse the following verbs; be sure to indicate ambiguities:

Verb	Root	"Tense"	Person	Gender	Number	Other	Translation
וַתַּ֫הַר							
חָסוּ							
יֹאבֶה							
וַתַּ֫חַז							
יֵרַע							
יִתְעוּ							
יֶחֱרֶה							
גֵּעַת							
נָ֫חוּ							
אֶהַב							
יְהִי							
יֹאפוּ							
וִיחִי							
יֵעָצִי							
יוֹרִים							
אָאֹר							
חָלוּ							
וַיֵּט							
וַיִּ֫חָן							
סְעוּ							
חַנֹּתֵ֫נוּ							
עֵר							
עֲנוֹת							
רֹעִי							
הָגֹה							
יִפַּע							
חָטָאָה							

2. Using the charts in Gesenius, write the following forms in Hebrew:

he killed you (ms)	I killed him
you (ms) killed me	she killed them (m)
he will dress me	he will kill you (mp)
your (ms) writing	we killed her
you (p) killed him	you (fs) killed them
they forgot me	they will kill them (m)
they saw her	he made it (ms)
he will redeem you	I will do it (fs)
I will see it (ms)	they made me
I saw you (ms)	he made them (m)
you (m) will see me	

3. Complete the following chart:

Verb	Root	"Tense"	Person	Gender	Number	Other	Translation
וְאֶזְבָּחֵם							
יֹאחֲזוּךְ							
יִלְבָּשֵׁם							
יְדַעְתִּיו							
וִיחֻנֶּךָּ							
תִּתְּנוּם							
יִשָּׂאֵנוּ							
יִצְרָהּ							
מְצָאתִיו							
וַיִּרְאֶהָ							
מְצָאַתְנוּ							
וִירִשְׁתָּהּ							
כָּתְבֵם							
קָחֶנָּה							
שְׁאִלְתִּיו							
יֹאכְלֶנּוּ							
זָכְרֵנִי							
רָאֹהוּ							
יִשָּׂאֹהוּ							
רָאָהּ							
יְשַׁמֵּנִי							
נְשָׂאתִים							
וַיַּעַזְבֵנִי							
יִצְּרֵהוּ							
נְתַתִּיךָ							
מְשָׁחֲךָ							

4. Translate the following biblical passages, parse all verbs and analyze all nouns with suffixes:

Exodus 19:20

וַיֵּ֧רֶד יְהוָ֛ה עַל־הַ֥ר סִינַ֖י אֶל־רֹ֣אשׁ הָהָ֑ר
וַיִּקְרָ֨א יְהוָ֧ה לְמֹשֶׁ֛ה אֶל־רֹ֥אשׁ הָהָ֖ר וַיַּ֥עַל מֹשֶֽׁה׃

Exodus 28:43

וְהָי֨וּ עַל־אַהֲרֹ֜ן וְעַל־בָּנָ֗יו בְּבֹאָ֣ם ׀ אֶל־אֹ֣הֶל מוֹעֵ֡ד
א֣וֹ בְגִשְׁתָּ֣ם אֶל־הַמִּזְבֵּחַ֩ לְשָׁרֵ֨ת בַּקֹּ֜דֶשׁ וְלֹא־יִשְׂא֥וּ
עָוֺ֛ן וָמֵ֑תוּ חֻקַּ֥ת עוֹלָ֛ם ל֖וֹ וּלְזַרְע֥וֹ אַחֲרָֽיו׃ ס

אֹ֣הֶל מוֹעֵ֡ד, "the tent of meeting"; מוֹעֵד is from יעד (historically וער), "to meet."

שָׁרֵת a פִּעֵל infinitive from שׁרת, "to serve."

יִשְׂאוּ > *יִשְׂאאוּ (see p. 264)

חֻקַּת from חֻקָּה. When used in priestly literature, it is the equivalent of the nonpriestly term חוֹק.

Deuteronomy 5:22-25 (in some Bibles, verses 19–22)

22 אֶֽת־הַדְּבָרִ֣ים הָאֵ֡לֶּה דִּבֶּר֩ יְהוָ֨ה אֶל־כָּל־קְהַלְכֶ֜ם
בָּהָ֗ר מִתּ֤וֹךְ הָאֵשׁ֙ הֶֽעָנָ֣ן וְהָֽעֲרָפֶ֔ל ק֥וֹל גָּד֖וֹל וְלֹ֣א יָסָ֑ף
וַֽיִּכְתְּבֵ֗ם עַל־שְׁנֵי֙ לֻחֹ֣ת אֲבָנִ֔ים וַֽיִּתְּנֵ֖ם אֵלָֽי׃
23 וַיְהִ֗י כְּשָׁמְעֲכֶ֤ם אֶת־הַקּוֹל֙ מִתּ֣וֹךְ הַחֹ֔שֶׁךְ וְהָהָ֖ר בֹּעֵ֣ר בָּאֵ֑שׁ וַתִּקְרְב֣וּן
אֵלַ֔י כָּל־רָאשֵׁ֥י שִׁבְטֵיכֶ֖ם וְזִקְנֵיכֶֽם׃ 24 וַתֹּאמְר֗וּ הֵ֣ן הֶרְאָ֜נוּ יְהוָ֤ה
אֱלֹהֵ֙ינוּ֙ אֶת־כְּבֹד֣וֹ וְאֶת־גָּדְל֔וֹ וְאֶת־קֹל֥וֹ שָׁמַ֖עְנוּ מִתּ֣וֹךְ הָאֵ֑שׁ הַיּ֤וֹם
הַזֶּה֙ רָאִ֔ינוּ כִּֽי־יְדַבֵּ֧ר אֱלֹהִ֛ים אֶת־הָאָדָ֖ם וָחָֽי׃ 25 וְעַתָּה֙ לָ֣מָּה נָמ֔וּת
כִּ֣י תֹֽאכְלֵ֔נוּ הָאֵ֥שׁ הַגְּדֹלָ֖ה הַזֹּ֑את אִם־יֹסְפִ֣ים ׀ אֲנַ֗חְנוּ לִשְׁמֹ֜עַ
אֶת־ק֨וֹל יְהוָ֧ה אֱלֹהֵ֛ינוּ ע֖וֹד וָמָֽתְנוּ׃

V. 22 דִּבֶּר is a פִּעֵל of דבר, "to speak."

עֲרָפֶל "heavy cloud, deep darkness."

לֻחֹת "tablets" (singular לוּחַ).

V. 24 הֵן a shortened form of הִנֵּה.

הֶרְאָנוּ "showed us," a הִפְעִיל of ראי with a 1cp suffix.

גֹּדֶל "greatness."

Judges 15:1–2

וַיְהִ֨י מִיָּמִ֜ים בִּימֵ֣י קְצִיר־חִטִּ֗ים וַיִּפְקֹ֨ד שִׁמְשׁ֤וֹן אֶת־אִשְׁתּוֹ֙ 15:1
בִּגְדִ֣י עִזִּ֔ים וַיֹּ֕אמֶר אָבֹ֥אָה אֶל־אִשְׁתִּ֖י הֶחָ֑דְרָה וְלֹֽא־נְתָנ֥וֹ אָבִ֖יהָ לָבֽוֹא׃
וַיֹּ֣אמֶר אָבִ֗יהָ אָמֹ֤ר אָמַ֙רְתִּי֙ כִּי־שָׂנֹ֣א שְׂנֵאתָ֔הּ וָאֶתְּנֶ֖נָּה לְמֵרֵעֶ֑ךָ הֲלֹ֨א 2
אֲחוֹתָ֤הּ הַקְּטַנָּה֙ טוֹבָ֣ה מִמֶּ֔נָּה תְּהִי־נָ֥א לְךָ֖ תַּחְתֶּֽיהָ׃

V. 1 וַיְהִ֨י מִיָּמִ֜ים idiomatic for "some time later."

גְּדִי "kid."

V. 2 מֵרֵעַ "friend, companion, (possibly) best man."

1 Samuel 14:36–37

וַיֹּ֣אמֶר שָׁא֡וּל נֵרְדָ֣ה אַחֲרֵי֩ פְלִשְׁתִּ֨ים ׀ לַ֜יְלָה וְֽנָבֹ֣זָה בָהֶ֣ם ׀ עַד־א֣וֹר 36
הַבֹּ֗קֶר וְלֹֽא־נַשְׁאֵ֤ר בָּהֶם֙ אִ֔ישׁ וַיֹּ֣אמְר֔וּ כָּל־הַטּ֥וֹב בְּעֵינֶ֖יךָ עֲשֵׂ֑ה ס
וַיֹּ֙אמֶר֙ הַכֹּהֵ֔ן נִקְרְבָ֥ה הֲלֹ֖ם אֶל־הָאֱלֹהִֽים׃ 37 וַיִּשְׁאַ֤ל שָׁאוּל֙ בֵּֽאלֹהִ֔ים
הַֽאֵרֵד֙ אַחֲרֵ֣י פְלִשְׁתִּ֔ים הֲתִתְּנֵ֖ם בְּיַ֣ד יִשְׂרָאֵ֑ל וְלֹ֥א עָנָ֖הוּ בַּיּ֥וֹם הַהֽוּא׃

V. 36 נַשְׁאֵר an unexpected jussive type form for נַשְׁאִיר.

ס There are two types of paragraph markers in printed Bibles, reflecting what is found in manuscripts: a ס (for סְתוּמָה), indicating a minor paragraph break, where the text is continued on the same line after leaving a small blank space, and a פ (for פְּתוּחָה), for a major break, where the end of the line is left blank and the next paragraph begins on the following line. (BHS, the standard scholarly Bible, typically ignores these masoretic conventions.) The example here is a relatively unusual case in which there is a paragraph break in the middle of a verse.

הֲלֹם "to here."

Isaiah 42:6

אֲנִ֧י יְהוָ֛ה קְרָאתִ֥יךָֽ בְצֶ֖דֶק וְאַחְזֵ֣ק בְּיָדֶ֑ךָ 6
וְאֶצָּרְךָ֗ וְאֶתֶּנְךָ֛ לִבְרִ֥ית עָ֖ם לְא֥וֹר גּוֹיִֽם׃

Isaiah 43:1–2

43:1 וְעַתָּ֞ה כֹּֽה־אָמַ֤ר יְהוָה֙ בֹּרַאֲךָ֣ יַעֲקֹ֔ב וְיֹצֶרְךָ֖ יִשְׂרָאֵ֑ל
אַל־תִּירָא֙ כִּ֣י גְאַלְתִּ֔יךָ קָרָ֥אתִי בְשִׁמְךָ֖ לִי־אָֽתָּה׃

2 כִּֽי־תַעֲבֹ֤ר בַּמַּ֙יִם֙ אִתְּךָ־אָ֔נִי וּבַנְּהָר֖וֹת לֹ֣א יִשְׁטְפ֑וּךָ
כִּֽי־תֵלֵ֤ךְ בְּמוֹ־אֵשׁ֙ לֹ֣א תִכָּוֶ֔ה וְלֶהָבָ֖ה לֹ֥א תִבְעַר־בָּֽךְ׃

V. 2 שׁטף "to overflow, wash away."

בְּמוֹ the syllable מוֹ is a filler and has no meaning. (Compare כְּמוֹ.)

תִכָּוֶה, "you will be burned," a נִפְעַל from כוי.

לֶהָבָה "flame" (poetic).

Haggai 2:22–23

22 וְהָ֣פַכְתִּי֮ כִּסֵּ֣א מַמְלָכוֹת֒ וְהִ֨שְׁמַדְתִּ֔י חֹ֖זֶק מַמְלְכ֣וֹת הַגּוֹיִ֑ם
וְהָפַכְתִּ֤י מֶרְכָּבָה֙ וְרֹ֣כְבֶ֔יהָ וְיָרְד֣וּ סוּסִ֧ים וְרֹכְבֵיהֶ֛ם אִ֖ישׁ בְּחֶ֥רֶב אָחִֽיו׃

23 בַּיּ֣וֹם הַה֣וּא נְאֻם־יְהוָ֣ה צְבָא֡וֹת אֶ֠קָּחֲךָ זְרֻבָּבֶ֨ל בֶּן־שְׁאַלְתִּיאֵ֤ל עַבְדִּי֙
נְאֻם־יְהוָ֔ה וְשַׂמְתִּ֖יךָ כַּֽחוֹתָ֑ם כִּֽי־בְךָ֣ בָחַ֔רְתִּי נְאֻ֖ם יְהוָ֥ה צְבָאֽוֹת׃

V. 22 חֹזֶק "strength."

מֶרְכָּבָה "chariot."

V. 23 חוֹתָם "signet ring."

Proverbs 1:28–29

28 אָ֣ז יִ֭קְרָאֻנְנִי וְלֹ֣א אֶעֱנֶ֑ה יְ֝שַׁחֲרֻ֗נְנִי וְלֹ֣א יִמְצָאֻֽנְנִי׃
29 תַּ֭חַת כִּי־שָׂ֣נְאוּ דָ֑עַת וְיִרְאַ֥ת יְ֝הוָ֗ה לֹ֣א בָחָֽרוּ׃

V. 28 יְשַׁחֲרֻנְנִי a פִּעֵל from שׁחר, "to seek early," with a 1cs suffix.

Proverbs 4:5–6

5 קְנֵ֣ה חָ֭כְמָה קְנֵ֣ה בִינָ֑ה אַל־תִּשְׁכַּ֥ח וְאַל־תֵּ֝֗ט מֵֽאִמְרֵי־פִֽי׃
6 אַל־תַּעַזְבֶ֥הָ וְתִשְׁמְרֶ֑ךָּ אֱהָבֶ֗הָ וְתִצְּרֶֽךָּ׃

V. 5 בִּינָה "understanding."

אֲמָרִים "speech, words" (poetic).

V. 6 נצר "to watch, guard."

Song of Songs 5:6–7

6 פָּתַ֤חְתִּֽי אֲנִי֙ לְדוֹדִ֔י וְדוֹדִ֖י חָמַ֣ק עָבָ֑ר נַפְשִׁי֙ יָֽצְאָ֣ה בְדַבְּר֔וֹ
בִּקַּשְׁתִּ֙יהוּ֙ וְלֹ֣א מְצָאתִ֔יהוּ קְרָאתִ֖יו וְלֹ֥א עָנָֽנִי׃
7 מְצָאֻ֧נִי הַשֹּׁמְרִ֛ים הַסֹּבְבִ֥ים בָּעִ֖יר הִכּ֣וּנִי פְצָע֑וּנִי
נָשְׂא֤וּ אֶת־רְדִידִי֙ מֵֽעָלַ֔י שֹׁמְרֵ֖י הַחֹמֽוֹת׃

V. 6   דּוֹד "lover" (more frequently "uncle").

     חמק "to turn away."

V. 7   הִכּוּנִי a הִפְעִיל perfect of נכי, "to hit," with 1cs suffix.

     פְּצָעוּנִי incorporating the root פצע, "to wound."

     רְדִיד an article of women's clothing, perhaps a "veil" or "shawl."

24 The Derived Conjugations (בִּנְיָנִים) Healthy Verbs

Traditional Hebrew grammar recognizes seven major בִּנְיָנִים or derived conjugations, typically named for the 3ms perfect form of the verb: קַל (or פָּעַל), נִפְעַל, פִּעֵל, פֻּעַל, הִפְעִיל, הָפְעַל, and הִתְפַּעֵל. This categorization is not accurate; based on form and meaning, there are really five בִּנְיָנִים: קַל (or פָּעַל), נִפְעַל, פִּעֵל, הִפְעִיל, and הִתְפַּעֵל; the פֻּעַל and הָפְעַל are not separate בִּנְיָנִים but are passives of the פִּעֵל and הִפְעִיל, respectively. The following morphological features typify each of the בִּנְיָנִים:

קַל (or פָּעַל) is unaugmented (thus קַל, or "simple"); it has no doubling (no דָּגֵשׁ חָזָק) and no prefixes. From כבד, "to be heavy," for example, we have כָּבֵד, "he is heavy, important" (perfect), and אֶכְבַּד, "I will be heavy, important" (imperfect).¹

נִפְעַל is typified by a prefix נוּן. In the perfect, it is visible, as in נִכְבַּד, "he/it was honored," while in the imperfect it is typically assimilated into the first root letter (פּ הַפֹּעַל), as in יִכָּבֵד (<*יִנְכָּבֵד), "he/it will be honored."

פִּעֵל (as well as פֻּעַל) is typified by doubling of the middle root letter (ע הַפֹּעַל). This may be seen in the perfect כִּבֵּד, "he honored" (or its passive, כֻּבַּד, "he was honored"), and in the imperfect, יְכַבֵּד, "he will honor" (or its passive, יְכֻבַּד, "it will be honored"). The difference between פִּעֵל and פֻּעַל is in the vocalization of the word, but both are typified by a דָּגֵשׁ חָזָק in ע הַפֹּעַל. (It is unfortunate that Hebrew grammarians chose the root פעל to illustrate the different בִּנְיָנִים, because the middle letter of that root cannot be doubled. The doubling, the typifying characteristic of the פִּעֵל, is thus not visible in the way the בִּנְיָן is spelled.)

הִפְעִיל (and הָפְעַל) is typified by a prefix הֵא. This may be seen in the perfect הִכְבִּיד, "he made heavy" (or its passive, הָכְבַּד, "he/it was made heavy"—note that the קָמֵץ throughout the paradigm is a קָמֵץ קָטָן). In the imperfect and related forms this הֵא is elided, and its

---

1. The דְּגֵשִׁים in כָּבֵד and אֶכְבַּד are all דְּגֵשִׁים קַלִּים.

vowel is thrown backward; we thus have יַכְבִּיד (< *יְהַכְבִּיד), "he will make heavy," and יֻכְבַּד (< *יְהֻכְבַּד), "he/it will be made heavy."

הִתְפַּעֵל is typified by a prefix הִת־ and by doubling of the middle root letter (עַ הַפֹּעַל). This may be seen in the perfect, הִתְכַּבֵּד, "he made himself heavy," and the imperfect, יִתְכַּבֵּד, "he will make himself heavy." (In the imperfect, the הֵא of the prefix הִת־ is elided, as in the הִפְעִיל.) With words that begin with sibilants (see p. 8), the תָּו of the הִתְפַּעֵל is found after the first root letter, and in some cases may become partially assimilated to the sibilant. (This reversal of letters is called metathesis.) For example, from שׂכר we have וְהַמִּשְׂתַּכֵּר (מִשְׂתַּכֵּר is a הִתְפַּעֵל participle) instead of *וְהַמִּתְשַׂכֵּר. With צָדִי (and later Hebrew זַיִן and סָמֶךְ), there is partial assimilation as well, as seen in the form נִצְטַדָּק.[2]

All of the direct-object suffixes that were discussed in the previous chapter may be added to verbs in any בִּנְיָן; predictable phonetic changes occur as a result of the change of stress, but the fundamental identifying features of each בִּנְיָן (for example, the doubling of the first letter of the נִפְעַל imperfect) are generally unaffected.

In addition, there are several rare בִּנְיָנִים, some of which occur only with hollow verbs. The main one found with healthy verbs, the קַל passive, will be discussed at the end of this chapter.

Several grammars suggest that the בִּנְיָנִים have a clear semantic function—that is, that each בִּנְיָן affects the meaning of the (קַל) verb in a particular way. There is some truth to this notion. If the meaning of a verb in the קַל is known, it is often possible to predict the meaning of the verb in other בִּנְיָנִים, but this is not always the case. It is therefore always best to look up in a lexicon the meaning assigned to a particular verb in the particular בִּנְיָן. Thus the observations in the following section are only general guidelines.[3]

The נִפְעַל is usually translated as an English passive; thus from the קַל, כָּתַב, "he wrote," we have the נִפְעַל, נִכְתַּב, "was written." However, there is a class of verbs, called the "middle voice," that are identical in form with the active voice but approach the passive in terms of meaning. They typically describe self-contained situations, such as *open* in sentences like "your mouth opened" (in contrast to the active "you opened your mouth"). The נִפְעַל may express such cases of middle voice, as in Ezekiel 24:27, יִפָּתַח פִּיךָ, "your mouth will open." It may also be reflexive, as in Exodus 22:2, וְנִמְכַּר בִּגְנֵבָתוֹ, "and he shall sell himself in exchange for his theft." Additionally, it may express potentiality. In such cases, it may be translated with the suffix "-a/ible," as in Exodus 16:10, וְהִנֵּה כְּבוֹד יְהוָה נִרְאָה בֶּעָנָן, "suddenly the glory of YHWH was visible/ appeared in the cloud," or Job 42:15, וְלֹא נִמְצָא נָשִׁים יָפוֹת כִּבְנוֹת אִיּוֹב בְּכָל־הָאָרֶץ, "women

---

2. The תָּו, a dental stop, partially assimilates to the צָדִי, a sibilant emphatic, and becomes the emphatic טֵית.

3. The following observations are especially indebted to the treatment of the derived conjugations in Lambdin's *Introduction to Biblical Hebrew*, 175–78, 193–95, 211–13, 249–50.

as beautiful as Job's daughters did not exist (= were not 'findable') in the whole land." It is important to remember all of these uses so that the נִפְעַל is not translated automatically as a passive; in fact, not all נִפְעַל verbs have corresponding קַל verbs, so it is difficult to understand the נִפְעַל as a passive of the קַל in the way the פֻּעַל is a passive of the פִּעֵל.

The frequent assertion that the פִּעֵל is intensive is probably based on an association between the doubling of the middle root letter and the meaning of the form; this assertion, however, is by and large incorrect, for the intensive use of the פִּעֵל, if found at all, is not its predominant use. The main function of the פִּעֵל is factitive or transitizing—that is, it makes intransitive verbs (verbs that do not require or cannot take a direct object) into transitive verbs (verbs that do take direct objects). For example, in the קַל we have וְטָמֵא עַד־הָעָרֶב, "and he will be impure until the evening" (Leviticus 11:25 and elsewhere), while in the פִּעֵל we have טִמְּאוּ אֶת־הֵיכַל קָדְשֶׁךָ, "they defiled (made impure) your holy temple" (Psalm 79:1). In addition, there are several common verbs that appear only in the פִּעֵל; these include דִּבֶּר, "spoke," סִפֵּר, "told," and צִוָּה, "commanded." The פֻּעַל is the passive of the פִּעֵל.

The הִפְעִיל is mostly causative in meaning; that is, the notion of causation may be added to the corresponding קַל root. From the קַל, אָכַל, "to eat," for example, we have the הִפְעִיל, הֶאֱכִיל, "to cause to eat," and thus "to feed," as in Exodus 16:32, לְמַעַן יִרְאוּ אֶת־הַלֶּחֶם אֲשֶׁר הֶאֱכַלְתִּי אֶתְכֶם בַּמִּדְבָּר, "so they may see the food that I fed you in the wilderness." Similarly, from the קַל, לָבַשׁ, wore, we have the הִפְעִיל, הִלְבִּישׁ, "clothe" (cause to wear), as in 1 Samuel 17:38, וַיַּלְבֵּשׁ אֹתוֹ שִׁרְיוֹן, "he dressed him with a breastplate." (Note that in English, *dressed* takes the piece of clothing as an indirect object, while in Hebrew, a direct object is used [here שִׁרְיוֹן]—this cannot, and should not, be reflected in translation.) As may be seen from these examples, it is often best to translate the הִפְעִיל idiomatically, without using the phrase "caused to." In some cases, a verb may have both a פִּעֵל and a הִפְעִיל that are similar in meaning. It is not unusual for a verb in the הִפְעִיל to have two direct objects (to be "doubly transitive"). This may be seen, for example, in the previous example from 1 Samuel, as well as in Exodus 40:13, וְהִלְבַּשְׁתָּ אֶת־אַהֲרֹן אֵת בִּגְדֵי הַקֹּדֶשׁ. The structure of English is fundamentally different from that of Hebrew, so such Hebrew double direct objects would typically be translated with the help of one direct and one indirect object. In this case, we would translate, "and you should clothe Aaron (English and Hebrew direct object) with the sacral vestments (English indirect object, reflecting a Hebrew direct object)."

The הִתְפַּעֵל is most often reflexive, as may be seen through the contrast of the הִתְפַּעֵל of קדשׁ in Exodus 19:22, הַכֹּהֲנִים הַנִּגָּשִׁים אֶל־יְהוָה יִתְקַדָּשׁוּ, "the priests who are approaching YHWH shall sanctify themselves," with the (stative) קַל (Exodus 29:37),

כָּל־הַנֹּגֵעַ בַּמִּזְבֵּחַ יִקְדָּשׁ, "whatever touches the altar shall become sanctified," or the (transitive) פִּעֵל (Exodus 28:41), וְקִדַּשְׁתָּ אֹתָם, "you should sanctify them." It may also be iterative, that is, representing a repeated or ongoing action, as in Genesis 13:17, קוּם הִתְהַלֵּךְ בָּאָרֶץ לְאָרְכָּהּ וּלְרָחְבָּהּ, "Come and walk throughout the land, to its length and width." Another use of the הִתְפַּעֵל that is not found in MIH is "to pretend," as when Amnon, who desires his sister Tamar, is told (2 Samuel 13:5), שְׁכַב עַל־מִשְׁכָּבְךָ וְהִתְחָל, "lie down on your bed and feign illness (the חֳלִי of הִתְפַּעֵל)."

The previous observations about the typical uses of the various בִּנְיָנִים should only be seen as a guide to likely meanings; a lexicon should be consulted to understand how a particular word is being used in a particular context.

The Perfect and the Converted Perfect

The following are typical perfect forms of healthy verbs in the major בִּנְיָנִים and their passives. The active form of כתב is included for the sake of comparison:

The Perfect in the Various בִּנְיָנִים

	קַל	נִפְעַל	פֻּעַל	פִּעֵל	הֻפְעַל	הִפְעִיל	הִתְפַּעֵל
3ms	כָּתַב	נִמְלַט	שֻׁבַּר/דֻּבַּר	גִּנַּב	הֻשְׁלַךְ	הִשְׁלִיךְ	הִתְיַצֵּב
3fs	כָּתְבָה	נִמְלְטָה	דֻּבְּרָה	גִּנְּבָה	הֻשְׁלְכָה	הִשְׁלִיכָה	הִתְיַצְּבָה
2ms	כָּתַבְתָּ	נִמְלַטְתָּ	דֻּבַּרְתָּ	גִּנַּבְתָּ	הֻשְׁלַכְתָּ	הִשְׁלַכְתָּ	הִתְיַצַּבְתָּ
2fs	כָּתַבְתְּ	נִמְלַטְתְּ	דֻּבַּרְתְּ	גִּנַּבְתְּ	הֻשְׁלַכְתְּ	הִשְׁלַכְתְּ	הִתְיַצַּבְתְּ
1cs	כָּתַבְתִּי	נִמְלַטְתִּי	דֻּבַּרְתִּי	גִּנַּבְתִּי	הֻשְׁלַכְתִּי	הִשְׁלַכְתִּי	הִתְיַצַּבְתִּי
3c	כָּתְבוּ	נִמְלְטוּ	דֻּבְּרוּ	גִּנְּבוּ	הֻשְׁלְכוּ	הִשְׁלִיכוּ	הִתְיַצְּבוּ
2mp	כְּתַבְתֶּם	נִמְלַטְתֶּם	דֻּבַּרְתֶּם	גִּנַּבְתֶּם	הֻשְׁלַכְתֶּם	הִשְׁלַכְתֶּם	הִתְיַצַּבְתֶּם
2fp	כְּתַבְתֶּן	נִמְלַטְתֶּן	דֻּבַּרְתֶּן	גִּנַּבְתֶּן	הֻשְׁלַכְתֶּן	הִשְׁלַכְתֶּן	הִתְיַצַּבְתֶּן
1cp	כָּתַבְנוּ	נִמְלַטְנוּ	דֻּבַּרְנוּ	גִּנַּבְנוּ	הֻשְׁלַכְנוּ	הִשְׁלַכְנוּ	הִתְיַצַּבְנוּ

All the בִּנְיָנִים share the following features: in all cases the 2p suffixes are heavy; in all cases the 2ms, 1cs, and 1cp have penultimate stress; and pretonic reduction is at work in the נִפְעַל, פֻּעַל, פִּעֵל, and הִתְפַּעֵל in the same places as in the קַל. In most forms of the פִּעֵל and הִתְפַּעֵל Philippi's law is operative (see p. 179), as the form becomes, for example, דִּבַּרְתָּ (< דִּבֵּרְתָּ*). In addition, the objective suffixes for the verbs are the same in all of the בִּנְיָנִים.

The paradigms above admit to several variations. The הֻפְעַל (note that the first vowel is a קָמֶץ קָטָן) may also be vocalized with a קִבּוּץ, as a הֻפְעַל. In addition, in some cases, the Hebrew syllables $C_1VC_2C_2\breve{e}$ may be reduced to C_1VC_2; in practical terms, this results in the loss of an expected דָּגֵשׁ חָזָק. Instead of בִּקְּשָׁה*, for example, we have בִּקְשָׁה. This loss of the דָּגֵשׁ חָזָק is found particularly with the letters ילמנק and the sibilants (זסצשׁשׂ); it is especially unfortunate in cases like בִּקְשָׁה because the דָּגֵשׁ חָזָק, that typifies the פִּעֵל, is absent. This principle, however, is not fully consistent—on some occasions the דָּגֵשׁ חָזָק is omitted in other letters, and other times it is found in these letters. The 3ms of the פִּעֵל usually is formed as in כִּבֵּס. A small number of verbs, including the common verb דבר, are vocalized as דִּבֶּר with a סֶגוֹל under the middle root letter, except at the pause, where it appears as דִּבֵּר.

The converted perfect is formed by adding a וְ vocalized with a שְׁוָא to the perfect. In the 2ms and 1cs, where the perfect has penultimate stress (but not the 1cp), the stress becomes ultimate in the converted perfect, as may be seen in these pairs: (Exodus 4:15) עָשִׂיתִי כַּאֲשֶׁר דִּבַּרְתָּ אֵלָי, וְדִבַּרְתָּ אֵלָיו "you will speak to him," and (Genesis 27:19) "I did what you spoke to me," and (Jeremiah 7:15) וְהִשְׁלַכְתִּי (ultimate stress) אֶתְכֶם מֵעַל פָּנָי (penultimate stress) כַּאֲשֶׁר הִשְׁלַכְתִּי אֶת־כָּל־אֲחֵיכֶם אֵת כָּל־זֶרַע אֶפְרָיִם:, "I will cast you from before me as I cast all of your brothers, the seed of Ephraim." In the third masculine singular, the final vowel may become short (thus כִּבֵּס, but וְכִבֶּס), as in the frequent priestly phrase וְכִבֶּס בְּגָדָיו, "he must wash his clothes."

The Imperfect and the Converted Imperfect

The following chart illustrates the typical imperfect forms of healthy verbs in the major בִּנְיָנִים and their passives. The active form of כתב is included for the sake of comparison:

The Imperfect in the Various בִּנְיָנִים

	קַל	נִפְעַל	פִּעֵל	פֻּעַל	הִפְעִיל	הָפְעַל	הִתְפַּעֵל
3ms	יִכְתֹּב	יִמָּלֵט	יְדַבֵּר	יְגֻנַּב	יַשְׁלִיךְ	יָשְׁלַךְ	יִתְיַצֵּב
3fs	תִּכְתֹּב	תִּמָּלֵט	תְּדַבֵּר	תְּגֻנַּב	תַּשְׁלִיךְ	תָּשְׁלַךְ	תִּתְיַצֵּב
2ms	תִּכְתֹּב	תִּמָּלֵט	תְּדַבֵּר	תְּגֻנַּב	תַּשְׁלִיךְ	תָּשְׁלַךְ	תִּתְיַצֵּב
2fs	תִּכְתְּבִי	תִּמָּלְטִי	תְּדַבְּרִי	תְּגֻנְּבִי	תַּשְׁלִיכִי	תָּשְׁלְכִי	תִּתְיַצְּבִי
1cs	אֶכְתֹּב	אֶמָּלֵט	אֲדַבֵּר	אֲגֻנַּב	אַשְׁלִיךְ	אָשְׁלַךְ	אֶתְיַצֵּב
3mp	יִכְתְּבוּ	יִמָּלְטוּ	יְדַבְּרוּ	יְגֻנְּבוּ	יַשְׁלִיכוּ	יָשְׁלְכוּ	יִתְיַצְּבוּ
3fp	תִּכְתֹּבְנָה	תִּמָּלַטְנָה	תְּדַבֵּרְנָה	תְּגֻנַּבְנָה	תַּשְׁלֵכְנָה	תָּשְׁלַכְנָה	תִּתְיַצֵּבְנָה
2mp	תִּכְתְּבוּ	תִּמָּלְטוּ	תְּדַבְּרוּ	תְּגֻנְּבוּ	תַּשְׁלִיכוּ	תָּשְׁלְכוּ	תִּתְיַצְּבוּ
2fp	תִּכְתֹּבְנָה	תִּמָּלַטְנָה	תְּדַבֵּרְנָה	תְּגֻנַּבְנָה	תַּשְׁלֵכְנָה	תָּשְׁלַכְנָה	תִּתְיַצֵּבְנָה
1cp	נִכְתֹּב	נִמָּלֵט	נְדַבֵּר	נְגֻנַּב	נַשְׁלִיךְ	נָשְׁלַךְ	נִתְיַצֵּב

The prefixes and suffixes of the verbs are the same in all of the בִּנְיָנִים. The בִּנְיָן of any particular verb may be recognized by features noted above: קַל has no doubling (no דָּגֵשׁ חָזָק) and no prefixes, and has a חִירֶק as a prefix vowel (for example, יִכְתֹּב). נִפְעַל also has חִירֶק as its prefix vowel, but the following letter takes a דָּגֵשׁ חָזָק, marking the assimilated נוּן (for example, יִמָּלֵט). The פִּעֵל and פֻּעַל are marked by doubling of the middle root letter, and the prefix vowel is a שְׁוָא נָע (for example, יְגֻנַּב, יְדַבֵּר). The prefix הֵא that typified the הִפְעִיל and הָפְעַל in the imperfect is elided, so these are characterized by the prefix vowels of פַּתַח for the הִפְעִיל and קָמֵץ קָטָן for the הָפְעַל (for example, יָשְׁלַךְ, יַשְׁלִיךְ). Finally, the הִתְפַּעֵל is typified by a prefix תִ and by doubling of the middle root letter (for example, יִתְיַצֵּב).

Regular phonological rules and spelling principles are operative throughout the paradigms. So, for example, most 2fs, 3mp, and 3fp forms show evidence of pretonic reduction, as may be seen from the following pairs: יִגְנַב ‖ תִּגְנְבִי, יְדַבֵּר ‖ תְּדַבְּרִי, יִמָּלֵט ‖ תִּמָּלְטִי, יִתְיַצֵּב ‖ תִּתְיַצְּבִי, יַשְׁלִיךְ ‖ תַּשְׁלִיכִי. In the fp of the נִפְעַל, Philippi's law (see p. 179) is operative, so we have תִּמָּלַטְנָה (< *תִּמָּלֵטְנָה). Finally, the spelling of the הִפְעִיל usually, but not always, has a יוֹד between the second and third root letter. For example, in the Hebrew Bible, "he will destroy," a הִפְעִיל from שחת is spelled יַשְׁחִית (with a יוֹד) four times and יַשְׁחֵת twice.

With the exception of the הִפְעִיל, the converted imperfect is typically formed by adding a וְ followed by a פַּתָח and a דָּגֵשׁ חָזָק to the imperfect (or, in the case of the 1cs, a וְ with a קָמֵץ). However, the syllable וְיְ* is shortened to וַיְ (see pp. 55, 264). Thus we have, for example, וַתְּדַבֵּרְנָה, "they spoke," וַיְדַבֵּר, "he spoke," וַיְדַבְּרוּ, "they spoke," but וָאֲדַבֵּר, "I spoke" (with compensatory lengthening under the וְ). In the הִפְעִיל, forms with no suffix end with □□ rather than □י□, so we have, for example, in the imperfect יַשְׁלִיךְ, "he will cast," but in the converted imperfect וַיַּשְׁלֵךְ, "he cast," as in Exodus 7:10, וַיַּשְׁלֵךְ אַהֲרֹן אֶת־מַטֵּהוּ, "Aaron cast his staff."

It is crucial to develop an active knowledge of the various בִּנְיָנִים in the perfect and imperfect, and to memorize the distinctive vowel patterns of each בִּנְיָן. Nevertheless, the following chart, outlining the main characteristics of each בִּנְיָן, will be helpful for identifying healthy verbs found in the biblical text.

Identifying the בִּנְיָן of Perfect and Imperfect Verbs

קַל has no prefix and no doubling in the perfect and imperfect (for example, כָּתַב יִכְתֹּב). The characteristic vowel of the prefix of the imperfect is a חִירֶק.

נִפְעַל has a prefix נוּן in the perfect; in the imperfect, this נוּן is assimilated into the first root letter (for example, נִמְלַט יִמָּלֵט). The characteristic vowel of the prefix of the imperfect is a חִירֶק which is followed by a דָּגֵשׁ חָזָק.

פִּעֵל and פֻּעַל have a doubled middle root letter (for example, דִּבֵּר/דֻּבַּר יְדַבֵּר גָּנַב יְגַנֵּב). The characteristic vowel of the prefix of the imperfect is a שְׁוָא.

הִפְעִיל and הָפְעַל have a prefix הֵא in the perfect; in the imperfect, this הֵא is elided, and its vowel is thrown backward (for example, הִשְׁלִיךְ יַשְׁלִיךְ הָשְׁלַךְ). The characteristic vowel of the prefix of the imperfect of the הִפְעִיל is a פַּתָח, and of the הָפְעַל is a קָמֵץ קָטָן (or a קִבּוּץ).

הִתְפַּעֵל has a prefix תָו and a doubled middle root letter (for example, הִתְיַצֵּב יִתְיַצֵּב).

The Jussive, the Imperative, and the Cohortative

These forms are as expected. The jussive is identical to the form of the converted imperfect without the וַ; the imperative, where it exists, is usually a shortened form of the imperfect (without a subjective prefix); and the cohortative is formed by adding a הָ, which may result in some vowel changes.

Thus the 3ms jussives would follow these forms:

קַל	נִפְעַל	פֻּעַל	פִּעֵל	הִפְעִיל	הֻפְעַל	הִתְפַּעֵל
יִכְתֹּב	יִמָּלֵט	יְדֻבַּר	יְגַנֵּב	יַשְׁלִךְ	יָשְׁלַךְ	יִתְיַצֵּב

The Jussive in the Various בִּנְיָנִים

Except for הִפְעִיל, context then must determine whether a form is an imperfect or a jussive. The forms would be conjugated in the second person, and would thus have a תִּ prefix if used after an אַל in a negative imperative or prohibitive.

Because the פֻּעַל and הֻפְעַל are passives, they do not appear in the imperative. The forms of the imperatives are presented below.

The Imperative in the Various בִּנְיָנִים

	קַל	נִפְעַל	פִּעֵל	הִפְעִיל	הִתְפַּעֵל
2ms	כְּתֹב	הִמָּלֵט	דַּבֵּר	הַשְׁלֵךְ	הִתְיַצֵּב
2fs	כִּתְבִי	הִמָּלְטִי	דַּבְּרִי	הַשְׁלִיכִי	הִתְיַצְּבִי
2mp	כִּתְבוּ	הִמָּלְטוּ	דַּבְּרוּ	הַשְׁלִיכוּ	הִתְיַצְּבוּ
2fp	כְּתֹבְנָה	הִמָּלַטְנָה	דַּבֵּרְנָה	הַשְׁלֵכְנָה	very rare

As noted, these are closely related to the imperfect in form. Only the form of the נִפְעַל is somewhat unexpected. It has a prefixed הָא; this allows the דָּגֵשׁ חָזָק that remains from the assimilated נוּן to be expressed. The imperatives have the typical signs of the בִּנְיָן that they belong to: the קַל has no doubling, the נִפְעַל has doubling of the first root letter, the פִּעֵל has doubling of the second root letter, the הִפְעִיל has a פַּתַח as its prefix vowel, and the הִתְפַּעֵל has doubling of the second root letter and a prefix תִּו. Although both the נִפְעַל and הִפְעִיל have a prefix הָא, their vocalization is quite different (הִמָּלֵט:נִפְעַל versus הַשְׁלִיךְ:הִפְעִיל).

The forms for the cohortative are presented below:

	הִתְפַּעֵל	הִפְעִיל	פִּעֵל	נִפְעַל	קַל
1cs	אֶתְיַצְּבָה	אַשְׁלִיכָה	אֲדַבְּרָה	אֶמָּלְטָה	אֶכְתְּבָה
1cp	נִתְיַצְּבָה	נַשְׁלִיכָה	נְדַבְּרָה	נִמָּלְטָה	נִכְתְּבָה

With the exception of the הִפְעִיל, the imperfect loses its final vowel through pretonic reduction because the added הָ is accented (compare אֲמַלֵּט and אֲמַלְּטָה). In the הִפְעִיל, however, there is no vowel reduction (thus אַשְׁלִיכָה, from אַשְׁלִיךְ). In בִּנְיָנִים other than the הִפְעִיל, the accent is penultimate at the pause, and there is no vowel reduction. Thus we have the two forms for "so I may speak": וַאֲדַבְּרָה (for example, Genesis 18:32—nonpausal) and וַאֲדַבֵּרָה (for example, Deuteronomy 32:1—pausal).

The Participles

Verbs in the קַל have both an active and a passive participle; in the other בִּנְיָנִים, verbs have one participle only, which is active or passive depending on the nature of the בִּנְיָן. Outside of the קַל and נִפְעַל, all of the participles begin with מְ. A chart with the participles appears on the following page; alternative fs forms are given, though the form that ends with הֶ is much more common.

The Participle in the Various בִּנְיָנִים

	קַל	נִפְעַל	פִּעֵל	פֻּעַל	הִפְעִיל	הָפְעַל	הִתְפַּעֵל
ms	כֹּתֵב	נִמְלָט	מְדַבֵּר	מְגֻנָּב	מַשְׁלִיךְ	מָשְׁלָךְ	מִתְיַצֵּב
fs	כֹּתֶבֶת	נִמְלֶטֶת	מְדַבֶּרֶת	מְגֻנֶּבֶת	מַשְׁלֶכֶת	מָשְׁלֶכֶת	מִתְיַצֶּבֶת
fs	כֹּתְבָה	נִמְלָטָה	מְדַבְּרָה	מְגֻנָּבָה	מַשְׁלִיכָה		מִתְנַכְּרָה
mp	כֹּתְבִים	נִמְלָטִים	מְדַבְּרִים	מְגֻנָּבִים	מַשְׁלִיכִים	מָשְׁלָכִים	מִתְיַצְּבִים
fp	כֹּתְבוֹת	נִמְלָטוֹת	מְדַבְּרוֹת	מְגֻנָּבוֹת	מַשְׁלִיכוֹת	מָשְׁלָכוֹת	מִתְיַצְּבוֹת

It is noteworthy that all participles that end in an *a* vowel are vocalized with a קָמֵץ in the נִפְעַל; this creates a distinction between the perfect נִמְלַט and the participle נִמְלָט. (This distinction is lost at the pause, where both forms are נִמְלָט.) In the הָפְעַל the forms מֻשְׁלָךְ (sometimes spelled plene [full], מוּשְׁלָךְ) and מָשְׁלָךְ both exist.

The Infinitives

Each בִּנְיָן has its own form for the infinitive construct and infinitive absolute; as in the קַל, the infinitive construct often has suffixes, in which case its vowels are subject to change. Although each בִּנְיָן has its own form of the infinitive absolute, it is not unusual to see the קַל infinitive absolute used with a verb from a different בִּנְיָן. The chart below shows the infinitive construct, the infinitive construct with the 3ms possessive suffix, and the infinitive absolute. The signs that typify each בִּנְיָן may be seen in the infinitives as well.

The Infinitives in the Various בִּנְיָנִים

	קַל	נִפְעַל	פִּעֵל	פֻּעַל	הִפְעִיל	הָפְעַל	הִתְפַּעֵל
inf const	כְּתֹב	הִמָּלֵט	דַּבֵּר	none	הַשְׁלִיךְ	none	הִתְיַצֵּב
w/3ms	כָּתְבוֹ	הִמָּלְטוֹ	דַּבְּרוֹ	none	הַשְׁלִיכוֹ	none	הִתְיַצְּבוֹ
inf abs	כָּתֹב	הִמָּלֵט /נִמְלֹט	rare	rare	הַשְׁלֵךְ	הָשְׁלֵךְ	none

The פָּעַל infinitive construct דַּבֵּר is identical in form to the פָּעֵל ms imperative; context determines the difference. Additionally, this infinitive construct form is typically used instead of the rare infinitive absolute form, קַטֹּל.

Additional בִּנְיָנִים

This chapter so far has focused on the five major בִּנְיָנִים and their internal passives. There are several less commonly recognized בִּנְיָנִים as well; some of these are found only with hollow verbs, but several are found with triliteral verbs. The most common of these is the קַל passive. As we have seen, the נִפְעַל should not be seen as the passive of the קַל; it therefore should not be surprising that like the פָּעֵל and הִפְעִיל, the קַל should have had its own internal passive.

Genesis 3:19, עַד שׁוּבְךָ אֶל־הָאֲדָמָה כִּי מִמֶּנָּה לֻקָּחְתָּ, "until you return to the earth, because you were taken from it," offers a convincing example of the קַל passive. The word לֻקָּחְתָּ looks like a (pausal form of the) פָּעֵל perfect. However, the verb לקח, which is very common, never appears in the פָּעֵל, so it would be surprising for it to appear in the related פֻּעַל. לקח is common in the קַל, so we may say that לֻקָּחְתָּ is a קַל passive. The קַל passive is generally vocalized according to the masoretic tradition as a פֻּעַל in the perfect, and as a הֻפְעַל in the imperfect; it is not clear when the קַל passive was lost and became assimilated into the patterns of these other בִּנְיָנִים. It may be recognized by the absence of a corresponding פָּעֵל or הִפְעִיל. The following verbs most often appear in the קַל passive: לקח, שדד, ילד, and נתן.

Vocabulary for chapter 24

Many of the verbs that we have seen in the קַל are conjugated in other בִּנְיָנִים as well. It is impossible to list all their meanings in these בִּנְיָנִים. At this point students should use a standard biblical lexicon, such as Francis Brown, S. R. Driver, and Charles A. Briggs, *A Hebrew and English Lexicon of the Old Testament,* often called BDB after its three authors. With the help of BDB, the paradigms from Gesenius, and the suggestions given at the beginning of this chapter about how various בִּנְיָנִים affect the meaning of roots, the meanings and forms of all biblical verbs can be determined. The vocabulary in this and the following chapter comprises words that are mainly or exclusively attested outside of the קַל.

[הִפְעִיל] בדל	to separate (lacking	הִבְדִּיל מַבְדִּיל יַבְדִּיל)
[פִּעֵל] בקש	to seek	(בִּקֵּשׁ מְבַקֵּשׁ יְבַקֵּשׁ בַּקֵּשׁ)
[פִּעֵל] בשל	to boil	(בִּשֵּׁל מְבַשֵּׁל יְבַשֵּׁל בַּשֵּׁל)
[פִּעֵל] דבר	to speak	(דִּבֶּר מְדַבֵּר יְדַבֵּר דַּבֵּר)
[פִּעֵל] זמר	to sing (יְזַמֵּר זַמֵּר lacking lacking)	
[הִתְפַּעֵל] יצב	to take one's stand	(הִתְיַצֵּב מִתְיַצֵּב יִתְיַצֵּב הִתְיַצֵּב)
[פִּעֵל] כבס	to wash	(כִּבֵּס מְכַבֵּס יְכַבֵּס כַּבֵּס)
[נִפְעַל] כלם	to be ashamed	(נִכְלַם נִכְלָם יִכָּלֵם הִכָּלֵם)
[הִפְעִיל]	to put to shame, humiliate (lacking הִכְלִים מַכְלִים יַכְלִים)	
[פִּעֵל] כפר	to atone (כִּפֶּר lacking יְכַפֵּר כַּפֵּר)	
[נִפְעַל] לחם	to fight	(נִלְחַם נִלְחָם יִלָּחֵם הִלָּחֵם)
[נִפְעַל] מלט	to escape	(נִמְלַט נִמְלָט יִמָּלֵט הִמָּלֵט)
[פִּעֵל]	to deliver	(מִלֵּט מְמַלֵּט יְמַלֵּט מַלֵּט)
[נִפְעַל] סתר	to be concealed	(נִסְתַּר נִסְתָּר יִסָּתֵר הִסָּתֵר)
[הִפְעִיל]	to conceal	(הִסְתִּיר מַסְתִּיר יַסְתִּיר הַסְתֵּר)
[הִתְפַּעֵל] פלל	to pray	(הִתְפַּלֵּל מִתְפַּלֵּל יִתְפַּלֵּל הִתְפַּלֵּל)
[נִפְעַל] פרד	to divide	(נִפְרַד נִפְרָד יִפָּרֵד הִפָּרֵד)
[הִפְעִיל]	to make a division (lacking הִפְרִיד מַפְרִיד יַפְרִיד)	
[הִפְעִיל] צלח	to succeed, thrive	(הִצְלִיחַ מַצְלִיחַ יַצְלִיחַ הַצְלֵחַ)

[פִּעֵל] קדם	to come to meet (קִדֵּם יְקַדֵּם lacking קָדַם)	
[פִּעֵל] קטר	offer incense (usually to foreign gods) (קִטֵּר מְקַטֵּר יְקַטֵּר קַטֵּר)	
[הִפְעִיל]	to offer incense (usually to YHWH) (הִקְטִיר מַקְטִיר יַקְטִיר הַקְטֵר)	
[הִפְעִיל] שׂכל	to prosper, act prudently (הִשְׂכִּיל מַשְׂכִּיל יַשְׂכִּיל הַשְׂכֵּל)	
[נִפְעַל] שׁאר	to remain (lacking נִשְׁאַר יִשָּׁאֵר)	
[הִפְעִיל] שׁכמ	to get up early (הִשְׁכִּים מַשְׁכִּים יַשְׁכִּים הַשְׁכֵּם)	
[הִפְעִיל] שׁלכ	to cast, throw (הִשְׁלִיךְ מַשְׁלִיךְ יַשְׁלִיךְ הַשְׁלֵךְ)	
[נִפְעַל] שׁמד	to be destroyed (lacking יִשָּׁמֵד lacking נִשְׁמַד)	
[הִפְעִיל]	to destroy (הִשְׁמִיד יַשְׁמִיד הַשְׁמֵד lacking)	

Exercises for chapter 24

1. Parse the following verbs, explaining how you know the בִּנְיָן of each verb:

נִשְׁמַדְתָּ	
כִּפַּרְתָּ	
תְּכַלֵּם	
יַקְטֵר	
הִתְיַצְּבוּ	
תִּכָּלַמְנָה	
נִלְחֲמָה	
מֻשְׁלָכוֹת	
בַּקְּשׁוּ	

2. Write out the paradigms for the perfect, imperfect, imperative, participles and infinitives using the following verbs:

הִתְפַּעֵל	הֻפְעַל	הִפְעִיל	פֻּעַל	פִּעֵל	נִפְעַל	קַל
כבד	בדל	בדל	בקשׁ	זמר	פרד	שׁפך

3. Using the chart below, parse the following verbs:

Verb	בִּנְיָן	Root	"Tense"	Person	Gender	Number	Other/suffix	Translation
קָדְמוּ								
הִצְלַח								
וּמִלַּטְנוּ								
זֻמַּר								
מְכַפֵּר								
וְנִכְלַמְתִּי								
מְדַבְּרוֹת								
תַּפְרִיד								
יָשְׁמַד								
הִשְׁמָדָם								
אַסְתִּירָה								
וַיַּשְׁכֵּם								
תָּשְׁמַד								
וָאֶלְחֵם								
הִמָּלְטִי								
תַּסְתִּיר								
בַּקֵּשׁ								
וְנַכְלִים								
תַּבְדֵּלְנָה								
וַתְּכַבֵּס								
הִתְיַצְּבוּ								
נְזַמְּרָה								
נִפְרַדְתֶּם								
הִתְפַּלֵּל								
מַשְׂכִּילִים								
וַיִּסָּתְרוּ								

4. Write the following forms in Hebrew; if there is more than one way of expressing the form (for example, for translations that may be expressed by the perfect and converted imperfect), write all the ways:

let's act prudently		
she prospered		
they (m) will separate (= divide)		
speak! (fp)		
they (fp) separated		
I (f) am seeking		
they took their (mp) stand		
be ashamed! (ms)		
he is arising		
I will come to meet		
in his praying		
they are hidden (m)		
it (m) was destroyed		
let me cast		
they (f) fought		
may he deliver		
they (f) make atonement		
it (f) thrives		
we washed		

5. Translate the following biblical passages, parse all verbs, and analyze all nouns with suffixes. Look up all words that you do not know in a biblical lexicon such as BDB:

Genesis 1:3–8

3 וַיֹּ֣אמֶר אֱלֹהִ֔ים יְהִ֣י א֑וֹר וַֽיְהִי־אֽוֹר: 4 וַיַּ֧רְא אֱלֹהִ֛ים אֶת־הָא֖וֹר כִּי־ט֑וֹב וַיַּבְדֵּ֣ל אֱלֹהִ֔ים בֵּ֥ין הָא֖וֹר וּבֵ֥ין הַחֹֽשֶׁךְ: 5 וַיִּקְרָ֨א אֱלֹהִ֤ים ׀ לָאוֹר֙ י֔וֹם וְלַחֹ֖שֶׁךְ קָ֣רָא לָ֑יְלָה וַֽיְהִי־עֶ֥רֶב וַֽיְהִי־בֹ֖קֶר י֥וֹם אֶחָֽד: פ 6 וַיֹּ֣אמֶר אֱלֹהִ֔ים יְהִ֥י רָקִ֖יעַ בְּת֣וֹךְ הַמָּ֑יִם וִיהִ֣י מַבְדִּ֔יל בֵּ֥ין מַ֖יִם לָמָֽיִם: 7 וַיַּ֣עַשׂ אֱלֹהִים֮ אֶת־הָרָקִיעַ֒ וַיַּבְדֵּ֗ל בֵּ֤ין הַמַּ֨יִם֙ אֲשֶׁר֙ מִתַּ֣חַת לָרָקִ֔יעַ וּבֵ֣ין הַמַּ֔יִם אֲשֶׁ֖ר מֵעַ֣ל לָרָקִ֑יעַ וַֽיְהִי־כֵֽן: 8 וַיִּקְרָ֧א אֱלֹהִ֛ים לָֽרָקִ֖יעַ שָׁמָ֑יִם וַֽיְהִי־עֶ֥רֶב וַֽיְהִי־בֹ֖קֶר י֥וֹם שֵׁנִֽי: פ

V. 5. Note the penultimate accent in קָ֣רָא in the phrase קָ֣רָא לָ֑יְלָה. Hebrew typically does not have two consecutive accented syllables, and in such situations, the accent of the first word moves back. This is called נָסוֹג אָחוֹר.

Exodus 10:1–2

10:1 וַיֹּ֤אמֶר יְהוָה֙ אֶל־מֹשֶׁ֔ה בֹּ֖א אֶל־פַּרְעֹ֑ה כִּֽי־אֲנִ֞י הִכְבַּ֤דְתִּי אֶת־לִבּוֹ֙ וְאֶת־לֵ֣ב עֲבָדָ֔יו לְמַ֗עַן שִׁתִ֛י אֹתֹתַ֥י אֵ֖לֶּה בְּקִרְבּֽוֹ: 2 וּלְמַ֡עַן תְּסַפֵּר֩ בְּאָזְנֵ֨י בִנְךָ֜ וּבֶן־בִּנְךָ֗ אֵ֣ת אֲשֶׁ֤ר הִתְעַלַּ֨לְתִּי֙ בְּמִצְרַ֔יִם וְאֶת־אֹתֹתַ֖י אֲשֶׁר־שַׂ֣מְתִּי בָ֑ם וִֽידַעְתֶּ֖ם כִּי־אֲנִ֥י יְהוָֽה:

V. 1 Note the defective spelling of the infinitive construct in שִׁתִ֛י.

Leviticus 16:20–26

20 וְכִלָּה֙ מִכַּפֵּ֣ר אֶת־הַקֹּ֔דֶשׁ וְאֶת־אֹ֥הֶל מוֹעֵ֖ד וְאֶת־הַמִּזְבֵּ֑חַ וְהִקְרִ֖יב אֶת־הַשָּׂעִ֥יר הֶחָֽי׃ 21 וְסָמַ֨ךְ אַהֲרֹ֜ן אֶת־שְׁתֵּ֣י יָדָ֗ו [יָדָיו֙] עַ֤ל רֹאשׁ֙ הַשָּׂעִ֣יר הַחַ֔י וְהִתְוַדָּ֣ה עָלָ֗יו אֶת־כָּל־עֲוֺנֹת֙ בְּנֵ֣י יִשְׂרָאֵ֔ל וְאֶת־כָּל־פִּשְׁעֵיהֶ֖ם לְכָל־חַטֹּאתָ֑ם וְנָתַ֤ן אֹתָם֙ עַל־רֹ֣אשׁ הַשָּׂעִ֔יר וְשִׁלַּ֛ח בְּיַד־אִ֥ישׁ עִתִּ֖י הַמִּדְבָּֽרָה׃ 22 וְנָשָׂ֨א הַשָּׂעִ֥יר עָלָ֛יו אֶת־כָּל־עֲוֺנֹתָ֖ם אֶל־אֶ֣רֶץ גְּזֵרָ֑ה וְשִׁלַּ֥ח אֶת־הַשָּׂעִ֖יר בַּמִּדְבָּֽר׃ 23 וּבָ֤א אַהֲרֹן֙ אֶל־אֹ֣הֶל מוֹעֵ֔ד וּפָשַׁט֙ אֶת־בִּגְדֵ֣י הַבָּ֔ד אֲשֶׁ֥ר לָבַ֖שׁ בְּבֹא֣וֹ אֶל־הַקֹּ֑דֶשׁ וְהִנִּיחָ֖ם שָֽׁם׃ 24 וְרָחַ֨ץ אֶת־בְּשָׂר֤וֹ בַמַּ֙יִם֙ בְּמָק֣וֹם קָד֔וֹשׁ וְלָבַ֖שׁ אֶת־בְּגָדָ֑יו וְיָצָ֗א וְעָשָׂ֤ה אֶת־עֹֽלָתוֹ֙ וְאֶת־עֹלַ֣ת הָעָ֔ם וְכִפֶּ֥ר בַּעֲד֖וֹ וּבְעַ֥ד הָעָֽם׃ 25 וְאֵ֛ת חֵ֥לֶב הַחַטָּ֖את יַקְטִ֥יר הַמִּזְבֵּֽחָה׃ 26 וְהַֽמְשַׁלֵּ֤חַ אֶת־הַשָּׂעִיר֙ לַעֲזָאזֵ֔ל יְכַבֵּ֣ס בְּגָדָ֔יו וְרָחַ֥ץ אֶת־בְּשָׂר֖וֹ בַּמָּ֑יִם וְאַחֲרֵי־כֵ֖ן יָב֥וֹא אֶל־הַֽמַּחֲנֶֽה׃

V. 21 עִתִּ֖י will be found in the lexicon under ענה.

V. 23 וְהִנִּיחָ֖ם will be found in the lexicon under the הִפְעִיל of נוח (with a suffix).

Deuteronomy 4:9–11

9 רַ֡ק הִשָּׁ֣מֶר לְךָ֩ וּשְׁמֹ֨ר נַפְשְׁךָ֜ מְאֹ֗ד פֶּן־תִּשְׁכַּ֣ח אֶת־הַדְּבָרִ֡ים אֲשֶׁר־רָא֣וּ עֵינֶיךָ֩ וּפֶן־יָס֜וּרוּ מִלְּבָבְךָ֗ כֹּ֚ל יְמֵ֣י חַיֶּ֔יךָ וְהוֹדַעְתָּ֥ם לְבָנֶ֖יךָ וְלִבְנֵ֥י בָנֶֽיךָ׃ 10 י֗וֹם אֲשֶׁ֨ר עָמַ֜דְתָּ לִפְנֵ֨י יְהוָ֣ה אֱלֹהֶיךָ֮ בְּחֹרֵב֒ בֶּאֱמֹ֨ר יְהוָ֜ה אֵלַ֗י הַקְהֶל־לִי֙ אֶת־הָעָ֔ם וְאַשְׁמִעֵ֖ם אֶת־דְּבָרָ֑י אֲשֶׁ֨ר יִלְמְד֜וּן לְיִרְאָ֣ה אֹתִ֗י כָּל־הַיָּמִים֙ אֲשֶׁ֨ר הֵ֤ם חַיִּים֙ עַל־הָ֣אֲדָמָ֔ה וְאֶת־בְּנֵיהֶ֖ם יְלַמֵּדֽוּן׃ 11 וַתִּקְרְב֣וּן וַתַּֽעַמְד֔וּן תַּ֖חַת הָהָ֑ר וְהָהָ֞ר בֹּעֵ֤ר בָּאֵשׁ֙ עַד־לֵ֣ב הַשָּׁמַ֔יִם חֹ֖שֶׁךְ עָנָ֥ן וַעֲרָפֶֽל׃

V. 9 וְהוֹדַעְתָּ֥ם is found under the הִפְעִיל of ידע; it is originally a פ״ו verb.

V. 10 וְאַשְׁמִעֵ֖ם is spelled defectively. Also, note that the "tense" is not converted (that is, it is not וָאַשְׁמִעֵם), and it occurs after the imperative; hence, it is part of a purpose clause, and should be translated "so that . . ."

1 Kings 18:25–29

25 וַיֹּאמֶר אֵלִיָּהוּ לִנְבִיאֵי הַבַּעַל בַּחֲרוּ לָכֶם הַפָּר הָאֶחָד וַעֲשׂוּ רִאשֹׁנָה כִּי אַתֶּם הָרַבִּים וְקִרְאוּ בְּשֵׁם אֱלֹהֵיכֶם וְאֵשׁ לֹא תָשִׂימוּ: 26 וַיִּקְחוּ אֶת־הַפָּר אֲשֶׁר־נָתַן לָהֶם וַיַּעֲשׂוּ וַיִּקְרְאוּ בְשֵׁם־הַבַּעַל מֵהַבֹּקֶר וְעַד־הַצָּהֳרַיִם לֵאמֹר הַבַּעַל עֲנֵנוּ וְאֵין קוֹל וְאֵין עֹנֶה וַיְפַסְּחוּ עַל־הַמִּזְבֵּחַ אֲשֶׁר עָשָׂה: 27 וַיְהִי בַצָּהֳרַיִם וַיְהַתֵּל בָּהֶם אֵלִיָּהוּ וַיֹּאמֶר קִרְאוּ בְקוֹל־גָּדוֹל כִּי־אֱלֹהִים הוּא כִּי שִׂיחַ וְכִי־שִׂיג לוֹ וְכִי־דֶרֶךְ לוֹ אוּלַי יָשֵׁן הוּא וְיִקָץ: 28 וַיִּקְרְאוּ בְּקוֹל גָּדוֹל וַיִּתְגֹּדְדוּ כְּמִשְׁפָּטָם בַּחֲרָבוֹת וּבָרְמָחִים עַד־שְׁפָךְ־דָּם עֲלֵיהֶם: 29 וַיְהִי כַּעֲבֹר הַצָּהֳרַיִם וַיִּתְנַבְּאוּ עַד לַעֲלוֹת הַמִּנְחָה וְאֵין־קוֹל וְאֵין־עֹנֶה וְאֵין קָשֶׁב:

Zechariah 8:1–6

8:1 וַיְהִי דְּבַר־יְהוָה צְבָאוֹת לֵאמֹר: 2 כֹּה אָמַר יְהוָה צְבָאוֹת קִנֵּאתִי לְצִיּוֹן קִנְאָה גְדוֹלָה וְחֵמָה גְדוֹלָה קִנֵּאתִי לָהּ:
3 כֹּה אָמַר יְהוָה שַׁבְתִּי אֶל־צִיּוֹן וְשָׁכַנְתִּי בְּתוֹךְ יְרוּשָׁלִָם וְנִקְרְאָה יְרוּשָׁלִַם עִיר־הָאֱמֶת וְהַר־יְהוָה צְבָאוֹת הַר הַקֹּדֶשׁ: ס
4 כֹּה אָמַר יְהוָה צְבָאוֹת עֹד יֵשְׁבוּ זְקֵנִים וּזְקֵנוֹת בִּרְחֹבוֹת יְרוּשָׁלִָם וְאִישׁ מִשְׁעַנְתּוֹ בְּיָדוֹ מֵרֹב יָמִים:
5 וּרְחֹבוֹת הָעִיר יִמָּלְאוּ יְלָדִים וִילָדוֹת מְשַׂחֲקִים בִּרְחֹבֹתֶיהָ: ס
6 כֹּה אָמַר יְהוָה צְבָאוֹת כִּי יִפָּלֵא בְּעֵינֵי שְׁאֵרִית הָעָם הַזֶּה בַּיָּמִים הָהֵם גַּם־בְּעֵינַי יִפָּלֵא נְאֻם יְהוָה צְבָאוֹת פ

Psalm 8:5–10

5 מָֽה־אֱנ֥וֹשׁ כִּֽי־תִזְכְּרֶ֑נּוּ וּבֶן־אָ֝דָ֗ם כִּ֣י תִפְקְדֶֽנּוּ׃

6 וַתְּחַסְּרֵ֣הוּ מְּ֭עַט מֵאֱלֹהִ֑ים וְכָב֖וֹד וְהָדָ֣ר תְּעַטְּרֵֽהוּ׃

7 תַּ֭מְשִׁילֵהוּ בְּמַעֲשֵׂ֣י יָדֶ֑יךָ כֹּ֝ל שַׁ֣תָּה תַֽחַת־רַגְלָֽיו׃

8 צֹנֶ֣ה וַאֲלָפִ֣ים כֻּלָּ֑ם וְ֝גַ֗ם בַּהֲמ֥וֹת שָׂדָֽי׃

9 צִפּ֣וֹר שָׁ֭מַיִם וּדְגֵ֣י הַיָּ֑ם עֹ֝בֵ֗ר אָרְח֥וֹת יַמִּֽים׃

10 יְהוָ֥ה אֲדֹנֵ֑ינוּ מָֽה־אַדִּ֥יר שִׁ֝מְךָ֗ בְּכָל־הָאָֽרֶץ׃

Vv. 6–7   תַּמְשִׁילֵהוּ, תְּעַטְּרֵהוּ and וַתְּחַסְּרֵהוּ have a 3ms objective suffix; their בִּנְיָן is as expected.

V. 7   שַׁתָּה is from שׁ(י)ת, and the final הֵא is a *mater lectionis*. The order of the phrase כֹּל שַׁתָּה תַחַת־רַגְלָיו: is direct object + verb (w/ subject) + prepositional phrase.

25 The Derived Conjugations (בִּנְיָנִים) Other Verbs

It is impossible within the scope of this textbook to detail all of the forms of the verbs in all of the בִּנְיָנִים; for a complete treatment of that material, I recommend Thomas O. Lambdin, *Introduction to Biblical Hebrew* (New York: Scribner's, 1971), lessons 37–51. In this chapter I shall assume mastery of the forms taught in the past several chapters—that is, the קַל verbs of all types and the healthy verb in all of the בִּנְיָנִים; based on phonological principles developed in the earlier chapters, this chapter deals with the changes affected by weak verbs, in particular בִּנְיָנִים. My emphasis is recognition rather than construction, and toward that goal this chapter should be used in conjunction with the verb paradigms from *Gesenius' Hebrew Grammar as Edited and Enlarged by the Late E. Kautzsch . . . Second English Edition . . . by A. E. Cowley* (Oxford: Oxford University Press, 1910), some of which were seen in chapter 24. In contrast to previous chapters, this chapter is organized according to verb classes rather than verb "tenses."

Guttural Verbs

The forms of these verbs will reflect two types of changes: there are several vowels that the gutturals prefer, and the gutturals cannot be doubled, so in the נִפְעַל imperfect and the פִּעֵל (all forms), we must have either compensatory lengthening or virtual doubling.

For first gutturals, see p. 514 of the Gesenius paradigms. As noted there, the נִפְעַל perfect is introduced with נֶ or נֶ, as in נֶעֱמַד, in contrast to the nonguttural נִקְטַל; this vowel change is caused by the guttural. The initial נוּן of the נִפְעַל remains. The same is true for the participle, where we have נֶעֱמָד as opposed to נִקְטָל. In the imperfect, however, the initial guttural cannot take the expected דָּגֵשׁ חָזָק (compare יִקָּטֵל). Instead we have compensatory lengthening, with the short חִירֶק חָסֵר lengthened to the long צֵרִי; this results in the form יֵעָמֵד. The same is true for the infinitive construct (הִקָּטֵל ‖ הֵעָמֵד) and the imperatives (for example, הִקָּטֵל ‖ הֵעָמֵד). Thus for first gutturals these forms of the נִפְעַל are recognized by the characteristic *i* vowel of the prefix that is elongated through compensatory lengthening.

The הָפְעַל and הִפְעִיל are typified by closed first syllables—for example, הִקְטִיל and יָקְטַל. Although gutturals may close a syllable, they tend not to, so instead the הִפְעִיל forms are הֶעֱמִיד and יַעֲמִיד and the הָפְעַל forms הָעֳמַד and יָעֳמַד. These forms are easy to recognize because they retain the characteristic signs of their respective בִּנְיָנִים: the prefixed הָא for the perfect and the פַּתַח and קָמֶץ prefix vowels for the imperfect.

For second gutturals, see p. 515 of the Gesenius paradigm. The נִפְעַל is relatively straightforward—it is identical with healthy verbs, except when an expected שְׁוָא נָע is replaced by a חֲטַף פַּתַח, as in נִשְׁחֲטוּ (compare נִקְטְלוּ). The פִּעֵל, פֻּעַל, and הִתְפַּעֵל present a more serious problem, however, because all of these בִּנְיָנִים are characterized by doubling of the middle root letter. In the case of ברכ, which is used for the Gesenius paradigm, compensatory lengthening occurs. Thus we have, for example, בֵּרֵךְ instead of קִטֵּל and יִתְבָּרֵךְ instead of יִתְקַטֵּל. Verbs with a middle חע are not represented in this paradigm, however—they usually are subject to virtual doubling, as may be seen, for example, in the perfect פִּעֵל forms שִׁחֵת and בִּעֵר. With words that are middle אלך, we typically find compensatory lengthening (for example, בֵּאֵר), though there are cases here of virtual doubling as well. In cases of second guttural verbs, then, the פִּעֵל and פֻּעַל may be recognized only by the characteristic vowel patterns, because the typical doubling may not be expressed.

For third gutturals, see pp. 516–17 of the Gesenius paradigms. Because none of the בִּנְיָנִים is characterized by doubling of the third radical, the only change of these forms is connected to the vocalic preferences of the guttural. Specifically, the vowel before the guttural is typically changed to a פַּתַח (partial assimilation), and if the guttural appears at the end of the word after an *i* vowel, it receives a פַּתַח גְּנוּבָה. For example, we have in the נִפְעַל: יִשָׁלַח (compare יִקָּטֵל) and in the הִפְעִיל: הִשְׁלִיחַ (compare הִקְטִיל). In spite of these minor changes, however, the main distinguishing characteristics of the various בִּנְיָנִים are visible.

First Weak Verbs

The conjugation of פ״נ and פ״י verbs in the various בִּנְיָנִים is relatively straightforward as long as several basic principles are remembered: נוּן is prone to assimilation in cases where it is adjacent to a consonant, leaving behind a דָּגֵשׁ חָזָק (see pp. 45–46), and many פ״י verbs are historically פ״ו verbs, and the original וָו "returns" when it does not begin the word (see p. 209). פא״ verbs form a special class only in the קַל; otherwise, they are treated like first gutturals, which have been discussed.

For פנ״ verbs, see p. 520 of the Gesenius paradigms. The behavior of these verbs is regular given the rules governing the assimilation of the נוּן. Assimilation occurs in most forms of the הִפְעִיל ,נִפְעַל, and הָפְעַל. (Because of the nature of the inflectional prefixes in the פָּעֵל, פֻּעַל, and הִתְפַּעֵל verbs, פנ״ verbs are regular in these בִּנְיָנִים.) For example, in נִפְעַל perfect we have נִגַּשׁ (*נִנְגַּשׁ >) (|| נִקְטַל), and in the הִפְעִיל imperfect we have יַגִּישׁ (*יַנְגִּישׁ >). These forms are relatively easy to recognize and parse: they may be recognized by the דָּגֵשׁ חָזָק, and they may be parsed by writing out the reconstructed pre-דָּגֵשׁ form and comparing it with the paradigm of healthy verbs (for example, יַגֵּשׁ > *יַנְגֵּשׁ || יִקְטֹל). In some cases, however, there may be confusion between the 3ms perfect of פנ״ verbs in the נִפְעַל and the פָּעֵל. This is the case, for example, with the verb נחם, which is intransitive in the נִפְעַל, and means "to be sorry," but in the פָּעֵל is transitive, "to comfort." In both, the 3ms perfect is נִחַם (note the virtual doubling of the חֵית and the influence of the guttural on the final vowel of the פָּעֵל); context may determine how the verb should be parsed and translated.

For פי״ verbs, see pp. 522–23 of the Gesenius paradigms; most of the paradigm deals with the verbs that are originally פו״, while the last two columns concern true פי״ verbs (see p. 209). Original פו״ verbs are regular in the פָּעֵל and פֻּעַל. In the הִתְפַּעֵל, either a וָו or יוֹד may appear; compare the forms הִתְוַדָּה and הִתְיַלֵּד. In the הִפְעִיל, נִפְעַל, and הָפְעַל, the original וָו returns. In cases in which the first root letter takes a דָּגֵשׁ חָזָק, like the נִפְעַל imperfect, the וָו is written, as in יִוָּשֵׁב (|| יִקָּטֵל). More commonly, the original וָו closed the syllable, and the CVw>CV[long]. The prefixes of the נִפְעַל perfect and the הִפְעִיל perfect and imperfect are וֹ, while the הָפְעַל prefixes are וּ. The rest of the word is unaffected by these changes at the beginning of the word. For example, we have in the נִפְעַל 3ms perfect נוֹשַׁב (|| נִקְטַל), in the הִפְעִיל 3ms imperfect יוֹשִׁיב (|| יַקְטִיל), and in the הָפְעַל ms participle מוּשָׁב (|| מָקְטָל). (The last syllable of the הִפְעִיל may be shortened in the jussive and converted imperfect, as in healthy verbs; we thus have וַיֹּשֶׁב and וַיּוֹשֵׁב.) Thus, when an unexpected וָו appears in the initial position of a conjugated verb, it is most likely historically a פו״ verb. Although these are *historically* פו״ verbs, by convention they are listed in the lexica and in other grammatical tools as פי״ verbs.

Original or "proper" פי״ verbs occur only in the קַל and the הִפְעִיל. In the הִפְעִיל, instead of Ciy or Cay, we have Cê. For example, the הִפְעִיל 3ms perfect of יטב is הֵיטִיב (|| הִקְטִיל), and the corresponding imperfect is יֵיטִיב (|| יַקְטִיל).

Hollow Verbs

For hollow verbs, see pp. 524–25 of the Gesenius paradigms; as these paradigms indicate, the so-called ע״י and ע״ו are conjugated differently only in the קַל; in all the other בִּנְיָנִים they have merged. This means that if you find a hollow verb in a בִּנְיָן other than קַל, it is impossible from that context alone to determine whether it would be listed in the lexica as ק׳׳ם or ק׳׳ום. (In terms of finding the correct root, it is noteworthy that there are many more ע״וs than ע״יs, and most of these verbs are cross-listed in the lexica.)

As indicated in the Gesenius paradigm, these verbs are distinguished by having two special בִּנְיָנִים: the *Pôlēl* (פֹּלֵל) and the *Pôlal* (פֹּלַל), that are used instead of the פִּעֵל and פֻּעַל. (There is also a reflexive הִתְפֹּלֵל, comparable to the הִתְפַּעֵל.) The פִּעֵל of these verbs is rare, though it is found in LBH texts; when it is found, the יוֹד is treated as a consonant, and the verb is conjugated as a regular פִּעֵל, as in לְקַיֵּם (|| לְדַבֵּר).

The נִפְעַל is characterized by a חוֹלֶם between the two strong consonants, as well as a prefix נוּן. This נוּן is assimilated in the imperfect, infinitives, and imperatives. In the perfect, the prefix vowel of the נוּן is a קָמֵץ, as in the 3ms נָקוֹם (except where it is reduced proprotonically—for example, with the addition of a suffix), while in the imperfect, it is the expected חִירֶק, as in יִקּוֹם (|| יִקָּטֵל).

The הִפְעִיל is characterized by a long-i vowel between the two consonants—this helps us recognize these verbs as הִפְעִיל. The perfect has a prefix הֵ (elongated from the הִ in a closed syllable of regular verbs), while the imperfect takes a קָמֵץ (elongated from the פַּתַח in a closed syllable of regular verbs). Thus the 3ms forms are הֵקִים (|| הִקְטִיל) and יָקִים (|| יַקְטִיל). Forms like יָקִים, however, are ambiguous—they might be found as a ק׳׳ם perfect verb in the קַל or הִפְעִיל, as well as a ק׳׳ום verb in the הִפְעִיל perfect. For example, יָשִׂים (from שׂ[י]ם) is a קַל, while יָקִים (from ק[ו]ם) is a הִפְעִיל. The word יָבִין (from ב[י]ן) is truly ambiguous—context determines whether it is a קַל, "he discerned," or a הִפְעִיל, "he taught" (a causative).

In the jussive and converted imperfect, these forms are shortened, just like the hollow קַל ע״י verb (for example, in the קַל, יָשִׂים but וַיָּשֶׂם or וַיָּשֶׁם). Thus in the הִפְעִיל, the imperfect is יָקִים the jussive is יָקֵם, as in Jeremiah 28:6, יָקֵם יְהוָה אֶת־דְּבָרֶיךָ אֲשֶׁר נִבֵּאתָ, "may YHWH fulfill the words that you have prophesied," and the converted imperfect is וַיָּקֶם. A guttural will change the vowel of הַפֹּעַל ע to the preferred פַּתַח; we thus have וַיָּרַח, "he smelled" (from ר[ו]ח) and וַיָּעַד, "he testified" (from ע[ו]ד).

The הָפְעַל is conjugated identically to that of פ״י verbs, thus הוּקַם ([ק][ו][מ]) || הוּשַׁב (יש״ב). Attestations of the root in other בִּנְיָנִים determine whether the root is hollow or פ״י.

The special בִּנְיָנִים known as פֹּלֵל, פֹּלַל, and הִתְפֹּלֵל are characterized by duplication of the final consonant—for example, קוֹמֵם, יְקוֹמֵם, and הִתְבֹּשֵׁשׁ; this may be compared to the doubling of the middle radical in פִּעֵל/פֻּעַל. This doubling makes these forms easy to identify.

Geminate Verbs

For geminate (or ע״ע) verbs, see pp. 518–19 of the Gesenius paradigms. Although it is not indicated on the chart, the פָּעֵל (and very infrequently, the פָּעַל) of the geminates does exist; like the hollow verbs, geminates usually take a special form, *Poʿēl* (and its passive *Poʿal*). The בִּנְיָן of a geminate can typically be recognized by the usual signs of each בִּנְיָן. For example, in the נִפְעַל perfect we find a prefix נוּן, as in נָסַב, and in the imperfect, a דָּגֵשׁ חָזָק in the first root letter preceded by a חִירֶק, as in יִסַּב; in the הִפְעִיל perfect we find a prefix הֵא, as in הֲסִבּוֹת, and in the imperfect, the prefix is marked with an a-class vowel (except where it reduced), as in תָּסֵב. In the הָפְעַל, both perfect and imperfect are characterized by a u-class vowel, as in הוּסַבָּה and יֻסַּב. With the exception of the *Poʿēl* and *Poʿal*, the forms of the geminates are typically the most difficult to recognize and parse, because the gemination often does not appear in the conjugated verb.

ל״י Verbs

For ל״י see pp. 528–29 of the Gesenius paradigms, where they are known by their traditional title of ל״ה verbs. Their conjugation in the various בִּנְיָנִים is straightforward if the conjugation of the קַל is understood: all of the בִּנְיָנִים take the same inflectional suffixes in the perfect as the קַל. Because the weakness of ל״י verbs is at the end of the word, the various distinguishing signs of each of the בִּנְיָנִים are clearly visible. For example, in the 3ms perfect, all of the forms end in ◌ָה. The various בִּנְיָנִים are then distinguished in the typical ways: קַל has no doubling or prefixes (גָּלָה); נִפְעַל has a prefixed נוּן (נִגְלָה); פִּעֵל and פֻּעַל have a doubled middle root letter (גִּלָּה, גֻּלָּה); הִפְעִיל and הָפְעַל have a prefix הֵא (הִגְלָה, הָגְלָה); and הִתְפַּעֵל has a prefixed הִת as well as a doubled middle root letter (הִתְגַּלָּה).

In the jussive and converted imperfect, the final syllable is typically dropped, just as we saw in the קַל, where יִבְנֶה "changes to" וַיִּבֶן (with a helping vowel). In the נִפְעַל we have the jussive תִּגָּל (compare תִּגָּלֶה). In the פִּעֵל the shortening of the form causes the loss of the doubling of the middle root letter, making these verbs difficult to parse. We thus have וַיְצַו "he commanded" from יְצַוֶּה, "he will command." Such forms, which are quite common, must be recognized by their vowel patterns as converted imperfect פִּעֵלs of ל״ה verbs.

In the הִפְעִיל we have וַיַּשְׁקְ (compare יַשְׁקֶה) and a secondary form וַיֶּגֶל (compare יַגְלֶה). With many verbs that are ל״ה and first gutturals, the קַל and הִפְעִיל shortened forms are identical (for example, וַיַּעַל), just as the imperfects are identical (יַעֲלֶה—these forms are identical because the initial guttural causes the prefix vowel to be a פַּתַח even in the קַל, though פַּתַח typifies the הִפְעִיל, and the final original יוֹד causes an i-class vowel, which elsewhere typifies the הִפְעִיל, to appear even in the קַל). Context alone determines how to parse these identical forms. For example, in Exodus 24:13, וַיַּעַל מֹשֶׁה אֶל־הַר הָאֱלֹהִים, "Moses ascended the mountain of God," context and the intransitivity of the verb suggest that עלי is in the קַל, while in Genesis 8:20, וַיַּעַל עֹלֹת בַּמִּזְבֵּחַ, "He offered up burnt offerings on the altar," context and the transitivity of the verb (it takes the direct object עֹלֹת) suggest that עלי is in the הִפְעִיל. In a substantial number of cases the הִפְעִיל converted imperfect of ל״ה verbs is not shortened, as in 2 Kings 3:2, where the typical formula וַיַּעַשׂ הָרַע בְּעֵינֵי יְהוָה, "He did what was evil before YHWH," appears as וַיַּעֲשֶׂה הָרַע בְּעֵינֵי יְהוָֹה.

ל״א Verbs

For ל״א verbs, see pp. 526–27 of the Gesenius paradigms. The recognition of these verbs is relatively straightforward because the signs of the various בִּנְיָנִים are not affected by the final weakness of the אָלֶף. These verbs are similar to regular verbs, with two main exceptions: (1) because the final syllable is open, a short vowel in that syllable is lengthened (for example, נִפְעַל 3ms perfect נִקְטַל∥נִמְצָא); (2) in several cases, the vocalization of the ל״א verbs seems to have assimilated partially to that of the common ל״ה verbs (for example, נִפְעַל 2fp imperfect תִּקָּטַלְנָה∥תִּמָּצֶאנָה as opposed to תִּגָּלֶינָה—all of the בִּנְיָנִים show this feature).

Other Irregular Verbs

The word used for "to bow down" takes forms like וְהִשְׁתַּחֲוִיתָ (2ms converted perfect), לְהִשְׁתַּחֲוֹת (infinitive construct), וַיִּשְׁתַּחוּ (2ms converted imperfect), and וַיִּשְׁתַּחֲווּ (2mp converted imperfect). There has been considerable debate concerning the root and בִּנְיָן of these forms: some consider them to be a הִתְפַּעֵל of שׁחי, while others claim they are a הִשְׁתַּפְעֵל of חוי.

There are additional בִּנְיָנִים that are barely attested; these are described in the BH reference grammars.

In some cases, the same defective verb may appear to have various roots. For example, "to be silent" seems to be formed from the roots ד(ו)מ, דמם, and דמי. In other cases, we have suppletion, where specific roots are used in particular בִּנְיָנִים or tenses; for example, we have ט(ו)ב in the perfect and יטב in the imperfect ("to be good"), and יקצ, "to awake," in the קַל, while ק(ו)צ is the root in the הִפְעִיל.

Vocabulary for chapter 25

[פָּעֵל] אוי	to desire (lacking אִוָּה lacking יְאַוֶּה)	
[הִתְפַּעֵל]	to desire strongly, lust after (lacking הִתְאַוָּה מִתְאַוֶּה יִתְאַוֶּה)	
[הִפְעִיל] אזנ	to listen, hear (הֶאֱזִין יַאֲזִין הַאֲזֵן rare)	
[נִפְעַל] אמנ	to be established, firm (lacking נֶאֱמַן נֶאֱמָן יֵאָמֵן)	
[הִפְעִיל]	to trust, believe (הֶאֱמִין מַאֲמִין יַאֲמִין הַאֲמֵן)	
[פָּעֵל] ברכ	to bless (בֵּרַךְ מְבָרֵךְ יְבָרֵךְ בָּרֵךְ)	
[פָּעֵל] הלל	to praise (הִלֵּל מְהַלֵּל יְהַלֵּל הַלֵּל)	
[נִפְעַל] חבא	to hide (lacking נֶחְבָּא נֶחְבָּא יֵחָבֵא)	
[פָּעֵל] חלל	to pollute, defile (lacking חִלֵּל מְחַלֵּל יְחַלֵּל)	
[הִפְעִיל]	to begin (lacking הֵחֵל מֵחֵל יָחֵל)	
[הִפְעִיל] חרמ	to destroy, proscribe (הֶחֱרִים יַחֲרִים הַחֲרֵם lacking)	
[הִפְעִיל] ידי	to give thanks (הוֹדָה מוֹדֶה יוֹדֶה הוֹדֵה)	
[פָּעֵל] יחל	to wait (יִחַל מְיַחֵל יְיַחֵל יַחֵל)	
[הִפְעִיל] יכח	to reprove, rebuke (הוֹכִיחַ מוֹכִיחַ יוֹכִיחַ הוֹכַח)	
[פָּעֵל] יסר	to discipline, chastise (יִסַּר מְיַסֵּר יְיַסֵּר יַסֵּר)	
[הִפְעִיל] ישע	to deliver, help (הוֹשִׁיעַ מוֹשִׁיעַ יוֹשִׁיעַ הוֹשַׁע)	
[נִפְעַל] יתר	to be left over (lacking נוֹתַר נוֹתָר יִוָּתֵר)	
[הִפְעִיל]	to leave over (הוֹתִיר יוֹתִיר הוֹתֵר lacking)	
[נִפְעַל] כ(ו)נ	to be firm (נָכוֹן נָכוֹן יִכּוֹן הִכּוֹן)	
[הִפְעִיל]	to establish, make firm (הֵכִין מֵכִין יָכִין הָכֵן)	
[פָּעֵל] כסי	to cover (כִּסָּה מְכַסֶּה יְכַסֶּה כַּסֵּה)	
[פָּעֵל] מאנ	to refuse (lacking מֵאֵן lacking יְמָאֵן)	
[פָּעֵל] מהר	to hasten (מִהַר מְמַהֵר יְמַהֵר מַהֵר)	
[נִפְעַל] נבא	to prophesy (נִבָּא נִבָּא יִנָּבֵא הִנָּבֵא)	
[הִפְעִיל] נבט	to look (הִבִּיט מַבִּיט יַבִּיט הַבֵּט)	
[הִפְעִיל] נגד	to tell (הִגִּיד מַגִּיד יַגִּיד הַגֵּד)	

נדח	to be thrust out (lacking lacking נָדַח נִדַּח)	[נִפְעַל]
	to thrust out (הֵדִיחַ יָדִיחַ הַדַּח lacking)	[הִפְעִיל]
נ(ו)ף	to raise, wave (הֵנִיף מֵנִיף יָנִיף הָנֵף)	[הִפְעִיל]
נכי	to hit, kill (הִכָּה מַכֶּה יַכֶּה הַכֵּה)	[הִפְעִיל]
נכר	(to recognize הִכִּיר מַכִּיר יַכִּיר הַכֵּר)	[הִפְעִיל]
נצב	to stand (lacking lacking נִצַּב נִצָּב)	[נִפְעַל]
	to erect (הִצִּיב מַצִּיב יַצִּיב הַצֵּב)	[הִפְעִיל]
נצל	to deliver, take away (הִצִּיל מַצִּיל יַצִּיל הַצֵּל)	[הִפְעִיל]
נשׂג	to reach, overtake (lacking הִשִּׂיג מַשִּׂיג יַשִּׂיג)	[הִפְעִיל]
ע(ו)ד	to testify (הֵעִיד מֵעִיד יָעִיד הָעֵד)	[הִפְעִיל]
פלא	to be extraordinary (lacking נִפְלָא יִפָּלֵא)	[נִפְעַל]
	to do wondrously (lacking הִפְלִיא מַפְלִיא יַפְלִיא)	[הִפְעִיל]
צוי	to command (צִוָּה מְצַוֶּה יְצַוֶּה צַוֵּה)	[פִּעֵל]
קהל	to assemble (lacking נִקְהָל נִקְהַל יִקָּהֵל)	[נִפְעַל]
קוי	to wait (קִוָּה יְקַוֶּה קַוֵּה lacking)	[פִּעֵל]
קנא	to be jealous, zealous (lacking קִנֵּא lacking יְקַנֵּא)	[פִּעֵל]
ר(ו)ע	to raise a shout (הֵרִיעַ מֵרִיעַ יָרִיעַ lacking)	[הִפְעִיל]
רחם	to have pity on (רִחַם מְרַחֵם יְרַחֵם רַחֵם)	[פִּעֵל]
שחת	to spoil, ruin, corrupt (שִׁחֵת lacking lacking שַׁחֵת)	[פִּעֵל]
	to spoil, ruin, corrupt (הִשְׁחִית מַשְׁחִית יַשְׁחִית הַשְׁחֵת)	[הִפְעִיל]
שקי	to give drink (הִשְׁקָה מַשְׁקֶה יַשְׁקֶה הַשְׁקֵה)	[הִפְעִיל]
שרת	to minister, serve (lacking שֵׁרֵת מְשָׁרֵת יְשָׁרֵת)	[פִּעֵל]

THE DERIVED CONJUGATIONS (בִּנְיָנִים): OTHER VERBS

TRANSLATION TIP #5:

Sometimes verbs look the same in different בִּנְיָנִים; note these ambiguities, and use the context to determine the correct בִּנְיָן and translation.

Judges 14:19: וַיִּחַר אַפּוֹ וַיַּעַל בֵּית אָבִיהוּ

The root עלי is identical in the converted imperfect in the קַל and the הִפְעִיל. The קַל is "to ascend," while the הִפְעִיל is causative, "to raise up." Even though the subject of this verb is the strong Samson, the broader context suggests the translation "He became angry and ascended to his father's house," rather than "He became angry and lifted up his father's house." This verse is especially confusing because there is no preposition introducing בֵּית אָבִיהוּ; the direct object in BH may also indicate motion toward a place (the accusative of place).

Exercises for chapter 25

1. Parse the following verbs, explaining how you know what בִּנְיָן each verb is in. Note all ambiguous forms and, if relevant, explain why that particular root is ambiguous:

יַבִּיט	
נִדַּח	
תָּבִין	
יְצַו	
וַיֵּךְ	
יוֹדֶה	
הוּשַׁב	
אָנִיף	
יָעִידוּ	
מֵאֵן	
נוֹתְרָה	
נִצָּב	
וַיַּעַל	

2. Parse and translate the verbs and verb-related forms (for example, participles and infinitives) from the following verses in Genesis:

17:20

וּלְיִשְׁמָעֵאל֮ שְׁמַעְתִּיךָ֒ הִנֵּ֣ה ׀ בֵּרַ֣כְתִּי אֹת֗וֹ וְהִפְרֵיתִ֥י אֹת֛וֹ וְהִרְבֵּיתִ֥י אֹת֖וֹ בִּמְאֹ֣ד מְאֹ֑ד שְׁנֵים־עָשָׂ֤ר נְשִׂיאִם֙ יוֹלִ֔יד וּנְתַתִּ֖יו לְג֥וֹי גָּדֽוֹל׃

18:29

וַיֹּ֨סֶף ע֜וֹד לְדַבֵּ֤ר אֵלָיו֙ וַיֹּאמַ֔ר אוּלַ֛י יִמָּצְא֥וּן שָׁ֖ם אַרְבָּעִ֑ים וַיֹּ֨אמֶר֙ לֹ֣א אֶֽעֱשֶׂ֔ה בַּעֲב֖וּר הָאַרְבָּעִֽים׃

24:48

וָאֶקֹּ֥ד וָֽאֶשְׁתַּחֲוֶ֖ה לַֽיהוָ֑ה וָאֲבָרֵ֗ךְ אֶת־יְהוָה֙ אֱלֹהֵי֙ אֲדֹנִ֣י אַבְרָהָ֔ם אֲשֶׁ֤ר הִנְחַ֙נִי֙ בְּדֶ֣רֶךְ אֱמֶ֔ת לָקַ֛חַת אֶת־בַּת־אֲחִ֥י אֲדֹנִ֖י לִבְנֽוֹ׃

29:13

וַיְהִי֩ כִשְׁמֹ֨עַ לָבָ֜ן אֶת־שֵׁ֣מַע ׀ יַעֲקֹ֣ב בֶּן־אֲחֹת֗וֹ וַיָּ֤רָץ לִקְרָאתוֹ֙ וַיְחַבֶּק־לוֹ֙ וַיְנַשֶּׁק־ל֔וֹ וַיְבִיאֵ֖הוּ אֶל־בֵּית֑וֹ וַיְסַפֵּ֣ר לְלָבָ֔ן אֵ֥ת כָּל־הַדְּבָרִ֖ים הָאֵֽלֶּה׃

34:30

וַיֹּ֨אמֶר יַעֲקֹ֜ב אֶל־שִׁמְע֣וֹן וְאֶל־לֵוִי֮ עֲכַרְתֶּ֣ם אֹתִי֒ לְהַבְאִישֵׁ֙נִי֙ בְּיֹשֵׁ֣ב הָאָ֔רֶץ בַּֽכְּנַעֲנִ֖י וּבַפְּרִזִּ֑י וַאֲנִי֙ מְתֵ֣י מִסְפָּ֔ר וְנֶאֶסְפ֤וּ עָלַי֙ וְהִכּ֔וּנִי וְנִשְׁמַדְתִּ֖י אֲנִ֥י וּבֵיתִֽי׃

37:32

וַֽיְשַׁלְּח֞וּ אֶת־כְּתֹ֣נֶת הַפַּסִּ֗ים וַיָּבִ֙יאוּ֙ אֶל־אֲבִיהֶ֔ם וַיֹּאמְר֖וּ זֹ֣את מָצָ֑אנוּ הַכֶּר־נָ֗א הַכְּתֹ֧נֶת בִּנְךָ֛ הִ֖וא אִם־לֹֽא׃

37:35

וַיָּקֻמוּ֩ כָל־בָּנָ֨יו וְכָל־בְּנֹתָ֜יו לְנַחֲמ֗וֹ וַיְמָאֵן֙ לְהִתְנַחֵ֔ם וַיֹּ֕אמֶר כִּֽי־אֵרֵ֧ד אֶל־בְּנִ֛י אָבֵ֖ל שְׁאֹ֑לָה וַיֵּ֥בְךְּ אֹת֖וֹ אָבִֽיו׃

38:13–15

13 וַיֻּגַּ֥ד לְתָמָ֖ר לֵאמֹ֑ר הִנֵּ֥ה חָמִ֛יךְ עֹלֶ֥ה תִמְנָ֖תָה לָגֹ֥ז צֹאנֽוֹ׃

14 וַתָּסַר֩ בִּגְדֵ֨י אַלְמְנוּתָ֜הּ מֵעָלֶ֗יהָ וַתְּכַ֤ס בַּצָּעִיף֙ וַתִּתְעַלָּ֔ף וַתֵּ֙שֶׁב֙ בְּפֶ֣תַח עֵינַ֔יִם אֲשֶׁ֖ר עַל־דֶּ֣רֶךְ תִּמְנָ֑תָה כִּ֤י רָאֲתָה֙ כִּֽי־גָדַ֣ל שֵׁלָ֔ה וְהִ֕וא לֹֽא־נִתְּנָ֥ה ל֖וֹ לְאִשָּֽׁה׃

15 וַיִּרְאֶ֣הָ יְהוּדָ֔ה וַֽיַּחְשְׁבֶ֖הָ לְזוֹנָ֑ה כִּ֥י כִסְּתָ֖ה פָּנֶֽיהָ׃

42:7

וַיַּ֥רְא יוֹסֵ֛ף אֶת־אֶחָ֖יו וַיַּכִּרֵ֑ם וַיִּתְנַכֵּ֨ר אֲלֵיהֶ֜ם וַיְדַבֵּ֧ר אִתָּ֣ם קָשׁ֗וֹת וַיֹּ֤אמֶר אֲלֵהֶם֙ מֵאַ֣יִן בָּאתֶ֔ם וַיֹּ֣אמְר֔וּ מֵאֶ֥רֶץ כְּנַ֖עַן לִשְׁבָּר־אֹֽכֶל׃

42:25

וַיְצַ֣ו יוֹסֵ֗ף וַיְמַלְא֤וּ אֶת־כְּלֵיהֶם֙ בָּ֔ר וּלְהָשִׁ֤יב כַּסְפֵּיהֶם֙ אִ֣ישׁ אֶל־שַׂקּ֔וֹ וְלָתֵ֥ת לָהֶ֛ם צֵדָ֖ה לַדָּ֑רֶךְ וַיַּ֥עַשׂ לָהֶ֖ם כֵּֽן׃

43:9

אָֽנֹכִי֙ אֶֽעֶרְבֶ֔נּוּ מִיָּדִ֖י תְּבַקְשֶׁ֑נּוּ אִם־לֹ֨א הֲבִיאֹתִ֤יו אֵלֶ֙יךָ֙ וְהִצַּגְתִּ֣יו לְפָנֶ֔יךָ וְחָטָ֥אתִֽי לְךָ֖ כָּל־הַיָּמִֽים׃

43:18

וַיִּֽירְא֣וּ הָֽאֲנָשִׁ֗ים כִּ֤י הֽוּבְאוּ֙ בֵּ֣ית יוֹסֵ֔ף וַיֹּאמְר֗וּ עַל־דְּבַ֤ר הַכֶּ֙סֶף֙ הַשָּׁ֣ב בְּאַמְתְּחֹתֵ֔ינוּ בַּתְּחִלָּ֖ה אֲנַ֣חְנוּ מֽוּבָאִ֑ים לְהִתְגֹּלֵ֤ל עָלֵ֙ינוּ֙ וּלְהִתְנַפֵּ֣ל עָלֵ֔ינוּ וְלָקַ֧חַת אֹתָ֛נוּ לַעֲבָדִ֖ים וְאֶת־חֲמֹרֵֽינוּ׃

44:11–13

11 וַֽיְמַהֲר֗וּ וַיּוֹרִ֛דוּ אִ֥ישׁ אֶת־אַמְתַּחְתּ֖וֹ אָ֑רְצָה וַֽיִּפְתְּח֖וּ אִ֥ישׁ אַמְתַּחְתּֽוֹ׃

12 וַיְחַפֵּ֕שׂ בַּגָּד֣וֹל הֵחֵ֔ל וּבַקָּטֹ֖ן כִּלָּ֑ה וַיִּמָּצֵא֙ הַגָּבִ֔יעַ בְּאַמְתַּ֖חַת בִּנְיָמִֽן׃

13 וַֽיִּקְרְע֖וּ שִׂמְלֹתָ֑ם וַֽיַּעֲמֹס֙ אִ֣ישׁ עַל־חֲמֹר֔וֹ וַיָּשֻׁ֖בוּ הָעִֽירָה׃

3. Using the chart below, parse the following verbs, and note ambiguities:

Verb	בִּנְיָן	Root	"Tense"	Person	Gender	Number	Other/suffix	Translation
הִצַּלְתָּ								
וָאוֹתֵר								
הַלְלוּהוּ								
נִבְּאוּ								
נֶחְבָּא								
וַיַּשְׁקְ								
רִחַם								
מְמַהֵר								
יָחֵל								
הַאֲזִינִי								
וַיַּגֵּד								
יָפֶה								
שֵׁרְתוּ								
יָרִיעַ								
בָּרֵךְ								
קִוִּיתִי								
הִתְאַוָּה								
נִצְּבוּ								
מַכִּירְךָ								
נֶאֱמָן								
יִסַּרְתָּ								
שֵׁרְתוּ								
הַצֵּל								
יוֹשַׁע								
יוֹכִיחַ								
וַתַּשְׁקְ								
הַצִּיבִי								
הַחֲרֵם								
וַיַּשְׁגֵּם								
יָחֵלְנוּ								

4. Translate the following biblical passages, parse all verbs, and analyze all nouns with suffixes. Look up all words that you do not know in a lexicon:

Genesis 24:16–23

16 וְהַֽנַּעֲרָ֗ טֹבַ֤ת מַרְאֶה֙ מְאֹ֔ד בְּתוּלָ֕ה וְאִ֖ישׁ לֹ֣א יְדָעָ֑הּ וַתֵּ֣רֶד הָעַ֔יְנָה וַתְּמַלֵּ֥א כַדָּ֖הּ וַתָּֽעַל: 17 וַיָּ֥רָץ הָעֶ֖בֶד לִקְרָאתָ֑הּ וַיֹּ֕אמֶר הַגְמִיאִ֥ינִי נָ֛א מְעַט־מַ֖יִם מִכַּדֵּֽךְ: 18 וַתֹּ֖אמֶר שְׁתֵ֣ה אֲדֹנִ֑י וַתְּמַהֵ֗ר וַתֹּ֧רֶד כַּדָּ֛הּ עַל־יָדָ֖הּ וַתַּשְׁקֵֽהוּ: 19 וַתְּכַ֖ל לְהַשְׁקֹת֑וֹ וַתֹּ֗אמֶר גַּ֤ם לִגְמַלֶּ֙יךָ֙ אֶשְׁאָ֔ב עַ֥ד אִם־כִּלּ֖וּ לִשְׁתֹּֽת: 20 וַתְּמַהֵ֗ר וַתְּעַ֤ר כַּדָּהּ֙ אֶל־הַשֹּׁ֔קֶת וַתָּ֥רָץ ע֛וֹד אֶל־הַבְּאֵ֖ר לִשְׁאֹ֑ב וַתִּשְׁאַ֖ב לְכָל־גְּמַלָּֽיו: 21 וְהָאִ֥ישׁ מִשְׁתָּאֵ֖ה לָ֑הּ מַחֲרִ֕ישׁ לָדַ֗עַת הַֽהִצְלִ֧יחַ יְהוָ֛ה דַּרְכּ֖וֹ אִם־לֹֽא: 22 וַיְהִ֗י כַּאֲשֶׁ֨ר כִּלּ֤וּ הַגְּמַלִּים֙ לִשְׁתּ֔וֹת וַיִּקַּ֣ח הָאִ֗ישׁ נֶ֣זֶם זָהָב֮ בֶּ֣קַע מִשְׁקָלוֹ֒ וּשְׁנֵ֤י צְמִידִים֙ עַל־יָדֶ֔יהָ עֲשָׂרָ֥ה זָהָ֖ב מִשְׁקָלָֽם: 23 וַיֹּ֙אמֶר֙ בַּת־מִ֣י אַ֔תְּ הַגִּ֥ידִי נָ֖א לִ֑י הֲיֵ֧שׁ בֵּית־אָבִ֛יךְ מָק֖וֹם לָ֥נוּ לָלִֽין:

Genesis 29:16–28

16 וּלְלָבָ֖ן שְׁתֵּ֣י בָנ֑וֹת שֵׁ֤ם הַגְּדֹלָה֙ לֵאָ֔ה וְשֵׁ֥ם הַקְּטַנָּ֖ה רָחֵֽל: 17 וְעֵינֵ֥י לֵאָ֖ה רַכּ֑וֹת וְרָחֵל֙ הָֽיְתָ֔ה יְפַת־תֹּ֖אַר וִיפַ֥ת מַרְאֶֽה: 18 וַיֶּאֱהַ֥ב יַעֲקֹ֖ב אֶת־רָחֵ֑ל וַיֹּ֗אמֶר אֶֽעֱבָדְךָ֙ שֶׁ֣בַע שָׁנִ֔ים בְּרָחֵ֥ל בִּתְּךָ֖ הַקְּטַנָּֽה: 19 וַיֹּ֣אמֶר לָבָ֗ן ט֚וֹב תִּתִּ֣י אֹתָ֣הּ לָ֔ךְ מִתִּתִּ֥י אֹתָ֖הּ לְאִ֣ישׁ אַחֵ֑ר שְׁבָ֖ה עִמָּדִֽי: 20 וַיַּעֲבֹ֧ד יַעֲקֹ֛ב בְּרָחֵ֖ל שֶׁ֣בַע שָׁנִ֑ים וַיִּהְי֤וּ בְעֵינָיו֙ כְּיָמִ֣ים אֲחָדִ֔ים בְּאַהֲבָת֖וֹ אֹתָֽהּ: 21 וַיֹּ֨אמֶר יַעֲקֹ֤ב אֶל־לָבָן֙ הָבָ֣ה אֶת־אִשְׁתִּ֔י כִּ֥י מָלְא֖וּ יָמָ֑י וְאָב֖וֹאָה אֵלֶֽיהָ: 22 וַיֶּאֱסֹ֥ף לָבָ֛ן אֶת־כָּל־אַנְשֵׁ֥י הַמָּק֖וֹם וַיַּ֥עַשׂ מִשְׁתֶּֽה: 23 וַיְהִ֣י בָעֶ֔רֶב וַיִּקַּח֙ אֶת־לֵאָ֣ה בִתּ֔וֹ וַיָּבֵ֥א אֹתָ֖הּ אֵלָ֑יו וַיָּבֹ֖א אֵלֶֽיהָ: 24 וַיִּתֵּ֤ן לָבָן֙ לָ֔הּ אֶת־זִלְפָּ֖ה שִׁפְחָת֑וֹ לְלֵאָ֥ה בִתּ֖וֹ שִׁפְחָֽה: 25 וַיְהִ֣י בַבֹּ֔קֶר וְהִנֵּה־הִ֖וא לֵאָ֑ה וַיֹּ֣אמֶר אֶל־לָבָ֗ן מַה־זֹּאת֙ עָשִׂ֣יתָ לִּ֔י הֲלֹ֤א בְרָחֵל֙ עָבַ֣דְתִּי עִמָּ֔ךְ וְלָ֖מָּה רִמִּיתָֽנִי: 26 וַיֹּ֣אמֶר לָבָ֔ן לֹא־יֵעָשֶׂ֥ה כֵ֖ן בִּמְקוֹמֵ֑נוּ לָתֵ֥ת הַצְּעִירָ֖ה לִפְנֵ֥י הַבְּכִירָֽה: 27 מַלֵּ֖א שְׁבֻ֣עַ זֹ֑את וְנִתְּנָ֨ה לְךָ֜ גַּם־אֶת־זֹ֗את בַּעֲבֹדָה֙ אֲשֶׁ֣ר תַּעֲבֹ֣ד עִמָּדִ֔י ע֖וֹד שֶֽׁבַע־שָׁנִ֥ים אֲחֵרֽוֹת: 28 וַיַּ֤עַשׂ יַעֲקֹב֙ כֵּ֔ן וַיְמַלֵּ֖א שְׁבֻ֣עַ זֹ֑את וַיִּתֶּן־ל֛וֹ אֶת־רָחֵ֥ל בִּתּ֖וֹ ל֥וֹ לְאִשָּֽׁה:

Deuteronomy 13:13–19

13 כִּֽי־תִשְׁמַ֞ע בְּאַחַ֣ת עָרֶ֗יךָ אֲשֶׁר֩ יְהוָ֨ה אֱלֹהֶ֧יךָ נֹתֵ֛ן לְךָ֖ לָשֶׁ֥בֶת שָׁ֖ם לֵאמֹֽר: 14 יָצְא֞וּ אֲנָשִׁ֤ים בְּנֵֽי־בְלִיַּ֙עַל֙ מִקִּרְבֶּ֔ךָ וַיַּדִּ֖יחוּ אֶת־יֹשְׁבֵ֣י עִירָ֑ם לֵאמֹ֔ר נֵלְכָ֗ה וְנַעַבְדָ֛ה אֱלֹהִ֥ים אֲחֵרִ֖ים אֲשֶׁ֥ר לֹא־יְדַעְתֶּֽם: 15 וְדָרַשְׁתָּ֣ וְחָקַרְתָּ֗ וְשָׁאַלְתָּ֖ הֵיטֵ֑ב וְהִנֵּ֤ה אֱמֶת֙ נָכ֣וֹן הַדָּבָ֔ר נֶעֶשְׂתָ֛ה הַתּוֹעֵבָ֥ה הַזֹּ֖את בְּקִרְבֶּֽךָ: 16 הַכֵּ֣ה תַכֶּ֗ה אֶת־יֹֽשְׁבֵ֛י הָעִ֥יר הַהוּא [הַהִ֖יא] לְפִי־חָ֑רֶב הַחֲרֵ֨ם אֹתָ֧הּ וְאֶת־כָּל־אֲשֶׁר־בָּ֛הּ וְאֶת־בְּהֶמְתָּ֖הּ לְפִי־חָֽרֶב: 17 וְאֶת־כָּל־שְׁלָלָ֗הּ תִּקְבֹּץ֙ אֶל־תּ֣וֹךְ רְחֹבָ֔הּ וְשָׂרַפְתָּ֨ בָאֵ֜שׁ אֶת־הָעִ֤יר וְאֶת־כָּל־שְׁלָלָהּ֙ כָּלִ֔יל לַיהוָ֖ה אֱלֹהֶ֑יךָ וְהָיְתָה֙ תֵּ֣ל עוֹלָ֔ם לֹ֥א תִבָּנֶ֖ה עֽוֹד: 18 וְלֹֽא־יִדְבַּ֧ק בְּיָדְךָ֛ מְא֖וּמָה מִן־הַחֵ֑רֶם לְמַעַן֩ יָשׁ֨וּב יְהוָ֜ה מֵחֲר֣וֹן אַפּ֗וֹ וְנָֽתַן־לְךָ֤ רַחֲמִים֙ וְרִֽחַמְךָ֣ וְהִרְבֶּ֔ךָ כַּאֲשֶׁ֥ר נִשְׁבַּ֖ע לַאֲבֹתֶֽיךָ: 19 כִּ֣י תִשְׁמַ֗ע בְּקוֹל֙ יְהוָ֣ה אֱלֹהֶ֔יךָ לִשְׁמֹר֙ אֶת־כָּל־מִצְוֹתָ֔יו אֲשֶׁ֛ר אָנֹכִ֥י מְצַוְּךָ֖ הַיּ֑וֹם לַעֲשׂוֹת֙ הַיָּשָׁ֔ר בְּעֵינֵ֖י יְהוָ֥ה אֱלֹהֶֽיךָ:

Jeremiah 17:19–27

19 כֹּה־אָמַ֨ר יְהוָ֜ה אֵלַ֗י הָלֹךְ֙ וְעָֽמַדְתָּ֙ בְּשַׁ֣עַר בְּנֵֽי־עָם [הָעָ֔ם] אֲשֶׁ֨ר יָבֹ֤אוּ בוֹ֙ מַלְכֵ֣י יְהוּדָ֔ה וַאֲשֶׁ֖ר יֵצְא֣וּ ב֑וֹ וּבְכֹ֖ל שַׁעֲרֵ֥י יְרוּשָׁלִָֽם: 20 וְאָמַרְתָּ֣ אֲלֵיהֶ֗ם שִׁמְע֤וּ דְבַר־יְהוָה֙ מַלְכֵ֣י יְהוּדָ֔ה וְכָל־יְהוּדָ֕ה וְכֹ֖ל יֹשְׁבֵ֣י יְרוּשָׁלִָ֑ם הַבָּאִ֖ים בַּשְּׁעָרִ֥ים הָאֵֽלֶּה: ס 21 כֹּ֚ה אָמַ֣ר יְהוָ֔ה הִשָּׁמְר֖וּ בְּנַפְשׁוֹתֵיכֶ֑ם וְאַל־תִּשְׂא֤וּ מַשָּׂא֙ בְּי֣וֹם הַשַּׁבָּ֔ת וַהֲבֵאתֶ֖ם בְּשַׁעֲרֵ֥י יְרוּשָׁלִָֽם: 22 וְלֹא־תוֹצִ֨יאוּ מַשָּׂ֤א מִבָּתֵּיכֶם֙ בְּי֣וֹם הַשַּׁבָּ֔ת וְכָל־מְלָאכָ֖ה לֹ֣א תַֽעֲשׂ֑וּ וְקִדַּשְׁתֶּם֙ אֶת־י֣וֹם הַשַּׁבָּ֔ת כַּאֲשֶׁ֥ר צִוִּ֖יתִי אֶת־אֲבוֹתֵיכֶֽם: 23 וְלֹ֣א שָׁמְע֔וּ וְלֹ֥א הִטּ֖וּ אֶת־אָזְנָ֑ם וַיַּקְשׁוּ֙ אֶת־עָרְפָּ֔ם לְבִלְתִּ֣י שׁוֹמֵ֔עַ [שְׁמ֔וֹעַ] וּלְבִלְתִּ֖י קַ֥חַת מוּסָֽר: 24 וְ֠הָיָה אִם־שָׁמֹ֨עַ תִּשְׁמְע֤וּן אֵלַי֙ נְאֻם־יְהוָ֔ה לְבִלְתִּ֣י ׀ הָבִ֣יא מַשָּׂ֗א בְּשַׁעֲרֵ֞י הָעִ֤יר הַזֹּאת֙ בְּי֣וֹם הַשַּׁבָּ֔ת וּלְקַדֵּ֖שׁ אֶת־י֣וֹם הַשַּׁבָּ֑ת לְבִלְתִּ֥י עֲשׂוֹת־בָּ֖ה [ב֖וֹ] כָּל־מְלָאכָֽה: 25 וּבָ֣אוּ בְשַׁעֲרֵ֣י הָעִ֣יר הַזֹּ֡את מְלָכִ֣ים ׀ וְשָׂרִ֡ים יֹשְׁבִים֩ עַל־כִּסֵּ֨א דָוִ֜ד רֹכְבִ֣ים ׀ בָּרֶ֣כֶב וּבַסּוּסִ֗ים הֵ֚מָּה וְשָׂ֣רֵיהֶ֔ם אִ֥ישׁ יְהוּדָ֖ה וְיֹשְׁבֵ֣י יְרוּשָׁלִָ֑ם וְיָשְׁבָ֥ה הָֽעִיר־הַזֹּ֖את לְעוֹלָֽם: 26 וּבָ֣אוּ מֵעָרֵֽי־יְהוּדָ֡ה

וּמִסְּבִיב֣וֹת יְרוּשָׁלִַ֡ם וּמֵאֶ֣רֶץ בִּ֠נְיָמִן וּמִן־הַשְּׁפֵלָ֨ה וּמִן־הָהָ֜ר וּמִן־הַנֶּ֗גֶב מְבִאִ֣ים עוֹלָ֣ה וְזֶ֣בַח וּמִנְחָ֣ה וּלְבוֹנָ֑ה וּמְבִאֵ֥י תוֹדָ֖ה בֵּ֥ית יְהוָֽה: 27 וְאִם־לֹ֨א תִשְׁמְע֜וּ אֵלַ֗י לְקַדֵּשׁ֙ אֶת־י֣וֹם הַשַּׁבָּ֔ת וּלְבִלְתִּ֣י ׀ שְׂאֵ֣ת מַשָּׂ֗א וּבֹ֛א בְּשַׁעֲרֵ֥י יְרוּשָׁלִַ֖ם בְּי֣וֹם הַשַּׁבָּ֑ת וְהִצַּ֧תִּי אֵ֣שׁ בִּשְׁעָרֶ֗יהָ וְאָֽכְלָה֙ אַרְמְנ֣וֹת יְרוּשָׁלִַ֔ם וְלֹ֖א תִכְבֶּֽה: פ

Job 1:1–5

1:1 אִ֛ישׁ הָיָ֥ה בְאֶֽרֶץ־ע֖וּץ אִיּ֣וֹב שְׁמ֑וֹ וְהָיָ֣ה ׀ הָאִ֣ישׁ הַה֗וּא תָּ֧ם וְיָשָׁ֛ר וִירֵ֥א אֱלֹהִ֖ים וְסָ֥ר מֵרָֽע: 2 וַיִּוָּ֥לְדוּ ל֛וֹ שִׁבְעָ֥ה בָנִ֖ים וְשָׁל֥וֹשׁ בָּנֽוֹת: 3 וַיְהִ֣י מִ֠קְנֵהוּ שִֽׁבְעַ֨ת אַלְפֵי־צֹ֜אן וּשְׁלֹ֧שֶׁת אַלְפֵ֣י גְמַלִּ֗ים וַחֲמֵ֨שׁ מֵא֤וֹת צֶֽמֶד־בָּקָר֙ וַחֲמֵ֣שׁ מֵא֣וֹת אֲתוֹנ֔וֹת וַעֲבֻדָּ֖ה רַבָּ֣ה מְאֹ֑ד וַיְהִי֙ הָאִ֣ישׁ הַה֔וּא גָּד֖וֹל מִכָּל־בְּנֵי־קֶֽדֶם: 4 וְהָלְכ֤וּ בָנָיו֙ וְעָשׂ֣וּ מִשְׁתֶּ֔ה בֵּ֖ית אִ֣ישׁ יוֹמ֑וֹ וְשָׁלְח֗וּ וְקָרְאוּ֙ לִשְׁלֹ֣שֶׁת אַחְיֽוֹתֵיהֶ֔ם [אַחְיוֹתֵיהֶ֔ם] לֶאֱכֹ֥ל וְלִשְׁתּ֖וֹת עִמָּהֶֽם: 5 וַיְהִ֡י כִּ֣י הִקִּיפוּ֩ יְמֵ֨י הַמִּשְׁתֶּ֜ה וַיִּשְׁלַ֧ח אִיּ֣וֹב וַֽיְקַדְּשֵׁ֗ם וְהִשְׁכִּ֣ים בַּבֹּ֘קֶר֮ וְהֶעֱלָ֣ה עֹלוֹת֮ מִסְפַּ֣ר כֻּלָּם֒ כִּ֚י אָמַ֣ר אִיּ֔וֹב אוּלַי֙ חָטְא֣וּ בָנַ֔י וּבֵרֲכ֥וּ אֱלֹהִ֖ים בִּלְבָבָ֑ם כָּ֛כָה יַעֲשֶׂ֥ה אִיּ֖וֹב כָּל־הַיָּמִֽים: פ

Proverbs 3:1–4

3:1 בְּ֭נִי תּוֹרָתִ֣י אַל־תִּשְׁכָּ֑ח וּ֝מִצְוֺתַ֗י יִצֹּ֥ר לִבֶּֽךָ:
2 כִּ֤י אֹ֣רֶךְ יָ֭מִים וּשְׁנ֣וֹת חַיִּ֑ים וְ֝שָׁל֗וֹם יוֹסִ֥יפוּ לָֽךְ:
3 חֶ֥סֶד וֶאֱמֶ֗ת אַֽל־יַ֫עַזְבֻ֥ךָ קָשְׁרֵ֥ם עַל־גַּרְגְּרוֹתֶ֑יךָ כָּ֝תְבֵ֗ם עַל־ל֥וּחַ לִבֶּֽךָ:
4 וּמְצָא־חֵ֥ן וְשֵֽׂכֶל־ט֑וֹב בְּעֵינֵ֖י אֱלֹהִ֣ים וְאָדָֽם: פ

Proverbs 30:7–9

7 שְׁ֭תַּיִם שָׁאַ֣לְתִּי מֵאִתָּ֑ךְ אַל־תִּמְנַ֥ע מִ֝מֶּ֗נִּי בְּטֶ֣רֶם אָמֽוּת:
8 שָׁ֤וְא ׀ וּֽדְבַר־כָּזָ֡ב הַרְחֵ֬ק מִמֶּ֗נִּי רֵ֣אשׁ וָ֭עֹשֶׁר אַל־תִּֽתֶּן־לִ֑י הַ֝טְרִיפֵ֗נִי לֶ֣חֶם חֻקִּֽי:
9 פֶּ֥ן אֶשְׂבַּ֨ע ׀ וְכִחַשְׁתִּי֮ וְאָמַרְתִּי֮ מִ֪י יְה֫וָ֥ה וּפֶֽן־אִוָּרֵ֥שׁ וְגָנַ֑בְתִּי וְ֝תָפַ֗שְׂתִּי שֵׁ֣ם אֱלֹהָֽי: פ

Cumulative Exercises

Using the chart below, parse the following verbs, and note ambiguities:

Verb	בִּנְיָן	Root	"Tense"	Person	Gender	Number	Other/suffix	Translation
נִמְצָא								
יָנֻסוּ								
נָבוֹן								
יֵעָשֶׂה								
גָּר								
אֶזְכָּרְךָ								
סַפֵּר								
וָאֹחֶז								
וְנוֹדַע								
וַתֵּבְךְּ								
זִבְחוּ								
יְרוֹמֵם								
שָׂם								
תִּתִּי								

Verb	בִּנְיָן	Root	"Tense"	Person	Gender	Number	Other/suffix	Translation
אִסְרוּ								
נָקוּמָה								
דַּבֵּר								
יָבְשָׁה								
קָמָה								
וַיָּחָן								
יָרֹם								
דְּרוּשָׁה								
יָרִים								
יֵיטִיב								
יַבְדֵּל								
טִמֵּא								
מָשׁוֹחַ								
נְבָאוּ								
בֵּרֵךְ								
וַיֹּבֶט								
לְכָה								
יְחִי								
וַיִּרְא								
תִּוָּרֵא								
הֵשִׁיב								
הֵשִׁיבוּ								
וַיְבִיאֵנִי								
מַחֲזִיק								
וּבְקָעוּהוּ								

Verb	בִּנְיָן	Root	"Tense"	Person	Gender	Number	Other/suffix	Translation
אָכְלוּ								
הֱיוֹת								
תּוֹצֵא								
בֹּאָם								
בּוֹשׁוּ								
זֹנִים								
הוֹרֵד								
וַתַּעַל								
מְהַלֵּל								
יַהֲפֹךְ								
תֹּאפוּ								
גָּדְלוּ								
וַיּוֹלֶד								

Following the example below, describe the phonological principles that explain why the second word in each pair differs from the first:

דְּבָרִים ‖ דְּבַר Propretonic reduction of ָ to ְ .

בַּמִּדְבָּר ‖ בָּעֲרָבָה
וְרִבְכֶם ‖ וּלְזַרְעָם
וָאֲצַוֶּה ‖ וַיְבָרֶךְ
וַיִּשְׁמְרוּ ‖ וַיִּקְחוּ
וַיַּשְׁמִידוּ ‖ וַיּוֹרִדוּ
שָׁמְרוּ ‖ תַּמּוּ
כָּתַבְתִּי ‖ נָתַתִּי
בְּיָדְךָ ‖ תִּתּוֹ בְיָדְךָ
וַיִּכְתֹּב ‖ וַיִּקְרָא
יִשְׁמֹר ‖ יַעֲשֶׂה

Analyze the following nouns with suffixes, as in the examples below:

BH Word	Analysis	Translation
דְּבָרִי	דָּבָר +1cs suffix	my word
כַּפֵּיהֶם	כַּפַּיִם (dual) +3ms suffix	their palms
אֹהֲבַי	אֹהֲבִים +1cs suffix	my lovers, those who love me
לַאֲבֹתֵיכֶם		
וּלְזַרְעָם		
וְרִיבְכֶם		
שִׁבְטֵיכֶם		
לְהַשְׁמִידֵנוּ		
וּלְבָנָיו		
מִלְחַמְתּוֹ		
בְּקִרְבְּכֶם		
אֹיְבֵיכֶם		
מֵאַרְצָם		
בְּיָדֵנוּ		
כְּמַעֲשֶׂיךָ		
חָכְמַתְכֶם		
בְּרִיתוֹ		
וְחֻקָּיו		
מִזְבְּחֹתֵיהֶם		
לְאֹהֲבָיו		
אַדְמָתְךָ		
אֱלֹהֵיהֶם		
וְרַגְלְךָ		
בְּצִדְקָתְךָ		

CUMULATIVE EXERCISES

Read Exodus 1:1–7 (reproduced below). Translate the passage using the attached glossary; feel free to skip the personal names in vv. 2–4.

1:1 וְאֵ֗לֶּה שְׁמוֹת֙ בְּנֵ֣י יִשְׂרָאֵ֔ל הַבָּאִ֖ים מִצְרָ֑יְמָה אֵ֣ת יַעֲקֹ֔ב אִ֥ישׁ וּבֵית֖וֹ בָּֽאוּ: 2 רְאוּבֵ֣ן שִׁמְע֔וֹן לֵוִ֖י וִיהוּדָֽה: 3 יִשָּׂשכָ֥ר זְבוּלֻ֖ן וּבִנְיָמִֽן: 4 דָּ֥ן וְנַפְתָּלִ֖י גָּ֥ד וְאָשֵֽׁר: 5 וַֽיְהִ֗י כָּל־נֶ֛פֶשׁ יֹצְאֵ֥י יֶֽרֶךְ־יַעֲקֹ֖ב שִׁבְעִ֣ים נָ֑פֶשׁ וְיוֹסֵ֖ף הָיָ֥ה בְמִצְרָֽיִם: 6 וַיָּ֤מָת יוֹסֵף֙ וְכָל־אֶחָ֔יו וְכֹ֖ל הַדּ֥וֹר הַהֽוּא: 7 וּבְנֵ֣י יִשְׂרָאֵ֗ל פָּר֧וּ וַֽיִּשְׁרְצ֛וּ וַיִּרְבּ֥וּ וַיַּֽעַצְמ֖וּ בִּמְאֹ֣ד מְאֹ֑ד וַתִּמָּלֵ֥א הָאָ֖רֶץ אֹתָֽם: פ

1. Which of the following nouns are unbound and which are constructs? How do you know?

   V. 1 שְׁמוֹת֙ בְּנֵ֣י יִשְׂרָאֵ֔ל _____

   _____

   V. 5 יֹצְאֵ֥י יֶֽרֶךְ־יַעֲקֹ֖ב _____

   _____

2. Using the grid below, parse the following verbs and verb-related forms: וַֽיְהִ֗י, בָּֽאוּ, הַבָּאִ֖ים, יֹצְאֵ֥י, וַיַּֽעַצְמ֖וּ, וַיִּרְבּ֥וּ, וַֽיִּשְׁרְצ֛וּ, פָּר֧וּ, וַתִּמָּלֵ֥א.

Verb	בִּנְיָן	Root	"Tense"	Person	Gender	Number	Other/suffix	Translation
הַבָּאִים								
בָּאוּ								
וַיְהִי								
יֹצְאֵי								
וַיַּעַצְמוּ								
וַיִּרְבּוּ								
וַיִּשְׁרְצוּ								
פָּרוּ								
וַתִּמָּלֵא								

3. Explain why there is a דָּגֵשׁ in some of the following initial letters but not in others:

בְּנֵי (v. 1) _____

_____

בָּאוּ (v. 1) _____

_____

בְּמִצְרָיִם (v. 5) _____

_____

4. The word וַיָּמָת (v. 6) has two קְמָצִים; how is each one pronounced? Why?

_____

_____

5. Why is the word נפשׁ vocalized in two different ways in v. 5?

_____

_____

6. Identify the nature of the דָּגֵשׁ in the following words:

וְאֵלֶּה בְּנֵי הַבָּאִים (v. 1) _____

_____

פָּרוּ וַיִּרְבּוּ בִּמְאֹד וַתִּמָּלֵא (v. 7) _____

_____

7. Explain the different forms of the conjunction in the following words:

וְאֵ֫לֶּה (v. 1) _____

_____

וִיהוּדָה (v. 2) _____

_____

וּבְנְיָמִן (v. 3) _____

_____

8. Explain the two different forms of וכל in v. 6.

_____

_____

Glossary of Grammatical Terms and Abbreviations

˓ This sign indicates penultimate stress—that is, stress on the next-to-last (penultimate) syllable (for example, מָ֫וֶת).

* This sign indicates that the following form is not attested. It is reconstructed, hypothetical, or presented to illustrate a pedagogical point.

\> This sign indicates that a word has changed from the form at left to the one at right.

< This sign indicates that a word has changed from the form at right to the one at left.

∅ This sign indicates the absence of an expected feature, or the presence of a silent sound.

´ This sign, used in transliterated Hebrew, indicates penultimate stress (for example, *máwet* for מָ֫וֶת).

ABP: *See* Archaic biblical poetry.

Active verb: A verb that describes an activity rather than a state.

Adjective: A word used to describe, qualify, or modify a noun.

Allophone: An alternative pronunciation of a phoneme.

Apocopated: Shortened in the final position. This term is usually used for cases in which the converted imperfect or jussive is a shortened form of the imperfect. This is most frequent in ל״ה verbs.

Apposition: A relation in which two nominals are adjacent and the second modifies the first. The first nominal may not be in the construct, and the word *namely* can often be inserted between the nominals in translating.

Archaic biblical poetry: A BH dialect reflected in some ancient poetic texts in the Bible, such as Judges 5.

Aspect: A category that indicates whether a verb's action is completed (perfect) or incomplete (imperfect).

Assimilation: The change of one sound to a different sound under the influence of another (typically adjacent) sound, as in the typical assimilation of the נוּן of the preposition מִן (e.g. *מִן־מֶלֶךְ > מִמֶּלֶךְ). In general, נוּן is prone to assimilation, and typically $C_1Vn+C_2V(C_3) > C_1VC_2+C_2V(C_3)$.

Attributive adjective: An adjective that directly modifies the noun, as in the English phrase "the good book" or the BH הַסֵּפֶר הַטּוֹב.

BH: *See* Biblical Hebrew.

Biblical Hebrew: The dialects of Hebrew reflected in the Hebrew Bible.

Biliteral: Two-lettered. A minority of Hebrew roots are biliteral, such as אֵם, "mother," or שׂ(י)ם, "to place."

Bound form: *See* Construct.

Bound preposition: A preposition that is written as part of the noun it precedes. The prepositions בְּ, כְּ, and לְ are bound prepositions.

C: Consonant.

c: Common, a form used for both the masculine and the feminine.

Cantillation marks: Signs written above and below the consonantal text that indicate how the word is to be chanted and where the word is accented.

Closed syllable: A syllable that ends in a consonant.

Cognate accusative: The use of the same root (cognate) for a verb and its direct object (accusative), as in (Genesis 11:3), נִלְבְּנָה לְבֵנִים, "let's make bricks," literally, "let's brick bricks."

Cohortative: A first-person volitional form, translated "May I/we" and typically marked by a final ָה (for example, אֶכְתְּבָה, "may I write").

Collective: A singular noun which refers to a group, such as *sheep* in English or אָדָם, "humanity," in Hebrew.

Common: A form used for both the masculine and the feminine.

Comparative: A form that expresses the possession of an attribute to a greater or lesser degree than something else. *See also* Superlative.

Compensatory lengthening: The change from a short vowel to a long vowel, usually when a syllable that would typically be closed is open (for example, the first syllable of הָאִישׁ; contrast הַטּוֹב).

Conjunctive accents: Cantillation marks that tell the reader to continue. (Opposite of disjunctive accents.)

Consonant cluster: Consecutive consonants in a syllable, in Hebrew separated only by a שְׁוָא, as in יֵשְׁתְּ.

Construct (סְמִיכוּת): A nominal joined to a following noun. It may be translated by "of" (for example, דְּבַר־הַנָּבִיא, "the word of the prophet"). Phonologically, it acts as if it has lost its accent.

Conversive *waw*: See Waw consecutive.

Converted imperfect: A verb in the imperfect preceded by a וְ with a פַּתַח and a doubled verbal prefix letter (for example, וַיִּכְתֹּב); in a narrative sequence, this is typically translated as a perfect.

Converted perfect: A verb in the perfect preceded by a וְ with a שְׁוָא (for example, וְכָתַב); in a narrative sequence, this is typically translated in the past.

Dagesh (Hebrew דָּגֵשׁ): A dot written in a Hebrew consonant (with the exception of a final הא).

Dagesh forte (Hebrew דָּגֵשׁ חָזָק): A *dagesh* that doubles the consonant in which it appears. The *dagesh forte* typically may not appear in a guttural letter.

Dagesh lene (Hebrew דָּגֵשׁ קַל): A *dagesh* that appears in the letters ב, ג, ד, כ, פ, and ת, indicating the allophonic pronunciation of ב, ג, ד, כ, פ, and ת.

Defective (Hebrew חָסֵר) spelling: the spelling of a word without a usual vowel letter.

Definite article (Hebrew הֵא הַיְדִיעָה): A הֵא preceding a noun, typically vocalized with a פַּתַח and a following דָּגֵשׁ חָזָק, indicating that the noun represents a specific object or concept.

Definiteness: Referring to a specific person, thing, or idea. In Hebrew, definiteness is often indicated with the definite article; proper nouns, nouns with pronominal suffixes, and nouns in construct with definite nouns are also definite.

Demonstrative pronoun: A deictic (pointing) pronoun that refers to a specific entity (for example, English *this* or BH זֶה).

Dentals: The consonants ד, ט, and ת, pronounced with the tongue touching the tips of the upper teeth.

Direct object: The grammatical object directly affected by the action of the verb; in BH, the *definite* direct object is usually preceded by אֵת.

Directive: A nominal form with an unaccented הָ suffix indicating that the action is toward the place specified by the word to which the directive is added, for example, שְׁכְמָה, to(ward) שְׁכֶם. Sometimes called locative.

Disjunctive accents: Cantillation marks that tell the reader to pause.

Dissimilation: The change of one sound to a different sound in the environment of an identical or similar sound.

Disyllabic: Consisting of two syllables.

Doubly transitive: Taking two direct objects.

Dual: A suffix indicating two paired items (for example, רַגְלַיִם, "two feet").

Durative: An action that takes place over time.

Elision: The loss of a sound. This is most frequent with הֵא in the middle of a word; thus instead of *בְּהַמָּקוֹם, "in the place," we get בַּמָּקוֹם. In contrast to the loss of a letter through assimilation, elision does not leave a דָּגֵשׁ חָזָק to mark the lost letter or sound.

Elongated imperative: An imperative with an added הָ afformative (for example, כָּתְבָה, "write!").

Emphatics: The consonants ט, צ, and ק, pronounced in the soft palate, in a region farther back than the corresponding letters כ, ס, and ת. Also called velars.

Energic נוּן: A נוּן inserted between a verb and its pronominal (object) suffix (for example, יְבָרְכֶנְהוּ, "he will bless him"); its use in BH is unclear and does not affect meaning.

F: Feminine.

Factitive: Turning an intransitive, typically stative verb into a transitive verb.

Finite verb: A verb that is conjugated with respect to person, such as the perfect or imperfect, in contrast to the *in*finitive.

Full (Hebrew מָלֵא) spelling: The spelling of a word using a vowel letter (for example, כּוֹתֵב, as opposed to כֹּתֵב). Also called *plene* spelling.

Furtive *pataḥ* (Hebrew פַּתַח גְּנוּבָה): A פַּתַח written under a final ה, ח, or ע, which is always pronounced before the final consonant, as in שָׁמֵחַ. (In proper Biblical manuscripts, it is written a bit to the right of the consonant it is under.)

Geminates: Roots that have identical second and third letters (for example, סבב).

Gemination: The doubling of a consonant, expressed through a דָּגֵשׁ חָזָק. This may be seen, for example, in פִּעֵל verbs like טִמֵּא, where the מֵם is geminated.

Gender: The grammatical class of a word as masculine or feminine.

Gentilic: The use of the suffix ִי (ms form) to indicate that a person belongs to a particular people (for example, פְּלִשְׁתִּי, "a Philistine man").

GN: Geographical name, the name of a place.

Gutturals: The consonants א, ה, ח, and ע, whose sound originates in the throat.

Healthy verbs: Verbs deriving from triliteral roots that have no gutturals.

Heavy suffix: A pronominal suffix (such as הֶם־) comprising a closed syllable that always retains its accent. These suffixes often cause changes in the word to which they are added (note סֵפֶר but סִפְרֵיהֶם).

Imperative: A second-person volitional form (a command), for example, שְׁמֹר, "guard!"

Imperfect tense: A verbal form referring to incomplete actions (for example, יִשְׁמֹר, "he will guard"). The form is typified by a prefix added to the root letters.

Independent preposition: *See* Unbound preposition.

Indirect object: The object indirectly affected by the action of the verb; in BH, the indirect object is preceded by a preposition.

Infinitive absolute: A nominal form of the verb often used with a cognate verb for emphasis (for example, Deuteronomy 11:13 וְהָיָה אִם־שָׁמֹעַ תִּשְׁמְעוּ), or by itself as a pseudoimperative (for example, Exodus 20:8 זָכוֹר אֶת־יוֹם הַשַּׁבָּת לְקַדְּשׁוֹ).

Infinitive construct: A nominal form of the verb, often translated as an English infinitive ("to . . .") or gerund ("-ing"). Suffixes are often added to this form; for example, from שְׁמֹר, "to guard," "guarding," we get שָׁמְרִי, "my guarding."

Infix: A letter, letters, syllable, or syllables added in the middle of a word.

Ingressive: An action focused on entering its initial stages, often translated "becoming," as in מָלַךְ, "(he) has become king."

Inseparable preposition: *See* Bound preposition.

Interrogative הָא (Hebrew הָא הַשְּׁאֵלָה): An initial הָא, typically vocalized הֲ, indicating that what follows is a yes-no question.

Intransitive verb: A verb expressing a self-contained action or state. Intransitive verbs generally do not take a direct object.

Iterative: Representing a repeated action.

Jussive: A volitional form, typically in the third person, though second person jussives are used with אַל to express prohibitives. The jussive form sometimes is a shortened form of the imperfect; for example, from the root הי״י, יִהְיֶה, "he will be," is the קַל imperfect, and יְהִי, "may he be," is the jussive.

Kethib (Hebrew/Aramaic כְּתִיב): The reading written in the main text of the Bible, which is corrected in the marginal note (the *Qere*).

Labials: The consonants ב, ו, מ, and פ, pronounced using the lips.

Late Biblical Hebrew: A BH dialect reflected in some of the later books of the Hebrew Bible, such as Chronicles, Ezra-Nehemiah, and Esther.

Law of the שְׁוָא: Initial *Cĕ +Cĕ > CiC*, as in לִשְׁלֹמֹה > *לְשְׁלֹמֹה ("to Solomon"). No Hebrew word may begin with two שְׁוָאִים.

Law of the שְׁוָא with gutturals: In cases where an initial שְׁוָא should immediately precede a חֲטָף vowel, that שְׁוָא takes the full vowel of the following חֲטָף, as in בֶּאֱמֶת > *בְּאֱמֶת, "in truth."

LBH: Late biblical Hebrew. *See* Standard biblical Hebrew.

Light suffix: A pronominal suffix (such as וֹ‎) that is not composed of a closed syllable that always retains its accent. Opposite of heavy suffix.

Linking vowel: A vowel that links a verb to its object suffix.

Locative: *See* Directive.

M: Masculine.

Mappîq (Hebrew מַפִּיק): A dot in a final הָא, indicating that it is not a vowel letter and should be pronounced with slight aspiration, as in בְּנָהּ, "her son."

Maqqēp (Hebrew מַקֵּף or מַקָּף): A short raised horizontal line (like a raised hyphen) joining two or more words into a single accentual unit, as in אֶת־יִצְחָק.

Masoretes: Jewish scholars living at the end of the first millennium CE who introduced vowels and other features into the biblical text to assure that the correct tradition for reading and copying the text would be preserved.

Matres lectionis: *See* Vowel letters.

Medial *shewa* (Hebrew שְׁוָא מְרַחֵף): A שְׁוָא that shares certain characteristics of both a שְׁוָא נָח and a שְׁוָא נָע.

MIH: *See* Modern Israeli Hebrew.

Mobile *shewa*: A שְׁוָא נָע that represents an ultrashort vowel sound.

Modal: Verbal forms expressing the nuances of "could," "would," "should."

Modern Israeli Hebrew: The dialects of Hebrew reflected in spoken and written Hebrew in the modern state of Israel.

Monosyllabic: Consisting of one syllable.

Morphology: The study of linguistic forms.

Narrative sequence: A sequence of verbs that are connected with a set of *waw* consecutives. A narrative sequence with converted imperfects narrates past events, while a narrative sequence with converted perfects narrates future or ongoing events.

Nominal: Relating to a noun, pronoun, or adjective.

Nominal patterns (Hebrew מִשְׁקָלִים; singular מִשְׁקָל): Morphological patterns shared by a group of nouns.

Nominal sentence: In BH, a sentence lacking a verb. Hebrew nominal sentences are usually translated into English with some form of the verb of being (*is*).

Noun: A word expressing an entity.

Open syllable: A syllable that ends in a vowel.

P: Plural.

Paragogic נוּן: A final נ added after the final long vowel of an imperfect (for example, יִשְׁמְרוּן instead of the expected יִשְׁמְרוּ); it does not affect meaning.

Participle: A declined form of a root; it typically takes four forms (ms, fs, mp, fp) and may be used verbally or nominally.

Pasēq (Hebrew פָּסֵק): A vertical line separating two adjacent words, as in Genesis 22:11, אַבְרָהָ֥ם ׀ אַבְרָהָ֖ם.

Passive participle: In the *Qal*, a nominal form of the verb indicating that the action is done to the verb, for example, כָּתוּב, "is/was/will be written."

Pausal forms: Special forms that words take at major disjunctive accents, as in כָּסֶף (rather than כֶּסֶף) at the אַתְנַחְתָּא in Gen 37:28.

Pause: The major stopping places in a biblical verse, as indicated by the major disjunctive accents סִלּוּק (ק֔) and אַתְנַחְתָּא (ק֑), and often זָקֵף קָטֹן (ק֔) and סְגוֹל (ק֒).

Penultima: The next-to-last syllable of a word.

Penultimate stress: Accent or stress on the next-to-last syllable of a word (Hebrew מִלְעֵיל). The sign ˋ marks this type of accent in this text.

Perfect tense: A verbal form referring to complete actions. The form is typified by a suffix added to the root letters, for example, כָּתַבְתִּי, "I wrote."

Perpetual *qere*: A word that is always read differently than its consonantal spelling, such as יהוה, which is read as either אֲדֹנָי or אֱלֹהִים.

Personal pronoun: A pronoun referring to a person.

Philippi's law: I-class vowels in closed accented syllables became a-class vowels (for example, *דִּבַּרְתָּ > דְּבַרְתָּ).

Phoneme: A sound that is significant in terms of differentiating the meaning of one word from another. (Hebrew has twenty-three consonantal phonemes, as שׁ and שׂ are distinct.)

Phonology: The study of sound patterns.

Plene spelling: *See* Full spelling.

Pluperfect: An action completed before another action that is described, as in "I had eaten when she arrived." In BH the pluperfect may be indicated by an *un*converted perfect that breaks the narrative sequence.

PN: Personal name.

Postpositive cantillation marks: Cantillation marks that appear on the last syllable of a word, and thus do not mark where the word is accented.

Predicative adjective: An adjective that functions as a predicate, as in the English sentence "The book is good" (הַסֵּפֶר טוֹב).

Prefix: A letter, letters, syllable, or syllables attached to the beginning of a word.

Preposition: A word that takes a nominal as object in a phrase that functions adjectivally or adverbially.

Prepositive cantillation marks: Cantillation marks that appear on the first syllable of a word and thus do not mark where the word is accented.

Pretonic reduction: Vowel reduction one syllable before the tone.

Proclitic: A word or syllable closely dependent on the following word (for example, the preposition עַל־).

Prohibitive: A negative command, "Do not . . . ," typically expressed by אַל followed by a jussive.

Pronominal suffix: A suffix consisting of a pronoun.

Pronoun: A word used instead of a noun.

Propretonic reduction: Vowel reduction two syllables before the tone (for example, דְּבָרִים from דָּבָר).

Punctual: An action that takes place at a particular point in time.

Qere (Hebrew/Aramaic קְרֵי): The text written as a marginal note in the Bible, which corrects the main text (the *Kethib*).

Quiescent *shewa*: A שְׁוָא נָח that is silent and represents the end of a syllable (as in the first syllable of יִכְתֹּב).

Rāpeh (Hebrew רָפֶה): A horizontal stroke over a consonant indicating the absence of a *dagesh*.

Relative pronoun: A pronoun that connects a dependent clause to a nominal in another clause (for example, English *which* or Hebrew אֲשֶׁר).

S: Singular.

SBH: *See* Standard biblical Hebrew.

Segholates: A class of nouns, often with a סֶגוֹל in each syllable (for example, כֶּסֶף). These words are characterized by penultimate stress and derive from earlier monosyllabic nouns.

Semitic languages: The language family that includes Hebrew, Aramaic, Arabic, Akkadian, Ugaritic, and other related languages. The predominance of triliteral roots is one of the characteristic features of this family.

Sibilants: The consonants ז, ס, צ, שׁ, and שׂ, pronounced by narrowing the air passages between the tongue and the hard palate.

Sonants: The consonants ל, מ, נ, and ר, which are voiced—that is, pronounced with a vibration of the vocal cords.

Spirant: The pronunciation of one of the letters ב, ג, ד, כ, פ, or ת without a דָּגֵשׁ.

Spirantization: The loss of a דָּגֵשׁ in the letters ב, ג, ד, כ, פ, and ת.

Standard biblical Hebrew: The predominant dialect of Hebrew found in the Bible, likely reflecting Judean Hebrew of the late pre-exilic century (seventh to early sixth century BCE).

Stative verb: A verb that describes a state rather than an action (for example, כָּבֵד, "he was heavy").

Stop: The pronunciation of one of the letters ב, ג, ד, כ, פ, and ת with a דָּגֵשׁ.

Substantive: A noun or pronoun.

Suffix: A letter, letters, syllable, or syllables added to the end of a word.

Superlative: A form which expresses an attribute to the greatest possible degree.

Suppletion: The use of complementary forms from two roots (for example, ילך in the imperfect and הלך in the perfect).

Syncope: *See* Elision.

Syntax: The study of relations between words in a phrase or sentence.

Theme vowel: The vowel between the second and third root letters of a verb, for example, $\bar{e}$ in כָּבֵד or *a* in שָׁמַר, *a* in יִכְבַּד, or $\bar{o}$ in יִשְׁמֹר.

Tonic syllable: The syllable that has the tone or accent. In BH this may be either the ultima or the penultima.

Transitive verb: A verb that normally takes a direct object.

Triliteral: Three-lettered; most Hebrew roots are triliteral, for example, אכל, "to eat."

Ultima: The last syllable of a word.

Ultimate stress: Accent or stress on the last syllable of a word (Hebrew מִלְרַע).

Unbound form: A noun not in the construct. Some also call this form absolute.

Unbound preposition: A preposition written as its own word, separately from the noun that it precedes (for example, עַל).

V: Vowel.

Velars: *See* Emphatics.

Verbal adjective: An adjective derived from a verb.

Virtual doubling: An imaginary ("virtual") doubling of a consonant, which is posited to explain why a short vowel is found in an open unaccented syllable.

Volitional forms: Forms expressing wish, intention, or desire. In BH these are expressed through the cohortative in the first person (for example, אֶשְׁמְרָה, "may I guard"), the imperative in the second person (for example, שְׁמֹר, "guard"), and the jussive (for example, יְהִי, "may it/he be") in the third person.

Vowel class: The division of Semitic vowels into the three classes of *a, i, u*.

Vowel length: The division of Semitic vowels into long (for example, קָמֵץ גָּדוֹל) and short (for example, פַּתַח). In some languages, this label refers to how long the vowel sound is held when pronounced.

Vowel letters (also called *matres lectionis* or אִמּוֹת הַקְּרִיאָה). The letters א, ה, ו, and י are sometimes consonantal but are also used to indicate the presence of a vowel at the end of the syllable, as in the word בָּנָה.

Vowel reduction: A change from a long vowel to a short vowel, typically a שְׁוָא נָח (for example, מָקוֹם to מְקוֹמִי).

Vowel retraction: The movement of a vowel to the previous syllable.

Waw consecutive: A וַ preceding a perfect or imperfect verb in a narrative sequence (for example, the first letter of וַיִּשְׁלַח). Also called conversive *waw*.

Hebrew Grammatical Terms and Their English Equivalents

Vowel letters	אִמּוֹת הַקְּרִיאָה
Dagesh forte	דָּגֵשׁ חָזָק
Dagesh lene	דָּגֵשׁ קַל
Definite article	הֵא הַיְדִיעָה
Interrogative הֵא	הֵא הַשְׁאֵלָה
Conversive *waw*	וָו הַמְהַפֶּכֶת
Conversive *waw*	וָו הַהִפּוּךְ
Kethib	כְּתִיב
Defective spelling	כְּתִיב חָסֵר
Full spelling	כְּתִיב מָלֵא
Penultimate stress	מִלְעֵיל
Ultimate stress	מִלְרַע
Nominal pattern	מִשְׁקָל
Mappîq	מַפִּיק
Infinitive absolute	מָקוֹר מוּחְלָט
Infinitive construct	מָקוֹר נָטוּי
Maqqēp	מַקֵּף (or מַקָּף)
Unbound form	נִפְרָד
Furtive *pataḥ*	פַּתַח גְּנוּבָה
Construct	סְמִיכוּת

Geminates	ע״ע	
Qere	קְרִי	
Rāpeh	רָפֶה	
Medial shewa	שְׁוָא מְרַחֵף	
Quiescent shewa	שְׁוָא נָח	
Mobile shewa	שְׁוָא נָע	

Hebrew-English Glossary

All words are listed alphabetically, so nouns such as מִקְדָּשׁ are found under מֶ rather than קוֹף. All verbs are followed by their conjugated forms in parentheses. These forms are 3ms perfect, ms active participle, 3ms imperfect and ms imperative. The abbreviation *n/a*, for not applicable, suggests that the particular verb is not found, or is very rare, in that particular "tense." When a verb has been noted in a בִּנְיָן other than קַל, this בִּנְיָן is listed in square brackets. Exceptional forms of nouns and adjectives are noted in parentheses.

א

אָב (irr. pl. אָבוֹת)	father
אבד (אָבַד אֹבֵד יֹאבַד אֲבַד)	perish
אבי (אָבָה אֹבֶה יֹאבֶה n/a)	desire
אֶבְיוֹן	poor person
אבל (אָבַל n/a יֶאֱבַל n/a)	mourn
אֶבֶן (fem., pl. אֲבָנִים)	rock
אָדוֹן	master, lord
אָדָם (coll.; no pl.)	humanity, person
אֲדָמָה	cultivable land
אֲדֹנָי	God
אהב (אָהַב אֹהֵב יֶאֱהַב אֱהַב)	like, love
אֹהֶל	tent
אוי ([פִּעֵל] אִוָּה n/a יְאַוֶּה n/a)	desire
אוי ([הִתְפַּעֵל] הִתְאַוָּה מִתְאַוֶּה יִתְאַוֶּה n/a)	desire strongly, lust after
אוֹצָר (irr. pl. אוֹצָרוֹת)	storehouse, treasure

light	אוֹר
sign	אוֹת
then	אָז
hear, listen	אזנ ([הִפְעִיל] הֶאֱזִין יַאֲזִין הַאֲזֵן) rare
ear	אֹזֶן
brother	אָח
sister	אָחוֹת
grasp, hold	אחז (אָחַז אָחֵז יֹאחַז אֱחֹז)
after	אַחַר
another, different	אַחֵר (אֲחֵרוֹת and אֲחֵרִים pl. ;אַחֶרֶת fem.)
last	אַחֲרוֹן
after	אַחֲרֵי
where?	אַיֵּה
how?	אֵיךְ
ram	אַיִל (אֵילִים pl.)
where?	אֵיפֹה
man, person	אִישׁ (אֲנָשִׁים irr. pl.)
eat	אכל (אָכַל אָכֵל יֹאכַל אֱכֹל)
god, God	אֵל
to, toward	אֶל־
these	אֵלֶּה
god, gods, God	אֱלֹהִים
widow	אַלְמָנָה
mother	אֵם
concubine, female slave	אָמָה
cubit	אַמָּה
firm, to be established	אמנ ([נִפְעַל] נֶאֱמַן נֶאֱמָן יֵאָמֵן) (n/a)
believe, trust	אמנ ([הִפְעִיל] הֶאֱמִין מַאֲמִין יַאֲמִין הַאֲמֵן)
say	אמר (אָמַר אֹמֵר יֹאמַר אֱמֹר)
to where?	אָנָה
humanity	אֱנוֹשׁ (coll., mostly poetic)
we	אֲנַחְנוּ
I	אֲנִי
I	אָנֹכִי
gather	אספ (אָסַף אֹסֵף יֶאֱסֹף אֱסֹף)
bind	אסר (אָסַר אֹסֵר יֶאֱסֹר אֱסֹר)
nose (also used in idioms concerning anger)	אַף
bake	אפי (אָפָה אֹפֶה יֹאפֶה אֲפֵה)
beside	אֵצֶל
Ark, chest	אֲרוֹן
lion	אֲרִי
lion	אַרְיֵה

HEBREW-ENGLISH GLOSSARY

אֹרֶךְ .... length
אֶרֶץ (אֲרָצוֹת .fem., with expected pl) .... Earth, land
ארר (אָרַר אֹרֵר יָאֹר אֹר) .... curse
אֵשׁ .... fire
אִשָּׁה (נָשִׁים .irr. pl) .... woman
אשׁם (אָשֵׁם and אָשַׁם n/a יֶאְשַׁם n/a) .... be guilty
אֲשֶׁר .... which (relative particle)
אַתְּ (.fem. sing) .... you
אֵת, אֶת־ .... with (definite direct object marker)
אַתָּה (.masc. sing) .... you
אַתֶּם (.masc. pl) .... you
אַתֵּן (.fem. pl) .... you

ב

בְּ .... in
בגד (בָּגַד בֹּגֵד יִבְגֹּד n/a) .... deal or act treacherously
בֶּגֶד .... garment
בדל ([הִפְעִיל] הִבְדִּיל מַבְדִּיל יַבְדִּיל n/a) .... separate
בְּהֵמָה .... animal (domesticated)
ב(ו)א (בָּא בָּא יָבֹא בֹּא) .... come
בּוֹר (בֹּרוֹת .irr. pl) .... cistern, pit
ב(ו)שׁ (בּוֹשׁ בּוֹשׁ יֵבוֹשׁ בּוֹשׁ) .... be ashamed
בזז (בָּזַז בֹּזֵז יָבֹז בֹּז) .... plunder
בזי (בָּזָה בֹּזֶה יִבְזֶה n/a) .... despise
בחן (בָּחַן בֹּחֵן יִבְחַן בְּחַן) .... examine, test
בחר (בָּחַר בֹּחֵר יִבְחַר בְּחַר) .... choose
בטח (בָּטַח בֹּטֵחַ יִבְטַח בְּטַח) .... trust
בֶּטֶן .... stomach, uterus
בְּיַד .... by, via
ב(י)נ n/a (בָּן יָבִין בִּין) .... understand
בֵּין .... between
בַּיִת (בָּתִּים .masc.; irr. pl) .... house
בְּכוֹר .... firstborn
בכי (בָּכָה בֹּכֶה יִבְכֶּה בְּכֵה) .... cry
בלע (בָּלַע n/a יִבְלַע n/a) .... swallow
בָּמָה .... high place (for worship)
בֵּן (בָּנִים .irr. pl:) .... son
בני (בָּנָה בֹּנֶה יִבְנֶה בְּנֵה) .... build
בַּעַל .... husband, owner, Baal (a Canaanite deity)
בער (בָּעַר בֹּעֵר יִבְעַר n/a) .... burn
בקע (בָּקַע בֹּקֵעַ יִבְקַע בְּקַע) .... cleave, split

בָּקָר (coll.)	large cattle
בֹּקֶר	daybreak, morning
בקש ([פִּעֵל] בִּקֵּשׁ מְבַקֵּשׁ יְבַקֵּשׁ בַּקֵּשׁ)	seek
ברא (בָּרָא בֹּרֵא יִבְרָא בְּרָא)	create
ברח (בָּרַח בֹּרֵחַ יִבְרַח בְּרַח)	flee
בְּרִית	covenant, treaty
ברכ ([פִּעֵל] בֵּרֵךְ מְבָרֵךְ יְבָרֵךְ בָּרֵךְ)	bless
בְּרָכָה	blessing
בשל ([פִּעֵל] בִּשֵּׁל מְבַשֵּׁל יְבַשֵּׁל בַּשֵּׁל)	boil
בָּשָׂר	flesh, meat
בַּת (irr. pl. בָּנוֹת)	daughter

ג

גאל (גָּאַל גֹּאֵל יִגְאַל גְּאַל)	redeem
גבה (גָּבַהּ n/a יִגְבַּהּ n/a)	be high
גְּבוּל	border
גִּבּוֹר	warrior
גְּבוּרָה	might
גִּבְעָה	hill
גֶּבֶר	man
גדל (גָּדַל n/a יִגְדַּל גְּדַל)	be great, grow up
גָּדוֹל	big, great
גּוֹי	nation
ג(ו)ר (גָּר גָּר יָגוּר גּוּר)	sojourn
ג(י)ל (גָּל n/a יָגִיל גִּיל)	rejoice
גלי (גָּלָה גֹּלֶה יִגְלֶה גְּלֵה)	exile, uncover
גנב (גָּנַב גֹּנֵב יִגְנֹב n/a)	steal
גֶּפֶן	vine
גֵּר	sojourner
גרש (n/a גֵּרֵשׁ n/a n/a)	chase out

ד

דבק (דָּבַק n/a יִדְבַּק n/a)	cling
דבר ([פִּעֵל] דִּבֵּר מְדַבֵּר יְדַבֵּר דַּבֵּר)	speak
דָּבָר	word, matter, thing
דּוֹר (pl. דּוֹרוֹת and דּוֹרִים)	generation
דֶּלֶת	door
דָּם	blood
דממ (דָּם n/a יִדֹּם דֹּם)	be silent

HEBREW-ENGLISH GLOSSARY

knowledge	דַּעַת
manner, path	דֶּרֶךְ (both masc. and fem.)
inquire, seek	דרשׁ (דָּרַשׁ דָּרֵשׁ יִדְרֹשׁ דְּרֹשׁ)

ה

groan, utter, meditate	הגי (הָגָה n/a יֶהְגֶּה n/a)
he, it (masc.), that (masc.)	הוּא
woe	הוֹי
she, it (fem.), that (fem.)	הִיא
to be	היי (הָיָה הֹוִיָה [rare] יְהֶיה הֱיֵה)
palace, temple	הֵיכָל
walk, go	הלכ (הָלַךְ הֹלֵךְ יֵלֵךְ לֵךְ)
praise	הלל ([פִּעֵל] הִלֵּל מְהַלֵּל יְהַלֵּל הַלֵּל)
they, those	הֵמָּה, הֵם (masc.)
they, those	הֵנָּה, הֵן (fem.)
see, wow, indeed (a presentative particle, untranslated or depending on context)	הִנֵּה
turn, overturn	הפכ (הָפַךְ הֹפֵךְ יַהֲפֹךְ הֲפֹךְ)
mountain	הַר (הָרִים pl.)
much	הַרְבֵּה
kill	הרג (הָרַג הֹרֵג יַהֲרֹג הֲרֹג)
conceive	הרי (הָרָה n/a תַּהֲרֶה [fs] n/a)

ו

and (other translations possible)	וְ (vocalization varies, see pages 63–64)

ז

this	זֹאת (fem.)
sacrifice	זבח (זָבַח זֹבֵחַ יִזְבַּח זְבַח)
sacrifice	זֶבַח
this	זֶה (masc.)
gold	זָהָב
remember	זכר (זָכַר זֹכֵר יִזְכֹּר זְכֹר)
male	זָכָר
sing	זמר ([פִּעֵל] n/a n/a יְזַמֵּר זַמֵּר)
to be or act as a whore (metaphorically, to abandon YHWH)	זני (זָנָה זֹנֶה יִזְנֶה n/a)
scream	זעק (זָעַק n/a יִזְעַק זְעַק)
be old	זקנ (זָקֵן n/a יִזְקַן n/a)
elder, old	זָקֵן

foreigner	זָר
arm	זְרֹועַ (fem.)
plant, sow	זרע (זָרַע זֹרֵעַ יִזְרַע זְרַע)
descendants, seed	זֶרַע

ח

hide	חבא ([נִפְעַל] נֶחְבָּא נֶחְבָּא יֵחָבֵא n/a)
bind	חבש (חָבַשׁ חֹבֵשׁ יַחֲבֹשׁ חֲבֹשׁ)
pilgrimage festival	חַג (with suffixes, e.g., חַגִּי)
cease	חדל (חָדַל n/a יֶחְדַּל חֲדַל)
new	חָדָשׁ
month, new moon	חֹדֶשׁ
wall	חֹומָה
outside (pl. streets)	חוּץ (pl. חוּצֹות)
see, have a vision	חזה (חָזָה חֹזֶה יֶחֱזֶה חֲזֵה)
be strong	חזק (חָזַק n/a יֶחֱזַק חֲזַק)
sin	חטא (חָטָא חֹטֵא יֶחֱטָא n/a)
purification offering (traditionally "sin offering")	חַטָּאת (pl. חַטָּאֹות)
wheat	חִטָּה
alive, living	חַי
be alive	חיי (חַי n/a יִחְיֶה חֲיֵה)
life	חַיִּים
writhe	ח(י)/ח(ו)/ל (חָל rare יָחִיל חִיל)
power, strength	חַיִל
be wise	חכמ (חָכַם n/a יֶחְכַּם חֲכַם)
skillful, wise	חָכָם
wisdom	חָכְמָה (קָמֵץ קָטָן is a the initial קָמֵץ)
dream	חֲלֹום
get/be sick	חלי (חָלָה חֹלֶה n/a n/a)
defile, pollute	חלל ([פִּעֵל] חִלֵּל מְחַלֵּל יְחַלֵּל n/a)
begin	חלל ([הִפְעִיל] הֵחֵל מֵחֵל יָחֵל n/a)
divide	חלק (חָלַק חֹלֵק יַחֲלֹק חֲלֹק)
anger	חֵמָה
donkey	חֲמֹור
violence	חָמָס
favor	חֵן (with suffix, חִנּוֹ)
encamp	חני (חָנָה חֹנֶה יַחֲנֶה חֲנֵה)
show favor	חננ (חָנַן חֹנֵן יָחֹן חֹן)
kindness, loyalty	חֶסֶד
seek refuge	חסי (חָסָה חֹסֶה יֶחֱסֶה חֲסֵה)
delight in	חפצ (חָפֵץ n/a יַחְפֹּץ n/a)

HEBREW-ENGLISH GLOSSARY

חֵץ (חִצִּים .pl) . . . arrow
חָצֵר . . . courtyard
חֹק (חֻקִּים .pl) . . . ordinance
חֶרֶב (.fem) . . . sword
חרי (חָרָה n/a יֶחֱרֶה n/a) . . . be angry
חרם ([הִפְעִיל] הֶחֱרִים n/a יַחֲרִים הַחֲרֵם) . . . destroy, proscribe
חרשׁ (חָרַשׁ חֹרֵשׁ יַחֲרֹשׁ n/a) . . . engrave, plow
חשׁב (חָשַׁב חֹשֵׁב יַחְשֹׁב n/a) . . . think
חֹשֶׁךְ . . . darkness
חתת (חַת n/a יֵחַת חֹת) . . . be dismayed, shattered

ט

טָהוֹר . . . ritually pure
טהר (טָהֵר n/a יִטְהַר טְהַר) . . . be pure
טוֹב . . . good
טמא (טָמֵא n/a יִטְמָא n/a) . . . be impure
טָמֵא . . . ritually impure
טמן (טָמַן n/a יִטְמֹן n/a) . . . hide

י

יבשׁ (יָבֵשׁ n/a יִיבַשׁ n/a) . . . be dry
יגע (יָגַע n/a יִיגַע n/a) . . . be tired, work
יָד (dual, יָדַיִם, hands, pl. יָדוֹת, times) . . . hand
ידי ([הִפְעִיל] הוֹדָה מוֹדֶה יוֹדֶה הוֹדֵה) . . . give thanks
ידע (יָדַע יֹדֵעַ יֵדַע דַּע) . . . know
יהוה . . . Yahweh
יוֹם (irr. pl. יָמִים) . . . day
יוֹמָם . . . by day
יַחַד . . . together
יַחְדָּו . . . together
יחל ([פִּעֵל] יִחֵל מְיַחֵל יְיַחֵל יַחֵל) . . . wait
יטב (יִיטַב n/a n/a) . . . be good
יַיִן . . . wine
יכח ([הִפְעִיל] הוֹכִיחַ מוֹכִיחַ יוֹכִיחַ הוֹכַח) . . . rebuke, reprove
יכל (יָכֹל n/a יוּכַל n/a) . . . be able
ילד (יָלַד יֹלֵד יֵלֵד לֵד) . . . give birth
יֶלֶד . . . boy, child
ילכ (see הלכ) . . . go
יָם . . . sea
יָמִין . . . right

ינק (יָנַק יֹנֵק יִינַק) n/a	nurse
יסד (יָסַד יֹסֵד) n/a n/a	establish
יסף (יֹסֵף) n/a n/a	do again, do more
יסר ([פִּעֵל] יִסֵּר מְיַסֵּר יְיַסֵּר יַסֵּר)	chastise, discipline
יַעַן	because of
יעץ (יָעַץ יוֹעֵץ יִיעַץ) n/a	advise
יַעַר	forest
יצא (יָצָא יֹצֵא יֵצֵא צֵא)	leave
יצב ([הִתְפַּעֵל] הִתְיַצֵּב מִתְיַצֵּב יִתְיַצֵּב הִתְיַצֵּב)	take one's stand
יצק (יָצַק n/a יִצֹק צַק and יְצֹק)	pour out
יצר (יָצַר יֹצֵר יִצֹּר) n/a	fashion, form
ירא (יָרֵא n/a יִירָא יְרָא)	fear
ירד (יָרַד יוֹרֵד יֵרֵד רֵד)	descend
ירי (יָרָה יֹרֶה rare יִרֶה)	shoot
ירש (יָרַשׁ יוֹרֵשׁ יִירַשׁ רֵשׁ)	inherit, possess
ישב (יָשַׁב יֹשֵׁב יֵשֵׁב שֵׁב)	dwell, sit
יְשׁוּעָה	salvation
ישע ([הִפְעִיל] הוֹשִׁיעַ מוֹשִׁיעַ יוֹשִׁיעַ הוֹשַׁע)	deliver, help
יָשָׁר	straight, upright
יתר ([נִפְעַל] נוֹתַר נוֹתָר יִוָּתֵר) n/a	be left over
יתר ([הִפְעִיל] הוֹתִיר n/a יוֹתִיר הוֹתֵר)	leave over
יֶתֶר	remainder

כ

כְּ	like, as
כבד (כָּבֵד n/a יִכְבַּד כְּבַד)	be heavy
כָּבוֹד	glory, honor
כבס ([פִּעֵל] כִּבֵּס מְכַבֵּס יְכַבֵּס כַּבֵּס)	wash
כֶּבֶשׂ (כַּבְשָׂה or כִּבְשָׂה fem.)	lamb
כֹּה	thus
כֹּהֵן	priest
כ(ו)ן ([נִפְעַל] נָכוֹן נָכוֹן יִכּוֹן הִכּוֹן)	be firm
כ(ו)ן ([הִפְעִיל] הֵכִין מֵכִין יָכִין הָכֵן)	establish, make firm
כֹּחַ	strength
כִּי	because
כֹּל, כָּל־	all, every, any, everything
כלי (כָּלָה n/a יִכְלֶה) n/a	cease, be finished
כְּלִי (כֵּלִים pl.)	vessel
כלם ([נִפְעַל] נִכְלַם נִכְלָם יִכָּלֵם הִכָּלֵם)	be ashamed
כלם ([הִפְעִיל] הִכְלִים מַכְלִים יַכְלִים) n/a	humiliate, put shame

HEBREW-ENGLISH GLOSSARY

wing	כָּנָף
seat, throne	כִּסֵּא
cover	כסי ([פִּעֵל] כִּסָּה מְכַסֶּה יְכַסֶּה כַּסֵּה)
fool	כְּסִיל
silver (contrast MIH, money)	כֶּסֶף
be angry	כעס (כָּעַס n/a יִכְעַס n/a)
palm	כַּף (כַּפּוֹת .pl)
atone	כפר ([פִּעֵל] כִּפֶּר n/a יְכַפֵּר כַּפֵּר)
vineyard	כֶּרֶם
kneel, bow down	כרע (כָּרַע כֹּרֵעַ יִכְרַע n/a)
cut (often with בְּרִית)	כרת (כָּרַת כֹּרֵת יִכְרֹת כְּרֹת)
stumble	כשל (כָּשַׁל כֹּשֵׁל יִכְשַׁל n/a)
write	כתב (כָּתַב כֹּתֵב יִכְתֹּב כְּתֹב)

ל

to	לְ
heart	לֵב or לֵבָב (לִבָבוֹת and לִבּוֹת .pl)
put on a garment	לבש (לָבַשׁ n/a יִלְבַּשׁ לְבַשׁ)
fight	לחם ([נִפְעַל] נִלְחַם נִלְחָם יִלָּחֵם הִלָּחֵם)
bread, food	לֶחֶם (no pl.; may be coll.)
night	לַיְלָה (לֵילוֹת .irr. pl)
stay overnight	לי(ן)/לו(ן) (לָן לָן יָלִין לִין)
capture	לכד (לָכַד לֹכֵד יִלְכֹּד לְכֹד)
learn	למד (לָמַד לֹמֵד יִלְמַד לְמַד)
why?	לָמָה (לָמָּה before א ה ע)
so that	לְמַעַן
according to	לְפִי
before	לִפְנֵי
take	לקח (לָקַח לֹקֵחַ יִקַּח קַח)
toward	לִקְרַאת
tongue (rarely, language)	לָשׁוֹן (masc. but pl. is לְשֹׁנוֹת)

מ

very	מְאֹד
from where?	מֵאַיִן
refuse	מאן ([פִּעֵל] מֵאֵן n/a יְמָאֵן n/a)
reject, spurn, despise	מאס (מָאַס מֹאֵס יִמְאַס n/a)
tower	מִגְדָּל
open land	מִגְרָשׁ

wilderness (not desert in the sense of totally dry)	מִדְבָּר
measure (מָדַד n/a יָמוֹד n/a)	מדד
why?	מַדּוּעַ
what? (vocalization varies, see page 57)	מַה
hasten ([פִּעֵל] מִהַר מְמַהֵר יְמַהֵר מַהֵר)	מהר
totter (מָט מָט יָמוּט n/a)	מ(ו)ט
opposite	מוּל
appointed place, feast time	מוֹעֵד
die (מֵת מֵת יָמוּת מוּת)	מ(ו)ת
death	מָוֶת
altar (masc., pl. מִזְבְּחוֹת)	מִזְבֵּחַ
psalm	מִזְמוֹר
camp	מַחֲנֶה
tomorrow	מָחָר
staff, tribe	מַטֶּה
who(m)	מִי
water	מַיִם
sell (מָכַר מֹכֵר יִמְכֹּר מְכֹר)	מכר
be full (מָלֵא מָלֵא יִמְלָא מְלֹא)	מלא
angel (= divine messenger), messenger	מַלְאָךְ
work	מְלָאכָה
war	מִלְחָמָה
escape ([נִפְעַל] נִמְלַט נִמְלָט יִמָּלֵט הִמָּלֵט)	מלט
deliver ([פִּעֵל] מִלֵּט מְמַלֵּט יְמַלֵּט מַלֵּט)	מלט
reign (מָלַךְ מֹלֵךְ יִמְלֹךְ מְלֹךְ)	מלך
king	מֶלֶךְ
kingdom, kingship, reign	מַלְכוּת
kingdom	מַמְלָכָה
from	מִן
cereal offering, gift, offering	מִנְחָה
number	מִסְפָּר
deed, work	מַעֲשֶׂה
because	מִפְּנֵי
find (מָצָא מֹצֵא יִמְצָא מְצֹא)	מצא
commandment	מִצְוָה
sanctuary, Temple	מִקְדָּשׁ
place (masc.; irr. pl. מְקוֹמוֹת)	מָקוֹם
cattle	מִקְנֶה
appearance, vision	מַרְאֶה
anoint (מָשַׁח מֹשֵׁחַ יִמְשַׁח מְשֹׁחַ)	משח
dwelling, Tabernacle	מִשְׁכָּן

HEBREW-ENGLISH GLOSSARY

rule	מָשַׁל (מָשַׁל מֹשֵׁל יִמְשֹׁל מְשֹׁל)
family, extended family (clan)	מִשְׁפָּחָה
justice	מִשְׁפָּט
weight	מִשְׁקָל
when?	מָתַי

נ

utterance	נְאֻם
commit adultery	נאף (נָאַף נֹאֵף יִנְאַף n/a)
prophesy	נבא ([נִפְעַל] נִבָּא נִבָּא יִנָּבֵא הִנָּבֵא)
look	נבט ([הִפְעִיל] הִבִּיט מַבִּיט יַבִּיט הַבֵּט)
prophet	נָבִיא
south, southern Israel	נֶגֶב
tell	נגד ([הִפְעִיל] הִגִּיד מַגִּיד יַגִּיד הַגֵּד)
opposite	נֶגֶד
touch	נגע (נָגַע נֹגֵעַ יִגַּע גַּע)
smite	נגף (נָגַף נֹגֵף יִגֹּף n/a)
approach	נגש (n/a n/a יִגַּשׁ גֵּשׁ)
wander	נדד (נָדַד נֹדֵד יְדוֹד n/a)
be thrust out	נדח ([נִפְעַל] נָדַּח נִדָּח n/a n/a)
thrust out	נדח ([הִפְעִיל] הִדִּיחַ n/a יַדִּיחַ הַדַּח)
vow	נדר (נָדַר נֹדֵר יִדֹּר נְדֹר)
river, stream	נָהָר (masc., but pl. is usually נְהָרוֹת)
rest	נ(ו)ח (נָח n/a יָנוּחַ n/a)
flee	נ(ו)ס (נָס נָס יָנוּס נוּס)
raise, wave	נ(ו)ף ([הִפְעִיל] הֵנִיף מֵנִיף יָנִיף הָנֵף)
inherit, possess	נחל (נָחַל n/a יִנְחַל n/a)
stream, wadi	נַחַל
inheritance	נַחֲלָה
we	נַחְנוּ
bronze, copper	נְחֹשֶׁת
extend	נטי (נָטָה נֹטֶה יִטֶּה נְטֵה)
plant	נטע (נָטַע נֹטֵעַ יִטַּע נְטַע)
abandon	נטש (נָטַשׁ n/a יִטֹּשׁ נְטוֹשׁ)
kill, hit	נכי ([הִפְעִיל] הִכָּה מַכֶּה יַכֶּה הַכֵּה)
recognize	נכר ([הִפְעִיל] הִכִּיר מַכִּיר יַכִּיר הַכֵּר)
depart, journey	נסע (נָסַע נֹסֵעַ יִסַּע סַע)
young man	נַעַר
young girl	נַעֲרָה
fall	נפל (נָפַל נֹפֵל יִפֹּל נְפֹל)

breath, life-force, person	נֶפֶשׁ (fem.)
stand	נצב ([נִפְעַל] נִצַּב נִצָּב n/a n/a)
erect	נצב ([הִפְעִיל] הִצִּיב מַצִּיב יַצִּיב הַצֵּב)
deliver, take away	נצל ([הִפְעִיל] הִצִּיל מַצִּיל יַצִּיל הַצֵּל)
guard, watch	נצר (נָצַר נֹצֵר יִצֹּר נְצֹר)
female	נְקֵבָה
carry	נשׂא (נָשָׂא נֹשֵׂא יִשָּׂא שָׂא)
overtake, reach	נשׂג ([הִפְעִיל] הִשִּׂיג מַשִּׂיג יַשִּׂיג n/a)
chief	נָשִׂיא
kiss	נשׁק (נָשַׁק נֹשֵׁק יִשַּׁק שַׁק)
give	נתן (נָתַן נֹתֵן יִתֵּן תֵּן)

ס

turn, go around	סבב (סָבַב סוֹבֵב יָסֹב סֹב or יָסֹב סֹב)
around	סָבִיב
close	סגר (סָגַר סֹגֵר יִסְגֹּר סְגֹר)
turn aside	ס(ו)ר (סָר סָר יָסוּר סוּר)
horse	סוּס
forgive	סלח (סָלַח סֹלֵחַ יִסְלַח סְלַח)
count	ספר (סָפַר סֹפֵר יִסְפֹּר סְפֹר)
document, scroll	סֵפֶר
be concealed	סתר ([נִפְעַל] נִסְתַּר נִסְתָּר יִסָּתֵר הִסָּתֵר)
conceal	סתר ([הִפְעִיל] הִסְתִּיר מַסְתִּיר יַסְתִּיר הַסְתֵּר)

ע

serve, work	עבד (עָבַד עֹבֵד יַעֲבֹד עֲבֹד)
servant, slave	עֶבֶד
service, work, labor	עֲבוֹדָה
pass	עבר (עָבַר עֹבֵר יַעֲבֹר עֲבֹר)
until, up to	עַד־
witness	עֵד
congregation	עֵדָה
testify	ע(ו)ד ([הִפְעִיל] הֵעִיד מֵעִיד יָעִיד הָעֵד)
again, still	עוֹד
eternity (not world, as in MIH)	עוֹלָם
sin	עָוֹן (pl. עֲוֹנֹת)
fly	ע(ו)פ (עָף עָף יָעוּף n/a)
bird	עוֹף (collective)
rouse oneself	ע(ו)ר (עֵר יָעוֹר עוֹר n/a)
strength	עֹז (עֻזִּי or עָזִּי typically, with suffixes)

HEBREW-ENGLISH GLOSSARY

עזב (עָזַב עֹזֵב יַעֲזֹב עֲזֹב)	abandon, leave
עזר (עָזַר עֹזֵר יַעֲזֹר עֲזֹר)	help
עַיִן	eye
עִיר (עָרִים fem.; irr. pl.)	city
עַל-	on
עֹלָה	burnt offering
עלי (עָלָה עֹלֶה יַעֲלֶה עֲלֵה)	go up
עֶלְיוֹן	highest, supreme
עַם (עַמִּים pl.)	nation, people
עִם-	with
עמד (עָמַד עֹמֵד יַעֲמֹד עֲמֹד)	stand
ענה (עָנָה עֹנֶה יַעֲנֶה עֲנֵה)	answer
עָנִי	humble, poor
עָנָן	cloud
עָפָר	dust, soil
עֵץ	tree, wood
עֵצָה	advice, counsel
עֶצֶם (fem.)	bone
עֶרֶב	evening, dusk
ערכ (עָרַךְ עֹרֵךְ יַעֲרֹךְ עֲרֹךְ)	arrange
עשׂי (עָשָׂה עֹשֶׂה יַעֲשֶׂה עֲשֵׂה)	do
עֵת	time
עַתָּה	now

פ

פגע (פָּגַע n/a יִפְגַּע פְּגַע)	meet
פדי (פָּדָה פֹּדֶה יִפְדֶּה פְּדֵה)	redeem
פֶּה (פִּיפִיּוֹת פִּיּוֹת פִּיּוֹת irr. pl.)	mouth
פֹּה	here
פ(ו)צ (n/a n/a יָפוּץ פּוּץ)	be scattered
פחד (פָּחַד n/a יִפְחַד)	fear
פלא ([נִפְעַל] נִפְלָא נִפְלָא יִפָּלֵא n/a)	be extraordinary
פלא ([הִפְעִיל] הִפְלִיא מַפְלִיא יַפְלִיא n/a)	do wondrously
פלל ([הִתְפַּעֵל] הִתְפַּלֵּל מִתְפַּלֵּל יִתְפַּלֵּל הִתְפַּלֵּל)	pray
פני (פָּנָה פֹּנֶה יִפְנֶה פְּנֵה)	turn
פָּנִים (plural only)	face
פעל (פָּעַל פֹּעֵל יִפְעַל n/a)	do
פַּעַם	time, footstep
פקד (פָּקַד פֹּקֵד יִפְקֹד פְּקֹד)	visit, remember, count
פַּר (פָּרָה fem.)	bull
פרד ([נִפְעַל] נִפְרַד נִפְרָד יִפָּרֵד הִפָּרֵד)	divide

make a division	פרד ([הִפְעִיל] הִפְרִיד מַפְרִיד יַפְרִיד n/a)
be fruitful	פרי (פָּרָה פֹּרֶה יִפְרֶה פָּרָה)
fruit	פְּרִי
spread out	פרשׂ (פָּרַשׂ פֹּרֵשׂ יִפְרֹשׂ n/a)
rebel, sin	פשׁע (פָּשַׁע פֹּשֵׁעַ יִפְשַׁע פָּשַׁע)
entrance, opening	פֶּתַח

צ

small cattle (typically goats, sheep)	צֹאן (frequently coll.)
army	צָבָא (צְבָאוֹת masc., pl.)
righteous	צַדִּיק
be right	צדק (צָדַק n/a יִצְדַּק n/a)
righteousness	צֶדֶק
righteousness	צְדָקָה
command	צוי ([פִּעֵל] צִוָּה מְצַוֶּה יְצַוֶּה צַוֵּה)
succeed, thrive	צלח ([הִפְעִיל] הִצְלִיחַ מַצְלִיחַ יַצְלִיחַ הַצְלֵחַ)
sprout	צמח (צָמַח צֹמֵחַ יִצְמַח n/a)
cry out	צעק (צָעַק צֹעֵק יִצְעַק צָעַק)
north	צָפוֹן
keep watch	צפי (צָפָה n/a יִצְפֶּה n/a)
enemy, narrow, straits	צַר
distress, straits	צָרָה
show hostility toward	צרר (צָרַר צֹרֵר יָצֹר n/a)

ק

assemble	קבץ (קָבַץ קֹבֵץ יִקְבֹּץ קְבֹץ)
bury	קבר (קָבַר קֹבֵר יִקְבֹּר קְבֹר)
grave	קֶבֶר
holy	קָדוֹשׁ
come meet	קדמ ([פִּעֵל] קִדֵּם n/a יְקַדֵּם קַדֵּם)
be holy	קדשׁ (קָדַשׁ n/a יִקְדַּשׁ n/a)
holy thing	קֹדֶשׁ
assemble	קהל ([נִפְעַל] נִקְהַל נִקְהָל יִקָּהֵל קָהֵל n/a)
assembly	קָהָל
wait	קוי ([פִּעֵל] קִוָּה n/a יְקַוֶּה קַוֵּה)
voice	קוֹל (קֹלֹת masc.; irr. pl.)
rise (with other verbs, indicates beginning of an action)	ק(ו)מ (קָם קָם יָקוּם קוּם)
small	קָטֹן, קָטָן (קְטַנּוֹת and קְטַנִּים pl.; קְטַנָּה fem.)
offer incense (usually to foreign gods)	קטר ([פִּעֵל] קִטֵּר מְקַטֵּר יְקַטֵּר קַטֵּר)
offer incense (usually to YHWH)	קטר ([הִפְעִיל] הִקְטִיר מַקְטִיר יַקְטִיר הַקְטֵר)
incense	קְטֹרֶת

קִיר (קִירוֹת .irr. pl)	wall
קלל (קַל n/a יֵקַל n/a)	be light
קנא ([פָּעֵל] קִנֵּא n/a יְקַנֵּא n/a)	be jealous, zealous
קני (קָנָה קְנֵה יִקְנֶה קָנֹה)	purchase
קֵץ (with suffixes, e.g., קִצּוֹ)	end
קצר (קָצַר קְצֹר יִקְצֹר n/a)	reap, to be short
קרא (קָרָא קְרָא יִקְרָא קָרֹא)	call, read
קרב (קָרַב n/a יִקְרַב קָרֹב)	approach
קֶרֶב	midst
קָרְבָּן (קֹמֶץ קָטָן is a קָמֵץ the initial)	sacrifice
קרע (קָרַע קְרֹעַ יִקְרַע קָרֹעַ)	rip
קשׁי (קָשָׁה n/a יִקְשֶׁה n/a)	be hard
קשׁר (קָשַׁר קְשֹׁר יִקְשֹׁר n/a)	conspire, tie
קֶשֶׁת	rainbow, bow

ר

ראי (רָאָה רְאֵה יִרְאֶה רָאֹה)	see
רֹאשׁ (רָאשִׁים .irr. pl)	head
רֵאשִׁית	beginning of
רַב (רַבִּים .pl)	numerous
רֹב	greatness, multitude
רבי (רָבָה n/a יִרְבֶּה רָבֹה)	be great, numerous
רֶגֶל	foot, leg
רדפ (רָדַף רְדֹף יִרְדֹּף רָדֹף)	chase
רוּחַ (רוּחוֹת .fem., sometimes masc.; pl)	spirit, wind
ר(ו)מ (רָם רָם יָרוּם רוֹם)	be high
ר(ו)ע ([הִפְעִיל] הֵרִיעַ מֵרִיעַ יָרִיעַ n/a)	raise a shout
ר(ו)צ (רָץ רָץ יָרוּץ רוֹץ)	run
רֹחַב	breadth
רְחוֹב (רְחוֹבוֹת .irr. pl)	plaza (contrast MIH, "street")
רחמ ([פָּעֵל] רִחֵם מְרַחֵם יְרַחֵם רַחֵם)	have pity on
רחצ (רָחַץ רְחַץ יִרְחַץ רָחֹץ)	wash
רחק (רָחַק n/a יִרְחַק רָחֹק)	be far
ר(י)ב (רָב רָב יָרִיב רִיב)	engage in a legal battle, fight
רִיב	dispute, lawsuit, fight
רכב (רָכַב רְכַב יִרְכַּב רָכֹב)	ride
רֶכֶב (.coll)	charioteer, chariots
רננ (n/a n/a יָרֹן רֹן)	cry out (almost always in joy)
רַע (רָעִים .pl)	bad, evil
רֵעַ	friend, neighbor
רָעָב	famine
רעי (רָעָה רְעֵה יִרְעֶה רָעֹה)	tend sheep

be bad	רעע (רַע n/a יֵרַע n/a)
shake	רעשׁ (רָעַשׁ רֹעֵשׁ יִרְעַשׁ n/a)
heal	רפא (רָפָא רֹפֵא יִרְפָּא רְפָא)
murder	רצח (רָצַח רֹצֵחַ יִרְצַח n/a)
be pleased	רצי (רָצָה רֹצֶה יִרְצֶה רְצֵה)
wicked	רָשָׁע

שׂ

be sated	שׂבע (שָׂבַע n/a יִשְׂבַּע שְׂבַע)
field	שָׂדֶה
laugh	שׂחק (שָׂחַק n/a יִשְׂחַק n/a)
place	שׂ(י)מ (שָׂם שָׂם יָשִׂים שִׂים)
act prudently, prosper	שׂכל ([הִפְעִיל] הִשְׂכִּיל מַשְׂכִּיל יַשְׂכִּיל הַשְׂכֵּל)
left	שְׂמֹאל
be happy	שׂמח (שָׂמַח n/a יִשְׂמַח שְׂמַח)
happiness	שִׂמְחָה
hate	שׂנא (שָׂנֵא שֹׂנֵא יִשְׂנָא שְׂנָא)
lip, shore, speech	שָׂפָה
officer	שַׂר (שָׂרִים pl.)
burn	שׂרפ (שָׂרַף שֹׂרֵף יִשְׂרֹף שְׂרֹף)

שׁ

ask	שׁאל (שָׁאַל שֹׁאֵל יִשְׁאַל שְׁאַל)
Sheol, the underworld	שְׁאוֹל
remain	שׁאר ([נִפְעַל] נִשְׁאַר נִשְׁאָר יִשָּׁאֵר n/a)
break	שׁבר (שָׁבַר שֹׁבֵר יִשְׁבֹּר שְׁבֹר)
staff, tribe	שֵׁבֶט
capture	שׁבי (שָׁבָה שֹׁבֶה יִשְׁבֶּה שְׁבֵה)
cease	שׁבת (שָׁבַת n/a יִשְׁבֹּת n/a)
Sabbath	שַׁבָּת
devastate	שׁדד (שָׁדַד שֹׁדֵד יָשׁוּד n/a)
return	שׁ(ו)ב (שָׁב שָׁב יָשׁוּב שׁוּב)
ox	שׁוֹר
slaughter	שׁחט (שָׁחַט שֹׁחֵט יִשְׁחַט שְׁחַט)
corrupt, spoil, ruin	שׁחת ([פִּעֵל] שִׁחֵת n/a n/a) ([הִפְעִיל] הִשְׁחִית מַשְׁחִית יַשְׁחִית הַשְׁחֵת)
sing	שׁ(י)ר (שָׁר שָׁר יָשִׁיר שִׁיר)
song	שִׁיר
place	שׁ(י)ת (שָׁת n/a יָשִׁית שִׁית)
lie down, have sex with	שׁכב (שָׁכַב שֹׁכֵב יִשְׁכַּב שְׁכַב)
forget	שׁכח (שָׁכַח שֹׁכֵחַ יִשְׁכַּח שְׁכַח)
get up early	שׁכמ ([הִפְעִיל] הִשְׁכִּים מַשְׁכִּים יַשְׁכִּים הַשְׁכֵּם)

HEBREW-ENGLISH GLOSSARY

שכנ (שָׁכַן שֹׁכֵן יִשְׁכֹּן שְׁכֹן)	dwell
שָׁלוֹם	peace, well-being
שלח (שָׁלַח שֹׁלֵחַ יִשְׁלַח שְׁלַח)	send
שלכ ([הִפְעִיל] הִשְׁלִיךְ מַשְׁלִיךְ יַשְׁלִיךְ הַשְׁלֵךְ)	cast, throw
שלמ (שָׁלֵם n/a יִשְׁלַם n/a)	be whole
שָׁם	there
שֵׁם (שֵׁמוֹת) (masc.; irr. pl.	name
שמד ([נִפְעַל] נִשְׁמַד n/a יִשָּׁמֵד n/a)	be destroyed
שמד ([הִפְעִיל] הִשְׁמִיד n/a יַשְׁמִיד הַשְׁמֵד)	destroy
שָׁמַיִם	heavens, sky
שממ (שָׁמַם שׁוֹמֵם יִשֹּׁם שֹׁם)	appalled, be desolated
שְׁמָמָה	desolation
שֶׁמֶן	oil
שמע (שָׁמַע שֹׁמֵעַ יִשְׁמַע שְׁמַע)	hear, heed
שמר (שָׁמַר שֹׁמֵר יִשְׁמֹר שְׁמֹר)	guard, observe
שֶׁמֶשׁ (mostly fem.; rarely masc.)	sun
שָׁנָה (שָׁנִים) (fem.; irr. pl.	year
שַׁעַר	gate
שִׁפְחָה	maidservant
שפט (שָׁפַט שֹׁפֵט יִשְׁפֹּט שְׁפֹט)	judge
שפכ (שָׁפַךְ שֹׁפֵךְ יִשְׁפֹּךְ שְׁפֹךְ)	pour out
שקט (שָׁקַט שֹׁקֵט יִשְׁקֹט n/a)	be quiet, undisturbed
שקי ([הִפְעִיל] הִשְׁקָה מַשְׁקֶה יַשְׁקֶה הַשְׁקֵה)	give drink
שֶׁקֶל	Shekel (a weight, approximately 11–13 grams)
שרת ([פִּעֵל] שֵׁרֵת מְשָׁרֵת יְשָׁרֵת n/a)	serve, minister
שתי (שָׁתָה שֹׁתֶה יִשְׁתֶּה שְׁתֵה)	drink

ת

תּוֹךְ	middle
תּוֹךְ (construct of תָּוֶךְ)	middle of
תּוֹעֵבָה	abomination
תּוֹרָה	instruction, law, teaching, Torah (rare and LBH)
תַּחַת	under, instead of
תלי (תָּלָה תֹּלֶה יִתְלֶה תְּלֵה)	hang
תָּמִיד	continually
תָּמִים	complete, faultless
תממ (תַּם n/a יִתֹּם n/a)	be complete
תעה (תָּעָה תֹּעֶה יִתְעֶה n/a)	wander, err
תְּפִלָּה	prayer
תפש (תָּפַשׂ תֹּפֵשׂ יִתְפֹּשׂ תְּפֹשׂ)	capture
תקע (תָּקַע תֹּקֵעַ יִתְקַע תְּקַע)	blow (a horn), strike

English-Hebrew Glossary

All verbs are followed by their conjugated forms in parentheses. These forms are 3ms perfect, ms active participle, 3ms imperfect, and ms imperative. The abbreviation *n/a*, for not applicable, suggests that the particular verb is not found, or is very rare, in that particular "tense." When a verb has been noted in a בִּנְיָן other than קַל, this בִּנְיָן is listed in square brackets. Exceptional forms of nouns and adjectives are noted in parentheses.

A

abandon .... עזב (עָזַב עֹזֵב יַעֲזֹב עֲזֹב)׃ נטש (נָטַשׁ n/a יִטֹּשׁ נְטֹשׁ)
able, to be .... יכל (יָכֹל n/a יוּכַל n/a)
abomination .... תּוֹעֵבָה
according .... לְפִי
act as or to be a whore (metaphorically, to abandon YHWH) .... זני (זָנָה זֹנֶה יִזְנֶה n/a)
act prudently .... שׂכל ([הִפְעִיל] הִשְׂכִּיל מַשְׂכִּיל יַשְׂכִּיל הַשְׂכֵּל)
advice .... עֵצָה
advise .... יעץ (יָעַץ יוֹעֵץ יִיעַץ n/a)
after .... אַחֲרֵי׃ אַחַר
again .... עוֹד
alive, to be .... חיי (חַי n/a יִחְיֶה חֲיֵה)
alive .... חַי
all .... כֹּל, כָּל־
altar .... מִזְבֵּחַ (masc., pl. מִזְבְּחוֹת)
and (other translations possible) .... וְ (vocalization varies, see pages 63–64)
angel (= divine messenger) .... מַלְאָךְ
anger .... חֵמָה
angry, to be .... חרי (חָרָה n/a יֶחֱרֶה n/a)׃ כעס (כָּעַס n/a יִכְעַס n/a)

ENGLISH-HEBREW GLOSSARY

animal (domesticated) .... בְּהֵמָה
anoint .... מׁשׁח (מָשַׁח מֹשֵׁחַ יִמְשַׁח מְשֹׁחַ)
another .... אַחֵר (אֲחֵרוֹת and אֲחֵרִים pl.; אַחֶרֶת fem.)
answer .... ענה (עָנָה עֹנֶה יַעֲנֶה עֲנֵה)
any .... כֹּל, כָּל-
appalled, to be .... שׁמם (שָׁמַם שׁוֹמֵם יִשֹּׁם שֹׁם)
appearance .... מַרְאֶה
appointed place .... מוֹעֵד
approach .... קרב (קָרַב n/a יִקְרַב קְרָב): נגש (n/a n/a יִגַּשׁ גַּשׁ)
Ark .... אָרוֹן
arm .... זְרוֹעַ (fem.)
army .... צָבָא (צְבָאוֹת .pl ,.masc)
around .... סָבִיב
arrange .... ערכ (עָרַךְ עֹרֵךְ יַעֲרֹךְ עֲרֹךְ)
arrow .... חֵץ (חִצִּים .pl)
as .... כְּ
ashamed, to be .... ב(ו)שׁ (בּוֹשׁ בּוֹשׁ יֵבוֹשׁ בּוֹשׁ): כלמ ([נפעל] נִכְלַם נִכְלָם יִכָּלֵם הִכָּלֵם)
ask .... שׁאל (שָׁאַל שֹׁאֵל יִשְׁאַל שְׁאַל)
assemble .... קבצ (קָבַץ קֹבֵץ יִקְבֹּץ קְבֹץ): קהל ([נפעל] נִקְהַל נִקְהָל יִקָּהֵל n/a)
assembly .... קָהָל
atone .... כפר ([פעל] כִּפֵּר n/a יְכַפֵּר כַּפֵּר)

B

Baal (a Canaanite deity) .... בַּעַל
bad, to be .... רעע (רַע n/a יֵרַע n/a)
bad .... רַע (רָעִים .pl)
bake .... אפי (אָפָה אֹפֶה יֹאפֶה אֲפֵה)
be .... הײ (הָיָה הוֹיָה [rare] יִהְיֶה הֱיֵה)
because .... כִּי, מִפְּנֵי
because of .... יַעַן
before .... לִפְנֵי
begin .... חלל ([הפעיל] הֵחֵל מֵחֵל יָחֵל n/a)
beginning of .... רֵאשִׁית
believe .... אמנ ([הפעיל] הֶאֱמִין מַאֲמִין יַאֲמִין הַאֲמֵן)
beside .... אֵצֶל
between .... בֵּין
big .... גָּדוֹל
bind .... אסר (אָסַר אֹסֵר יֶאְסֹר אֱסֹר): חבשׁ (חָבַשׁ חֹבֵשׁ יַחֲבֹשׁ חֲבֹשׁ)
bird .... עוֹף (coll.)
bless .... ברכ ([פעל] בֵּרַךְ מְבָרֵךְ יְבָרֵךְ בָּרֵךְ)
blessing .... בְּרָכָה
blood .... דָּם
blow (a horn) .... תקע (תָּקַע תֹּקֵעַ יִתְקַע תְּקַע)

boil .... בשל ([פִּעֵל] בִּשֵּׁל מְבַשֵּׁל יְבַשֵּׁל בַּשֵּׁל)
bone .... עֶצֶם (fem.)
border .... גְּבוּל
bow .... קֶשֶׁת
bow down .... כרע (כָּרַע כֹּרֵעַ יִכְרַע n/a)
boy .... יֶלֶד
bread .... לֶחֶם (no pl.; may be coll.)
breadth .... רֹחַב
break .... שבר (שָׁבַר שֹׁבֵר יִשְׁבֹּר שְׁבֹר)
breath .... נֶפֶשׁ (fem.)
bronze .... נְחֹשֶׁת
brother .... אָח
build .... בני (בָּנָה בֹּנֶה יִבְנֶה בְּנֵה)
bull .... פַּר (fem. פָּרָה)
burn .... שרף (שָׂרַף שֹׂרֵף יִשְׂרֹף שְׂרֹף); בער (בָּעַר בֹּעֵר יִבְעַר n/a)
burnt offering .... עֹלָה
bury .... קבר (קָבַר קֹבֵר יִקְבֹּר קְבֹר)
by .... בְּיַד
by day .... יוֹמָם

C

call .... קרא (קָרָא קֹרֵא יִקְרָא קְרָא)
camp .... מַחֲנֶה
capture .... תפשׂ (תָּפַשׂ תֹּפֵשׂ יִתְפֹּשׂ תְּפֹשׂ); שׁבי (שָׁבָה שֹׁבֶה יִשְׁבֶּה שְׁבֵה); לכד (לָכַד לֹכֵד יִלְכֹּד לְכֹד)
carry .... נשׂא (נָשָׂא נֹשֵׂא יִשָּׂא שָׂא)
cast .... שלך ([הִפְעִיל] הִשְׁלִיךְ מַשְׁלִיךְ יַשְׁלִיךְ הַשְׁלֵךְ)
cattle .... מִקְנֶה
cease .... כלי (כָּלָה n/a יִכְלֶה n/a); חדל (חָדַל n/a יֶחְדַּל חֲדָל); שׁבת (שָׁבַת n/a יִשְׁבֹּת n/a)
cereal offering .... מִנְחָה
charioteer .... רֶכֶב (coll.)
chariot(s) .... רֶכֶב (usually coll.)
chase .... רדף (רָדַף רֹדֵף יִרְדֹּף רְדֹף)
chase out .... גרשׁ (n/a גֹּרֵשׁ n/a n/a)
chastise .... יסר ([פִּעֵל] יִסַּר מְיַסֵּר יְיַסֵּר יַסֵּר)
chest .... אָרוֹן
chief .... נָשִׂיא
child .... יֶלֶד
choose .... בחר (בָּחַר בֹּחֵר יִבְחַר בְּחַר)
cistern .... בּוֹר (irr. pl. בֹּרוֹת)
city .... עִיר (fem.; irr. pl. עָרִים)
cleave .... בקע (בָּקַע בֹּקֵעַ יִבְקַע בְּקַע)
cling .... דבק (דָּבַק n/a יִדְבַּק n/a)

ENGLISH-HEBREW GLOSSARY

close	סָגַר (סָגַר סֹגֵר יִסְגֹּר סְגֹר)
cloud	עָנָן
come	ב(ו)א (בָּא בָּא יָבֹא בֹּא)
come meet	קדמ ([פִּעֵל] קִדֵּם n/a יְקַדֵּם קַדֵּם)
command	צוי ([פִּעֵל] צִוָּה מְצַוֶּה יְצַוֶּה צַוֵּה)
commandment	מִצְוָה
commit adultery	נאפ (נָאַף נֹאֵף יִנְאַף n/a)
complete, to be	תממ (תַּם n/a יִתֹּם n/a)
complete	תָּמִים
conceal	סתר ([הִפְעִיל] הִסְתִּיר מַסְתִּיר יַסְתִּיר הַסְתֵּר)
concealed, to be	סתר ([נִפְעַל] נִסְתַּר נִסְתָּר יִסָּתֵר הִסָּתֵר)
conceive	הרי (הָרְתָה n/a תַּהֲרֶה n/a)[form given is 3fs]
concubine	אָמָה
congregation	עֵדָה
conspire	קשר (קָשַׁר קֹשֵׁר יִקְשֹׁר n/a)
continually	תָּמִיד
copper	נְחֹשֶׁת
corrupt	שחת ([פִּעֵל] שִׁחֵת n/a n/a שַׁחֵת) ([הִפְעִיל] הִשְׁחִית מַשְׁחִית יַשְׁחִית הַשְׁחֵת)
counsel	עֵצָה
count	ספר (סָפַר סֹפֵר יִסְפֹּר סְפֹר); פקד (פָּקַד פֹּקֵד יִפְקֹד פְּקֹד)
courtyard	חָצֵר
covenant	בְּרִית
cover	כסי ([פִּעֵל] כִּסָּה מְכַסֶּה יְכַסֶּה כַּסֵּה)
create	ברא (בָּרָא בֹּרֵא יִבְרָא בְּרָא)
cry	בכי (בָּכָה בֹּכֶה יִבְכֶּה בְּכֵה)
cry out	צעק (צָעַק צֹעֵק יִצְעַק צְעַק); זעק is used and conjugated similarly
cry out (almost always in joy)	רננ (רָן n/a n/a יָרֹן רֹן)
cubit	אַמָּה
cultivable land	אֲדָמָה
curse	ארר (אָרַר אֹרֵר יָאֹר אֹר)
cut (often with בְּרִית)	כרת (כָּרַת כֹּרֵת יִכְרֹת כְּרֹת)

D

darkness	חֹשֶׁךְ
daughter	בַּת (בָּנוֹת) (irr. pl.)
day	יוֹם (יָמִים) (irr. pl.)
daybreak	בֹּקֶר
deal or act treacherously	בגד (בָּגַד בֹּגֵד יִבְגֹּד n/a)
death	מָוֶת
deed	מַעֲשֶׂה
defile	חלל ([פִּעֵל] חִלֵּל מְחַלֵּל יְחַלֵּל n/a)
definite direct object marker	אֵת, אֶת־

ENGLISH-HEBREW GLOSSARY

delight in	חפץ (חָפֵץ n/a יַחְפֹּץ n/a)
deliver	נצל ([הִפְעִיל] הִצִּיל מַצִּיל יַצִּיל הַצֵּל)؛ ישע ([הִפְעִיל] הוֹשִׁיעַ מוֹשִׁיעַ יוֹשִׁיעַ הוֹשַׁע)؛ מלט ([פִּעֵל] מִלֵּט מְמַלֵּט יְמַלֵּט מַלֵּט)
depart	נסע (נָסַע נֹסֵעַ יִסַּע סַע)
descend	ירד (יָרַד יוֹרֵד יֵרֵד רֵד)
descendants	זֶרַע
desire	אבי (אָבָה אֹבֶה יֹאבֶה n/a)؛ אוי ([פָּעֵל] אִוָּה n/a יְאַוֶּה n/a)
desire strongly	אוי ([הִתְפָּעֵל] הִתְאַוָּה מִתְאַוֶּה יִתְאַוֶּה n/a)
desolated, to be	שמם (שָׁמַם שׁוֹמֵם יִשֹּׁם שֹׁם)
desolation	שְׁמָמָה
despise	בזי (בָּזָה בֹּזֶה יִבְזֶה n/a)
destroy	שמד ([הִפְעִיל] הִשְׁמִיד n/a יַשְׁמִיד הַשְׁמֵד)؛ חרם ([הִפְעִיל] הֶחֱרִים n/a יַחֲרִים הַחֲרֵם)
destroyed, to be	שמד ([נִפְעַל] נִשְׁמַד n/a יִשָּׁמֵד n/a)
devastate	שדד (שָׁדַד שֹׁדֵד יָשׁוּד n/a)
die	מ(ו)ת (מֵת מֵת יָמוּת מוּת)
different	אַחֵר (אֲחֵרוֹת and אֲחֵרִים .pl؛ אַחֶרֶת .fem)
discipline	יסר ([פִּעֵל] יִסַּר מְיַסֵּר יְיַסֵּר יַסֵּר)
dismayed, to be	חתת (חַת n/a יֵחַת חֹת)
dispute	רִיב
distress	צָרָה
divide	חלק (חָלַק חֹלֵק יַחֲלֹק חֲלֹק)؛ פרד ([נִפְעַל] נִפְרַד נִפְרָד יִפָּרֵד הִפָּרֵד)
do	עשי (עָשָׂה עֹשֶׂה יַעֲשֶׂה עֲשֵׂה)؛ פעל (פָּעַל פֹּעֵל יִפְעַל n/a)
do again	יסף (יָסַף n/a n/a סַף)
do more	יסף (יָסַף n/a n/a סַף)
do wondrously	פלא ([הִפְעִיל] הִפְלִיא מַפְלִיא יַפְלִיא n/a)
document	סֵפֶר
donkey	חֲמוֹר
door	דֶּלֶת
dream	חֲלוֹם
drink	שתי (שָׁתָה שֹׁתֶה יִשְׁתֶּה שְׁתֵה)
dry, to be	יבש (יָבֵשׁ n/a יִיבַשׁ n/a)
dusk	עֶרֶב
dust	עָפָר
dwell	ישב (יָשַׁב יֹשֵׁב יֵשֵׁב שֵׁב)؛ שכן (שָׁכַן שֹׁכֵן יִשְׁכֹּן שְׁכֹן)
dwelling	מִשְׁכָּן

E

ear	אֹזֶן
Earth	אֶרֶץ (אֲרָצוֹת .fem., with expected pl)
eat	אכל (אָכַל אֹכֵל יֹאכַל אֱכֹל)
elder	זָקֵן
encamp	חני (חָנָה חֹנֶה יַחֲנֶה חֲנֵה)

ENGLISH-HEBREW GLOSSARY

end .... קֵץ (with suffixes, e.g., קִצּוֹ)
enemy .... צַר
engage in a (legal) battle .... ריב(י) (רָב רָב יָרִיב רִיב)
engrave .... חרשׁ (חָרַשׁ חֹרֵשׁ יַחֲרֹשׁ n/a)
entrance .... פֶּתַח
erect .... נצב ([הִפְעִיל] הִצִּיב מַצִּיב יַצִּיב הַצֵּב)
err .... תעה (תָּעָה תֹּעֶה יִתְעֶה n/a)
escape .... מלט ([נִפְעַל] נִמְלַט נִמְלָט יִמָּלֵט הִמָּלֵט)
establish .... כ(ו)ן ([הִפְעִיל] הֵכִין מֵכִין יָכִין הָכֵן); יסד (יָסַד יֹסֵד n/a n/a)
established, to be .... אמן ([נִפְעַל] נֶאֱמַן נֶאֱמָן יֵאָמֵן n/a)
eternity .... עוֹלָם
evening .... עֶרֶב
every .... כֹּל, כָּל-
everything .... כֹּל
evil .... רַע (pl. רָעִים)
examine .... בחן (בָּחַן בֹּחֵן יִבְחַן בְּחַן)
exile .... גלי (גָּלָה גֹּלֶה יִגְלֶה גְּלֵה)
extend .... נטי (נָטָה נֹטֶה יִטֶּה נְטֵה)
extended family (clan) .... מִשְׁפָּחָה
extraordinary, to be .... פלא ([נִפְעַל] נִפְלָא נִפְלָא יִפָּלֵא n/a)
eye .... עַיִן

F

face .... פָּנִים (plural only)
fall .... נפל (נָפַל נֹפֵל יִפֹּל נְפֹל)
family .... מִשְׁפָּחָה
famine .... רָעָב
far, to be .... רחק (רָחַק n/a יִרְחַק רְחַק)
fashion .... יצר (יָצַר יֹצֵר יִצֹּר n/a)
father .... אָב (irr. pl. אָבוֹת)
faultless .... תָּמִים
favor .... חֵן (with suffixes, e.g., חִנּוֹ)
fear .... ירא (יָרֵא n/a יִירָא יְרָא); פחד (פָּחַד n/a יִפְחַד n/a)
feast time .... מוֹעֵד
female .... נְקֵבָה
female slave .... אָמָה
field .... שָׂדֶה
fight .... ריב(י) (רָב רָב יָרִיב רִיב); לחם ([נִפְעַל] נִלְחַם נִלְחָם יִלָּחֵם הִלָּחֵם)
fight .... רִיב
find .... מצא (מָצָא מֹצֵא יִמְצָא מְצָא)
finished, to be .... כלי (כָּלָה n/a יִכְלֶה n/a)
fire .... אֵשׁ

firm, to be	אמן (נִפְעַל) נֶאֱמַן נֶאֱמָן יֵאָמֵן (n/a); אמן (נִפְעַל) נָכוֹן נָכוֹן יִכּוֹן הָכֵן) נ(ר)כ
first-born	בְּכוֹר
flee	ברח (בָּרַח בֹּרֵחַ יִבְרַח בְּרַח); נ(ר)ס (נָס נָס יָנוּס נוּס)
flesh	בָּשָׂר
fly	ע(ו)פ (עָף עָף יָעוּף n/a)
food	לֶחֶם (no pl.; may be coll.)
fool	כְּסִיל
foot	רֶגֶל
footstep	פַּעַם
foreigner	זָר
forest	יַעַר
forget	שכח (שָׁכַח שֹׁכֵחַ יִשְׁכַּח שְׁכַח)
forgive	סלח (סָלַח סֹלֵחַ יִסְלַח סְלַח)
form	יצר (יָצַר יֹצֵר יִצֹּר n/a)
friend	רֵעַ
from	מִן־
from where?	מֵאַיִן
fruit	פְּרִי
fruitful, to be	פרי (פָּרָה פֹּרֶה יִפְרֶה פְּרֵה)
full, to be	מלא (מָלֵא מָלֵא יִמְלָא מְלָא)

G

garment	בֶּגֶד
gate	שַׁעַר
gather	אספ (אָסַף אֹסֵף יֶאֱסֹף אֱסֹף)
generation	דּוֹר (דּוֹרוֹת and דּוֹרִים .pl)
get sick	חלי (חָלָה חֹלֶה n/a n/a)
get up early	שכמ ([הִפְעִיל] הִשְׁכִּים מַשְׁכִּים יַשְׁכִּים הַשְׁכֵּם)
gift	מִנְחָה
give	נתנ (נָתַן נֹתֵן יִתֵּן תֵּן)
give birth	ילד (יָלַד יֹלֵד יֵלֵד לֵד)
give drink	שקי ([הִפְעִיל] הִשְׁקָה מַשְׁקֶה יַשְׁקֶה הַשְׁקֵה)
give thanks	ידי ([הִפְעִיל] הוֹדָה מוֹדֶה יוֹדֶה הוֹדֵה)
glory	כָּבוֹד
go	הלכ / ילכ (הָלַךְ הֹלֵךְ יֵלֵךְ לֵךְ)
go around	סבב (סָבַב סוֹבֵב יָסֹב סֹב or יָסֹב סֹב)
go up	עלי (עָלָה עֹלֶה יַעֲלֶה עֲלֵה)
God (literally, my masters)	אֲדֹנָי
God, god	אֵל
God, god, gods	אֱלֹהִים
gold	זָהָב

good, to be	יטב (יָטַב n/a יִיטַב n/a n/a)
good	טוֹב
grasp	אחז (אָחַז אֹחֵז יֹאחַז אָחֹז)
grave	קֶבֶר
great, to be	רבה (רָבָה n/a יִרְבֶּה רְבֵה); גדל (גָּדֵל n/a יִגְדַּל גָּדַל)
great	גָּדוֹל
greatness	רֹב
groan	הגי (הָגָה n/a יֶהְגֶּה n/a)
grow up	גדל (גָּדֵל n/a יִגְדַּל גָּדַל)
guard	שמר (שָׁמַר שֹׁמֵר יִשְׁמֹר שָׁמֹר); נצר (נָצַר נֹצֵר יִצֹּר נְצֹר)
guilty, to be	אשמ (אָשַׁם and אָשֵׁם n/a יֶאְשַׁם n/a)

H

hand	יָד (dual, יָדַיִם, hands, pl. יָדוֹת, times)
hang	תלי (תָּלָה תֹּלֶה יִתְלֶה תָּלֹה)
happiness	שִׂמְחָה
happy, to be	שמח (שָׂמַח n/a יִשְׂמַח שָׂמֹחַ)
hard, to be	קשׁי (קָשָׁה n/a יִקְשֶׁה n/a)
hasten	מהר ([פִּעֵל] מִהַר מְמַהֵר יְמַהֵר מַהֵר)
hate	שׂנא (שָׂנֵא שֹׂנֵא יִשְׂנָא שְׂנֹא)
have a vision	חזה (חָזָה חֹזֶה יֶחֱזֶה חָזֹה)
have pity on	רחמ ([פִּעֵל] רִחַם מְרַחֵם יְרַחֵם רַחֵם)
have sex with	שכב (שָׁכַב שֹׁכֵב יִשְׁכַּב שָׁכֹב)
he	הוּא
head	רֹאשׁ (irr. pl. רָאשִׁים)
heal	רפא (רָפָא רֹפֵא יִרְפָּא רְפֹא)
hear	שׁמע (שָׁמַע שֹׁמֵעַ יִשְׁמַע שָׁמֹעַ); אזנ ([הִפְעִיל] הֶאֱזִין n/a יַאֲזִין הַאֲזֵן)
heart	לֵב, לֵבָב (לְבָבוֹת and לִבּוֹת pl.)
heavens	שָׁמַיִם
heavy, to be	כבד (כָּבֵד n/a יִכְבַּד כָּבֹד)
heed	שׁמע (שָׁמַע שֹׁמֵעַ יִשְׁמַע שָׁמֹעַ)
help	ישׁע ([הִפְעִיל] הוֹשִׁיעַ מוֹשִׁיעַ יוֹשִׁיעַ הוֹשֵׁעַ); עזר (עָזַר עֹזֵר יַעֲזֹר עָזֹר)
here	פֹּה
hide	חבא ([נִפְעַל] נֶחְבָּא נֶחְבָּא יֵחָבֵא n/a); טמנ (טָמַן n/a יִטְמֹן n/a)
high, to be	ר(ו)מ (רָם רָם יָרוּם רוֹם); גבה (גָּבַהּ n/a יִגְבַּהּ n/a)
high place (for worship)	בָּמָה
highest	עֶלְיוֹן
hill	גִּבְעָה
hit	נכי ([הִפְעִיל] הִכָּה מַכֶּה יַכֶּה הַכֵּה)
hold	אחז (אָחַז אֹחֵז יֹאחַז אָחֹז)
holy, to be	קדשׁ (קָדַשׁ n/a יִקְדַּשׁ n/a)

holy ... קָדוֹשׁ
holy thing ... קֹדֶשׁ
honor ... כָּבוֹד
horse ... סוּס
house ... בַּיִת (בָּתִּים .masc.; irr. pl)
how? ... אֵיךְ
humanity ... אָדָם (coll.; no pl.); אֱנוֹשׁ (coll., mostly poetic)
humble ... עָנִי
humiliate ... כלם ([הִפְעִיל] הִכְלִים מַכְלִים יַכְלִים n/a)
husband ... בַּעַל

I

I ... אָנֹכִי, אֲנִי
impure, to be ... טמא (טָמֵא n/a יִטְמָא n/a)
in ... בְּ
incense ... קְטֹרֶת
inherit ... ירש (יָרַשׁ יוֹרֵשׁ יִירַשׁ רֵשׁ); נחל (נָחַל n/a יִנְחַל n/a)
inheritance ... נַחֲלָה
inquire ... דרש (דָּרַשׁ דֹּרֵשׁ יִדְרֹשׁ דְּרֹשׁ)
instead of ... תַּחַת
instruction ... תּוֹרָה
it ... הוּא (masc.); הִיא (fem.)

J

jealous, to be ... קנא ([פִּעֵל] קִנֵּא n/a יְקַנֵּא n/a)
journey ... נסע (נָסַע נֹסֵעַ יִסַּע סַע)
judge ... שפט (שָׁפַט שֹׁפֵט יִשְׁפֹּט שְׁפֹט)
justice ... מִשְׁפָּט

K

keep watch ... צפי (צָפָה n/a יִצְפֶּה n/a)
kill ... הרג (הָרַג הֹרֵג יַהֲרֹג הֲרֹג); נכי ([הִפְעִיל] הִכָּה מַכֶּה יַכֶּה הַכֵּה)
kindness ... חֶסֶד
king ... מֶלֶךְ
kingdom ... מַמְלָכָה; מַלְכוּת
kingship ... מַלְכוּת
kiss ... נשׁק (נָשַׁק נֹשֵׁק יִשַּׁק שַׁק)
kneel ... כרע (כָּרַע כֹּרֵעַ יִכְרַע n/a)
know ... ידע (יָדַע יֹדֵעַ יֵדַע דַּע)
knowledge ... דַּעַת

L

labor	מְלָאכָה; עֲבוֹדָה
lamb	כֶּבֶשׂ (כַּבְשָׂה or כִּבְשָׂה fem.)
land	אֶרֶץ (אֲרָצוֹת .fem., with expected pl)
language	לָשׁוֹן (לְשֹׁנוֹת .masc. irr. pl)
large cattle	בָּקָר (.coll)
last	אַחֲרוֹן
laugh	שׂחק (שָׂחַק n/a יִשְׂחַק n/a)
law	תּוֹרָה
lawsuit	רִיב
learn	למד (לָמַד לָמֵד יִלְמַד לָמַד)
leave	יצא (יָצָא יָצֹא יֵצֵא צֵא); עזב (עָזַב עָזֹב יַעֲזֹב עֲזֹב)
leave over	יתר ([הִפְעִיל] הוֹתִיר n/a יוֹתִיר הוֹתֵר)
left	שְׂמֹאל
left over, to be	יתר ([נִפְעַל] נוֹתַר נוֹתָר יִוָּתֵר n/a)
leg	רֶגֶל
length	אֹרֶךְ
lie down	שכב (שָׁכַב שָׁכֵב יִשְׁכַּב שְׁכַב)
life	חַיִּים
life-force	נֶפֶשׁ (.fem)
light, to be	קלל (קַל n/a יֵקַל n/a)
light	אוֹר
like	אהב (אָהַב אָהֹב יֶאֱהַב אֱהֹב)
like, as	כְּ
lion	אַרְיֵה; אֲרִי
lip	שָׂפָה
listen	אזנ ([הִפְעִיל] הֶאֱזִין rare יַאֲזִין הַאֲזֵן)
living	חַי
lord	אָדוֹן
look	נבט ([הִפְעִיל] הִבִּיט מַבִּיט יַבִּיט הַבֵּט)
love	אהב (אָהַב אָהֹב יֶאֱהַב אֱהֹב)
loyalty	חֶסֶד
lust after	אוי ([הִתְפַּעֵל] הִתְאַוָּה מִתְאַוֶּה יִתְאַוֶּה n/a)

M

maidservant	שִׁפְחָה
make a division	פרד ([הִפְעִיל] הִפְרִיד מַפְרִיד יַפְרִיד n/a)
make firm	כ(ו)נ ([הִפְעִיל] הֵכִין מֵכִין יָכִין הָכֵן)
male	זָכָר
man	אִישׁ (אֲנָשִׁים .irr. pl); גֶּבֶר
manner	דֶּרֶךְ (both masc. and fem.)
master	אָדוֹן

matter	דָּבָר
measure	מדד (מָדַד n/a יָמוֹד n/a)
meat	בָּשָׂר
meditate	הגי (הָגָה n/a יֶהְגֶּה n/a)
meet	פגע (פָּגַע n/a יִפְגַּע פְּגַע)
messenger	מַלְאָךְ
middle	תָּוֶךְ
middle of	תּוֹךְ (תָּוֶךְ construct of)
midst	קֶרֶב
might	גְּבוּרָה
minister	שרת ([פִּעֵל] שֵׁרֵת מְשָׁרֵת יְשָׁרֵת n/a)
month	חֹדֶשׁ
morning	בֹּקֶר
mother	אֵם
mountain	הַר (הָרִים pl.)
mourn	אבל (אָבַל n/a יֶאֱבַל n/a)
mouth	פֶּה (פִּיפִיּוֹת פֵּיוֹת פִּיּוֹת irr. pl.)
much	הַרְבֵּה
multitude	רֹב
murder	רצח (רָצַח רֹצֵחַ יִרְצַח n/a)

N

name	שֵׁם (שֵׁמוֹת masc.; irr. pl.)
narrow	צַר
nation	עַם (עַמִּים pl.); גּוֹי
neighbor	רֵעַ
new	חָדָשׁ
new moon	חֹדֶשׁ
night	לַיְלָה (לֵילוֹת irr. pl.)
north	צָפוֹן
nose (also used in idioms concerning anger)	אַף
now	עַתָּה
number	מִסְפָּר
numerous, to be	רבי (רָבָה n/a יִרְבֶּה רְבֵה)
numerous	רַב (רַבִּים pl.)
nurse	ינק (יָנַק יֹנֵק יִינַק n/a)

O

observe	שמר (שָׁמַר שֹׁמֵר יִשְׁמֹר שְׁמֹר)
offer incense (usually to foreign gods)	קטר ([פִּעֵל] קִטֵּר מְקַטֵּר יְקַטֵּר קַטֵּר)
offer incense (usually to YHWH)	קטר ([הִפְעִיל] הִקְטִיר מַקְטִיר יַקְטִיר הַקְטֵר)

offering	מִנְחָה
officer	שַׂר (שָׂרִים .pl)
oil	שֶׁמֶן
old, to be	זקן (זָקֵן n/a יִזְקַן n/a)
old	זָקֵן
on	עַל-
open land	מִגְרָשׁ
opening	פֶּתַח
opposite	נֶגֶד; מוּל
ordinance	חֹק (חֻקִּים .pl)
outside	חוּץ (.pl, streets חוּצוֹת)
overtake	נשׂג (הִפְעִיל] הִשִּׂיג מַשִּׂיג יַשִּׂיג n/a]
overturn	הפך (הָפַךְ הֹפֵךְ יַהֲפֹךְ הֲפֹךְ)
owner	בַּעַל
ox	שׁוֹר

P

palace	הֵיכָל
palm	כַּף (כַּפּוֹת .pl)
pass	עבר (עָבַר עֹבֵר יַעֲבֹר עֲבֹר)
path	דֶּרֶךְ (both masc. and fem.)
peace	שָׁלוֹם
people	עַם (עַמִּים .pl)
perish	אבד (אָבַד אֹבֵד יֹאבַד אֲבֹד)
person	אָדָם (coll.; no pl.); נֶפֶשׁ (fem.); אִישׁ (.irr. pl אֲנָשִׁים)
pilgrimage festival	חַג (חַגִּי ,.with suffixes, e.g)
pit	בּוֹר (.irr. pl בֹּרוֹת)
place	שׂי(י)מ (שָׂם שָׂם יָשִׂים שִׂים); שׁי(י)ת (שָׁת n/a יָשִׁית שִׁית)
place	מָקוֹם (.masc.; irr. pl מְקוֹמוֹת)
plant	נטע (נָטַע נֹטֵעַ יִטַּע נְטַע); זרע (זָרַע זֹרֵעַ יִזְרַע זְרַע)
plaza	רְחוֹב (.irr. pl רְחוֹבוֹת)
pleased, to be	רצי (רָצָה רֹצֶה יִרְצֶה רְצֵה)
plow	חרשׁ (חָרַשׁ חֹרֵשׁ יַחֲרֹשׁ n/a)
plunder	בזז (בָּזַז בֹּזֵז יָבֹז בֹּז)
pollute	חלל ([פִּעֵל] חִלֵּל מְחַלֵּל יְחַלֵּל n/a)
poor	עָנִי
poor person	אֶבְיוֹן
possess	ירשׁ (יָרַשׁ יוֹרֵשׁ יִירַשׁ רֵשׁ); נחל (נָחַל n/a יִנְחַל n/a)
pour out	שפך (שָׁפַךְ שֹׁפֵךְ יִשְׁפֹּךְ שְׁפֹךְ); יצק (יָצַק n/a יִצֹּק צֹק and יַצֵּק)
power	חַיִל
praise	הלל ([פִּעֵל] הִלֵּל מְהַלֵּל יְהַלֵּל הַלֵּל)
pray	פלל ([הִתְפַּעֵל] הִתְפַּלֵּל מִתְפַּלֵּל יִתְפַּלֵּל הִתְפַּלֵּל)

prayer . . . . תְּפִלָּה
pregnant, to become . . . . [form given is 3fs](n/a) תַּהֲרֶה n/a (הָרְתָה) הרי
(see, wow, indeed) presentative particle, ... הִנֵּה
    untranslated depending on context
priest . . . . כֹּהֵן
prophesy . . . . נבא ([נִפְעַל] נִבָּא נִבָּא יִנָּבֵא הִנָּבֵא)
prophet . . . . נָבִיא
proscribe . . . . חרמ ([הִפְעִיל] הֶחֱרִים n/a יַחֲרִים הַחֲרֵם)
prosper . . . . שׂכל ([הִפְעִיל] הִשְׂכִּיל מַשְׂכִּיל יַשְׂכִּיל הַשְׂכֵּל)
Psalm . . . . מִזְמוֹר
purchase . . . . קני (קָנָה קֹנֶה יִקְנֶה קְנֵה)
pure, to be . . . . טהר (טָהֵר n/a יִטְהַר טְהָר)
purification offering (traditionally, sin offering) . . . . חַטָּאת (חַטָּאוֹת pl.)
put on a garment . . . . לבש (לָבַשׁ n/a יִלְבַּשׁ לְבַשׁ)
put to shame . . . . כלמ ([הִפְעִיל] הִכְלִים מַכְלִים יַכְלִים n/a)

Q

quiet, to be . . . . שקט (שָׁקַט שֹׁקֵט יִשְׁקֹט n/a)

R

rainbow . . . . קֶשֶׁת
raise . . . . נ(ו)ף ([הִפְעִיל] הֵנִיף מֵנִיף יָנִיף הָנֵף)
raise a shout . . . . ר(ו)ע ([הִפְעִיל] הֵרִיעַ מֵרִיעַ יָרִיעַ n/a)
ram . . . . אַיִל (אֵילִים pl.)
reach . . . . נשׂג ([הִפְעִיל] הִשִּׂיג מַשִּׂיג יַשִּׂיג n/a)
read . . . . קרא (קָרָא קֹרֵא יִקְרָא קְרָא)
reap . . . . קצר (קָצַר קֹצֵר יִקְצֹר n/a)
rebel . . . . פשׁע (פָּשַׁע פֹּשֵׁעַ יִפְשַׁע פְּשַׁע)
rebuke . . . . יכח ([הִפְעִיל] הוֹכִיחַ מוֹכִיחַ יוֹכִיחַ הוֹכַח)
recognize . . . . נכר ([הִפְעִיל] הִכִּיר מַכִּיר יַכִּיר הַכֵּר)
redeem . . . . גאל (גָּאַל גֹּאֵל יִגְאַל גְּאַל); פדי (פָּדָה פֹּדֶה יִפְדֶּה פְּדֵה)
refuse . . . . מאן ([פִּעֵל] מֵאֵן n/a יְמָאֵן n/a)
reign . . . . מלכ (מָלַךְ מֹלֵךְ יִמְלֹךְ מְלֹךְ)
reign . . . . מַלְכוּת
reject, spurn, despise . . . . מאס (מָאַס מֹאֵס יִמְאַס n/a)
rejoice . . . . ג(י)ל (גָּל n/a יָגִיל גִּיל)
remain . . . . שׁאר ([נִפְעַל] נִשְׁאַר נִשְׁאָר יִשָּׁאֵר n/a)
remainder . . . . יֶתֶר
remember . . . . זכר (זָכַר זֹכֵר יִזְכֹּר זְכֹר); פקד (פָּקַד פֹּקֵד יִפְקֹד יִפְקֹד)
reprove . . . . יכח ([הִפְעִיל] הוֹכִיחַ מוֹכִיחַ יוֹכִיחַ הוֹכַח)

ENGLISH-HEBREW GLOSSARY

rest	נ(ו)ח (נָח n/a יָנוּחַ n/a)
return	ש(ו)ב (שָׁב שָׁב יָשׁוּב שׁוּב)
ride	רכב (רָכַב רֹכֵב יִרְכַּב רְכַב)
right, to be	צדק (צָדַק n/a יִצְדַּק n/a)
right	יָמִין
righteous	צַדִּיק
righteousness	צְדָקָה; צֶדֶק
rip	קרע (קָרַע קֹרֵעַ יִקְרַע קְרַע)
rise (with other verbs, indicates beginning of an action)	ק(ו)מ (קָם קָם יָקוּם קוּם)
ritually impure	טָמֵא
ritually pure	טָהוֹר
river	נָהָר (נְהָרוֹת masc., but pl. is usually)
rock	אֶבֶן (אֲבָנִים fem., pl.)
rouse oneself	ע(ו)ר n/a עֵר יָעוֹר עוּר)
ruin	שחת ([פָּעֵל] שִׁחֵת n/a n/a שַׁחֵת) ([הִפְעִיל] הִשְׁחִית מַשְׁחִית יַשְׁחִית הַשְׁחֵת)
rule	משל (מָשַׁל מֹשֵׁל יִמְשֹׁל מְשֹׁל)
run	ר(ו)צ (רָץ רָץ יָרוּץ רוּץ)

S

Sabbath	שַׁבָּת
sacrifice	זבח (זָבַח זֹבֵחַ יִזְבַּח זְבַח)
sacrifice	זֶבַח; קָרְבָּן (קָמֶץ קָטָן is a קָמֶץ the initial)
salvation	יְשׁוּעָה
sanctuary	מִקְדָּשׁ
sated, to be	שׂבע (שָׂבַע n/a יִשְׂבַּע שְׂבַע)
say	אמר (אָמַר אֹמֵר יֹאמַר אֱמֹר)
scatter	פ(ו)צ (n/a n/a יָפוּץ פּוּץ)
scream	זעק (זָעַק n/a יִזְעַק זְעַק)
scroll	סֵפֶר
sea	יָם
seat	כִּסֵּא
see	ראי (רָאָה רֹאֶה יִרְאֶה רְאֵה); חזה (חָזָה חֹזֶה יֶחֱזֶה חֲזֵה)
seed	זֶרַע
seek	בקש ([פִּעֵל] בִּקֵּשׁ מְבַקֵּשׁ יְבַקֵּשׁ בַּקֵּשׁ); דרש (דָּרַשׁ דֹּרֵשׁ יִדְרֹשׁ דְּרֹשׁ)
seek refuge	חסי (חָסָה חֹסֶה יֶחֱסֶה חֲסֵה)
sell	מכר (מָכַר מֹכֵר יִמְכֹּר מְכֹר)
send	שלח (שָׁלַח שֹׁלֵחַ יִשְׁלַח שְׁלַח)
separate	בדל ([הִפְעִיל] הִבְדִּיל מַבְדִּיל יַבְדִּיל n/a)
servant	עֶבֶד
serve	עבד (עָבַד עֹבֵד יַעֲבֹד עֲבֹד); שׁרת ([פִּעֵל] שֵׁרֵת מְשָׁרֵת יְשָׁרֵת n/a)
service	עֲבוֹדָה

shake	רָעַשׁ (רָעַשׁ רֹעֵשׁ יִרְעַשׁ n/a)
shattered, to be	חתת (חַת n/a יֵחַת חֹת)
she	הִיא
Shekel (a weight, approximately 11–13 grams)	שֶׁקֶל
Sheol	שְׁאוֹל
shoot	ירי (יָרָה יֹרֶה יִירָה יְרֵה)
shore	שָׂפָה
short, to be	קצר (קָצַר קֹצֵר יִקְצַר n/a)
show favor	חנן (חָנַן חֹנֵן יָחֹן חֹן)
show hostility toward	צרר (צָרַר צֹרֵר יָצֹר n/a)
sick	חלי (חָלָה חֹלֶה n/a n/a)
sign	אוֹת
silent, to be	דמם (דָּם n/a יִדֹּם דֹּם)
silver	כֶּסֶף
sin	חטא (חָטָא חֹטֵא יֶחֱטָא n/a); פשע (פָּשַׁע פֹּשֵׁעַ יִפְשַׁע פְּשַׁע)
slave	עֶבֶד
small	קָטֹן, קָטָן (קְטַנּוֹת and קְטַנִּים pl.; קְטַנָּה fem.)
small cattle (typically goats, sheep)	צֹאן (frequently coll.)
smite	נגף (נָגַף נֹגֵף יִגֹּף n/a)
so that	לְמַעַן
soil	עָפָר
sojourn	ג(ו)ר (גָּר גָּר יָגוּר גּוּר)
sojourner	גֵּר
son	בֵּן (בָּנִים irr. pl.)
song	שִׁיר
south	נֶגֶב
southern Israel	נֶגֶב
sow	זרע (זָרַע זֹרֵעַ יִזְרַע זְרַע)
speak	דבר ([פִּעֵל] דִּבֶּר מְדַבֵּר יְדַבֵּר דַּבֵּר)
speech	שָׂפָה
spirit	רוּחַ (fem., sometimes masc.; pl. רוּחוֹת)
split	בקע (בָּקַע בֹּקֵעַ יִבְקַע בְּקַע)
spoil	שחת ([פִּעֵל] שִׁחֵת n/a n/a שַׁחֵת) ([הִפְעִיל] הִשְׁחִית מַשְׁחִית יַשְׁחִית הַשְׁחֵת)
spread out	פרש (פָּרַשׂ פֹּרֵשׂ יִפְרֹשׂ n/a)
sprout	צמח (צָמַח צֹמֵחַ יִצְמַח n/a)
staff	מַטֶּה; שֵׁבֶט
stand	עמד (עָמַד עֹמֵד יַעֲמֹד עֲמֹד n/a n/a): נצב ([נִפְעַל] נִצַּב נִצָּב)
stay overnight	לי(ן)/נ(ו)ן (לָן לָן יָלִין לִין)
steal	גנב (גָּנַב גֹּנֵב יִגְנֹב n/a)
still	עוֹד
stomach	בֶּטֶן
storehouse	אוֹצָר (אוֹצָרוֹת irr. pl.)

ENGLISH-HEBREW GLOSSARY

straight	יָשָׁר
straits	צָרָה; צַר
stream	נַחַל; נָהָר (masc., but pl. is usually נְהָרוֹת)
strength	חַיִל; כֹּחַ; עֹז (עֻזִּי or עָזִּי typically, with suffixes)
strike	תקע (תָּקַע תֹּקֵעַ יִתְקַע תְּקַע)
strong, to be	חזק (חָזַק n/a יֶחֱזַק חֲזַק)
stumble	כשל (כָּשַׁל כֹּשֵׁל יִכְשַׁל n/a)
succeed	צלח ([הִפְעִיל] הִצְלִיחַ מַצְלִיחַ יַצְלִיחַ הַצְלַח)
sun	שֶׁמֶשׁ (mostly fem.; rarely masc.)
supreme	עֶלְיוֹן
swallow	בלע (בָּלַע n/a יִבְלַע n/a)
sword	חֶרֶב (fem.)

T

Tabernacle	מִשְׁכָּן
take	לקח (לָקַח לֹקֵחַ יִקַּח קַח)
take away	נצל ([הִפְעִיל] הִצִּיל מַצִּיל יַצִּיל הַצֵּל)
take one's stand	יצב ([הִתְפָּעֵל] הִתְיַצֵּב מִתְיַצֵּב יִתְיַצֵּב הִתְיַצֵּב)
teaching	תּוֹרָה
tell	נגד ([הִפְעִיל] הִגִּיד מַגִּיד יַגִּיד הַגֵּד)
temple	הֵיכָל
Temple	מִקְדָּשׁ
tend sheep	רעי (רָעָה רֹעֶה יִרְעֶה רְעֵה)
tent	אֹהֶל
test	בחן (בָּחַן בֹּחֵן יִבְחַן בְּחַן)
testify	ע(ו)ד ([הִפְעִיל] הֵעִיד מֵעִיד יָעִיד הָעֵד)
that (demonstrative pronoun)	הַהוּא (masc.); הַהִיא (fem.)
that (relative pronoun)	אֲשֶׁר
then	אָז
there	שָׁם
these	אֵלֶּה
they	הֵמָּה, הֵם (masc.); הֵנָּה, הֵן (fem.)
thing	דָּבָר
think	חשב (חָשַׁב חֹשֵׁב יַחֲשֹׁב n/a)
this	זֶה (masc.), זֹאת (fem.)
those	הֵמָּה, הֵם (masc.); הֵנָּה, הֵן (fem.)
thrive	צלח ([הִפְעִיל] הִצְלִיחַ מַצְלִיחַ יַצְלִיחַ הַצְלַח)
throne	כִּסֵּא (masc., irr. pl. כִּסְאוֹת)
throw	שלכ ([הִפְעִיל] הִשְׁלִיךְ מַשְׁלִיךְ יַשְׁלִיךְ הַשְׁלֵךְ)
thrust out	נדח ([הִפְעִיל] הִדִּיחַ n/a יַדִּיחַ הַדַּח)
thrust out, to be	נדח ([נִפְעַל] נִדַּח n/a נִדָּח)

thus	כֹּה
tie	קשׁר (קָשַׁר קֹשֵׁר יִקְשֹׁר n/a)
time	עֵת
time	פַּעַם
tired, to be	יגע (יָגַע n/a יִיגַע n/a)
to	לְ; אֶל־
to where?	אָנָה
together	יַחְדָּו; יַחַד
tomorrow	מָחָר
tongue	לָשׁוֹן (masc. irr. pl. לְשֹׁנוֹת)
Torah	תּוֹרָה
totter	מו(ו)ט (מָט מָט יָמוּט n/a)
touch	נגע (נָגַע נֹגֵעַ יִגַּע גַּע)
toward	לְ; אֶל־; לִקְרַאת
tower	מִגְדָּל
treasure	אוֹצָר (irr. pl. אוֹצָרוֹת)
treaty	בְּרִית
tree	עֵץ
tribe	מַטֶּה; שֵׁבֶט
trust	בטח (בָּטַח בֹּטֵחַ יִבְטַח בְּטַח); אמנ ([הִפְעִיל] הֶאֱמִין מַאֲמִין יַאֲמִין הַאֲמֵן)
turn	פני (פָּנָה פֹּנֶה יִפְנֶה פְּנֵה); הפכ (הָפַךְ הֹפֵךְ יַהֲפֹךְ הֲפֹךְ); סבב (סָבַב סוֹבֵב יָסֹב or יָסֵב סֹב)
turn aside	סו(ו)ר (סָר סָר יָסוּר סוּר)

U

uncover	גלי (נִגְלָה גָּלָה יִגְלֶה גְּלֵה)
under	תַּחַת
understand	ב(י)נ (בָּן יָבִין בִּין n/a)
underworld	שְׁאוֹל
undisturbed	שקט (שָׁקַט שֹׁקֵט יִשְׁקֹט n/a)
until	עַד־
up to	עַד־
upright	יָשָׁר
uterus	בֶּטֶן
utter	הגי (הָגָה n/a יֶהְגֶּה n/a)
utterance	נְאֻם

V

very	מְאֹד
vessel	כְּלִי (pl. כֵּלִים)
via	בְּיַד

ENGLISH-HEBREW GLOSSARY

vine	גֶּפֶן
vineyard	כֶּרֶם
violence	חָמָס
vision	מַרְאֶה
visit	פקד (פָּקַד פֹּקֵד פָּקֻד יִפְקֹד)
voice	קוֹל (קֹלֹת masc.; irr. pl.)
vow	נדר (נָדַר נֹדֵר יָדֹר נְדֹר)

W

wadi	נַחַל
wait	קוי ([פִּעֵל] קִוָּה n/a יְקַוֶּה קַוֵּה); יחל ([פִּעֵל] יִחַל מְיַחֵל יְיַחֵל יַחֵל)
walk	הלכ / ילכ (הָלַךְ הֹלֵךְ יֵלֵךְ לֵךְ)
wall	חוֹמָה; קִיר (קִירוֹת masc; irr. pl.)
wander	תעה (תָּעָה תֹּעֶה יִתְעֶה n/a); נדד (נָדַד נֹדֵד יָדֹד n/a)
war	מִלְחָמָה
warrior	גִּבּוֹר
wash	רחצ (רָחַץ רֹחֵץ יִרְחַץ רְחַץ); כבס ([פִּעֵל] כִּבֵּס מְכַבֵּס יְכַבֵּס כַּבֵּס)
watch	נצר (נָצַר נֹצֵר יִצֹר נְצֹר)
water	מַיִם
wave	נ(ו)פ ([הִפְעִיל] הֵנִיף מֵנִיף יָנִיף הָנֵף)
we	אֲנַחְנוּ, נַחְנוּ
weight	מִשְׁקָל
well-being	שָׁלוֹם
what?	מַה (vocalization varies, see page 57)
wheat	חִטָּה
when?	מָתַי
where?	אַיֵּה; אֵיפֹה
which (relative particle)	אֲשֶׁר
who(m)?	מִי
whole, to be	שלמ (שָׁלֵם n/a יִשְׁלַם n/a)
why?	לָמָּה (לָ֫מָּה before א ה ע); מַדּוּעַ
wicked	רָשָׁע
widow	אַלְמָנָה
wilderness (not desert in the sense of totally dry)	מִדְבָּר
wind	רוּחַ
wine	יַיִן
wing	כָּנָף
wisdom	חָכְמָה (קָמֶץ קָטָן is a קָמֶץ the initial)
wise, to be	חכמ (חָכַם n/a יֶחְכַּם חֲכַם)
wise	חָכָם
with	עִם; אֵת, אֶת־

witness	עֵד
woe	הוֹי
woman	אִשָּׁה (נָשִׁים .irr. pl)
wood	עֵץ
word	דָּבָר
work	עבד (עָבַד עֹבֵד יַעֲבֹד עֲבֹד); יגע (יָגַע n/a יִיגַע n/a)
work	מַעֲשֶׂה; מְלָאכָה; עֲבוֹדָה
write	כתב (כָּתַב כֹּתֵב יִכְתֹּב כְּתֹב)
writhe	ח(י)ל / ח(ו)ל (חָל rare יָחִיל חִיל)

Y

Yahweh	יהוה
year	שָׁנָה (fem.; irr. pl. שָׁנִים)
you	אַתָּה (masc. sing.), אַתְּ (fem. sing.), אַתֶּם (masc. pl.), אַתֶּן (fem. pl.)
young girl	נַעֲרָה
young man	נַעַר

Z

zealous, to be	קנא ([פִּעֵל] קִנֵּא n/a יְקַנֵּא n/a)

Index

See also the Glossary of Grammatical Terms and Abbreviations.

Accents. *See* Cantillation marks; Stress
Active verbs, 112, 178–84, 204
Adjectives: attributive, 80–81; comparative, 82–83, 126; gender, 80; general, 70, 80–82, 96; number, 80; predicative, 70, 80–81, 82; verbal, 112
Allophones, 5, 6, 26
Apocopated verbs, 229–30, 285
Apposition, 222
Archaic Biblical Poetry, 2–3
Aspect, 169
Assimilation: general, 45, 46; *nun,* 44, 45–46, 65, 204, 211, 213, 214, 243, 245, 265, 266, 268, 281, 283; other consonants, 260; partial assimilation, 46–47, 261; vocalic assimilation, 46–47, 281
Attributive adjectives. *See* Adjectives, attributive

Biliteral roots, 108, 226
Binyanim. *See* Derived conjugations
Bound form. *See* Constructs
Bound prepositions. *See* Prepositions, bound

Cantillation marks: conjunctive, 20, 22; disjunctive, 20, 21, 25, 47, 130; general, 19–23, 27, 47, 92; postpositive, 21; prepositive, 21
Cognate accusative, 222
Cohortative verbs, 169, 170, 197, 212, 242, 267–68
Collective nouns, 74, 162

Combined deficiencies in verbs, 243–44
Comparative adjectives. *See* Adjectives, comparative
Compensatory lengthening, 45, 55, 57, 65, 75, 121, 172, 181, 227, 229, 280–81
Compound *shewa*. *See Shewa,* compound
Conjunctive accents. *See* Cantillation marks, conjunctive
Consonant clusters, 73, 229
Constructs: general, 41, 92, 111, 162; morphology, 92–94; stress, 42, 92; syntax, 54, 95–97
Conversive *waw*: *See Waw,* consecutive
Converted imperfects
—forms: *qal* of healthy verbs, 181; *qal* of verbs with gutturals, 196; *qal* of פֿ, יפֿ, and פֿא verbs, 211; *qal* of hollow verbs, לא and לי verbs, and geminates, 229; derived conjugations of healthy verbs, 266; derived conjugations other verbs, 282, 283, 285, 286
—functions, 169–70, 172–74
Converted perfects
—Forms: *qal* of healthy verbs, 180, 183; *qal* of verbs with gutturals, 194–95; *qal* of פֿ, יפֿ, and פֿא verbs, 210; *qal* of hollow verbs, לא and לי, and geminates, 228; derived conjugations of healthy verbs, 264; derived conjugations other verbs, 286
—functions, 169–70, 172–74

Dagesh forte, 26, 31, 44, 45, 46, 54, 56, 57, 75, 172, 181, 211, 225–28, 230, 244, 245, 260, 264, 266, 268, 281–82, 284
Dagesh lene, 26, 32, 33, 46, 61, 63, 131, 132, 180, 213, 227
Defective spelling, 15, 72, 235, 276
Defined direct objects, 66, 111, 129, 150, 186, 244
Definite article: forms, 45, 47, 54–56, 62, 63, 64; functions, 54, 83
Definition, 54, 80, 96, 150
Demonstrative pronouns. *See* Pronouns, demonstrative
Dental consonants, 8, 261
Derived conjugations, 71, 176, 260–70, 280–86
Disjunctive accents. *See* Cantillation marks, disjunctive
Dissimilation, 55, 63
Disyllabic nouns, 132
Doubly transitive verbs, 262
Dual nouns. *See* Nouns, dual
Durative verbs, 111

Elision, 47, 48, 62, 63, 64, 260–61, 265, 266
Elongated imperatives. *See* Imperatives, elongated
Emphasis, 81, 82, 121
Emphatic consonants, 8
Energic endings, 175, 245

Factitive verbs, 262
Final letters, 7

Final weak (ל״א and ל״י) verbs: *qal*, 225–32; derived conjugations, 284–85
Full spelling, 15, 72, 269
Furtive *pátaḥ*, 12, 14, 46, 94, 107, 175, 281

Geminate verbs: *qal*, 225–32; derived conjugations, 284
Gemination, 26, 31, 32, 44–45, 55, 56, 75, 131–32, 133, 215, 226–29, 232, 260, 261, 262, 265, 266, 268, 281, 284, 285. *See also* Dagesh forte
Gender, 1–2, 72–74, 80, 82, 96, 105, 120, 121, 162–63
Gentilic suffixes, 222, 223
Geographical names, 54, 73, 80, 117, 150, 223
Guttural consonants, 8, 31, 44, 46, 48, 55–57, 63, 65, 94, 106, 132–33, 194, 280–81
Guttural verbs: *qal*, 194–99; derived conjugations, 280–81

Ḥaṭṭap vowels. *See* Shewa, compound
Heavy suffixes, 42, 130, 131, 132, 144, 145, 179, 226–27, 264
Ḥîreq, 12, 13, 45, 144, 196
hlk (הלך), 215
Ḥólem, 12, 13, 131, 132, 227, 283
Hollow verbs: *qal*, 225–32; derived conjugations, 283–84

Imperatives
—elongated, 182–83, 197
—forms: *qal* of healthy verbs, 182; *qal* of verbs with gutturals, 197; *qal* of פ״נ, פ״י, and פ״א verbs, 212; *qal* of hollow verbs, ל״א and ל״י verbs, and geminates, 230–31; derived conjugations of healthy verbs, 267–68, 270; derived conjugations other verbs, 281, 283
—functions, 170
Imperfect verbs
—forms: *qal* of healthy verbs, 180–81; *qal* of verbs with gutturals, 195–96; *qal* of פ״נ, פ״י, and פ״א verbs, 210–11; *qal* of hollow verbs, ל״א and ל״י, and geminates, 228–29; derived conjugations of healthy verbs, 264; derived conjugations other verbs, 280–81, 282, 283, 284, 285
—functions, 170, 173, 174–75
Indirect objects, 262
Infinitive absolute
—forms: *qal* of healthy verbs, 175, 186; *qal* verbs with gutturals, 199; *qal* of hollow verbs, ל״א and ל״י, and geminates, 232; derived conjugations of healthy verbs, 269; derived conjugations other verbs, 283
—functions, 175
Infinitive construct
—forms: *qal* of healthy verbs, 175, 184–86; *qal* of verbs with gutturals, 199; *qal* of פ״נ, פ״י, and פ״א verbs, 213; *qal* of hollow verbs, ל״א and ל״י, and geminates, 232; derived conjugations of healthy verbs, 269–70; derived conjugations other verbs, 281, 283, 286
—functions, 175, 185
Initial weak (פ״נ, פ״י, and פ״א) verbs: *qal*, 211–15; derived conjugations, 281–83
Interrogative pronouns: הֲ, 56–57; other interrogative pronouns, 56, 57
Intransitive verbs, 262, 282, 285
Iterative verbs, 263

Jussives
—forms: *qal* of healthy verbs, 182; *qal* of verbs with gutturals, 197; *qal* of פ״נ, פ״י, and פ״א verbs, 212; *qal* of hollow verbs, ל״א and ל״י, and geminates, 230; derived conjugations of healthy verbs, 267; derived conjugations other verbs, 282, 283, 285
—functions, 171

Kethib, 27–28

Labial consonants, 8, 63, 64
Laryngeal consonants. *See* Guttural consonants
Late Biblical Hebrew, 2, 224, 242, 244
Law of the *shewa*, 42, 48, 61, 63, 93–94, 99, 133, 144, 197
Law of the *shewa* with gutturals, 46–47, 61, 194, 196, 197
Linking vowel, 227, 229
Locative הָ, 171
Lqḥ (לקח), 172, 214, 270

Mappîq, 26–27
Maqqāp, 27, 31, 42, 65, 66, 92
Masoretes, 11, 26
Matres lectionis. See Vowel letters
Medial *shewa*. *See* Shewa, medial
Mobile *shewa*. *See* Shewa, mobile
Modal verbs, 173. *See also* Cohortative verbs; Imperatives; Jussives
Monosyllabic nouns, 27, 64, 131–32

Narrative sequence, 174
Nominal patterns, 70–71, 188; consonantal prefixes, 70, 71
Nominal sentences, 81, 121
Nouns: dual, 75; masculine and feminine, 72–74, 76; singular and plural, 74, 76; unbound forms, 92; with suffixes, 54, 73, 80, 129–35, 143–50. *See also* Constructs
ntn (נתן), 214, 270
Numerals: cardinal, 159–63; ordinal, 163

Oath formula, 241
Objects. *See* Defined direct objects; Indirect objects

Paragogic *nun*, 175, 181, 221
Participles, active
—forms: *qal* of healthy verbs, 106, 183, 109–10; *qal* of verbs with gutturals, 107; *qal* of פ״נ, פ״י, and פ״א verbs, 213; *qal* of hollow verbs, ל״א and ל״י, and geminates, 108–9, 231; derived conjugations of healthy verbs, 268–69; derived conjugations other verbs, 280, 282
—functions, 105, 111
Participles, passive, forms: *qal* of healthy verbs, 175, 183–84; *qal* of verbs with gutturals, 198; *qal* of פ״נ, פ״י, and פ״א verbs, 213; *qal* of hollow verbs, ל״א and ל״י, and geminates, 232
Pāsēq, 27
Pataḥ, 12, 13, 46, 48, 54, 93, 94, 95, 196, 198, 245, 266, 281
Pausal forms, 47, 118, 120, 159, 162, 181, 183, 221, 264, 269
Pause, 47–48
Penultimate stress, 20, 41, 64, 73, 132, 180–81, 211, 226–27, 230, 264, 268
Perfect verbs
—forms: *qal* of healthy verbs, 179; *qal* of verbs with gutturals, 194–95; *qal* of פ״נ, פ״י, and פ״א verbs, 209–10; *qal* of hollow verbs, ל״א and ל״י verbs, and geminates, 226–28; derived conjugations of healthy verbs, 263; derived conjugations other verbs, 280–81, 282, 283, 284
—functions, 170, 173, 174
Perpetual *qere*, 28
Personal names, 54, 80, 96, 116, 117, 150
Philippi's law, 179, 227, 264–65
Phonemes, 5, 13, 26
Plene spelling. *See* Full spelling
Pluperfect, 172, 174, 221

Postpositive cantillation marks. *See* Cantillation marks, postpositive
Predicative adjectives. *See* Adjectives, predicative
Prepositions: bound, 61, 63, 65; general, 61, 66; unbound, 61; with suffixes, 129–30, 143–44
Prepositive cantillation marks. *See* Cantillation marks, prepositive
Pretonic reduction, 42, 47, 106, 144, 179, 181, 183, 197, 212, 227, 264–65, 268
Prohibitive forms, 171, 182, 230, 267
Pronominal suffixes: bound to infinitives, 184–85, 213, 232, 269; bound to nouns, 129–35, 143–50; bound to verbs, 129, 183, 244–51, 261, 264
Pronouns: demonstrative, 121–22; independent, 82, 120–21, 246; relative, 122
Propretonic reduction, 41–42, 44, 48, 73, 75, 93, 95, 99, 106, 131, 133, 144, 179, 227, 229, 245, 283
Punctual actions, 111
Purpose clause, 174–75, 222, 277

Qal passive, 270
Qāmeṣ, 12, 13, 41, 42, 46, 48, 57, 64, 73, 93, 95, 131–32, 179, 229, 245, 269, 281
Qāmeṣ qāṭān, 13, 46, 94, 132, 175, 179–80, 183, 184, 229, 232, 264
Qere, 27–28
Quiescent *shewa*. See *Shewa*, quiescent

Rāpeh, 26
Reduction. *See* Pretonic reduction; Propretonic reduction

SBH. *See* Standard Biblical Hebrew
Segholates, 73–74, 75, 92, 94, 95, 132, 145; in pause, 47

Semitic languages, 7, 13, 40, 70, 73, 75, 108, 162
Shewa: compound, 12, 13, 14, 31, 34, 44, 46, 48, 57, 63, 106, 131, 132–33, 194, 197, 212, 227, 243–44, 281; general, 12, 14, 30–31, 56, 57, 61–64, 132–33, 144, 160, 174, 227, 229, 264; medial, 33, 94; mobile, 12, 30, 31, 32, 41, 44, 46, 48, 106, 131, 194, 197, 227, 265, 281; quiescent, 12, 13, 30, 31, 33, 37, 48, 94, 132, 194
Sibilant consonants, 7, 8, 261, 264
Sonant consonants, 8
Spelling. *See* Defective spelling; Full spelling
Spirants, 7, 26, 33
Standard Biblical Hebrew, 2, 4
Stative verbs, 82, 112, 172, 178–84, 194–95, 210–12, 226, 229
Stops, 7, 26, 33
Stress, Consecutive stressed syllables avoided, 276. *See also* Cantillation marks; Penultimate stress; Ultimate stress
Substantives. *See* Nouns
Suffixes. *See* Nouns, with suffixes; Verbs with suffixes
Superlatives, 83
Suppletion, 286
Syllables: closed, 30–32, 33, 34, 41, 61, 63, 93, 94, 131, 132, 133, 179, 183, 184, 196, 215, 227, 282, 283; general, 5, 20, 30–34, 45, 55, 73, 107, 264, 282; open, 30–32, 33, 41, 93, 94, 131, 179–80, 196, 215, 227, 228, 245, 285; tonic, 20, 21, 22, 41, 129, 131, 245

Theme vowels, 179–84, 194, 211–12, 227, 229
Transitive verbs, 112, 262–63, 282, 285
Transliteration, 5, 14, 26, 27, 30, 31
Triliteral roots, 70

Ultimate stress, 20, 31, 41, 180, 264

Velar consonants, 8
Verbal adjectives. *See* Adjectives, verbal
Verbs. *See* Active verbs; Apocopated verbs; Cohortative verbs; Combined deficiencies in verbs; Converted imperfects; Converted perfects; Doubly transitive verbs; Durative verbs; Factitive verbs; Final weak (ל״א and ל״י) verbs; Guttural verbs; Hollow verbs; Imperatives; Imperfect verbs; Initial weak (פ״ן, פ״י, and פ״א) verbs; Intransitive verbs; Iterative verbs; Jussives; Perfect verbs; Pluperfect; Prohibitive forms; Stative verbs; Transitive verbs; Verbs with suffixes
Verbs with suffixes, 244–51
Virtual doubling, 45, 55, 65, 280–81, 282
Volitional forms, 170–71. *See also* Cohortative Verbs; Imperatives; Jussives
Vowel letters, 14–15, 26, 72, 109, 225, 229, 279
Vowel reduction, 41–42, 92–93, 106, 124, 131–32. *See also* Pretonic reduction; Propretonic reduction
Vowel retraction, 47, 183, 184, 232, 261, 266
Vowels: classes, 13, 14, 132; general, 11, 12; length, 13, 30–32, 41. *See also* Furtive *pátaḥ*; *Ḥîreq*; *Ḥólem*; *Pátaḥ*; Philippi's law; *Qāmeṣ*; *Qāmeṣ qāṭān*; *Shewa*; Theme vowels; Vowel letters

Waw: conjunctive, 8, 12, 63, 174; consecutive, 170, 171–74
Word order, xi, 81–82, 121, 174, 279

ykl (יכל), 215
ylk (ילך). See *hlk* (הלך)